LAW IN CONTEXT

LAW IN CONTEXT

Enlarging A Discipline

WILLIAM TWINING

CLARENDON PRESS · OXFORD
1997

*This book has been printed digitally and produced in a standard specification
in order to ensure its continuing availability*

OXFORD
UNIVERSITY PRESS

Great Clarendon Street, Oxford OX2 6DP

Oxford University Press is a department of the University of Oxford.
It furthers the University's objective of excellence in research, scholarship,
and education by publishing worldwide in

Oxford New York

Auckland Bangkok Buenos Aires Cape Town Chennai
Dar es Salaam Delhi Hong Kong Istanbul Karachi Kolkata
Kuala Lumpur Madrid Melbourne Mexico City Mumbai Nairobi
São Paulo Shanghai Singapore Taipei Tokyo Toronto

with an associated company in Berlin

Oxford is a registered trade mark of Oxford University Press
in the UK and in certain other countries

Published in the United States
by Oxford University Press Inc., New York

© William Twining 1997

The moral rights of the author have been asserted
Database right Oxford University Press (maker)

Reprinted 2002

ISBN 0-19-826483-6

For Jessica and Joshua

Acknowledgements

These essays were written over a period of nearly thirty years, during which I benefited from help, comments, advice, and criticism from more people than it is possible to list. Some of these debts were acknowledged when particular essays were first published. Thanks are also due to the Faculty of Law, University of Dar-es-Salaam, Oxford University Press, Sweet and Maxwell Ltd., Butterworths and Co., London and Toronto, Basil Blackwell Ltd., Valparaiso University Law Review, The Windsor Yearbook of Access to Justice, Dartmouth Publishing Co., the Northern Ireland Legal Quarterly, John Wylie and Sons, and Neil McCormick for permission to reproduce copyright material. Chapter 10 is reprinted from 48 *University of Miami Law Review* 119 (1993) which holds copyright on this article. A more general debt is also due to Terry Anderson, David Sugarman, and Robert Stevens. I am particular grateful to Holly Johnson for help with editing and to Evelyn Medina and Harriette Maddy for their patience in word processing, imaging, and generally coping with the frustrations of modern technology. As ever, I owe most to my wife for all her support, advice, practical help, and good judgement.

W.L.T.

Iffley
June 1996

Contents

Abbreviations

1. The following abbreviations are used in the text and the notes:

op. cit.   cited previously in the notes for this chapter
ibid.   same work and same page as that cited directly above
id.   same work as that cited directly above, different page
i.e.   in other words
e.g.   for example
passim   throughout the cited work
above   cited in a preceding chapter
below   cited in a following chapter
ff.   and pages following
ed.   editor

2. Some of the points and themes in the text are treated at greater length in other writings by the author. The following abbreviations are used in the notes:

ALELP   *Access to Legal Education and the Legal Profession* (with R. Dhavan and N. Kibble, edd., London, 1989)

ALLD   *Academic Law and Legal Development* (Lagos, 1977)

ANALYSIS *Analysis of Evidence* (with Terence Anderson, Boston and London, 1991)

BT   *Blackstone's Tower: The English Law School* (London, 1994)

HDTWR   *How to Do Things With Rules* (with David Miers, 3rd edn., London, 1991)

JJM   'The Job of Juristic Method: A Tribute to Karl Llewellyn', 48 *University of Miami Law Review* 601 (1993)

KLRM   *Karl Llewellyn and the Realist Movement* (London and Oklahoma, 1973, 1985)

LLS   *Learning Lawyers' Skills* (with Neil Gold and Karl Mackie, edd., London, 1989)

LTCL   *Legal Theory and Common Law* (ed., Oxford, 1986)

RB   'Reading Bentham', Maccabean Lecture, 75 *Proceedings of the British Academy* (1989), at 97–141

RE   *Rethinking Evidence* (Oxford, 1990; Chicago and London, 1994)

TAR   'Talk about Realism', 60 *New York University Law Review* 329 (1985)

TEBW   *Theories of Evidence: Bentham and Wigmore* (London, 1985; and Stanford, 1986)

1

Introduction: Wandering Jurist

This book deals with the institutionalized discipline of law as an enterprise which includes legal education, legal scholarship, legal theorizing, and the production of legal literature. It represents the reflections of an involved insider rather than the product of a more detached scholar trying, in Pierre Bourdieu's phrase, to exoticize the domestic.[1] The essays are more pragmatic than systematic. They span a period of nearly thirty years in several countries. They can be read as a reasonably coherent interpretation of developments, problems, and trends in law schools in common law countries during a formative period in the history of the discipline. Several deal with topical issues. Some may help law students to interpret the environment in which they spend at least three and often five or six years early in their careers. Non-lawyers may treat them as contributions to the archaeology and ethnography of knowledge. However, the main aim is to provide a detailed exploration of what is involved in trying to develop broader approaches to the study of law. Some of the chapters are new, but most have been published before. Nearly all of the latter are presented in their original form with only minor editorial corrections and additions.[2] Each was written as a self-standing paper at a particular time and place for specific reasons. The purpose of this introduction is to set them in context.

Only very few career academics have had personal or professional lives of sufficient interest to warrant a biography or autobiography. R. G. Collingwood's *Autobiography* is one rare exception which was seminal in my own intellectual development. Neither my life nor my ideas warrant such treatment, but I have been exceptionally fortunate to have been in a series of significant institutions at key points in their history: Oxford at the start of the great revival of Jurisprudence inspired by Herbert Hart; Chicago in the heyday of the Deanship of Edward Levi; Khartoum and Dar-es-Salaam in the heady years immediately after Independence; the Queen's University, Belfast during the flourishing of a remarkable law faculty, a period that coincided with the revival of the tragic 'troubles' in Northern Ireland; ten years at Warwick Law School as it tried to implement programmatically a broad approach to academic law; and, since 1983, at University College, London, the first modern English law school, the home of Bentham and Austin, and an institution which has for more than 150 years played a leading role in extending access to higher education to non-Anglicans,

---

[1] Pierre Bourdieu, *Homo Academicus* (trs. P. Collier, Stanford, 1988).
[2] For the sake of consistency, I have stayed with the original ways of designating gender.

women, ethnic minorities, and students from overseas. For nearly twenty years I have also been a fairly regular visitor to the University of Miami Law School, starting when Soia Mentschikoff (Karl Llewellyn's widow) was Dean and watching the institution develop from a respectable, largely local, professional school into a national law school which is noted for its intellectual liveliness as well as for its commitment to enlightened professionalism and to educational opportunity. In addition to these congenial and supportive bases, I have had all of the advantages of the modern wandering scholar. During the past twenty-five years I have held positions as a visitor at the universities of Yale, Chicago, Pennsylvania, Virginia, Uppsala, Northwestern, Canberra, Nairobi, Windsor (Ontario), the Netherlands Institute for Advanced Study, and Boston College. Largely through association with the International Legal Center (now the International Center for Law and Development) in the 1970s and with the Commonwealth Legal Education Association since 1975, I have also visited law schools throughout the Commonwealth and the English-speaking world as consultant, external examiner, lecturer, researcher, and professional tourist.

These essays are largely products of these experiences. Each was motivated at least in part by activist concerns, typically to develop, interpret, justify, and promote a particular approach to academic law and to explore some of its theoretical and practical implications. I am a legal theorist as well as an academic activist and in most contexts, including Northern Ireland, I have been an expatriate with all the limitations, privileges, and inhibitions that this entails. One hopes that this has resulted in an approach that is more reflective than polemical and a posture that approximates to relative detachment. The purpose of bringing these essays together is not to fight old political battles, but rather to provide some historical and intellectual insights into the background to the current situation of law as a discipline, particularly in the British Isles, but more generally, in the common law world. The essays fall into three main groups. The first four chapters establish a historical context and start to articulate an approach to 'broadening the study of law from within' in accordance with the classic values of liberal education. The second group (chapters 5–12) is concerned with implementing that programme in particular fields, notably legal theory, evidence, legal method and, more generally, skills teaching. The third group (chapters 13–17) deals with international trends and issues of policy in legal education and scholarship, mainly in common law countries.

In order to set these pieces in an appropriate and coherent context it is necessary to say something about my personal odyssey and the locales that were the settings of these essays. What follows is akin to the reminiscences of a foreign correspondent describing situations in which he has found himself doing work that stimulated him to write.

I chose to read law at Oxford for largely negative reasons. I was determined to escape the torments of a rigorous classical education; my father was opposed to my reading history; and my elder brother offered me his notes. I 'went up' to

Brasenose College, Oxford in October 1952, graduated in 1955, but remained there on and off until 1957. The 1950s saw the beginning of what Noel Annan called 'the Age of the don', which continued until the early or mid-seventies.[3] The decade was also later referred to as 'the silent fifties' by a generation of students who thought that their predecessors were apolitical and unduly submissive to authority, perhaps because they did not participate in marches, had not conceived of sit-ins, and were not interested in university governance. This interpretation is at best a half-truth. Some of my most vivid memories of the 1950s relate to the Cold War, McCarthyism, the class system, nationalization, Suez, Hungary, decolonization, apartheid, and concerns about nuclear power. The first Aldermarston march was in 1956, the same year as Sudan and Ghana achieved independence.

These were hardly apolitical diversions, but it is true that I can recall little discussion of higher education and none of university governance beyond C. P. Snow's *The Masters*.[4] There were few perceived connections between politics and studying law. There was little sustained discussion of legal education by law teachers, let alone by law students.[5] It was, however, a period of very significant change in higher education, but with very much less public debate and controversy than in the years that followed. There was, in a sense, a silent revolution in which the ground was laid and the momentum was built up for the more spectacular changes of the sixties.

For some, the most visible revolution in universities was 'the revolution in philosophy'. This had a direct impact on academic law, which otherwise seemed to be somewhat comatose. In 1952 H. L. A. Hart, a philosophy fellow at New College, who had practised as a barrister before the war, was appointed to the Corpus Chair of Jurisprudence at Oxford. At the time Hart was hardly known outside a small, but influential, circle of philosophers in Oxford, which included J. L. Austin, Gilbert Ryle, and Friedrich Waismann. This was a crucial moment in English academic law. Hart linked the new movement in analytical philosophy to legal theory. Within a remarkably short time he not only made a profound impact on Jurisprudence, but also introduced a new note of vigorous intellectualism into the study of law.[6]

I was bored and confused by law until 1954 when, towards the end of my second year, I first read Herbert Hart's inaugural lecture[7] and then attended his general lectures which were in large part forerunners of *The Concept of Law*.[8]

---

[3] Noel Annan, *Our Age* (London, 1990).   [4] C. P. Snow, *The Masters* (London, 1952).

[5] There was one notable exception to this quietism. In his inaugural lecture, published in extended form in 1950, Professor L. C. B. Gower of the London School of Economics launched a powerful attack on 'English Legal Training' (13 *MLR* 137 (1950)) discussed *BT*, at 30.

[6] For my assessment of Hart's contribution, see 'Academic Law and Legal Philosophy: the Significance of Herbert Hart', 95 *LQR* 557 (1979).

[7] H. L. A. Hart, 'Definition and Theory in Jurisprudence', Inaugural Lecture at Oxford, 1952. The most readily accessible version is published in 70 *LQR* 37 (1953).

[8] H. L. A. Hart, *The Concept of Law* (Oxford, 1961).

From then on I was committed to legal theory. Some of my writings, for example chapters 3 and 4, may give the impression that in espousing the realism of Karl Llewellyn and in criticising the Expository Tradition of academic law I was reacting against law as it was taught in Oxford in the 1950s. That is only partly correct. It is true that with many of my contemporaries I shared a deep ambivalence towards some of the more fustian and élitist features of the University of Oxford. It is also true that, especially in the final examinations, the predominant approach was analytical and expository. I later reacted against narrow conceptions of law, but not against the underlying educational philosophy. I still consider that analytical jurisprudence has some value.[9] My experiences as an undergraduate were for the most part positive. The Oxford tutorial system was based on the premise that undergraduate education should be largely self-education. One's main obligations were to write and present essays at one or two tutorials a week and to take occasional mock examinations called 'collections'. One was largely free to choose what one read, how and when one studied, and which lectures, if any, to attend. I took full advantage of that freedom, reading widely in literature, philosophy, and legal history and, until my final year, devoting a bare minimum of time to 'straight law'. I attended relatively few lectures and the only formal instruction that I received in Constitutional Law was four tutorials at weekends given by a bibulous and entertaining part-timer.

Few of my teachers fitted the model of the prototypical black-letter lawyer: one of my main tutors, Ronald Maudsley, had recently returned from Harvard and tried, with mixed success, to introduce us to his interpretation of policy analysis. Derek Hall was an elegant and inspiring tutor in legal history. Contact with Professors Hart and Lawson was liberating rather than narrowing. My main tutor, Barry Nicholas, while adopting what seemed to be a rigorously scholastic approach to Roman Law, was a model of the Oxford version of a Socratic tutor. Moreover, we were positively encouraged 'to read around the subject'. A reading-list which included works by Wolfgang Friedmann, Sir Henry Maine, F. W. Maitland, Sir Ivor Jennings, Sir David Keir, and A. P. d'Entrèves could hardly be criticized for being narrowly analytical. Indeed, the main criticism of my Oxford education might be that I was able to obtain a first class degree on the basis of good performances in Jurisprudence, Legal History, and two papers in Roman Law with no more than an adequate showing in three private law subjects (Contract, Tort, and Land Law) and a rather vague mixture of Constitutional Law and History. My Oxford education taught me the value of independent study, helped to develop certain general analytical skills, and gave extensive practice in writing to deadlines. It left me largely innocent of legal knowledge and almost totally unaware of the realities of legal practice or the relationship between law and social life.

At that time most law graduates who did not intend to qualify as solicitors

---

[9] See below, Ch. 8.

took the easier route of eating dinners and sitting Bar Finals a few months after graduation, with the help of a cram course. Many followed this path before deciding on a career. At the time being called to the Bar was considered to be little more than a tedious formality. Although I had no intention of practising as a barrister, I joined Lincoln's Inn and began to eat dinners. On graduation I planned to spend some time in East Africa before deciding what to do about a career. Dropping out had not yet come into vogue, so I enrolled for a correspondence course for Bar Finals with Messrs. Gibson and Weldon, the leading commercial law tutors, mainly to give a cover of respectability to this interlude. I intended to sit the examination eventually, but I was in no great hurry. I had already developed a strong dislike for the empty and jejune ritual of eating dinners, which brought back unhappy memories of public school. An encounter in the offices of Gibson and Weldon brought me face to face with the cynical anti-intellectualism of the professional examinations. A little later I decided that the Inns of Court were exploiting overseas students by providing them with the façade of a legal education, often at great personal expense.

The correspondence course did in fact fill in some elementary gaps in my knowledge of substantive law, but I devoted most of the next nine months to travel and to reading extensively in philosophy, jurisprudence, and general literature. Eventually after a long period of indecision and two terms standing in for my former tutor at Oxford, I obtained a fellowship to do postgraduate work at the University of Chicago, mainly under Karl Llewellyn. By then I knew that I did not wish to practise law nor even to become a paper barrister (in retrospect a diplomatic misjudgement more than a political gesture), nor did I wish to teach law in England. I wanted to work in Africa, preferably in higher education, and I ended up teaching law because that was all that I could claim to be equipped to teach.

The year in Chicago was a watershed. It began in 1957, shortly before the launch of the first Sputnik. Although I spent nearly half my time working with Karl Llewellyn,[10] I was fully integrated into the Law School both socially and intellectually.[11] This was toward the end of Edward Levi's extraordinary Deanship: in addition to having built up a star-studded faculty, Chicago was the base for a pioneering clinical programme and for large-scale interdisciplinary work in law and the social sciences,[12] including what later became the Law and Economics movement. This last was spearheaded by Levi himself and Aaron Director, shortly to be joined by Ronald Coase and George Stigler.[13] I immediately realized that Director's political ideas were almost the reverse of my own and I

[10] My relations with Llewellyn are described in *The Karl Llewellyn Papers* (Chicago, 1968).

[11] I took courses from a number of individuals most of whom I later learned were well-known: Edward Levi, Edward Shils, Max Rheinstein, Nicholas Katzenbach, Roscoe Stefan, Alison Dunham, Malcolm Sharp, William Winslow Crosskey, Soia Mentschikoff, and, of course, Karl Llewellyn.

[12] My wife worked on the Jury Project and I had some contact with the Arbitration Project.

[13] For an excellent account of the history of the American Law and Economics Movement, see Neil Duxbury, *Patterns of American Jurisprudence* (Oxford, 1995), Ch. 5.

refused to be pressured into taking his basic course on economic analysis. This
was a political stand that was almost certainly a strategic mistake. One needs to
study one's opponents and a grounding in economics should be part of the
equipment of most law teachers. After I had recovered from the initial culture
shock and shed some of my Oxford arrogance, I realized that this was a more
sophisticated, lively, and demanding institution than I had even conceived as
possible. The University of Chicago also provided an alternative model to Oxford
of an institution of higher learning devoted to excellence.[14]

Conversion to the idea of the American Law School at its best and to the ideas
of Karl Llewellyn at no stage involved a wholesale rejection of Oxford. It was,
after all, largely a capacity to write English and to study on my own that enabled
me to cope with the pace and the bewildering range of new ideas and experiences that Chicago offered.[15] I was concerned to reconcile and build on Hart and
Llewellyn rather than to choose between them. And Oxford rather than Chicago
had taught me the importance of history. But this experience both exposed and
provided for some key missing ingredients in my legal education up to then: the
linking of law to the social sciences; a dialectical approach to every issue; a
highly intellectualized but nevertheless realistic approach to legal practice and
the law in action; a demonstration of the interdependence of theory and practice;
and a concern for justice.

In September, 1958 I went almost directly from Chicago to the University of
Khartoum. There I spent three rich, exhilarating, and turbulent years during
which I learned a great deal about the operation of the courts, Arab politics,
editing, and diplomacy. In 1961 I seized the opportunity to become a founding
member of the Faculty of Law in Dar-es-Salaam three months before Independence. There I spent four of the most rewarding and educative years of my life.
The first essay in this collection, 'The Camel in the Zoo', was written in 1981

---

[14] The spirit of the institution is captured very well in Edward Shils, *Remembering The University
of Chicago: Teachers, Scientists and Scholars* (Chicago, 1992).

[15] One anecdote about coping may serve as a parable about the differences between English and
American law students at that time. In Chicago I took a course on Conflicts of Laws, taught by
Nicholas De Belleville Katzenbach, who later became Attorney-General of the US. The whole class
seemed to be at a loss to understand what the instructor was getting at. Panic set in as we got nearer
to the examination, which was to be 'open-book'. The reaction of my American colleagues was to
prepare course outlines based exclusively on the casebook and their class notes, even though it was
not clear what was being outlined. I took a different tack. I looked up whether Katzenbach had
published anything in this field. I discovered that he had recently published an article entitled
'Conflicts on an Unruly Horse' (65 *Yale Law Jo.* 1087 (1956)). I interpreted the gist of the piece
to be that there are no rules of Conflicts of Laws—a fairly extreme 'realist' position. Armed with
this information, I borrowed the only library copy of a standard black-letter text (i.e. one which
started with a general formulation of a principle or rule in black type), G. W. Stumberg, *Principles
of Conflicts of Laws*, 1st edn. (1951). I copied out the formulations on the topics we had covered.
In the examination I started each of my answers to problem questions: 'It has been said . . .', quoted
Stumberg *verbatim*, and then continued: 'However, . . .'. I obtained a straight A. Whether this was
a reward for an Oxonian's reputed ability to articulate black-letter rules or whether it shows that my
English education had equipped me with some schoolboy skills for playing the system is an open
question.

and published in 1986 as a fairly light-hearted contribution to the twenty-fifth anniversary celebrations of the Law Faculty in Dar-es-Salaam. It is included because it attempts to show how the experience of teaching in African law schools contributed to the formation of a generation of younger British law teachers who set out to break with tradition when they returned. It deals with only one aspect of that experience, other facets of which will at least be glimpsed in later essays.

The period 1958–65 saw the rise and decline of post-Independence euphoria in Sudan and East Africa. Enthusiastic expatriates, mainly from the British Isles and the United States, were able to experiment and innovate in relatively comfortable surroundings, sometimes with substantial financial backing from the Ford Foundation and other Western sources. We were conscious of some of the contradictions of this kind of cultural imperialism, nearly all expatriate university teachers were genuinely sympathetic to the aspirations of African nationalism, and by and large the more virulent critiques of neocolonialism had not yet made themselves felt.[16] Euphoria in this period was by no means confined to Africa. In the United States 1955–65 was the era of Kennedy and then of Lyndon Johnson's 'Great Society', of the Warren court, BROWN V. THE BOARD OF EDUCATION and the War on Poverty—all of which directly affected the ethos, activities, and culture of law schools. In the United Kingdom this was the period of the Robbins Report,[17] which focused attention on and guided the great expansion of higher education that was already under way. Stewart suggests that the keynotes in higher education in Britain in the period 1960–5 were 'optimism, new ideas, expansion, and opportunity'.[18] Law schools got off to a relatively slow start in this process, but they were inevitably caught up in the spirit of the times.[19] Stewart's words more accurately apply to law in the next period, but by 1965 there were some early indications that at last the discipline might be on the move.[20] Two examples will suffice. In 1963 Gerald Gardiner and Andrew Martin

[16] For general accounts of legal education in anglophone Africa in the post-independence period see, L. C. B. Gower, *Independent Africa: The Challenge to the Legal Profession* (Cambridge, Ma., 1967) and John S. Bainbridge, *The Study and Teaching of Law in Africa* (S. Hackensack, 1972). In Dar-es-Salaam the first serious student unrest surfaced in October, 1966 and was not initially directed at expatriates.

[17] *Higher Education: Report of the Committee Appointed by the Prime Minister under the Chairmanship of Lord Robbins 1961–63*, Cmnd. 2154 (1963).

[18] W. A. C. Stewart, *Higher Education in Postwar Britain* (London, 1989), at 154.

[19] The Robbins Report hardly mentions Law and the Heyworth Committee on Social Studies (Report, Cmnd. 2660, 1965) noted that in the UK 'the study of law has been mainly concerned with the professional training of barristers and solicitors' and that it lagged behind other countries in considering the wider implications of the subject. (para. 38).

[20] The period 1958–65 saw, for example, publication of the first editions of Cross on *Evidence* (London, 1958), de Smith on *Judicial Review of Administrative Action* (London, 1959), Hart's, *The Concept of Law* (London, 1961), Julius Stone's three volume successor to the *Province and Function of Law* (London, 1964–6), Sir Leon Radzinowicz's three volume study of the history of criminal law, a number of notable works on Public International Law and one of the first genuinely interdisciplinary books on law to be published in England, Robert Stevens and Basil Yamey, *The Restrictive Practices Court* (London, 1965). A new postwar generation of legal scholars was getting into its stride.

published *Law Reform NOW*, which presaged some of Gardiner's reforms as Lord
Chancellor, including the establishment of the Law Commission (1965) and the
appointment of the Ormrod Committee on Legal Education (1967, reported
1971).[21] In 1963 the Society of Public Teachers of Law, having felt handicapped
by lack of reliable information on legal education in presenting evidence to the
Robbins Committee and the National Incomes Commission, recruited Professor
John Wilson to prepare, with the help of a high-powered Advisory Committee,
a survey of legal education in the United Kingdom.[22] Although this survey was
almost entirely factual, it ranks as the first major stocktaking of legal education
in England since 1856.[23] Thus, when I returned to the United Kingdom in January
1966, expansion and reform were already, if belatedly, on the agenda.

After the death of Karl Llewellyn in 1962, I became involved in putting his
papers in order and writing about him. This necessitated several visits from
Dar-es-Salaam to Chicago. This in turn brought me into contact with the New
Nations Program, which was run by Denis Cowen, a South African liberal, with
a strong emphasis on Africa. The contrast between Friedmanite Chicago and
Nyerere's African Socialist Dar-es-Salaam put me in a state of almost continuous culture shock; it did not undermine my loyalty to independent Tanzania, but
it reinforced my scepticism of all forms of dogma.

I left Dar-es-Salaam in 1965. I then spent six months at Yale as a Visiting
Fellow before taking up the Chair of Jurisprudence at the Queen's University,
Belfast. The period in New Haven provided a bridge between my African and
Anglo-American phases. Through a link between the Yale Law School and the
Law Faculty in Dar-es-Salaam I had already encountered the Law and Modern-
ization Program, which was similar in conception to the Chicago New Nations
Program, but more radical intellectually and politically. This had attracted some
exceptionally talented young scholars, some of whom, notably Richard Abel and
David Trubek, were later leading members of the Critical Legal Studies Movement. While in New Haven, I mainly worked on Karl Llewellyn and anxiously
prepared to teach in Belfast; but I was still involved in African studies and had
close contact with the Law and Modernization Program and a number of African
postgraduates, including some of my former students from Khartoum and Dar-
es-Salaam.[24] Like Chicago, Yale was small, hospitable, and immensely stimulating. I had the chance to broaden and deepen my knowledge of American law

[21] *Law Reform NOW* (London, 1963); *Report of the Committee on Legal Education* (Ormrod
Report, 1971 Cmnd. 4594).
[22] J. F. Wilson, 'A Survey of Legal Education in the United Kingdom' (1966) 9 *JSPTL* (*NS*) 1.
[23] *The Report of the Legal Education Committee*, chaired by Lord Atkin, (Cmd. 4663, 1934) was
cursory, complacent, and had no visible influence. The best general history of legal education in
England and Wales up to 1965 is still Brian Abel-Smith and Robert Stevens, *Lawyers and the Courts*
(London, 1967). The story from 1945 to 1993 is surveyed in *BT*, Ch. 2, but there is room for much
more detailed work to be done.
[24] I had close contact with Robert Stevens, Myres McDougal, Harold Lasswell, Charles Black Jr.,
Charles Runyon, Quintin Johnstone, Francis Deng, and Willliam Felstiner and a number of others,
some of whom have since become well-known.

schools. It is easier to identify the physical differences between Chicago and New Haven than to pinpoint the more nuanced contrasts between the intellectual ambience and institutional culture of two élite law schools. Both were committed to broad, highly intellectualized approaches to law. Yale catered more for the élite of the legal profession; but I came away feeling, as an outsider, that the similarities between the ideas of Karl Llewellyn and of Lasswell and McDougal, and between Yale and Chicago students, were greater than the differences in style initially suggested. Similarly, both Law and Modernization at Yale and the New Nations Program at Chicago seemed to me to be stimulating, but destined to be peripheral and transient. The Yale programme also ran into political opposition, but for American law schools generally interest in Africa was little more than a passing fashion.[25]

In January, 1966 I moved to Belfast to take up the Chair of Jurisprudence in succession to James Louis Montrose. Montrose had been one of the most forceful and eloquent British protagonists of law as a subject of liberal education. He had resigned from Belfast after suffering a series of embittering political defeats at the end of a period of nearly thirty years as Dean and he died abroad not long afterwards. He had, however, left as part of his legacy a new curriculum, which was in many respects ahead of its time in the United Kingdom: a four-year degree; a full first year course on Juristic Technique and two compulsory courses on legal theory; one of the first courses in the British Isles on welfare law (entitled 'Social Legislation'); and a number of other arrangements that were considered to be progressive.[26] Queen's was also in the process of building up an exceptionally talented young faculty, as is illustrated by the fact that nearly all of my former colleagues in Belfast have since been appointed to Chairs of Law, many of them while relatively young. Others have become prominent in public life.

Queen's provides the primary context for the next two chapters. Taken together, these can be read as an early programmatic statement of my views on legal scholarship, legal education, and legal literature as the central interconnected activities of law schools. Chapter 3, 'Reflections on Law in Context', contains a manifesto for the 'Law in Context' series, which was first planned with Robert Stevens at Yale as a series of 'counter textbooks' and was officially launched in 1967. The introduction and conclusion were written in 1991 for a *festschrift* for Patrick Atiyah, who was a colleague in both Khartoum and Warwick, and who contributed the first and perhaps the most distinguished book to the series. Chapter 4, 'Pericles and the Plumber', used the platform of an inaugural lecture to issue a general manifesto for a broader approach to legal education. It was also a public affirmation that Montrose's agenda and approach were still alive at Queen's.

---

[25] On different interpretations of the demise of the American Law and Development Movement see below n. 43.

[26] A selection of Montrose's writings, together with a brief biography, was published in *Precedent in English Law and other essays* (ed. H. G. Hanbury, Shannon, 1968).

These two chapters can for the most part speak for themselves, but it is worth making some retrospective comments on them. First, given the positive things I have said above about Oxford, Chicago, Khartoum and Dar-es-Salaam and the fact that Queen's was already potentially receptive to a broad and liberal approach to the study of law, what was I reacting against? Why the polemical stance and the reforming zeal? My concerns were as much intellectual as ethical and political. At first there was a vague sense of dissatisfaction; later it became a conviction that the law schools were not doing justice to a very rich subject that was pervasive, important, intellectually challenging, and continuously raising moral and political issues in concrete ways. One reason is summed up in the central tenet of legal realism: for almost any legal purpose, and especially for understanding, focusing on rules alone is not enough. There was definitely a prevailing orthodoxy in academic law in the United Kingdom, even if it was difficult to pin down and describe. The clearest examples were to be found in the professional examinations and in law publishing, but it permeated most legal education and legal scholarship. My main direct exposure to this orthodoxy had been with Gibson and Weldon and the standard student textbooks, but I was aware that I had escaped fairly lightly. Although the general approach had intellectual roots in Austinian positivism,[27] it was rarely defended explicitly and, because some deviations and experiments were tolerated in universities, it provided a rather elusive target to attack. As with reactions against the Langdellian orthodoxy in the United States, it was necessary to establish an ideal type to which actual programmes and practices more or less conformed in order to develop a critique and to propose alternatives. My depiction of 'the Expository Tradition' does capture a congeries of assumptions, attitudes, and practices which some of us were trying to challenge, but, as I hope is made clear throughout these essays, the detailed history of English academic law is more complex than the ideal type.[28] Academic politics needs its myths and legends.[29]

A second retrospective comment concerns what is not said in these two chapters—the silences. In each there is little or no mention of the relevance of the African experience or of political-ideological concerns. The reason for downplaying Africa was simple: I learned quickly on my return to the United Kingdom that it was not considered diplomatic by potential allies or opponents among one's colleagues to suggest that the Law Faculty in Dar-es-Salaam might provide

[27] David Sugarman, 'Legal Theory and the Common Law Mind: The Making of the Textbook Tradition', in *LTCL*, Ch. 3.

[28] Pressure of space has led to the omission of one historical essay, '1836 and All That: Laws in the University of London 1836–1986' (40 Current Legal Problems 261 (1987)), a central theme of which is how recent is the development of 'critical mass' in university legal education in England compared to most Western countries. The broad patterns of university education and élite law schools were established in the US in the late 19th cent. By contrast, as leading commentators on higher education have emphasized, the modern English university is largely a post-World War II creation, e.g. Martin Trow, 14 *Oxford Review of Education* 81 (1988). The same is true of our law schools (See generally, *BT*, Ch. 2).

[29] For further reflections on exposition, and some second thoughts, see *BT* at 141–6.

some lessons for UK law schools. The explanation for the other omission is more complex. My personal political views have been reasonably 'progressive' throughout my adult life, but, unlike many colleagues, I have normally tried to distance these views when writing about academic matters, partly because my academic ideology gives primacy to values of tolerance and open-mindedness in this context, partly because the kind of approach I favour can itself accommodate a wide spectrum of political views, and partly because most of my working life has been spent as an expatriate in situations in which one has been expected to exhibit diplomatic restraint.[30]

Except for these two early essays, the period 1966–72 is not directly represented here, largely because I published little on the subject of this volume. My main efforts were directed to writing an intellectual biography of Karl Llewellyn and to developing and implementing my general ideas through teaching, editing, and research. On the whole, writing about them came later. It was an important period in Northern Ireland politics, in higher education internationally, and in legal education in the United Kingdom. In all of these politics were pervasive. In Belfast, we witnessed at close quarters the rise of Ian Paisley, the start of the Civil Rights Movement and the People's Democracy, the rapid intrusion of violence into the conflict, Bloody Sunday, internment, and the Compton, Widgery, and Diplock reports.[31]

These were just some of the salient events that dominated the foreground. Internationally, institutions of higher education in many countries were rocked by the turbulence that is popularly labelled '1968', but which dates back at least to incidents at Berkeley and the London School of Economics in 1966 and continued to have repercussions into the seventies and beyond. In this regard Queen's was in an unusual situation. First, student unrest in Belfast was at least as much associated with the local 'troubles' as with the international ferment. Secondly, as the main university in a radically divided society Queen's occupied a special position. Approximately 55 per cent of the local students were identifiable as Protestant and 45 per cent as Catholic. A significant number were from outside Northern Ireland, as were many of the academic staff. The University's public posture—and that of most academics—was that it should not take

---

[30] It is significant, and quite consistent, that 'The Camel in the Zoo' is the least 'political' of the contributions to the *Limits of Legal Radicalism* (ed., Issa Shivji, Dar-es-Salaam, 1986), a book which is even more revealing than its title. Similarly, it is my view that many recent commentators on the American Realist Movement have exaggerated the extent to which the jurisprudence of leading Realists, such as Llewellyn, Corbin, Cook, and Frank, was stimulated primarily by political concerns or was based upon shared political views. A great deal of American Legal Realism seems to me to have been strikingly apolitical, and individual realists have to be located on a fairly broad political spectrum. The Progressive Movement was an important part of the background, but Realism was as much motivated by a mixture of educational, scholarly, and technical concerns as by ideological or political issues. Suffice to say here that many of my contemporaries would have given rather more emphasis to political critique of the orthodoxy than I did in these essays.

[31] The main reports are discussed in 'Emergency Powers and Criminal Process: The Diplock Report' (1973) *Criminal L Rev.* 406.

sides on sectarian issues or tolerate sectarian intolerance or dogmatism on campus. To a remarkable extent during my time there, this aloofness from the
conflict was widely respected, including by those students and colleagues who
were involved in various kinds of activity off-campus. There even developed a
semi-articulated theory of the university as a sort of non-sectarian sanctuary.[32]
The troubles enhanced the feeling of non-locals, especially newcomers, that they
were really expatriates who could not understand and should not intervene in
local conflicts. The main relevance of all this here is that a strong version of the
classical liberal idea of a university as a somewhat aloof citadel of tolerance, if
not quite an ivory tower, was continually being articulated and reinforced in
response to challenges to 'come off the fence'. A standard response to students
and others was: 'on which side?' Ironically, at the height of the period of calls
for greater 'relevance', some academics at Queen's were being discouraged in
their teaching and writing from being too visibly concerned with local issues.[33]

The Northern Ireland troubles and '1968' overshadowed and diverted attention from the more parochial concerns of legal education policy, which seemed
rather trivial in the circumstances. In fact such issues became highly politicized
in legal circles during this period, especially in England. For this was the period
of the Ormrod Committee, which sat for twice as long as the Robbins Committee, only to produce a set of recommendations and a structure which reflected
the inability of the various sectors of the legal profession to agree on central
issues of professional formation. What was presented as a programmed sequence
of stages of legal education and training—academic, vocational, apprenticeship,
and continuing—reflected a scheme that had already been widely adopted in
other parts of the Commonwealth, except that in England the year of formal
vocational training was treated as a preparation for apprenticeship rather than as
a substitute. In reality the structure was little more than a carving up of spheres

---

[32] The student unrest at Queen's seemed tame compared to my experiences in Khartoum where
the university was several times surrounded by riot police and was closed down for substantial
periods. In Sudan a somewhat different concept of 'sanctuary' was invoked in defence of student
political activity on campus when political parties and most overt political activity were banned by
law.

[33] By no means all colleagues were inhibited, especially those who were locals. For example,
several of my colleagues were active in politics, including David Trimble, who became Leader of
the Ulster Unionists in 1996, and Kevin Boyle, who was a founder member of the People's Democracy and has since become a noted civil liberties lawyer; Tom Hadden launched the non-sectarian
periodical, *Fortnight*, while he was a lecturer in law at Queen's; and some outsiders, including,
Claire Palley and Harry Calvert were involved in constitutional debates. Toward the end of my stay,
in response to persistent student demands, we formed a joint staff-student non-sectarian working
group to study with 'relative detachment' controversial problems to do with interrogation and emergency powers. As an exercise in consensus politics this was highly educational, but politically it was
little more than a symbolic gesture. The main product was a pamphlet, *Emergency Powers: A Fresh
Start* (Fabian Tract 416, 1972). One lesson of the experience is that if one seeks to produce a
balanced package of recommendations based on consensus and compromise this will be used selec-
tively by politicians for their own sectarian ends. The general problems facing academics in polarized
societies will be familiar to teachers of Constitutional Law and other controversial subjects, especially in countries with repressive regimes.

of influence. The two branches of the practising profession could not agree on a joint system of training; instead, each branch insisted on retaining control over both of these stages as well as prescribing requirements for the recognition of degrees. The law degree was accepted as the 'normal' route of entry, but non-law graduate entry was retained (and has since prospered).[34] The academics managed to maintain a degree of autonomy and control over the first stage at the cost of being largely excluded from the three remaining stages. Thus university (and later polytechnic) law schools were assigned the modest role of primary schools, without even having a monopoly over primary legal education. The outcome was by no means all bad: the Ormrod exercise raised the level of debate; a relatively clear and stable structure was established; the development of an all-graduate legal profession was accelerated; and university law schools were given a relatively clear, though limited role, and some scope for innovation and diversification.[35]

In 1972 I was invited to join a committee on legal education in Northern Ireland, chaired by Professor (later Sir) Arthur Armitage, who had been a member of the Ormrod Committee. We learned from the experience of the Ormrod Committee and made recommendations that ensured substantial public funding for a Professional Training Institute within Queen's, but separate from the Law Faculty.[36] Scotland followed a similar path, with the result that it was only in England that professional training for law was almost entirely left to private financing, in sharp contrast with other professions such as Engineering and Medicine.

In 1972 I moved to the University of Warwick, one of the new universities established in the period of expansion and innovation that followed the Robbins Report. I had previously been informally involved in discussions with Professor Geoffrey Wilson about planning the Law School, which was established in 1968. Under his leadership the institution was committed to 'broadening the

---

[34] *BT* 36–7, 180.

[35] The pros and cons of the Ormrod structure are considered in *BT* at 37–42. However, the main motivation behind the scheme was political: neither branch of the profession nor the academics were prepared to surrender their share of control or agree on another form of power-sharing. The main beneficiary was the public purse, for by refusing to accept either the medical school model or even the location of the second ('vocational') stage in universities, the profession sacrificed any chance they might have had of that stage being publicly funded. The result has been a serious underinvestment in the vocational stage and a scandalously unfair system of discretionary grants for that stage, which has arbitrarily limited access to the profession, on which see P. A. Thomas, 'The Poverty of Students', 27 *The Law Teacher* 152 (1993).

[36] *Report of the Committee on Legal Education in Northern Ireland* (The Armitage Report, Cmnd. 579, 1973). The subsequent, sometimes troubled history of legal education and training in Northern Ireland is not dealt with here. For a balanced account up to 1989 see Desmond Greer in *ALELP* Ch. 10. This was before the Law Faculty at Queen's surrendered one of its main assets, a four year undergraduate degree. A rather happier story is the success of Servicing the Legal System (SLS), which in 1994 won one of The Queen's Anniversary Prizes for Higher and Further Education. SLS is a model both of systematic legal information provision in a small jurisdiction and of co-operation between practitioners and academics.

study of law from within', a formula which was on the whole sufficiently clear to give us a shared sense of purpose and yet sufficiently vague to allow individuals to further the general aim according to their own lights. The ideas underlying the approach were much the same as those that had been espoused in Dar-es-Salaam and in my own writings. The general approach was to be implemented in every course and each member of faculty was expected to rethink their field in broader terms than exposition and analysis of doctrine. Although I have never worked in an institution which had such a clear commitment to programmatic implementation of an explicit educational ethos, in fact there was relatively little teamwork. Individual teachers were free to interpret the Warwick ethos as they pleased and they did so in highly individualistic ways.[37]

During ten years at Warwick my main assignment was to teach legal theory, legal method, and to rethink a field of my choice. After considering land law and torts, I fairly quickly settled on evidence and for the next fifteen years this took up a large part of my scholarly energies.[38] Chapters 5 and 6 deal with some of the educational and theoretical implications of this enterprise, but most of this work falls outside the scope of this book. If the first four essays can now be read in retrospect as a combination of history and programmatics, the next group deal with aspects of the praxis of implementing this programme in my special fields of interest—evidence, jurisprudence, and legal method—and the relationships between them. Chapter 5 was originally delivered as a lecture at the University of Victoria, British Columbia in 1980. It makes the case for 'taking facts seriously' largely through a historical account of previous attempts to do this and some reasons for their failure to date.[39] 'Evidence and Legal Theory', chapter 6, was my inaugural lecture at University College in 1983, but belongs in spirit to the Warwick period. It is included here in order to illustrate the intimate relationship between legal theory, legal education, and legal scholarship in a particular field. These two papers were offshoots of a project which was conceived

[37] For one interpretation of the early years at Warwick, see R. Folsom and N. Roberts, 'The Warwick Story: Being Led Down the Contextual Path of the Law', 30 *Jo. Leg. Ed.* 166 (1979). See now Geoffrey Wilson (ed.), *Frontiers of Legal Scholarship* (Chichester, 1995).

[38] The general project resulted in a number of papers and three books: *TEBW*; *RE*; and *ANALYSIS*. How to teach fact-analysis is developed at much greater length in the Teachers' Manual for *ANALYSIS*.

[39] This is the first of several papers in this volume in which the mythical jurisdiction of Xanadu is introduced. This belongs to the realms of the imagination, as in Coleridge, rather than to the real place in China. 'Xanadu' was first used as a diplomatic way of pointing to the absurdity of some practices in respect of law publishing and legal information in Commonwealth countries, without attributing them to any particular jurisdiction, institution or individual (See 'Keeping up-to-date in Xanadu', Seventh Commonwealth Law Conference, Hong Kong, *Papers* (1983)). Since then I have continued to use this method of indeterminate attribution both to satirize common fallacies, attitudes or practices which seem to me to be obviously absurd, but also as a convenient vehicle for suggesting a general approach or perspective that can be applied flexibly, in the light of local knowledge, in different contexts (See Chs. 7, 13, and 15 below and William Twining and Emma Quick, edd., *Legal Records in the Commonwealth* (Aldershot, 1994, Ch. 2). For example, Xanadu can be interpreted as an 'ideal type' which can be used for comparing and contrasting local conditions in different jurisdictions as a way of establishing 'context'. In chapters the main use is satirical.

from the start as a case-study of what might be involved in broadening the study of any field of law 'from within'.

'Theory in the Law Curriculum' (chapter 7) also belongs to this group.[40] It was written with Neil MacCormick in 1985 specifically for a symposium the main purpose of which was to respond to a concern that the liveliness and increasing sophistication of legal philosophy was creating an increasing gap between legal theory and nearly all other subjects in the law curriculum. Jurisprudence was becoming a subject apart.[41] This was shortly after the perennial question whether Jurisprudence should be compulsory had resurfaced in the Australian National University, Canberra and University College, London. In both institutions Jurisprudence remained compulsory. However, in Dar-es-Salaam, Belfast, and Warwick legal theory (under various names) had sat quite comfortably in the second year, often preceded by a substantial dose of theory in the first year; but later at UCL I lost the local battle to move the course to the second year . To leave Jurisprudence to the final year largely undermines the argument that it should be one of the main vehicles for integrating the under-graduate curriculum. If one is to persuade law students of the value of theory, it pays to catch them young. These concerns stimulated us to make a general statement about the nature of legal theory and it was pleasing to find how much my co-author and I were in agreement about the nature of the enterprise.

Chapter 8, 'General and Particular Jurisprudence: Three Chapters in a Story' was written in 1995 as the first in a series of essays on globalization and legal theory.[42] It is a deliberately local and historical account of the distinction between general and particular jurisprudence within the English analytical tradition. It is placed here, out of chronological order, because it continues the exploration of the nature of legal theory and of its relationship to the detailed study of substantive law. It makes the point that although the dominant tradition of academic law in England has been quite narrowly focused on doctrine its geographical reach has been broad and cosmopolitan—for fairly obvious histor-ical reasons. The essay criticizes Hart's posthumous postscript to *The Concept of Law*, in which he tried to reconcile his central ideas with those of Ronald Dworkin by resorting to this largely forgotten distinction: Hart argued that his jurisprudence was general, whereas Dworkin's is particular. This distinction, I suggest, will not bear much weight and the significance of Dworkin's central ideas cannot be sensibly restricted to a single jurisdiction; however, this and

---

[40] Neil MacCormick collaborated on this paper and his contribution is apparent in both the style and the substance. I am grateful to him for agreeing to its republication. See further, Alan Hunt, 'The role and place of legal theory in legal education; reflections on foundationalism', 9 *Legal Studies* 146 (1989); cf. Hunt in 6 *Legal Studies* 292 (1986).

[41] The W. G. Hart Workshop in London for 1984 was devoted to this theme and the project eventually resulted in a volume entitled *Legal Theory and Common Law* (1986) (*LTCL*).

[42] A sequel, entitled 'Globalization and Legal Theory' is due to appear in (1996) *Current Legal Problems*.

earlier debates raise important issues about cultural relativism and how far legal phenomena are only explicable in terms of specific social and cultural contexts.

The remaining chapters deal with some general issues affecting the discipline in the common law world. To set them in context, we need to return to my story. During the 1970s, I maintained my professional interest in Africa through occasional external examining and consultancy. This was the period of the rise and fall of 'The Law and Development Movement'. From 1972 to 1975, I was a member of one of two committees set up by the International Legal Center in New York to prepare reports on legal education and legal research with special reference to the Third World.[43] Working on this project was an extraordinary privilege. It broadened one's horizons and provided an opportunity to reflect on and extend one's African experience and to keep in touch with developments in legal education and scholarship in many parts of the world. Of all the committee reports with which I have been associated, *Legal Education in a Changing World*[44] seems to me to have best stood the test of time and to provide the most systematic and forward-looking approach to the subject. This was largely due to the extraordinary range and quality of experience of members of the Committee.[45] Much of my subsequent work in the area as an activist, consultant, and commentator has used that report as a starting-point. This is especially the case in regard to involvement in a series of Commonwealth Legal Education Association projects on particular, often neglected, topics such as access, law publishing, the localization of legal literature and information, preservation of legal records, skills development, law in multilingual societies, human rights education, and legal education for non-lawyers.[46] Some of these particular topics are

---

[43] The two committees worked in parallel with close liaison. Quite sharp differences of view emerged within the Research Committee, but these were somewhat glossed over in its final report, entitled *Law and Development* (New York and Uppsala, 1974). See, however, the contrasting views of Trubek and Galanter, 'Scholars in Self-estrangement: Some Reflections on the Crisis in Law and Development Studies in the United States' (1974) *Wisconsin L Rev.* 1062—(Trubeck was chair of the Research Committee); and the criticisms of J. Goldring, 'Law and Cultural Colonialism' (unpublished paper, Sydney, 1974) and Robert Martin, 4 *Melanesian L Jo.* 270 (1976). These are discussed in *ALLD*. A powerful critique of American involvement in Latin America is James A. Gardner, *Legal Imperialism: American Lawyers and Foreign Aid in Latin America* (U Wisconsin Press, 1980). The debates centred on criticisms of the use of 'development' as a concept, on the relevance of American and Western ideas to 'Third World' countries, on the relative importance of abstract theory and pragmatic policy perspectives, and on ideological differences between Marxists and non-Marxists. There was more of a consensus on the Legal Education Committee, but in retrospect it would have been more illuminating to present the two reports in the form of a dialogue rather than as attempts to distil a consensus.

[44] *Legal Education in a Changing World* (International Legal Center, New York and Uppsala, 1975).

[45] The committee was chaired by Professor Jorge Avendano of Peru. It was drawn from five continents and transcended common law/civil law, North/South, practitioner/academic divides and included a quite wide spectrum of political views.

[46] These projects were all international collaborative efforts. The main published results are W. Twining and J. Uglow (edd.), *Legal Literature in Small Jurisdictions* (Ottawa and London, 1981); *Law Publishing and Legal Information* (London, 1981); *LLS*; *ALELP*; *Legal Records in the Commonwealth* (op. cit., 1994); *Law for Non-lawyers: Some Preliminary Reflections* (Commonwealth

treated or touched on in these essays, but the experience with the International Legal Center had a more general influence on almost everything I have written about academic law since the early 1970s.

The 1970s marked a watershed in British higher education. The optimism and expansion of the sixties had created a momentum and expectations that blinded most academics to the signs that suggested that there was serious trouble ahead. The events of 1968 had generated a period of intense debate and conflict within universities, although it probably took a less virulent form in the United Kingdom than in some other Western countries. Most of these debates were inward looking and were threatening, exciting or frustrating according to taste. 'Nineteen sixty-eight' probably contributed significantly to the decline in popular political support for higher education, but the economic crises of 1973 and after were probably the main factor in the steady 'decline of donnish dominion' that started in the Heath period, continued through the unsettled years of Labour rule, and accelerated in the Thatcher era.[47]

Law expanded rather more slowly than most other disciplines in the immediate post-Robbins period and it was first the 1980s and later the early 1990s that represent the peak periods of expansion. By 1994 it has been estimated that the scale of university (including polytechnic) legal education was about four times what it had been at the time of Ormrod and nearly thirty times what it had been in 1945.[48] By and large the periods of expansion coincided almost exactly with a succession of economic crises and policies of squeezing public funding of higher education. Compared to other disciplines, law was relatively well-cushioned by high demand and low costs. Realization dawned only slowly of the full implications of successive cuts, the end of the quinquennial system, and other pressures on higher education. In retrospect, much of the writing and debate about academic law in that period, including my own, tended to be rather inwardlooking and obscured the extent to which developments in our discipline and context were a function of changes and problems in higher education generally.[49] In *Blackstone's Tower* I have argued that nearly all significant decisions affecting legal education in English universities since World War II were taken without specific reference to law.

The 1980s were an unhappy time for English universities which were in an almost continuous state of financial crisis. This was mainly before the introduction of academic audit, research assessment, teaching quality assurance, and

Secretariat, London, 1983), and Cassandra Goldie, *Legal Awareness* (Perth, 1992). The Commonwealth Human Rights Initiative's first report, *Put Our World to Rights* (1991) was largely drafted by Professor Yash Ghai, the Commonwealth Legal Education Association's nominee on the Committee. On law in multilingual societies, see M. Cooray, *Changing the Language of the Law: The Sri Lankan Experience* (Quebec, 1985). *ALLD* is a commentary on and an elaboration of some of the main themes in *Legal Education in a Changing World*.

[47] A. H. Halsey, *Decline of Donnish Dominion, The British Academic Professions in the Twentieth Century* (Oxford, 1992).
[48] *BT*, Ch. 2.   [49] See *BT*, Ch. 2.

the integration of polytechnics and universities into a single 'system', which so far seems to have reinforced the hierarchy of prestige and privilege represented by the former binary divide. It was also before the movement to break up the University of London into a series of independent universities had gathered momentum—a process which, thankfully, it survived in a slimmed down form. In retrospect one can see that the financial problems of universities, pressures to bureaucratize, and to make them more 'efficient' and more accountable, and in general to move from an élite scholarly model of universities toward a mass factory model, were part of a series of general international trends which were not attributable solely to reactionary political forces. It was also a period of great changes in legal practice and the organization and ethos of the legal profession.[50] The cries of pain from academics were to be heard in Australia, New Zealand, the United States, and many parts of Europe and these were the problems of the rich compared to what was happening in poorer countries. For example, after the oil crises of the 1970s, the infrastructure of most African law faculties was rapidly eroded to such an extent that it is remarkable that they managed to keep going at all.

In 1983 I moved from Warwick to University College, London. This was a more traditional law faculty, although it was moving in the direction of a broader and more liberal approach under the leadership of Jeffrey Jowell. It differed from Warwick in several other respects: for example, it was more metropolitan and diverse; it had closer links with judges and leaders of the practising profession; it had a large and rapidly expanding postgraduate programme; and it was part of a loose confederation of five rather different law schools within the framework of a very large federal university. Like Warwick, UCL provided a supportive atmosphere for research and writing and, particularly at postgraduate level, plenty of scope for development of new courses.

At UCL my intellectual and teaching interests continued to focus mainly on jurisprudence, legal method, and the theory of evidence. I was able to maintain my international activities as an officer of the Commonwealth Legal Education Association and through regular visiting appointments at the University of Miami and, for short periods, at the Universities of Windsor and Nairobi. All of these interests are reflected in the ensuing chapters, which were written during this period.

Chapters 9–12 deal with the development of 'skills' in formal legal education.[51] Maintaining a balance between knowledge, theory, and skills (know-what, know-why, and know-how) is a perennial concern within and beyond

---

[50] On the impact of commercialization and bureaucratization on legal practice in the US see Anthony Kronman, *The Lost Lawyer* (Cambridge, Ma., 1993) and Mary Ann Glendon, *A Nation Under Lawyers* (New York, 1994), discussed below in Ch. 16.

[51] It has not been possible to include here several related papers, notably: 'Taking Skills Seriously' (1986), *Commonwealth Legal Education Newsletter* No. 42, reprinted in several places including *LLS*, Ch. 1; 'Analysis of Evidence' (with Terence Anderson), id., Ch. 8.

legal education. Direct learning of skills has a longer history than is generally recognized: it has been at the centre of American legal education since Langdell's reforms and can be traced back to classical Greece through the history of rhetoric. During the 1980s there was a significant movement within the Commonwealth to substitute direct learning of skills for traditional knowledge-based instruction, especially at the vocational stage. This became widely accepted as a new, though not uncontroversial, orthodoxy centred on the idea that professional training should be based on a job analysis of what lawyers in fact do and of what is involved in performing standard operations to an acceptable level of competence. There was controversy on a number of issues: can skills be learned directly in formal educational settings or can they only be developed through experience in practice with live clients and real problems? Is skills teaching compatible with the ethos and objectives of universities or is it necessarily 'illiberal'? What are the relative merits of different approaches to skills development: clinical/simulated; direct versus indirect; transactional (or 'holistic') versus abstracted methods?[52] My own position has been that it is both feasible and desirable to lay a foundation for various aspects of professional competence through direct study, but that this needs to be reinforced by repeated practice; that we do not know very much about the relative efficiency and effectiveness of various strategies and methods of learning skills; and that this is an area badly in need of more sophisticated theory, research, and development. Similarly, while it is reasonable to maintain that universities are best suited to dealing with matters of the intellect, it is neither sensible nor desirable to try to maintain sharp distinctions between intellectual and other skills. However, far from there being a necessary conflict between liberal values and emphasis on skills, much of classical liberal education was skills-based. Universities should accordingly both be involved in teaching appropriate skills, and should also play a major role in research into and development of all kinds of professional training.

My interest in the area concerned both policy and implementation. It included, first, developing teaching of basic intellectual skills in respect of rule-handling, fact analysis, and methods of reading and using different materials of law study for a variety of purposes; second, to argue for sustained theorizing about, research into, and development of training in respect of both intellectual skills and professional legal skills generally; and, in England, to help resist the temptation to transfer more 'knowledge-based' subjects onto the undergraduate stage in order to make space for skills training at the vocational stage.

Chapter 9, 'Legal Skills and Legal Education', was intended to make the case to English academic colleagues that it is in our interest to claim that 'we are in the skills business too' in order to fend off pressures to further overload the undergraduate curriculum either by increasing the number of prescribed 'core

---

[52] In *ANALYSIS* an attempt is made to combine abstracted and holistic approaches by first dealing directly with the logic of proof with little reference to the rules of evidence and procedure and then reintegrating the methods of analysis into the complex context of trial practice.

subjects' or, more insidiously, by external encouragement of undergraduates to choose 'knowledge-based' options in preference to those which give priority to intellectual skills and critical perspectives.[53] 'Karl Llewellyn and the Modern Skills Movement' (chapter 10) is an extract from a longer essay on Karl Llewellyn's concept of 'juristic method'.[54] It is included here for two reasons: first, in order to show how the modern skills movement is historically connected to a general sociological theory of law; and, secondly, to sound a note of warning about an emerging orthodoxy which threatens to combine 'the primary school model' of law schools with the kind of bureaucratic rationalism that is invading universities and the professions as well as business. Like myself, Llewellyn would probably have welcomed many recent developments in legal education and training, but he would almost certainly have had reservations about some of the things that are being done in the name of 'skills'.

Throughout my career I have been interested in teaching intellectual skills in ways which integrate 'theory' and 'practice'. The main results are to be found in two books, *How To Do Things With Rules* and *Analysis of Evidence*. The topic is further developed in chapters 11 and 12, 'Reading Law' and 'The Reading Law Cookbook'. These bring together two general themes: that a broader concept of legal education should involve the regular use of a much wider range of materials of law study than cases, statutes, and textbooks, but for this to be implemented in a disciplined way there is a need for relatively systematic techniques for reading and using each kind of material for specific educational purposes. These two papers could also be interpreted as preliminary sketches for an attempt to rethink 'legal method' in broader terms than the traditional phrase 'thinking like a lawyer' has been interpreted.[55] A systematic approach to the

---

[53] In the early 1990s the pressures to overload the undergraduate curriculum again increased and in another paper, not included here, I tried to reinforce and develop the argument in a context in which pressures to overload the curriculum at both the academic and professional stages were becoming more intense than ever. ('Intellectual Skills at the Academic Stage: Twelve Theses', in *Examining the Law Syllabus* (ed., P. Birks, Oxford, 1993).) Contemporaneously a minor controversy had developed around the fact that in-house trainers and recruitment partners in large city firms were publicly saying that graduates in other disciplines who had taken a one year conversion course were often at least as attractive as recruits to the legal profession as law graduates, see further *BT* at 55, 162–4.

[54] The original paper was delivered in Chicago and Leipzig in May, 1993 as part of two occasions celebrating the centenary of Llewellyn's birth (22 May 1893). It was first published in *Chicago Papers in Legal History* as 'Karl Llewellyn's Unfinished Agenda: Law in Society and the Job of Juristic Method' (1993). Slightly different versions are to be found in 48 *University of Miami Law Rev.* 119 (1993) and in *Rechtsrealismus, multikulturelle Gesellschaft und Handelsrecht: Karl Llewellyn und seine Bedeutung heute* (edd., Ulrich Drobnig and Manfred Rehbinder, Berlin, 1994). 'Juristic method' in this context is very much broader than 'legal method' or lawyers' methods and embraces all legal technology—how 'the law jobs' are done. Some commentators have confused the idea of 'law jobs', the tasks to which the institution of law is specialized, with the much narrower 'lawyer jobs', the roles or job descriptions of certain kinds of functionaries. This theme is developed at greater length in the original paper.

[55] This phrase is misleading for a number of reasons: first, it is usually confined to reasoning about questions of law, which is only one of many kinds of 'lawyers' reasonings'. Second, 'legal method' is usually applied to some aspects of the basic skills of law study (such as legal analysis,

direct learning of generic intellectual skills, including how to do things with rules, values, facts, concepts, and texts, has never been developed. These two chapters can be read as steps in that direction. I believe that direct teaching of such skills can not only be more effective and economical than 'pick-it-up' approaches, but also that it offers the best hope of integrating legal method, broadly conceived, with ethical and theoretical issues and ideas.

Chapter 13 on access to legal education and the legal profession is included because it deals with a problem of general concern that has resurfaced prominently in the United States and England in the mid-1990s.[56] A central theme is the contrast between jurisdictions which have conceptualized problems of access in a legalistic fashion (such as the United States and India) and those which have treated the issues less formally (or ignored them). More generally, it also suggests an approach to constructing a general perspective for studying issues of common interest in many countries in a way which is sensitive to differences in local conditions, without aspiring to be rigorously 'comparative'. The paper was originally devised as a means of giving flexible guidance to the authors of a series of country studies on access, without imposing too rigid a conceptual or methodological framework.[57] The particular project did serve to identify some common trends and problems in a variety of jurisdictions. The approach makes no claim to be adequate as a basis for genuinely systematic comparative studies, but it has worked reasonably well as a way of informally co-ordinating a series of action-oriented international projects.

'Preparing Lawyers for the Twenty-first Century' (chapter 14) was presented at the Eighth Commonwealth Law Conference in New Zealand in 1990. The audience was mainly judges, government lawyers, and practitioners from around the Commonwealth and the title was assigned by the organizers. It is included here mainly because it provides a succinct overview of broad trends in legal education and training in the Commonwealth in the 1970s and eighties. Since 1990 there have been further significant developments which further underline the extent and pace of change in legal practice internationally and only to a slightly lesser extent legal education and training. This paper also makes the point that, especially in systems that have adopted the multi-stage process of

legal reasoning in a narrow sense, and perhaps using a law library) rather than to the methods of legal practice. In respect of the latter there is plenty of room for disagreement as to whether, how, when and where they should be developed. Third, it suggests that all lawyers think—and in the same way. See further *BT*, at 179–81.

[56] In the case of HOPWOOD ET AL. V. STATE OF TEXAS ET AL., 78 F 3d. 932 (1996) the US Court of Appeals held that the Fourteenth Amendment does not permit a law school to discriminate in favour of minority applicants by giving substantial racial preferences in its admissions programme. In England, the Lord Chancellor's Advisory Committee on Legal Education and Conduct (ACLEC) in its First Report on Legal Education and Training (London, 1996) has treated access as one of its main concerns in a context in which serious allegations of racial discrimination had been levelled against both branches of the legal profession.

[57] The outcome was a book on access to legal education and the profession in the Commonwealth (*ALELP*).

professional formation on the Gower-Ormrod model, undergraduate law students often receive conflicting messages from the legal profession about their
expectations of the first or academic stage and of law graduates. Some such
messages can seriously subvert the idea that the role of universities in professional development is to provide a general education in law in which generic
intellectual skills and broad perspectives are at least as important as detailed
knowledge of doctrine and specific, immediately usable techniques.

The final three chapters deal with some general themes that became issues
of public concern in the early 1990s. 'What are Law Schools for?' (chapter 15)
was stimulated partly by my involvement in issues of legal education policy
in Tanzania, England, and India in this period and partly by reflecting on the
neuroses induced by 'league tables' for university departments, notably by the
research assessment and teaching quality assurance exercises in the United
Kingdom and by the *US News and World Report* rankings which seemed even
more questionable. The former experiences alerted me to important differences
between reports which focus on the process of professional formation, such as
the recent MacCrate and ACLEC reports, and reports which look at law schools
as institutions in the round. The latter provoked some questions about the assumptions underlying current 'league tables', particularly in the United States.
The main argument of the paper is that, if the discipline of law is to realize its
potential, there is a need for a quite fundamental rethinking of basic assumptions
about the functions, ambitions, and clienteles of law schools as institutions.

Chapter 16, 'Pericles Regained?', deals critically with the revival of images of
'the lawyer' and 'good lawyering' that have developed in response to concerns
about ethics and competence, job satisfaction, the justification of monopoly and
restrictive practices, and the fragmentation of legal professions, as well as continuing debates about the aims and objectives of legal education. In the early
1990s, especially in the United States, such concerns tended to be lumped together
under the rubric of an alleged 'crisis of identity'. Taking Anthony Kronman's
Periclean model of 'the lawyer-statesman' as the main example, the essay suggests that the basic elements—a combination of technical competence, a service
ethic, and practical wisdom—are features of a traditional model of professionalism which underlines the similarities between occupational groups rather than
the uniqueness of lawyers or the unity of legal professions. The ideal may indeed provide one rationale for a meaningful and satisfying professional life—
though not necessarily in Kronman's particular version—but it hardly constitutes
a basis for justifying professional monopolies or prescribing a single, extensive
core of knowledge and competence. A fragmented profession requires the diversification of 'local knowledge'. The final chapter, 'A Nobel Prize for Law?',
ends on a relatively optimistic note about the potential of legal scholarship to
win, or regain, acceptance as one of the great humane disciplines. However,
while acknowledging the enormous advances in the last thirty years, not least
in the United Kingdom, the essay suggests that there is much more to be done

before that potential is realized in practice. There is, in short, an unfinished agenda.

These last three chapters develop themes dealt with in *Blackstone's Tower: The English Law School*. In 1992 I was invited to give the Hamlyn Lectures for 1994. It was suggested that they might be devoted to legal education. This would be timely because the Lord Chancellor's Advisory Committee on Legal Education and Conduct was about to start on the first comprehensive review of legal education and training in England since 1971. Under Miss Hamlyn's bequest, the lectures were to be delivered 'among the common people of the United Kingdom of Great Britain and Northern Ireland'. Unfortunately, the lectures are usually delivered in a law school and are published and distributed by a specialist law publisher. This arrangement reinforces the image of law as a dry, technical subject and law books as unreadable tomes that are only accessible to specialists. Over time, despite some efforts to break the mould, the lectures have attracted an almost exclusively legal audience. I decided to try to help to reverse the trend by making the case for reinstating the study of law into the mainstream of our intellectual life and by treating non-lawyers (and colleagues from other jurisdictions) as my primary audience. My efforts were conspicuously unsuccessful. As the project progressed, it became all too clear that the audience for both lectures and the book would still be almost exclusively legal. To argue to lawyers that their field is important and interesting would merely be preaching to the converted or the irredeemable. So I compromised by narrowing the focus to the small world of the English law school, while attempting to present it in a new light, in a form which would be readable and comprehensible to non-experts as well as saying something fresh to lawyers. One result of this self-confirming process was that over time the text of *Blackstone's Tower* grew steadily closer to the present book. So I have designed them to complement each other.[58]

The main object of this book is to explore in detail and in depth what is involved in broadening the discipline of law. The phrase 'law in context' seems to me to be a suitable label for the enterprise. However, this phrase and terms like 'contextualism' and 'realism' have been criticized as being vague or insubstantial or question-begging; they are sometimes treated as a half-hearted kind of jurisprudence. I have argued at length elsewhere that 'law in context' refers not to theory of or about law, but to a general, explicitly pluralistic, approach to a discipline.[59] Terms like context are not totally uninformative, but they are

---

[58] However, the focus is different: *BT* attempts to present a coherent statement of my perspective and views on law as a discipline in its institutional context in England and Wales in the early 1990s. It builds on and, in some respects, advances my thinking in earlier writings, including several reprinted here, but the treatment is more compressed and the focus is local rather than international. Conversely, the last three chapters of this book can be read as developments and glosses on *BT*.

[59] Especially 'Some Jobs for Jurisprudence', 1 *British Jo. of Law and Society* 149 (1974) (inaugural lecture at the University of Warwick); TAR at 374–80; and Ch. 3 below.

not sufficient on their own to form the basis of a distinctive legal theory.[60] However, the criticism persists. My friend, Roger Cotterrell, provides a recent example. In elucidating his conception of sociology of law, he states:

At the same time, sociology of law presupposes much more than 'contextualism': that is, the study of law in social context. Contextualism, which established itself as an alternative to traditional approaches to legal education in Britain in the late 1960s, has been accommodated within existing organizations of legal education. It requires only that particular legal subjects—as defined by lawyers—be studied with a broad awareness of social consequences and social origins of law. A sociological perspective on law presupposes, however, that lawyers' definitions and interpretations of the field are insufficient: that law itself needs to be understood not merely in terms of lawyers' categories, but in the light of a theoretical understanding of the nature of societies within which legal systems exist. In other words, law is to be understood in terms of social theory. Legal theory is to be seen as a particular branch of social theory.[61]

This seems to be a reasonable interpretation of 'law in context' in British law schools, except that 'context' refers not just to social context—it is very much broader than that. But Cotterrell seems to assume that lawyers and other occupants of law schools can only employ 'lawyers' categories'. If that were so, and it may sometimes be the case, the criticism is well-taken. However, I have two main responses to this criticism. First, Cotterrell is treating 'sociology of law' and 'contextualism' in epistemological terms which seem to presuppose some idea of the autonomy of forms of knowledge. Lawyers think in legal categories; sociologists in sociological ones.[62] However, my conception of 'law in context' characterizes an approach to an institutionalized discipline which seeks to undermine rigid boundaries between fields of study. This is an ethnographic or sociological conception of how the study of law has been, and might be, approached in practice. I am concerned as much with approaches to an activity as with the knowledge-claims of the products of such processes. Studying law and doing sociology are activities, not just forms of knowledge. To argue for the contextualization of a subject leaves open what 'contexts' may be appropriate for particular purposes. This is a deliberately liberal, pluralistic, and interdisciplinary conception of what is involved in understanding law. There are many routes to understanding, of which sociology is just one. My second objection is related to this: by adopting an epistemological conception of sociology of law as an enterprise Cotterrell is lured into the extraordinary assertion that 'legal theory is to be seen as a particular branch of social theory.' I am sure that Cotterrell, who

---

[60] 'Context' is derived from the Latin *contexere*, which means to weave together or to join: a contextual approach clearly favours multi-disciplinary perspectives; it includes some rules of thumb, such as 'think in terms of total pictures'; 'look at decisions in the context of total processes', 'provide a historical context', etc. However, what are appropriate connections or weavings depend on the purpose of the enterprise, or again, on context. The open-endedness of context is part of its attraction as a label.   [61] Roger Cotterrell, *Law's Community* (Oxford, 1995) 76–7.
[62] Such assumptions also underpin autopoiesis, about which Cotterrell is quite critical.

has written illuminatingly about Hart and Dworkin and property from other perspectives, does not accept such reductionism. Maybe, the way out for him is to adopt a more sociological perspective on the sociology of law.

Law in Context, then, is a plea for pluralism and for enlarging the vision that informs activities that take place mainly, but not exclusively, in law schools. The essays that follow deal in detail with what that involves. The question remains: 'Why is broadening the study of law important?' No doubt there are many possible answers. Let me respond in personal terms. As an educator, I accept the basic values of the academic ethos; as a jurist I wish to build on rather than to reject the ideas of my teachers, especially Hart and Llewellyn, but to go beyond them; and as a teacher and scholar I have been committed to the idea that breadth of vision is necessary to understanding law. 'Context' and 'breadth' involve multiple lenses, historical, geographical, ethical, logical, sociological, and so on. The basic commitment is the commitment of a liberal intellectual to advancing and disseminating understanding. This requires relative detachment and, if in these pages, there are occasional glimpses of frustration or passion, they stem mainly from the belief that in our law schools our vision and our practice do not do justice to a potentially marvellous subject of study.

2

The Camel in the Zoo*

KHARTOUM 1958–61

Once upon a time, about 1960, a Scotsman from Aberdeen was appointed to a
lectureship in philosophy at the University of Khartoum. When asked why he
had taken the job, he replied: 'Khartoum is more central than Aberdeen.' This
view of the world is no doubt closer to Sudanese then to Scottish philosophy and
for this reason he may have been well qualified for the post. For most of us the
centre of the world is where one happens to be.

When, in 1958, I accepted appointment as Lecturer in Private Law at the
University of Khartoum, I would not have been able, if asked, to give so direct
a response. In retrospect I think that my motives were mixed; on the positive
side I was interested in Africa and in education, and law was the only subject
that I was competent to teach. At that time the Faculty of Law at Khartoum was
the only law faculty in what might be termed acceptable Africa. The fact that
Sudan was recently independent was an added attraction; and the job sounded
both interesting and challenging. On the negative side I was strongly dissatisfied
with the legal education I had received in England and the prospect of a career
in law teaching in my own country had little appeal. English academic law in
the 1950s seemed to me to be guilty of two cardinal errors: it succeeded in
trivializing important issues and in making a potentially fascinating subject boring.
A year in the United States confirmed my biases. So I set out on my teaching
career with the intention of making my subject seem interesting, important, and
relevant to my students.

I arrived in Khartoum armed with good intentions, high educational ideals and
vast ignorance. I also brought with me some precepts from my American guru,
the legal realist, Karl Llewellyn: 'See it fresh'; 'See it whole'; 'See it as it
works.'[1] I was immediately brought face to face with reality. Most of my students were older than I was and they told me that I was too young to be their
teacher. They were right. I was expected to teach four or five subjects for about
fifteen hours a week. So my immediate problem was no longer how to pioneer

---

* This is a revised version of a lecture delivered at the University of Khartoum in December,
1981. It was originally published in a collection of essays celebrating the twenty-fifth anniversary
of the Faculty of Law in Dar-es-Salaam: *Limits of Legal Radicalism* (ed., Issa Shivji, Dar-es-Salaam,
1986). Some of the general themes are developed at greater length in 'Legal Education within East
Africa', in *East African Law Today*, (London, 1966); also, *KLRM*; *ALLD*; and TAR.
[1] See TAR, at 367–70, 376–78.

a radical new approach to legal education; instead it was how to keep a few pages ahead of the class.

The day came when events caught up with me and I found myself with only twenty minutes in which to prepare a lecture on the Law of Torts. I spent most of those twenty minutes wrapping up a copy of the textbook, *Salmond on Torts*, in order to disguise it. When the lecture started I dictated very slowly indeed the rule in RYLANDS V. FLETCHER[2] and then commented vacuously and even more slowly on each element. I finished the lecture early. At the end two students came up to me: 'Sir,' they said, for at that stage they were still calling me 'sir', 'why do you not always lecture like this? That was the best lecture you have ever given. We took down every word.'

I nearly decided to retire from teaching at that point. What I thought of as the jug-and-vessel view of education was anathema to me—the view that the teacher pours knowledge into an empty and entirely passive receptacle. I had been conditioned to believe that university education should be essentially self-education. The teacher should at most be a stimulator and a leader; ideally he should be a joint explorer with his students on a voyage of discovery. What I was after was discussion, argument, above all participation by the students. My Sudanese students did not share this view. After this first incident I was despondent, but I did not give up. Instead I redoubled my efforts to try to persuade, to cajole, to provoke, to tease, and even to insult the class into participating. I resorted to a number of devices. I asked questions; I set problems; I mystified them by saying such things as 'DONOGHUE V. STEVENSON is much too important a case for me to lecture on', implying that I expected them to read it (surely not all of it?). I did not make much headway. The students were bored, polite, and tolerant and they thought me a little crazy to be concerned about the unreality of what we were studying. Then, one day we came to study that complicated absurdity, the common law relating to liability of animals. We got through cases of horses jumping over hedges, stories of rabid monkeys and erring avers, of circus elephants trampling dwarfs, cases with memorable and evocative names like FILBURN V. PEOPLES PALACE[3] and BEHRENS V. BERTRAM MILLS CIRCUS.[4] We pondered whether cats and cocks were cattle. I even posed the question whether the owner of a talking parrot could be liable in defamation.

Then we came to M'QUAKER V. GODDARD.[5] In that case a visitor to the London Zoo had fed an Arabian camel and had been bitten. He sued the zoo. After hearing 'expert' evidence, Branson J held as a matter of law that camels are tame and harmless; he held that the zoo was not liable in the absence of proof of negligence. This was upheld by the Court of Appeal, whose judgments were criticized by no less an authority than Professor Glanville Williams, who claimed

[2] RYLANDS V. FLETCHER, (1866) LR 1 Ex. 265.
[3] FILBURN V. PEOPLES PALACE, (1890) 25 QBD 258.
[4] BEHRENS V. BERTRAM MILLS CIRCUS, [1957] 2 QB 1.
[5] M'QUAKER V. GODDARD, [1940] 1 KB 687.

in an absurdly learned article that not all camels are tame and that it was wrong to treat them as generally harmless.[6] In order to provoke the class I read out a quotation from another alleged 'expert', Sir F. Palgrave: 'He is from first to last an undomesticated and savage animal, rendered serviceable by stupidity alone . . . never tame, though not wide awake enough to be exactly wild.'[7] I threw down a challenge: is that how Sudanese feel about camels? A hand went up. 'Aha,' I thought, 'at last I have got a response.' But instead it was a question: 'Please, sir, why was the camel in a zoo?' At that moment some scales fell away from my eyes. What had a camel in a zoo to do with the Sudan? Or circus elephants or performing fleas or slanderous parrots or carbolic smoke balls or the rule against perpetuities? What was I doing teaching all this artificial and irrelevant frippery to Sudanese students? Maybe I overreacted, but at least I got a discussion going. I had got a response by playing the nationalist card. Indeed, it was now difficult to stop the students talking and I had subverted my own course.

The discussion led to the conclusion that the English law of torts was neither relevant nor suitable to Sudan. To be sure there were roads and factories where accidents might happen. People could be defamed or insulted. There was even a zoo—but how many people actually sued?[8] And did English rules and values make sense in this kind of situation? What of liability for animals? What happened in practice when someone's goat or bull or camel (or some animal in the Khartoum zoo) caused damage? 'It is governed by custom', said the students. But how could one find out about custom in order to teach it? 'Ask the people', came the reply.

In solving one problem—for now I could hardly stop the students from talking—I had uncovered another. How could anyone, let alone a too-young expatriate, teach about the realities of the law in action in Sudan? If customary law was important—as it clearly was—surely years of research would be needed before anyone could be qualified to teach it.

Shortly after this incident I was invited to visit a village near Wad Medani by one of my students. The local headman (*omda*) was present. He had heard that I was interested in customary law and he intimated that I could put some questions to him through an interpreter. I was doubly unprepared; I had no training in fieldwork and I had prepared no questions. But I was, after all, a pupil of Karl Llewellyn. However, I had not learned all that he had to teach. Instead of asking the *omda* to tell me about some actual disputes that had recently occurred in the village and how these had in fact been handled, I improvised a series of formalistic hypothetical problems based on the English law of torts. What happens if A's goat wanders onto B's land and butts C, a trespasser? What happens if X's bull

---

[6] Williams, 56 *LQR* 354 (1940).   [7] Quoted by Williams, op. cit.

[8] Shortly after this a judge fell into an open ditch in Khartoum and sued in negligence, KHARTOUM MUNICIPAL COUNCIL v. COTRAN, (1958) *SLJR* 85, discussed in (1959) *SLJR* 112. The case attracted a lot of publicity and there followed a significant rise in the number of actions for personal injuries.

escapes onto the highway and gores Y's camel? He answered all my questions promptly, confidently, and with a straight face—but at the end he said: 'Very interesting, but we have no bulls or camels in this village and our goats do not behave like that—no such cases ever arise.'

I decided that I was not equipped for fieldwork. But I was still concerned to find genuinely Sudanese materials on which to base my teaching. *The Sudan Law Journal and Reports* had recently been started—largely by the efforts of Egon Guttman and the Chief Justice, Mohamed Abu Rannat. I threw myself enthusiastically into the task of helping with the editing of cases—an excellent apprenticeship for a young lawyer—and when first Guttman and then Patrick Atiyah left, I became the General Editor.

One of the stranger English legal exports is the notion that the publication of legislation is a responsibility of Government, but the publication of cases—the next most important source of law—can be left to private enterprise and commercial publishers.[9] Fortunately, unlike some African countries, the Sudan had resisted the idea and the *SLJR* was subsidized from public funds. But another common law assumption—that only cases of superior courts have precedent value and are worth reporting—had been imported. After a time I noticed that the great majority of cases that I received for consideration were criminal cases and that nearly all of these concerned homicide. If one merely reported the cases one was sent, then before long Sudan would have had an overdeveloped body of doctrine on provocation and manslaughter and almost no reported cases on most other subjects. Even in respect of the Penal Code this seemed somewhat unbalanced.

About this time I was consulted by a recent graduate, then a junior magistrate, about the meaning of the word 'building' in the offence of house trespass, under section 381 of the Sudan Penal Code. On investigation it transpired that the reported cases—all Indian—were in conflict and that different interpretations had developed locally in the courts of the three adjacent towns of Khartoum, Omdurman, and Khartoum North. There were no reported Sudanese cases, but we learned that in Omdurman the concept of 'building' was being interpreted to include the '*hosh*'—that is the compound contained by a wall, equivalent to the English 'close'; in Khartoum, on the other hand, house trespass was confined to entries into structures that were both covered and enclosed by walls; whereas in Khartoum North section 381 had been extended to include stores and godowns with a roof, but no walls. These differing interpretations did not seem entirely inappropriate for each place, but the fact remained that three lots of courts within the same conurbation were giving three different interpretations to the same section that covered a quite common offence, yet there was no institutionalized way of communicating about or discussing those differing interpretations. My first reaction was to try to persuade the magistrate involved to give a written

---

[9] See further, *ALLD*, at 30 ff.

judgment in this case, so that I could report it in order to draw attention to the issue. However, his superiors indicated that it was above the station of a third class magistrate to submit judgments for reporting.[10]

Some years later, with the help of a research assistant, I made an analysis of reported criminal cases in the Sudan for the period. We came up with the following figures: (1) There are 447 sections in the Sudan Penal Code; (2) In a period of fifteen years, only thirty-eight of these sections were referred to in reported cases; (3) Nearly half of the section references related to culpable homicide or attempts to commit culpable homicide or to other aspects of homicide; (4) 58 per cent of the references were to offences affecting the human body; 13 per cent to offences against property—the second highest category. For the vast majority of offences there was not a single reported case.[11]

Sudan is not unusual in this respect. The purpose of this analysis was to illustrate the point that cases that reach the law reports tend to be unrepresentative of the work of the legal system as a whole. It would be unduly cynical to say that the more frequent the offence, the less likely it is to reach the law reports and the more unusual or exotic the case the greater the likelihood that it will reach the law reports. But it is true to say that most systems of law reporting give an uneven coverage of a legal system; other means of providing regular information about the workings of the law are needed, both for those who operate the system and for those who seek to study it. My experience of law reporting in Sudan challenged my English lawyer's assumption of the primacy of law reports as the central form of primary sources of law. It also illustrates the importance of other methods of communicating legal information within a legal system.

This sharpened awareness of the uneven coverage of the law in one form of legal literature led me to look with fresh eyes at the syllabus of the Khartoum LL B., which had been based—with a few changes, notably in respect of Sharia—on English models. Although in its details the influence of the University of London was apparent, what was particularly striking when one thought about it was that the syllabus was extraordinarily close to that of the English Solicitors' Examinations. This syllabus at the time reflected the then unchallenged view of the English solicitor as someone whose main work involved handling the property transactions and problems of the middle and upper classes in a capitalist society; probate, conveyancing, trusts, matrimonial property, and domestic commercial transactions in the private sector were emphasized. Public Law, legal process, and administration of criminal justice, were given relatively little emphasis. Welfare law, labour law, and economic law were almost unknown. The Khartoum LL B. had not followed this slavishly—it gave space to Sharia, Public and Private International Law, and Jurisprudence—but it was nevertheless heavily

---

[10] The matter could have been dealt with by judicial circular. In fact we managed to find a case on the issue and reported it: SUDAN GOVERNMENT V. SILVANO GOTTARDI (1960) *SLJR* 245.

[11] Compiled by Philip Boynton. The figures are approximate.

influenced by 'the private practitioner image' of legal education—and of one kind of English practitioner at that.[12] Yet at the time over 90 per cent of Khartoum graduates entered the Public Service—either the judiciary or the Attorney-General's Office where most of them spent most of their time administering criminal justice or matters which broadly fell within the province of Public Law. It would, of course, be absurd to suggest that a curriculum, especially in a university, should follow closely the future patterns of work of its students—if that were so, 60 per cent of the English Solicitors' Examinations would have been devoted to Probate and Conveyancing; and in Sudan at least a similar amount of attention would have been given to procedures relating to the administration of criminal justice; or with the wisdom of hindsight, and taking a sardonic view, since about 70 per cent of the people I taught in Khartoum are now in the Gulf States, more emphasis should have been placed on the law of those jurisdictions than on English or Sudanese law. Nevertheless, there was an imbalance and a lesson was learned. So when I moved from Khartoum to Dar-es-Salaam, I persuaded my colleagues to take account of the fact that nearly all of our graduates were destined for the Public Service—with the result that we placed much more emphasis on Public Law and on such matters as international commercial transactions and much less on private property subjects.

One final anecdote. In one of the first examinations I set on the Law of Torts, I composed a problem based on the English case of DANIELS V. WHITE, in which the plaintiff had become ill because some carbolic acid had found its way into a bottle of lemonade.[13] The defendants had argued that it was a sufficient defence to an action for negligence that they had, as they claimed, a 'fool-proof' system of working—that is that their safety and cleaning measures and the system of inspection were as near perfect as could be. In the problem I set a trap for the students by basing the facts on a manufacturer of ginger beer (suggesting that the issue had something to do with DONOGHUE V. STEVENSON), but I tried to help them by stating that the defendants had a 'fool-proof' system of working. No less than a third of the candidates interpreted this as stating that the drink involved was 'full proof' lemonade—i.e., 100 per cent alcohol; some suggested, quite correctly, that whether or not the drink was alcoholic was irrelevant to the issue. I have never been able to decide whether this error, which made nonsense of both DANIELS V. WHITE and my problem, was attributable to linguistic difficulties or to a students' view of expatriate lecturers as being obsessed with alcohol.

These anecdotes can all be interpreted as cross-cultural parables from which one could draw a variety of morals. Of course, such experiences drove home some familiar lessons: for example, that law needs to be studied in its specific cultural, political, and economic context; that when studying foreign law and

---

[12] See 'Legal Education within East Africa', op. cit., at 139 ff.
[13] DANIELS V. WHITE, [1938] 4 All ER 258.

foreign legal sources in a country like Sudan every rule, every institution, every idea needs to be examined and tested for its suitability and applicability for import to a different cultural environment; that one form of post-colonial dependency is dependency on foreign literature;[14] that the law in books often diverges from the law in action, but that the gap between the law in books written in country A and the law in action in country B can be very much greater, especially when the countries do not share a common language and culture; that teachers and students often have sharply divergent expectations of each other, especially if they are from different cultures, and that if the process of learning is to thrive, both have to make adjustments.[15]

There was a more general lesson than this for an expatriate teacher like myself. For this was a vivid application of the basic principle of all comparative study: in order to understand one's own country, culture or institutions one needs to experience another. While teaching in the Sudan for three years and in Tanzania for a further four, my daily experience was to find that ideas I had taken for granted were being constantly challenged. Day in, day out one had to ask the question: What is the reason or basis for this or that rule or idea or institution? Does it make sense *here*? and, at first insidiously and then more persistently, does it make sense back there, in its country of origin? In short one of the main lessons of teaching law abroad was to take a fresh look at and to consider the underlying assumptions of what one had learned at home. This has much the same function as theorizing—it leads one to articulate, to examine, and to criticize many of one's basic assumptions.

UNITED KINGDOM 1965–81: THE 'BEEN TOS'' RETURN

Of course, my experiences were by no means unique; in fact they were quite commonplace. So far as law teaching is concerned, an extraordinarily high percentage of my generation of British law teachers spent a period of studying and teaching abroad. I mentioned at the start that one of my motives for coming

[14] See generally *Legal Literature in Small Jurisdictions*, Commonwealth Secretariat (edd., W. Twining and J. Uglow, London, 1981).

[15] Many of the lessons outlined in the text could be interpreted as precepts to study law in context. When I moved to Dar-es-Salaam I tried to apply these lessons in a context that had some obvious differences: Khartoum was large, urban, long established, and evolutionary in respect of education. Dar was small, suburban (after two years), brand new and self-consciously seeking to break from established British patterns. Khartoum was both Arab and African in a single state; the Dar law faculty initially served four different African countries. Politics were seen to be directly relevant to furthering national goals based more clearly on a dominant ideology, at least in Tanzania. Despite the many contrasts in the social, political, and cultural contexts, the educational context and tasks were ostensibly much the same: English traditions of university and legal education provided the model which at once invited and constrained deviation. At the time we often felt that we were making radical breaks with tradition and that we had the opportunity to do so; twenty years on the attempted deviations look both obvious and cautious and the constraints (of language and available literature and our own ignorance, for example) look distinctly more formidable.

out to Khartoum was that I was dissatisfied with academic law in England. This was true of many of my contemporaries among younger law teachers, especially during the 1960s. Thus many of the dozens of young Britons who went out to teach law in Sudan, East Africa, Ethiopia, Ghana, Nigeria, the Far East, and elsewhere were not only exposed to a regular series of culture shocks; they were already predisposed to question and to challenge many existing assumptions about legal education, legal literature, legal scholarship, and about law in general. Their experience abroad gave them the stimulus and the opportunity both to re-examine many established ideas and to start to develop new or alternative approaches. When they returned home they were quite well-equipped to try to break with tradition. I want to report briefly on some of the developments that have occurred in academic law in the United Kingdom since the expatriates returned home.

When I was an undergraduate in England in the 1950s legal education, legal scholarship, and nearly all thinking about law were dominated by a single orthodoxy—variously known as legal formalism, conceptualism, or the black-letter approach. For the sake of simplicity I shall refer to this as the Expository Tradition—for the symbol of this approach was the standard expository work, the student's textbook, like *Salmond on Torts* or *Cross on Evidence*. This pervaded the whole intellectual life of the law—not just legal education. The basic characteristics and assumptions are familiar: the study of a law is equated with the study of legal rules; it concentrates on expounding and analysing the law as it is, which is typically seen as positive law, an artificial creation of the will of man; the subject-matter of study is cases and statutes and secondary works based almost exclusively on those sources; a high premium is placed on conceptual precision, on logical consistency within the system, and on technical excellence. This was the dominant English tradition of analytical positivism. A similar approach to law had dominated American law schools in the late nineteenth and early twentieth centuries. It had, at an early stage, produced a reaction in the form of the movement known as Legal Realism, of which Arthur Corbin, Karl Llewellyn, and Jerome Frank were among the leaders. Boiled down to its essentials the core of Legal Realism can be restated very simply: rules are an important, indeed a central, feature of law, but for almost any purpose—for understanding, for practice, and for reform—the study of rules alone is not enough; law must be studied in the context of social processes generally. To understand the law, one needs to study both the law in action and the law in books: one of the central objectives of Legal Realism was to get more of the action into the books and into the classroom.[16]

Legal Realism scored only a partial victory in the United States in the period 1915–60. During that period it made almost no impact at all on English legal thought. But since the mid-1960s the United Kingdom has seen a revolt against

---

[16] See generally *KLRM*.

the Expository Orthodoxy—a revolt against formalism and a narrow conceptual tradition—which in some important respects parallels the American Realist Movement. There are, however, some important differences. Perhaps the most important ones are that political and ideological influences have been more prominent in the British movement to broaden the study of law and that the diversity of the reactions to the Expository Tradition has been much more obvious and open than in the United States. To put the matter very simply: there has been a widespread reaction in the UK against the Expository Tradition, but there have been several different kinds of reasons for rejecting it:[17]

1. the practitioners complained that academic law had become out of touch with the realities of private legal practice;
2. liberal educators and intellectuals complained that rote learning and authoritative exposition of rules were illiberal and anti-intellectual;
3. reformists, radicals, revolutionaries, and sceptics complained that the exposition of the law as it is encouraged uncritical acceptance of the status quo—that the Expository Orthodoxy was conservative, even reactionary;
4. social scientists and others complained that academic law was too narrowly focused, unempirical, and out of touch with social realities—a very different perspective on law in action from that of the private practitioner;
5. many people complained that concern with performing fleas and talking parrots and the rule against perpetuities was trivial—more attention should be focused on the problems of the poor, on industrial conflict, on multinational corporations, for example. The problems of council house tenants and the homeless should be substituted for the problems of the inhabitants of Blackacre, a country mansion with six maids' bedrooms;
6. internationally, 'Law and Development' became a fashionable phrase and has gone through a number of convolutions. The International Legal Center Reports on Legal Education and Research of 1975–6 both explicitly contrast Law and Development approaches with the black-letter, expository tradition.[18]

A great deal has happened in Anglo-American legal thought in the past twenty years.[19] Interest in 'Law and Development' has died down, to be replaced by some more parochial perspectives. Many newer developments reflect a heightened awareness of ideology and a degree of political polarization, illustrated by neo-conservative economic analysis of law, the rights-based liberal theory of law of Ronald Dworkin, and the rather variegated critical legal studies movements.

[17] The following passage is adapted from 'Law and social science: The method of detail', *New Society*, 27 (June 1974), at 760.
[18] International Legal Center, *Legal Education in a Changing World* (New York, 1975); *Law and Development* (New York, 1975).
[19] Some of these trends are summarized in a report by the Committee of Heads of University Law Schools, 'Law as an Academic Discipline', *Soc. Pub. Tchs. L Newsletter*, (Summer 1984).

Sociology of law, socio-legal studies, and law in context have become respectable without ever being dominant. For better or worse, there is much less interaction between African and Western juristic ideas. In the light of contemporary perspectives some of the 'new' ideas of the immediate post-colonial period seem rather simple or even misconceived. Yet the general trend in the direction of broadening and diversifying the study of law has been quite constant, though the survival of the Expository Orthodoxy points to some of the limits of legal radicalism. Exposition and analysis may not be enough, but they still retain a central place; and radicalism has tended to be defined largely in terms of deviations from the orthodoxy.

A number of influences fed into this recent intellectual ferment in England, for example, the rapid development of some social sciences and of social history, American jurisprudence, and new forms of ideological consciousness. Experience of teaching and other work in post-Independent Africa was only one of these influences, but it has been a quite significant one: it is striking that a significant number of the academic leaders of broader approaches had substantial African experience: Patrick Atiyah in Sudan; L. C. B. Gower and many others in Ghana and Nigeria; Claire Palley in Rhodesia, now Zimbabwe; Patrick McAuslan, Yash Ghai, James Read, Sol Picciotto, and Aubrey Diamond in East Africa.[20] The Warwick Law School is the institution in England that has been most committed to the systematic development of broader approaches; it is significant that at times about half the staff there had substantial Third World experience. This is not, as has sometimes been suggested, that Warwick is a retirement home for been-tos—for old neocolonialists, or retired expatriates; rather the kind of experience and approaches that such people had acquired in the Third World—and especially in post-Independence African countries when almost every aspect of national life was being challenged, reshaped and sometimes rethought—made such people peculiarly fitted to developing new approaches to law in their own country. The 'been-tos' returned home and made some impact; perhaps this was another kind of neocolonialism.[21]

---

[20] This is merely a selection of individuals who returned or went to a single jurisdiction, England.

[21] A fascinating diversity of interpretations of the early years of the Faculty of Law in Dar-es-Salaam is to be found in the *Limits of Legal Radicalism*, op. cit.

3

Reflections on 'Law in Context' *

During 1958–9 Patrick Atiyah was my neighbour in Khartoum. This was my first year of full-time teaching and he closely affected my academic develop-ment as mentor, colleague, and friend. That friendship has survived our various wanderings, a second period as colleagues at Warwick, and another, happily con-tinuing phase, as neighbours in Iffley. Like many others, I owe him an enormous intellectual debt. This paper explores one phase of our relationship: the genesis of the 'Law in Context' series.

The story begins in the Atiyahs' swimming-pool at their house on Sharia el Jamhuria in Khartoum. We used to repair there regularly after work to cool off. That may give a misleadingly neo-colonial impression. Patrick sometimes ap-pears to be larger than life, but the Atiyah 'swimming-pool' was not much larger than a bath. It seemed almost as deep as it was long. The first edition of *Sale of Goods*[1] had already been published and he was working on *An Introduction to the Law of Contract*.[2] Much as he enjoyed some aspects of life in Sudan, he felt intellectually isolated and he expressed himself memorably in this context. He would swim a length in two or three strokes, stand up, and continuing a passable imitation of a crawl burst out: 'How can I find out whether English businessmen take consideration seriously when I am isolated in this place?' Splash. 'How can one make sense of FELTHOUSE v. BINDLEY[3] in Khartoum?' Splash. Or, he might have added, cases about camels in zoos, horses jumping over hedges, circus elephants, Carbolic Smoke Balls and other features of Eng-lish life that were conspicuously absent in Sudan.[4]

I do not recall whether terms such as 'context' or 'the law-in-action' were used, but the problem of making sense of the common law in Sudan was clear. So too was the relevance of finding out what happens in practice, in England as

---

* This essay was originally published in Peter Cane and Jane Stapleton (edd.) *Essays for Patrick Atiyah* (Oxford, 1991). Atiyah's version of the genesis of *Accidents, Compensation and the Law* is given in 'An Autobiographical Fragment', in Geoffrey Wilson (ed.) *Frontiers of Legal Scholarship* (Chichester, 1995). Atiyah's work has been developed splendidly by Peter Cane, who is the editor of recent editions of *Accidents, Compensation and the Law* and by Jane Stapleton, *Product Liability* (London, 1994), both in the 'Law in Context' series. On my later views on the nature and functions of exposition, see *BT*, Ch. 6.

[1] P. S. Atiyah, *The Sale of Goods*, 1st edn. (London, 1957).
[2] P. S. Atiyah, *An Introduction to the Law of Contract*, 1st edn. (Oxford, 1961).
[3] FELTHOUSE v. BINDLEY, (1862) 11 CB (NS) 869.
[4] This general theme is developed in Ch. 2 above; see also TAR, at 359–60.

well as Sudan, as part of understanding any legal doctrine. Patrick juggled ideas and splashed about with equal abandon. And I learned that this was no conventional 'black-letter' lawyer.

Several years later, in 1965, Robert Stevens invited me to join him in planning a new series of law books designed to challenge the existing textbook orthodoxy. We had first developed some of these ideas in Dar-es-Salaam. The need for such a venture seemed obvious to us and we had few doubts about the general approach that we favoured. But there was a problem of choosing a suitable title for the series. 'Law in Society' had been pre-empted by another series that was being launched concurrently. 'Law and Society' was too similar. 'Realism' was a discredited idea in England and people were still making puns about sociology and socialism. In any case sociology was too narrow for our purposes. Borrowing the idea from Addison Mueller's *Contract in Context*,[5] I had suggested 'Law in Context' which appealed to me more than to my co-editor. Eventually this was accepted *faute de mieux*.[6]

The main problem, as we saw it, was to find suitable authors. To our dismay we soon learned that some of the few obvious candidates had been pre-empted by Otto Kahn-Freund, Bill Wedderburn, and Harry Street for another publisher.[7] When I suggested Atiyah's name, doubts were expressed on the ground that he was an exemplar of the tradition we were seeking to subvert. I told of my experiences in his 'swimming-pool' and pointed out that, since he had recently completed several years at the Board of Trade, he was particularly well-qualified to explore the relationship between aspects of commercial law, commercial practice, and public regulation. So it was agreed that he should be invited to contribute a book within this general area. However, when I visited him in his rooms in New College, he declared that he was bored with contract and commerce (happily this proved to be a passing phase) and he wished to write a book on Torts. This suggestion was accepted and within a remarkably short time *Accidents, Compensation and the Law*[8] followed.

As plans for the series developed, I became increasingly concerned about its intellectual foundations. It was clear what it was not, but one of the lessons of the history of the American Realist Movement was that it had been more successful in its iconoclastic and negative aspects than in providing a basis for constructing coherent alternatives. We decided to hold a one-day meeting for potential authors and sympathetic colleagues and I undertook to write a general working paper.

The 'mini-conference' was held in London, at the Oxford and Cambridge Club, on 20 May 1967. Some papers were circulated in advance and presentations

---

[5] A. Mueller, *Contract in Context* (Brooklyn, 1952).   [6] For details, see TAR, at 372–8.

[7] 'The Law and Society' series, published by Penguin Books. See the Editorial Foreword in D. W. Elliott and Harry Street, *Road Accidents* (London, 1968). It seems to have been a coincidence that the first book in each series concerned accidents.

[8] P. S. Atiyah, *Accidents, Compensation and the Law*, 1st edn. (London, 1970).

were made by Patrick Atiyah, John Griffith, Alan Milner, Patrick McAuslan, and myself.[9] The editors felt that the seminar was a success. Ironically, in the course of a lively debate, it was Atiyah's proposal which attracted the sharpest criticism, mainly on the ground that it was 'too traditional'. He had not yet lived down his image.

In the next section my working paper is reproduced in its original, incomplete form. Some footnote references have been added, but the text has not been altered. The third section comments retrospectively on the text with particular reference to the idea of 'a contextual approach' as a juristic concept and the question whether an 'ideal type' of a 'Law in Context' book can be constructed. The essay ends with an examination of the first edition of *Accidents, Compensation and the Law* in relation to that ideal type.

II. LAW IN CONTEXT: A TENTATIVE RATIONALE (1967)

A. Introduction: The Stereotype

Conventional law textbooks tend to follow a stereotyped pattern. 'Law in Context' is envisaged as a series of books that will compete with, supplement, and occasionally even replace this stereotype. The series has been stimulated by a dissatisfaction with the state of legal education, of legal research and, in particular, of legal literature in England. This paper attempts to analyse some of the sources of this dissatisfaction and to provide a tentative theoretical basis for the series.

It is convenient to start with an examination of the stereotype that we seek to attack: the standard pattern of the English textbook. A historian has recently commented: 'The lawyer's textbook looks more like a chemistry book than a history book: The law is divided up into a number of elements or rules, and when these are traced back to their origins through strings of cases the logical pattern remains dominant and the separate strands are not woven into coherent history.'[10] Social scientists and others have commented in similar terms and one is sometimes given the impression by laymen that the legal textbook symbolizes for them a general aridity, dullness, narrowness, and philistinism in the house

---

[9] The papers were: P. S. Atiyah, 'Torts: Some preliminary thoughts'; Patrick McAuslan, 'Modern Land Law'; Alan Milner, 'On the University Teaching of Criminal Law', 7 *JSPTL* (*NS*) 192 (1963) (already published); William Twining and Robert Stevens, 'Law in Context: A tentative rationale' (reproduced here), together with three appendices: I. W. Twining, 'Llewellyn's Cases and Materials on the Law of Sales', (a revised version appeared in 30 *MLR* 514 (1967)); II. Willard Hurst, Preface to *Law and Economic Growth—The Legal History of the Lumber Industry in Wisconsin 1836–1915* (Washington, DC, 1964); III. Lawrence Friedman and Stewart Macauley, 'Contract Law and Contract Research: Past, Present and Future' (a revised version was published in 20 *Journal of Legal Education* 452 (1968)). Note: hereafter the original footnotes are indicated by an asterisk.

[10] *Alan Harding, *A Social History of English Law*, 9 (Harmondsworth, 1966).

of intellect of academic lawyers. Law teachers often seem to have a curiously ambivalent attitude towards legal textbooks: they encourage their students to rély heavily upon them, they may write them, they may even make money out of them; yet they disassociate themselves from the intellectual attitudes and educational values that the genre encourages: authoritarian dogmatism, simplification, distrust of speculation on the part of the authors, and for students predigestion, relief from the need to think for oneself, and a high premium on memory work.

As educational tools textbooks fly in the face of some of the fundamental values of university education and at the same time they are primitive as means of training effective practitioners; as works of scholarship they may be accurate but are rarely exhaustive; they are rarely sufficiently comprehensive to be efficient works of reference; as works of the intellect they are, with rare exceptions, unimaginative; they have no pretensions to be works of art.

That some admirable works have been produced within the convention is not denied. At various points in history treatise writers have performed a valuable job of creative synthesis, imposing order on a wilderness of precedents or statutory provisions. Not all textbooks have had all the faults listed above. Many are notable for other virtues, most commonly lucidity, accuracy, and a rigorous analytical posture. But if in a legal textbook one finds profundity, originality, imagination, stimulation, or insight it is usually in spite of the tradition of the genre rather than because of it. Perhaps saddest of all is the thought that so many outstandingly able men have devoted so much effort to working within so restrictive a medium.

B. The Context

(i) The juristic context

The dominant juristic influence in England is still analytical. Courses on jurisprudence, and jurists themselves, may recognize that there is more to jurisprudence than the analysis of doctrine, but to the limited extent that legal theory has been influential in the writing of textbooks, it has been mainly in relation to the analysis of legal concepts. The salient characteristics of the analytical tradition are well-known: the emphasis on the autonomy of law as an independent discipline or science; the centrality of doctrine (rules and principles) to the concept of 'law'; the clear differentiation of law as it is from law as it ought to be; exposition and 'neutral' analysis usually given pride of place over criticism and suggestions for reform; and a reluctance to discuss questions of policy in detail. The conservative values of consistency and certainty (in the sense of settled doctrine) repeatedly nudge out other values. In its external relations with other disciplines the closest ties have been with empirical philosophy, which places great emphasis on the analysis of language. Less frequently noted, but for our purposes, significant, is a tendency to maintain a clear-cut distinction between 'theory' and 'practice' and for 'theory' to be associated with a concern with rather general and abstract problems.

Textbook writers under pressure to provide confident statements of 'the law' have to gloss over the problems of interpreting cases and statutes; the blandness of many expositions suggests that even the existence of such problems is not always appreciated. This indifference to their own methodological assumptions is sustained by the authoritarian nature of a tradition that dictates that there is a single correct answer to almost every question.

The main strengths of the tradition have been lucidity, accuracy, and intellectual rigour; its weaknesses a narrow formalism, cultural isolationism, a propensity for unjustified dogmatism, and a tendency to be divorced from the contemporary world of affairs. A contextual approach which is to be disciplined involves the conscious exploitation of the strengths of both analytical and sociological jurisprudence. 'Law in Context' must proceed from a broader jurisprudential base than does the typical textbook, yet it must seek to preserve as far as possible the rigour associated with the narrower approach.

(ii) The educational context: the textbook and legal education

The textbook is still the most used form of students' book. This is largely due to the style of examinations that law students have to undergo; the professional examinations have traditionally been little more than tests of memory; this is largely true of examinations for non-lawyers, even within the universities. Despite a respectable tradition of resistance to parrot-learning by university teachers of law, the information content of university law examinations has tended to be significantly higher than in most other university subjects. This is to be explained in large part by the influence of the profession both direct and indirect. A student who has mastered the textbook in a particular subject can be confident of passing almost any law examination in that subject. It is not surprising that the majority of candidates for law examinations, professional, university or otherwise, rely heavily upon the textbook and its satellite, 'the nutshell'. In the universities students are normally expected to resort to primary sources (cases and legislation), to learned articles in periodicals, and, less often, to other kinds of book but very rarely to the extent that the textbook has been considered unnecessary.

The recent growth in importance of the casebook in England represents a move away from this pattern. But the English casebook tends to differ in function as well as in form from its American namesake. In the United States the main reason for the importance of casebooks is that the method of teaching is such that each student needs to have the primary sources in front of him in the classroom. The casebook therefore contains almost everything that a student needs for a particular course. This is one of the features of American legal education that the editors have no wish to encourage. In England on the other hand casebooks are only exceptionally used as teaching *materials* (a significant expression) which every student is required to bring with him into the classroom. English casebooks are mainly regarded as convenient collections of standard cases, the main function of which is to save pressure on the law reports in libraries and to encourage students to resort to the primary sources. Casebooks are used to supplement rather than replace textbooks.

To return to the textbook. The first point to notice is that the educational objectives that a particular textbook aims to serve are often obscure. Ironically this may have commercial attractions: a work with indeterminate educational aims may be held out as serving several functions at once; for instance as an elementary reference work or as an outlet for original research, or even as a potential authoritative source of law. The standard advertisement by law publishers claims that the advertised product is useful not only to students of several types but also to practitioners and interested laymen. Thus the stereotype textbook often seeks to serve several aims, some of which may be incompatible or at least remarkably difficult to reconcile.

While textbooks have been able to serve non-pedagogical functions, in other respects they have been strongly influenced by patterns of legal education. Not surprisingly they have been closely tied to curricula. Since English law curricula have usually followed a classification which divides law up into fields that are formal in the sense that the divisions do not necessarily reflect significant social categories, textbooks have tended to follow suit. Contract, Tort, Equity are examples of fields which lump together a wide variety of disparate social situations and categories. An approach that purports to relate law to its social context may find that some of the established 'fields of Law' are unmanageable or unsatisfactory in other respects.

In other words, volumes in the 'Law in Context' series may well take some narrow area from a traditional subject and treat it in depth or it may bring together various related social issues traditionally dealt with in different subjects.

Another point worth noting is that university curricula have tended until recently to be narrow in scope and conservative. The subjects offered have tended to be few in number and relatively constant. Taxation, social legislation, international commercial transactions, etc., have only recently started to appear in university calendars. At the same time there are some recognized 'fields', in the orthodox sense, that are badly served or not covered at all by existing textbooks. Here it is worth noting the existence of a vicious circle. When a new subject is proposed to curriculum planners, a commonly raised objection is: 'There is no textbook in the area.' Conversely publishers are reluctant to risk investing in a book on a subject that is not to be found in existing curricula.

In planning 'Law in Context' particular attention will be paid to neglected, new, and expected subjects of study. Such subjects are most likely to make their first appearance as options in the final year of the undergraduate curriculum or in postgraduate curricula (although we are equally anxious to develop new volumes with a 'new' outlook for even the most traditional of subjects). At the same time the more senior the student, the easier it should be to loosen the grip of the standard textbook, provided that bad habits have not been too firmly ingrained in his first year or two of study. This is not to say that the series will ignore the needs of first year students. In particular a strong case could be made out for contextual works on statutory interpretation, procedure, and the English legal system which would be appropriate for first year students.

(iii) The Commercial Context (omitted)[11]

(iv) Recent Trends

Recently there has been manifested a growing discontent with the state of legal scholarship and legal education in England, especially among the younger law teachers. One can only speculate about the causes: increased familiarity with foreign (particularly American) ideas and methods; greater awareness of the need for faster and faster legal change to keep pace with social and technological change; a complex social context, understanding of which can no longer be taken for granted; the interdisciplinary fashion, which is fast becoming a fad; the belated recognition of psychology and sociology as respectable pursuits. New law faculties are opening, some connected with social science departments; the number of full-time teachers has expanded at an enormous rate during the past few years, especially outside the universities; the paperback revolution, new teaching techniques, Robbins and its aftermath are all part of the picture. On the whole the advance guard of the trend has tended to be cautious; Kahn-Freund insists that, in teaching, each legal problem should be looked at as a social problem needing a solution, but only after it has been treated as a problem requiring a dogmatic 'legal' answer in the accepted manner;[12] Wedderburn has advocated advance 'only a millimetre at a time'; others have been careful to protect their rear from attack by more conservative-minded lawyers. Evolution rather than revolution seems to be the order of the day.

Insofar as this may help us to avoid the otiose polemics of the realist controversy the cautious approach is to be welcomed. There are, however, dangers in such a strategy. The difficulties and problems of a contextual approach may be underestimated; the urgent need for equipping the younger generation of legal scholars with a whole range of techniques which are unknown to their predecessors may be overlooked (as may be the difficulty of doing this); the crypto-conservative (the unreconstructed realist) may be as much of a threat as Bickel's

---

[11] This section was never completed. Another section, on 'The American Heritage', was omitted from the second draft, see below, n. 30.

[12] *O. Kahn-Freund, 'Reflections on Legal Education', 29 *MLR* 121 (1966), 125.

'arrested realist',[13] the revolutionary who gets stuck in a groove, his elementary programme elevated to unchangeable dogma. There is one stage in particular in the process of reconstruction where it is particularly easy to stick. The 'convert' has intellectually assented at the level of abstract theory, but he has not realized the full implications of his theoretical ideas for detailed work, still less has he been able to break intellectual habits that are founded on a different theory. (And for the record we should like to say that we are very conscious of this in our own thinking.) Habits of mind are hard to break, the necessary materials are not readily available, a field categorized in a traditional manner, like Torts or Equity, may not be well-suited to a contextual treatment, and our formal legal education has not given us all of the relevant technical equipment. Moreover, the research required for a contextual approach may well be more time-consuming than traditional legal research. Much work may have to be put into one empirical study to produce a very limited amount of data.

In his *Introduction to Jurisprudence* Lloyd discusses American legal realism with more understanding and sympathy than most English jurists have done. However, he concludes:

> Moreover, there is a great deal of traditional law, such as the rules for the formation and dissolution of contracts, which hardly seems to lend itself to any very profound sociological re-examination or reassessment on the basis of new techniques, and these represent legal spheres with which the ordinary lawyer still remains very much concerned in his daily practice. From this point of view it is not easy to see how the better type of modern textbook can be radically reconstituted in the light of fresh techniques so as better to serve the modern lawyer.[14]

This is a crucial challenge which the series faces.

C. Some Suggested Guidelines

At the very outset it is worth repeating: it is not our intention to replace one stereotype with another. Nor is it our function as editors to tell authors how to write their books. But, for the purpose of provoking discussion, we have not been inhibited or deterred by such considerations from expressing personal opinions on some of the problems of the series, as we see them.

(i) The Unifying Elements in the Series

(a) The Contextual Approach

The word 'contextual' has been chosen deliberately for its open-endedness. It is relatively easy to say what 'the contextual approach' is not: it is not narrow-

---

[13] A. Bickel, *The Least Dangerous Branch* (Indianapolis, 1962) 81–2.
[14] Dennis Lloyd, *Introduction to Jurisprudence*, 2nd edn. (London, 1965) 262. This passage was modified in later editions.

minded, it does not treat law as being 'just there' to be studied in isolation, it is opposed to 'formalism'. But what are these broader aspects? What constitutes the context? Our view is that these need not be, indeed probably cannot be, defined in general terms. Each book will present particular problems of its own in respect of delimitation and presentation of the subject-matter, etc. 'Context' in one case may include the practices and expectations of the people most directly affected by the rules under consideration (for example in relation to business law), in another the light to be thrown on particular problems by the techniques and findings of other disciplines;[15] in almost all 'context' will include the consideration of policies underlying the rules. That there is plenty of scope within 'the contextual approach' for differences of method, for disagreement, and for experiment should be considered a virtue, if a principal object is to liberate legal scholarship from artificial restrictions. But this virtue carries with it the risk for our series that it will be a formless hotchpot of works united only by a negative reaction against a narrow tradition. Quite apart from the weakness of building anything solely on a negative reaction, there is the additional threat in the present case that some works would be 'unreconstructed', with the contextual matter little more than a gloss or an ornament, and that others may go to the opposite extreme, incorporating distortions and exaggerations of the kind which brought the realist movement into disrepute.

One possible solution might be to spell out a theory of law as a basis for the series as a whole. This, however, would almost certainly turn out to be either too vague to be useful or so dogmatic as to be both controversial and constricting—and authors would rightly refuse to be bound by it. Nearly all legal theories are contextual, with the possible exception of Kelsen's Pure Theory and its poor relations. By a 'legal theory' we mean in this context an articulated statement of a coherent set of general ideas about law; an important feature of a contextual approach is that it bears a close and definite connection to legal theories in this sense. For part of the 'context' of any 'legal' discussion is the assumptions presupposed by statements about law, whether these be statements *of* rules of law, or other kinds of statements *about* law. A characteristic of the contextual approach is that these assumptions are articulated, examined, and subjected to critical scrutiny; a characteristic of the tradition we are reacting against is that it is not self-conscious about its assumptions or, when it is, 'theory' is not considered as having a direct bearing on 'practice', which would here include the practice of legal writing.

Viewed in this way any one of a number of legal theories may be acceptable

---

[15] *e.g., in relation to Evidence, theories of knowledge, the psychology of perception, the weighing of evidence by historians and other specialists in fact-finding and interpretation, the conclusions of the Chicago Jury Project re the jury as a fact-finding device; it is significant that *Cross on Evidence*, 1st edn. (London, 1958) only makes use of one 'contextual' work (Gulson's *Philosophy of Proof*, 2nd edn. (London, 1923)) and contains not even a reference to works of leading legal theorists like Bentham, Frank or Perelman—an interesting contrast is offered by A. Trusov's *An Introduction to the Theory of Evidence* (Moscow, 1963).

to someone working contextually. Pound, Llewellyn, Bentham, Lasswell and McDougal are just some of those who might provide a theoretical framework for one or more works in the series. The implications of the general ideas of these jurists for the writing of law books have not often been spelled out, but there are implications and they can be articulated. There is, of course, a danger that a general theory may be applied dogmatically, instead of being used as a source of ideas and as a guide, but the English tendency is to under-use rather than to over-use theory and we need not be unduly apprehensive of this particular danger.

It does not matter for the purposes of our series what theory, if any, a particular author adopts; what may be important, however, is that what would in a traditional textbook often be left unstated should be articulated. This may be particularly important in respect of (a) the objectives of the book, including educational objectives, if any; (b) the methods employed for attaining (a); (c) the standpoint(s) of the author (see below); (d) the choice of organizing concepts for classifying the material (See Appendix on Llewellyn's *Cases and Materials on the Law of Sales*[16]); and (e) the values by which particular legal institutions or doctrines are judged.

It may be wise to leave open-ended the matter of a general theoretical basis for books in the series. It is still possible to ask whether one may not expect some theoretical common ground. This is a difficult question, to which we can only give a tentative answer. Although there is logically no necessary connection between a contextual approach and a teleological view of law, it seems likely (and for the series, desirable), that there will be a close connection in fact. Most authors will probably look on law as a means to an end (they may disagree as to what the ends should be), in which case they will be more likely to make explicit the ends that they consider a particular body of law should be securing and will criticize consistently in terms of such stated ends.

In recent years, much has been written on the relationship of law and the social sciences. Alas the amount of 'doing' has not kept pace with the amount of 'talking'. Thus rather than insist that 'Law in Context' is an attempt to relate law and the social sciences, we would rather put it in a more mundane way. Our purposes in this area are twofold. We hope to see books in this series relating legal doctrines to what actually happens in practice. (In contract, for instance, trying to find out what businessmen and other participants actually do, what is done in arbitration, the effect of insurance, and the practical importance of such matters as consideration.) Second, we should like to see authors being more critical of the policies underlying statutes and judicial decisions, and raising more regularly and more extensively than at present what the law should be.

We are aware that many members of the profession and some academic lawyers are opposed to exposing students to such material. Obviously we do not share their views. But such critics have to be convinced that the inclusion of

---

[16] Op. cit., n. 9 [omitted here].

such material is not inconsistent with the retention of at least a major part of the advantages to be derived from the current approach to academic law. We think the two are not only reconcilable, but that there exists in England the opportunity for getting the best of both worlds. We trust that 'Law in Context' books will in no way encourage legal sloppiness, or discourage doctrinal analysis; but hopefully they will link this doctrinal analysis to what actually happens in practice, at the same time forcing law students to consider what policies the law should pursue and what the law ought to be.

(b) The audience

It is the policy of the series that the 'intellectual level' of the books should be that of the 'average' university undergraduate. Implicit in our criticisms of the traditional textbook is the suggestion that such books tend to underestimate the intellectual capacities of undergraduates and to lay too much stress on simplification and handing things to students on a plate. They also try to perform a reference function, which unnecessarily duplicates the efforts of such readily available and more efficient works as *Halsbury*. It is suggested that our image of The Reader should be of an intelligent person who is capable of understanding the How and the Why as well as the What and who is able to supplement the information provided by 'Law in Context' books by use of standard works of reference. In 'Law in Context' depth should take priority over coverage and detail; this does not mean to say that the information-content of books in the series should be kept deliberately low. The point is rather that, if we are to produce works which are as solid as *Salmond on Torts*, but which aim at a broader perspective and a deeper understanding, then something has to be sacrificed. As has already been suggested, most of our books will try to cover less ground (in terms of legal topics) than *Salmond*—in other words a narrower coverage; but this may not be enough and, in some works at least, the general level of information-content may have to be less detailed as well, although if dramatization or similar devices are used, much more detail may be given in respect of selected instances. One foresees that striking a balance between the competing claims of coverage, detail, and depth will be one of the most persistent problems of the series. There is no simple dogmatic solution. We suggest as a general guide that depth should normally be given priority.

If we aim single-mindedly at the undergraduate, the question arises: should the series have any specific pedagogical aims? Are we, for instance, to look on the books as teaching tools? If so, how is that to affect them? The policy of the series is flexible on this point: it has been decided that the books may vary both in length and form; for instance the series could include a 'Cases and materials' work along the lines of Donnelly, Goldstein, and Schwartz' *Criminal Law*, a monograph like Berle and Means' *The Modern Corporation and Private Property*, a collection of connected essays like Stevens and Yamey, *The Restrictive*

Practices Court, or something more resembling a treatise, like Gower's *Modern Company Law*, or even a 'contextual' learning programme comparable to Kelso's *A Programmed Introduction to the Study of Law*;[17] similarly, although the aim is to produce substantial works, the series could accommodate a book on a relatively narrow topic of as little as 100–150 pages. Obviously objectives will vary with each book, including pedagogical objectives, and for this reason no general guide can be given for the series as a whole.

(ii) Ephemerality

Within any intellectual tradition it is important to try to seek to differentiate the relatively stable from the ephemeral. Any work which is to have lasting value or wide significance needs to be based on some stable foundation. By and large people working in the tradition of legal formalism find this stable element in the allegedly unchanging principles of the common law. The old law teacher's idea that gentlemen should not study legislation in a university was no doubt rooted in a feeling that one could expect the common law to evolve at a staid and respectable pace, whereas the legislature might overnight at any time abolish a whole field of legal study. The pathos of the German civilian's complaint 'that the politicians could repeal my life work in a day' is matched by the bewilderment of authors and publishers of formalistic books on African Constitutions when a large part of the subject-matter of their work disappears soon after the date of publication, if not on the very day, as happened in the case of Morris and Read's *Uganda*.[18] One of the fatal weaknesses of formalism is its inability to cope with rapidly changing situations. One of the root causes of the present trend away from formalism must surely be the increase in the pace of change in modern life, and in particular, the recent burst of law reform.

How can the contextual approach cope with this problem? In some ways it is harder for it to do so. Social change is notoriously faster than legal change; contextual work necessitates keeping pace with advances in other disciplines; the patient grubber after facts is often as prone to find his research as outdated as the African Constitutional lawyer: 'Law in Context' books are law books and so the problems posed by an increase in the pace of law reform are almost as acute for us as for traditionalists. Almost, but not quite. For insofar as the contextual approach is concerned with Why and How as well as What, it is to some extent concerned with less ephemeral phenomena. Social problems,

[17] R. C. Donnelly, J. Goldstein and R. D. Schwartz, *Criminal Law* (New York, 1962); A. A. Berle and G. C. Means, *The Modern Corporation and Private Property* (New York, 1932); R. Stevens and B. Yamey, *The Restrictive Practices Court*, (London, 1965); L. C. B. Gower, *The Principles of Modern Company Law*, 2nd edn. (London, 1957); C. Kelso, *A Programmed Introduction to the Study of Law* (Indianapolis, 1965).

[18] H. F. Morris and J. S. Read, *Uganda: The Development of its Laws and Constitution* (London, 1966).

people's values, even methods tend to change rather more slowly than detailed social facts and legal doctrines. Bentham's *Rationale of Evidence*, for instance, still has contemporary significance because he organized it around a considera- tion of 'the ends of judicature' and possible ways of achieving those ends.[19] Specific doctrines, many of which have been superceded, were considered in the context of relatively stable problems and objectives. Peake's *Compendium of the Law of Evidence*,[20] the treatise to which he referred non-lawyers and law stu- dents, has long since been forgotten.

It is desirable that a high proportion of 'Law in Context' books should be of lasting value, not only because of the obvious attractions of such an objective to authors and publishers alike, but also for basic educational reasons. Insofar as a prime objective of the series is to provide books of more educational value than standard textbooks, and insofar as one of the crucial problems of legal education is how to cope with the ever-increasing pace of change, and insofar as the solution lies in concentrating on that which is relatively stable or which has broad implications—viz. problems, values, methods—books which are writ- ten in full appreciation of the problems of working in a changing context are likely to be the most valuable educationally.

The experience of writers on African constitutions suggests some devices for coping with rapidly changing situations. One avenue of escape is to resort to a historical treatment. Dr. Claire Palley completed her study of the Constitution of Rhodesia shortly before UDI and she only had time to insert a brief addendum dealing with the event.[21] Unlike many African legal works her book has a good survival potential for not only is a substantial part of it based on a moving time- scale (straight history) but much of the 'flat' description is sufficiently related to an evolutionary pattern that many sections will continue to have a significance that is not dependent upon the law remaining static. History may have to be rewritten in every generation, but not every two years. Another device that has been resorted to has been to select particular points of time (for example the date of Independence) as the reference point for a detailed study. The basis of selec- tion of the point of time need not be arbitrary, as is usually the case when the cut-off point is related to the date of publication; rather, a moment may be chosen by reference to the same kinds of consideration that affect the choice of subjects of 'case-studies'.

To sum up: time is part of the context of almost any study. In periods of rapid change it becomes of critical importance. This is especially so in our present educational situation. One of the most difficult problems is how to equip our students to be adaptable. Insofar as the 'Law in Context' series has pedagogical aims, it should be especially sensitive to this problem.

[19] J. Bentham, *Rationale of Judicial Evidence* (ed., J. S. Mill, London, 1827).
[20] T. Peake, *A Compendium of the Law of Evidence*, 1st edn. (London, 1801).
[21] Claire Palley, *The Constitutional History and Law of Southern Rhodesia, 1888–1965* (Oxford, 1966).

(iii) Standpoint

One important aspect of lack of self-consciousness in our textbook tradition is that it is often unclear with whom the author identifies himself and what is his image of his audience. To take a simple example: a book on 'Personal injuries and the law' could vary quite considerably in form and content, depending on whether the operative image of the typical reader were a barrister arguing an appeal on a point of law (who might not be able to mention the insurance aspects), a judge hearing the appeal (who might not be meant to know anything about the insurance aspects), a solicitor acting for a client (how much would he need to know that is not in *Salmond*?) or a specialist on accident prevention or a reformer who is interested in (possibly radical) reform of the whole system of distribution of risk in relation to accidents. Differences in standpoint produce different criteria of relevance and of importance. A famous passage on causation from R. G. Collingwood makes the basic point:

A car skids while cornering at a certain point, turns turtle, and bursts into flames. From the car-driver's point of view, the cause of the accident was cornering too fast, and the lesson is that one must drive more carefully. From the county surveyor's point of view, the cause was a defective road surface, and the lesson is that one must make skid-proof roads. From the motor manufacturers' point of view, the cause was defective design, and the lesson is that one must place the centre of gravity lower.[22]

Salmond on Torts, a book which, until the latest edition,[23] never even mentioned the insurance aspects of personal injuries claims, does not make explicit the standpoint of the work. As regards readership the Preface to the First Edition indicates that it is primarily directed towards 'lawyers and students of law';[24] 'the standpoint of the student' is not a clearly differentiated 'standpoint' in the sense the term is used here, because it does not tell us with whom the student is supposed to identify nor what are the objectives of his studying the law of Torts. We may speculate that, in the Oxbridge tradition, there may have been a tendency, perhaps unconscious, to identify with barristers and Lords of Appeal, rather than with solicitors or less senior members of the judiciary or with 'legislators'; certainly the omission of discussion of the insurance aspects is partly explained on this ground. But a complete explanation would also need to include reference to the author's self-image, which, insofar as it is clear, is that of 'the legal scientist' systematically expounding 'legal science', the subject-matter of which is legal doctrine only. The law student reader, it seems, is also expected to identify with 'the legal scientist' in that the basic educational assumption underlying *Salmond* is that the student's main task is to learn the systematically

[22] R. G. Collingwood, 'On the So-called Idea of Causation', 85 *Proc. Aristotelian Society* (1937–8), at 96.

[23] *Salmond on Torts*, 14th edn., R. F. V. Heuston, (London, 1965), 33–8.

[24] *Salmond*, op. cit., Preface to First Edition, reprinted in later editions.

expounded principles of the law of Torts. The fact that this accords most closely
with the standpoint of 'the judge' could be treated as being coincidental.

The above analysis should not be interpreted in the first instance as a criticism
of *Salmond*, although it could be used as a basis for criticism. Rather it is
intended to illustrate the conception of 'standpoint'. *Salmond assumes* certain
educational aims and *identifies* fairly consistently with the standpoint of one
particular kind of participant in legal processes. The book has probably served
those aims admirably. It has also been useful to a wide variety of people. But
we must not, for this reason, be led into thinking that *Salmond's* aims are the
only possible ones, or that the standpoint of 'the legal scientist' or 'the judge'
is the only possible standpoint or even always the most apposite.

At this stage it may be appropriate to look more closely at the concept of
'standpoint' as an analytical tool. Although it is rarely openly described as such,
differentiation of standpoint is a commonly used juristic tool for clearing up
confusions of thought. Part of the disagreement between 'retributivists' and
'utilitarians' in respect of the justification of punishment has been dissolved by
showing that retributivists make most sense when treated as answering 'the
judge's question', whereas utilitarians are most commonly concerned with 'the
legislator's question'. In other words failure to differentiate between the standpoints of 'the judge' and of 'the legislator' has been the source of some confusion of thought in philosophical discussions of punishment. It is commonly
pointed out that Bentham's principle of utility is much less vulnerable to criticism when viewed from the standpoint of 'the legislator' than from the standpoint
of the individual actor who has to decide how he alone should act. Examples
could be multiplied.[25]

Failure to make clear differentiations of standpoint helps to explain persistent
misunderstandings and misconceived criticisms of American jurists, such as
Holmes and Llewellyn, when they talk of law in terms of prediction. Brief analysis of a famous passage may help further to elucidate the concept of 'standpoint'.

It will be recalled that one of the first 'realist' writings was Holmes's noted
paper 'The Path of the Law'. The context of the reading of this paper is significant; Holmes was addressing [Boston University] law students after dinner during
the heyday of Langell's influence at Harvard. Holmes's message was that the
way in which the students were taught to look at law was different from the way
in which certain types of participants looked at it, and for this reason it was
unrealistic. To give punch to what he was saying Holmes set out to shock his
audience by use of a vivid and seemingly cynical image:

Take the fundamental question, what constitutes the law? You will find some text writers
telling you that it is something different from what is decided by the courts of Massachusetts or England, that it is a system of reason, that it is deduction from principles of
ethics or admitted axioms or what not, which may or may not coincide with the decisions.

<hr />

[25] See *HDTWR*, 2nd edn., 64–71.

But if we take the view of our friend the bad man we shall find that he does not care two straws for the axioms or deductions, but that he does want to know what the Massachusetts or English courts are likely to do in fact. I am much of his mind. The prophecies of what the courts will do in fact, and nothing more pretentious, are what I mean by the law.[26]

This famous passage has been criticized, most commonly on two grounds. First, it is said, Holmes seems to be advocating an amoral attitude to law. This need not concern us here, though it should be pointed out that Holmes's Bad Man looks more like a tax consultant than a character from Genet; second, to look at law in terms of prediction does not take account of the standpoint of the judge or the legislator. There is considerable force in both these criticisms, if Holmes was trying to put forward a rounded philosophy of law that accommodated all possible standpoints. But the context of his talk suggests that Holmes's main objective was more modest. He was addressing himself to a specific audience composed, as he saw it, of intending practitioners; the image of the practitioner that he projected in this paper was essentially the image of the office lawyer. The point that Holmes was trying to get across was that the standpoint of such a functionary was significantly different from the kind of standpoint that Harvard law students were being asked to adopt and that this was an unrealistic way of preparing students for private practice. In 'The Path of the Law' the standpoint of the Bad Man and the standpoint of the counsellor are roughly equated and are by implication differentiated from those of the judge, the legislator, and even the advocate. Holmes's message can be restated in the following fashion without much distortion: 'You are intending to be private practitioners of law; the standpoint of the private practitioner, especially in respect of his role as counsellor, is very different from that of the judge or legislator. Your legal education, by concentrating on legal rules, tends to teach you to look at law from the standpoint of the judge, insofar as any standpoint is differentiated.'

A similar analysis of the first chapter of Llewellyn's *Bramble Bush* in terms of his picture of his audience as intending private practitioners of law ('The Counsellor' image again predominating) may help to explain, if not totally to justify, some of the passages that have occasioned controversy.[27]

[In a famous passage Pound distinguished between six standpoints from which 'law in the sense of the body of authoritative precepts' may be looked at: the law maker; the individual subject to the legal precept (whether good citizen or bad man); a judge or administrative official making an authoritative determination; the counsellor or legal adviser; the jurist or teacher; and the enterpreneur or man of business.[28]]

Whereas Pound's characterization of different standpoints is quite useful, it is rather crude and is open to the criticism that he does not distinguish clearly

<hr />

[26] O. W. Holmes, Jr., 'The Path or the Law', 10 *Harv. L Rev.* 451 (1897), 460–1.

[27] See *KLRM*, 140–52.

[28] R. Pound, *Jurisprudence*, vol. II. (1959), at 129–31. The passage was quoted in full in the text, but has been omitted here for reasons of space.

between the standpoints of actual people (actual judges, actual members of a legislature, etc.) and the 'standpoints' of constructs which refer to certain functions, no matter who performs them. 'The legislator' for instance may refer not only to one who has power and authority to make law, such as a member of Parliament, but to anyone who is concerned with 'the law as it ought to be'. Actual judges 'make law' and when they do so their standpoint is that of 'the legislator'. The standpoint of 'the legislator' in fact covers at least two functions: (i) the formulation or clarification of goals and (ii) the creation or choice of laws or other instruments for achieving these goals. Similarly the standpoint of 'the judge' at least covers the functions of (i) deciding particular cases and (ii) advancing reasoned justifications for such decisions; again a much more differentiated analysis of functions could be made in this respect. There is clearly an overlap or at least a close relationship between many of these functions—in the case of 'persuading' (argument by an advocate on a point of law) and judicial justification, almost complete identity. Pound's suggestion that 'law in the sense of a body of authoritative precepts' can be verified in terms of the standpoint of the judge, should not be taken to mean that the standpoint of the judge can be taken as covering all standpoints for all purposes. For instance, predicting the outcome of a particular case is not normally associated with the standpoint of 'the judge', (although of course an actual judge with an eye to a possible appeal from his decision may be concerned with prediction); nor would preventative counselling or negotiating or drafting, or other functions performed by private practitioners, normally be associated with the standpoints either of 'the judge' or actual judges.

The concept of 'standpoint' may be used with reference either to constructs personifying particular functions ('the legislator' etc.) or to actual or imagined people ('what would a normal solicitor dealing with a typical personal injuries claim arising from a motor accident want to know?'). The former is more intellectualized and accordingly more susceptible to rigorous development; the latter may help to promote a more realistic identification of the author with typical participants in actual processes. But the point must not be overlooked that the extent to which the concept of 'standpoint' can be employed as a tool of refined analysis turns largely on the degree of refinement of the characterization of different standpoints. The difficulty of differentiating between 'judicial', 'administrative', and 'legislative' functions is a familiar illustration of the problem of finding a satisfactory scheme of classification of functions of participants in legal processes. For present purposes it will be adequate to accept Pound's characterization, treating the headings as constructs rather than as referring to actual people.

What is the application of all this to 'Law in Context'? The brief answer is that, if we are right in suggesting that self-consciousness is basic to a 'contextual approach', then it would probably be a healthy exercise for an author to ask: 'Who am I? What am I trying to do? Who is my potential audience?' The first question will help to clarify overall purposes ('I am a legal scientist, scientifically expounding "the law" as it is' (for what purposes?); 'I am a critic of the existing law recommending what the law should be' (ideally or in terms of what is immediately practicable?); 'I am a social scientist-lawyer, reporting on findings I have made' (about what? to what end?); 'I am a collector and organizer of useful information for easy reference' (useful to whom for what?) or a combination of these (to what extent are they compatible?). The question 'who is my potential audience?' should further clarify purpose and provide criteria of relevance: Am I, in writing about personal injuries, addressing (actual or intending) solicitors, barristers, Lords of Appeal, Law Commissioners, industrial efficiency experts, insurance men, plaintiffs, defendants, social scientists? What knowledge can be assumed? As participants in (typical) processes what do they need to know and understand? (Back to: who am I?) To what extent am I setting out to give them all they need? And so on. 'Standpoint' is a concept which makes the elementary point that different people have different purposes and roles and needs and that authors of books should bear this in mind.

(iv) Conclusion

These are just some of the ideas that we may feel may be helpful in the difficult task of trying to devise 'new' forms of legal literature. We put 'new' in inverted commas because, of course, what is being attempted is only relatively new. There is much relevant experience from which we can learn. In particular American lawyers have been struggling for nearly fifty years with the problems of converting a contextually-oriented jurisprudence into concrete work in particular areas. The differences between the American scene and our own, especially in respect of legal education, may point to the conclusion that America may not be able to provide many models for simple imitation on this side of the Atlantic. Nevertheless in many specific respects their successes and their failures may be instructive. There are attached as appendices to this paper, some pieces concerning certain aspects of American legal literature which may be suggestive.[29]

W. L. T.
R. B. S.[30]

May, 1967

III. RETROSPECT

If I were to draft a manifesto or rationale for a new series of 'contextual' books today, there would undoubtedly be differences in tone and emphasis and in a

---

[29] Op. cit., n. 9 [not included here].

[30] William Twining and Robert Stevens. The paper was presented in our joint names as co-editors. I was responsible for the text; Robert Stevens made some comments and censored a section on the American Heritage as being undiplomatic to present to an English audience.

few ideas. Among other things the situation has changed. What has surprised me most on rereading this product of twenty-three years ago has been the continuities. Today I might modify a few statements, elaborate on others, but recant on none. However, it is not my intention to explore how far the 'Law in Context' series has lived up to its original aspirations. My concern here is to examine the idea of 'a contextual approach' at a general level and to explore how far *Accidents, Compensation and the Law* exemplifies that approach.

First, a cautionary note. As editors we have tried consistently to encourage authors to write the books they really want to write, rather than conform to a rigid set of criteria or conventions. In the context of a particular publishing venture the label was not meant to be precise or constricting; indeed, one of our aims was to try to encourage a greater diversity in legal literature. Accordingly, too much should not be read into the title as such. Nor would it be likely to be helpful to try to find the lowest common denominator of 'a contextual approach' by analysing the assumptions underlying all the books in the series. This would be repeating the mistake of characterizing 'realism' by looking for ideas shared by a list of twenty legal scholars explicitly selected for their diversity.[31]

However, it would be disingenuous or unduly defensive to claim that 'law in context' and related phrases were intended to have no juristic significance at all. As editors, one test of proposals for the series has been: 'Is it (sufficiently) contextual?' The 'tentative rationale' acknowledged an intellectual ancestry and some specific general assumptions. It may be helpful to proceed by constructing an 'ideal type' for a book, research project or other work embodying a contextual approach. Today one might articulate a suggested method for constructing a contextual book in terms of an intellectual procedure along the following lines:

1. Clarify the author's objectives (including educational objectives), vantage point, role, and intended audience (clarification of standpoint).
2. Formulate the main questions to be addressed.
3. Clarify the general perspective and assumptions to be adopted in addressing these questions, together with the main methods and sources.
4. Choose an appropriate organizing category.
5. Identify the geographical scope of the work (geographical/jurisdictional context).
6. In the light of 1 and 2 identify the most important relevant contexts in which the particular questions and phenomena will be studied.
7. Construct a broad demographic picture of the phenomena to be studied (total pictures).
8. Summarize the main thesis and themes of the work (the plot).
9. State how this work relates to and differs from existing literature and what it should add to understanding or knowledge in the area (the literary

---

[31] *KLRM*, at 75 ff.

context). Indicate why you think that the work should deserve attention in ten years' time (the ten year test).

10. Insofar as particular (kinds of) decisions are a focal point of attention construct an ideal type of the main kinds of total process which form the context of such decisions (processual thinking).

In considering a proposal or advising an author I have tended to ask such questions regularly, but not as schematically.[32] At first sight most, if not all, of these questions might be asked of any academic book or research project. Supposing that these ten points taken together characterize 'a contextual' approach, one might ask: is there some connecting thread that links all of them? And, what, if anything, makes them characterize a distinctive approach to law? A brief answer to the first question is that all the points are concerned with establishing connections, relating the subject of study and what is said to something else.[33] But we need to look in more detail at some of the categories to be able to give satisfactory answers to either question. Some are clearly points to be taken into account in planning any scholarly work. Formulation of questions (2), clarification of perspective (3), summarizing the argument (8), and relating the work to existing literature (9) are standard elements of designing any book. They feature here as part of the self-consciousness of 'Law in Context'. Clarification of standpoint (1) was dealt with at length in the original paper, but requires a brief further comment along with the other points.

1. Clarification of standpoint (Who am I? At what stage in what process am I? What am I trying to do?) helps to locate the author in terms of vantage point, purposes, presumed relation to the reader, and so on. Many law books either lack a clear standpoint in this sense, or assume the same criteria of relevance and significance as an appellate court judge, for no apparent reason. Many 'Law in Context' books have in practice tended to assume something approaching the standpoint of a legislator or policy maker. This was the authors' choice, but it is not a necessary corollary of a contextual approach. What is needed is clarity about objectives and vantage point, for these provide the main criteria of relevance and significance. Writers of avowedly educational works should formulate explicit learning objectives and choose a legal standpoint appropriate to these. In my experience academic lawyers are strangely reluctant to do this or to face squarely why they are giving priority to certain educational objectives. Why, for example, should undergraduate law students be encouraged to

---

[32] In practice we suggest to authors that they follow the invaluable advice in Jenny Uglow, 'Preparing a proposal for a book', written for the SPTL Working Party on Academic Law Publishing in 1977.

[33] See further Twining, 'Some Jobs for Jurisprudence', 1 *Brit. Jo. Law and Society* 149 (1974), 164–6 and TAR, 371 ff.

think like policy-makers or appellate court judges? The answers to such questions are too often treated as self-evident.

4. Choice of an appropriate organizing category has, as a matter of historical contingency, been a matter of conscious concern in 'law in context'. A central idea, borrowed from American legal realism, and developed in the late 1960s by Jolowicz and others[34] was the need to be self-conscious about classification and in particular to question the appropriateness of abstract legal categories for fields of study: for example, substituting 'compensation for accidents' for 'torts' (Atiyah); 'public control of land' for 'real property' (MacAuslan)[35]; 'information in litigation' for 'evidence' (Twining).[36] Patrick Atiyah's original proposal for *Accidents, Compensation and the Law* began:

> My principal complaint against the existing textbooks on Tort is that their choice and arrangement of materials is almost entirely governed by conceptualism. This may seem a relatively mild deficiency, but it is in fact a fundamental weakness.[37]

In practice the re-examination of traditional organizing categories for fields of law and particular topics has not led to a wholesale move to 'fact-based classification', itself a problematic concept, but rather to a self-conscious effort to choose a way of designating and organizing the field or topic under consideration in a way that is appropriate to given purposes.[38] By no means all 'Law in Context' books have involved rejection of traditional legal categories (for example Trusts, Criminal Law, Contract(s) have all survived).[39] Indeed, titles in the series do not conform to a single taxonomy and Atiyah himself has stayed with Contract as one way of designating a field.

5. Specifying the geographical scope of a work would seem an obvious task, especially for lawyers conditioned to think in terms of jurisdictional limits. Less obvious is the question: Where along the spectrum of general and particular jurisprudence does it belong? Such questions are surprisingly often ducked in academic practice. That they are often difficult to answer is illustrated by disagreements about the 'Americanness' of Ronald Dworkin[40] or the alleged parochialism of critical legal studies.

6. Choice of appropriate context(s). Whether it is possible to specify *general* criteria of appropriateness is, perhaps, the most problematic and potentially controversial issue for it raises fundamental questions about the nature of academic enterprises. At one level the purpose of a particular

---

[34] *Division and Classification of the Law* (ed., J. A. Jolowicz, London, 1970).
[35] McAuslan, op. cit., n. 9.   [36] *RE*, Ch. 11.   [37] Atiyah, op. cit., n. 9.
[38] On 'fact-based classification' see Jolowicz and Twining, O'Donovan and Paliwala in Jolowicz (ed.) (1970), op. cit.
[39] G. Moffat and M. Chesterman, *Trusts Law: Text and Materials* (London, 1988); N. Lacey, C. Wells, and D. Meure, *Reconstructing Criminal Law: Text and Materials* (London, 1990); and H. Collins, *The Law of Contract* (London, 1986).   [40] See below, Ch. 8, at 173–5.

project or enquiry or book may provide some common sense indications of what may be appropriate. But one's choice of purpose and method are themselves based on assumptions that are susceptible to critical scrutiny in terms of some more general legal or other theory.

7. Construction of a demographic total picture of the relevant phenomena. It is a familiar complaint that traditional expository scholarship tends to treat the atypical, the unrepresentative, and sometimes the trivial as if they are typical, representative, and important. Jury trials are treated as the paradigm of all trials in evidence discourse; appellate cases are treated as representative of all 'cases'; Blackacre was, at least until recently, the prototype of English residential property. The rule of thumb is: set the phenomenon under consideration in the context of some 'total picture' with particular reference to the scale of the relevant phenomena. For example, consider appellate cases in the context of all contested cases, contested cases in the context of all litigation, and litigation in the context of a total picture of all disputes (or dispute-processing) in the relevant society. What percentage of confessions are in practice retracted? Who are the main victims of misidentification—a few persons convicted by juries of serious crimes or hundreds of (or more) juveniles in less visible settings?[41] How much land is there in England and Wales? What are the main uses to which it is put?[42] What is the distribution of people and housing in respect of residential use? How many are owner-occupiers, lessees, licensees, squatters, homeless? What are the main transactions and problems relating to each category? Where does Blackacre and the problems of its spendthrift heir fit into this picture?

Relating particular phenomena to some broader total picture is clearly 'contextual' in a straightforward way. Of course, the statistical incidence of a phenomenon is not the sole indicator of its importance or significance (for example some jury trials are among the most important of all trials; *Re Polemis*[43] *is* conceptually interesting). Thinking in terms of total pictures is a simple heuristic device for countering lawyers' propensity to tunnel vision.

10. Thinking in terms of total processes. It is a truism that decisions are a focal point of legal discourse and that they take place in the context of processes. The concept of a process as a flow of decisions and events over time has been usefully developed by Harold Lasswell (a prototypical contextual thinker?), although few have been prepared to follow Lasswell and MacDougal in making this the basis for a full-blown theory of law as a process of decision.[44] Looking at particular decisions as part of some

---

[41] *RE*, Ch. 5.

[42] This demographic approach to Land Law was originally developed by Patrick McAuslan.

[43] *Re Polemis*, [1921] 3 *KB* 560.

[44] See Myres S. McDougal and W. Michael Reisman, *International Law Essays*, (Mineola, New York, 1981).

longer total process (for example litigation, an ongoing feud, a political strategy, some other social process) is clearly 'contextual' and equally clearly a necessary part of the intellectual equipment of anyone concerned with law.

These guidelines are sufficient to ground some elementary points: first, the range of possible connections, and hence of contexts, is almost limitless. Those mentioned are just a sample. Secondly, several of the questions are open-ended. Which of many possible standpoints, perspectives etc. is to be adopted is not prescribed. Thirdly, most of these ideas may seem pretty obvious, tempting one to say that they are 'just common sense'. I would agree that they make sense and are sensible, but how common they are in practice, especially in combination, is open to question. Like 'realism', 'law in context' is not a distinctive form of legal theory nor are these precepts on their own sufficient to constitute a comprehensive methodology for legal scholarship either in general or of a particular kind. However, they embody sufficient good sense to warrant the claim that they should be a necessary part of the equipment of every student of law and that failure to observe any of them may be a ground for criticism.[45]

IV. *ACCIDENTS, COMPENSATION AND THE LAW* AS A CONTEXTUAL WORK

Unlike most authors, Patrick Atiyah delivered his manuscript ahead of schedule. *Accidents, Compensation and the Law* was published in 1970 as the first book in the 'Law in Context' series. We could hardly have got off to a better start. It won almost instant recognition as a brilliantly designed and executed departure from tradition. Now in its fourth edition (edited by Peter Cane) it still holds its own in the market. Atiyah was highly influential in the campaign to establish the Royal Commission on Civil Liability and Compensation for Personal Injury in 1973 under Lord Pearson in the aftermath of the thalidomide affair.[46] The Pearson Commission's proposals were, in Atiyah's view, 'relatively unadventurous'[47] and even these have been largely shelved. So his criticisms of the tort 'system' in England and Wales are as pertinent as ever.

The purpose of this section is to explore how far *Accidents, Compensation and the Law* fits the 'ideal type' of a law in context book.

Conforming to the requirement to be self-conscious in design and method the first edition contained a foreword to the series (two pages) by the editors and a substantial preface (six pages) by the author. The first paragraph of the Preface gives a clear indication of Atiyah's conception of his enterprise:

---

[45] This theme is developed in TAR.

[46] *Report of the Royal Commission on Civil Liability and Compensation for Personal Injury* (Chairman, Lord Pearson), Cmnd. 7054 (1978).   [47] Atiyah, op. cit., 3rd edn., 18.

This is a law book but a law book with a difference. It deals with part of the area covered by what is traditionally thought of as the law of torts, namely compensation for the consequences of accidents, but it is at once wider and narrower than conventional books on torts. It is wider in three ways. First it deals with many aspects of the tort system which are not normally treated as a part of the law of torts at all, and are therefore not included in books or syllabuses on the law of torts. In particular this book attempts to deal with the way in which the law of torts operates in practice, by paying full regard to the relationship between the law of torts and the institution of liability insurance, and also by examining the role of settlements as well as litigation in the compensation process. Secondly, this book is wider than the traditional torts book in that it deals with the many ways in which people may be compensated for accidents otherwise than through the law of torts; it deals with private insurance, with the criminal injuries compensation scheme, and with the social security benefits of the welfare state, and it also touches on the more personal social services which were recently the subject of the Seebohm Report. And thirdly, this book is wider than the traditional torts book in that it is as much a book *about* the law as a book detailing the law. It attempts, in other words, not merely to expound the ways in which people may be compensated under the law, but also to provide a serious attempt to study and evaluate the policies which underlie the different compensation systems operating today. On the other hand, this book is narrower than the traditional torts book in that it does not attempt anything like the same comprehensive coverage of every doctrinal principle that passes under the name of torts. Nothing will be found in this book about the economic torts, very little about nuisance and RYLANDS V. FLETCHER, practically nothing about defamation and many other matters discussed in torts books. Moreover, even the discussion of negligence which is not much shorter than that in many torts books, is of a very different kind. This book does not attempt to deal in the same detail with all the myriad rules laid down by the courts in actions of negligence, including in this field problems arising from contributory negligence, remoteness of damage and the assessment of damages. Although these matters are all dealt with at some length, the treatment is directed towards stating the broad legal position, and evaluating the principal features of the legal position, rather than to a minute statement of every detailed rule.[48]

The book is divided into seven parts. The main headings are revealing: 1. The issues in perspective. 2. The Tort system. 3. The Tort system in operation. 4. Other compensation systems. 5. The overall picture. 6. Objectives. 7. The future.

The 'plot' of the book might be summarized as follows: England and Wales has a plethora of different compensation systems which, like Topsy, have just 'growed' largely independently of each other. These systems are based on different political ideologies and scales of values and their coexistence results in many anomalies and inconsistencies. The Tort system does not fulfil its objectives in practice and these objectives are to a large extent incompatible with the objectives of the other main compensation systems. Accordingly the common law action for personal injuries ought to be abolished, but there are practical difficulties associated with all the main alternative schemes that have been proposed

---

[48] Id., XIII–XIV.

to date. It can also be anticipated that there will be strong opposition to significant change from the Bar and other powerful interests.

The conception of the book fits most of the elements of the ideal type. So the title indicates a change of organizing category (4, in section III above); the Preface indicates the implications of this in respect of scope. Although the book was completed in Canberra and draws heavily on American and Australasian materials, the focus is explicitly on the details of the English situation and the implications of the analysis for other jurisdictions are not explored. The tort system is looked at in the context of 'the total compensation picture' in England and Wales (6) and is compared and contrasted with other compensation systems (such as social security and insurance) with devastating effect. A section entitled 'Some facts and figures' (expanded in later editions) gives a brief demography of the main phenomena of accidents and their compensation in England and Wales (7). Part 2 gives an account of the conceptual structure of the law of torts as it relates to accidents; Part 3 looks at this body of law in action in the context of the total process of personal injuries litigation, including the operation of out-of-court settlement and insurance (10). Parts 4 and 5 consider critically the phenomenon of the growth of virtually independent compensation systems, how they relate to each other and the anomalies that result (6 again); Part 6 explores the underlying ideologies of the various systems and proposes a rationale for a single coherent system of compensation for accidents; and Part 7 considers reforms and proposals for reform in other countries and their merits and prospects in the context of England and Wales. The Preface relates the book to existing literature (9). One might say that this is a work that sets the common law action for personal injuries caused by negligence, both in conception and in practice, in its historical, procedural, economic, ideological, and political contexts, as well as comparing it with other types of compensation and with arrangements in other common law countries (6). We have already seen that the book passed the ten year test with flying colours. Ironically this is an indication of its lack of political success. If there had been any significant reform, few would want to read the book as it then stood (or now stands). Most of the anomalies and inconsistencies identified in the first edition still survive. If all or most of the measures Atiyah favoured had been implemented, the book would have had to be almost completely redesigned.

The most difficult points about the relationship of *Accidents, Compensation and the Law* to our ideal type concern the theoretically most interesting questions: in particular, what standpoint, perspective, and methods did Atiyah adopt? *Accidents, Compensation and the Law* could plausibly be interpreted as a book about 'the problem of compensation for accidents' viewed from the standpoint of a mildly Fabian (?) law reformer, who supports the welfare state in a mixed economy. It diagnoses the problem, it analyses and criticizes current responses as incoherent and inefficient, and considers alternative strategies, though without making very detailed proposals for reform. Unlike an official law reform document or Terence Ison's *The Forensic Lottery*[49] it is not mainly an argument directed to resolving a problem or recommending a particular solution. The section on 'The Future' is, significantly, the shortest in the book and, like the rest of the analysis, is rather more detached than the argument of a reformer proposing a particular solution. The reason for this is made clear in the Preface. The enterprise is conceived of mainly as a contribution to legal education and legal scholarship, and only incidentally to reform. The primary audience are law students and academic specialists in torts. Although the author is not explicit about the precise educational objectives, one can infer that they include critical understanding of the law of negligence. Part of the argument is that the additional (non-legal or at least non-traditional) material, for example about insurance and settlement out of court, is at least as important in understanding the law of negligence as other topics in standard torts courses. The preface emphasizes two further points: that in a university course students should study and debate policy issues; and that a study of the law of torts through appellate cases (and a few statutes) does not lead to an understanding of this branch of the law as it affects practising solicitors and barristers and claimants. Their criteria of relevance are different from those of appellate court judges. Thus Atiyah's standpoint is that of an academic lawyer trying to provide the basis for a critical understanding of the law of negligence in action and, incidentally, to indicate points at which that understanding might be advanced by further research. The book is unusually coherent, unlike some other contextual works, because the author sticks consistently to this standpoint.

This formulation may sound almost commonplace today. It was relatively unorthodox in England in the 1960s. What was remarkable was the way in which the objective was pursued at a number of levels. One might be tempted to say that the book sets the law of negligence in context by comparing and contrasting it with other compensation systems. This captures what is perhaps its most original feature, but only gives a partial description of the perspective and method. Perhaps a more balanced account can be made in terms of questions and answers. The opening paragraph of the Introduction outlines the agenda of questions clearly and succinctly:

This book deals with certain kinds of misfortune, and in particular those arising from accidents. What "accidents' does the law concern itself with? How does it seek to avoid them? Which accidents are or should be met by payment of compensation? How is that compensation assessed? How should it be assessed? Who pays for the compensation? Who should pay for it? How is a compensation system administered? These are the questions with which we are principally concerned.[50]

In answering these questions Atiyah drew on a wide range of sources from law and other disciplines (and added to them in later editions). He employed a

[49] T. G. Ison, *The Forensic Lottery*, (London, 1967).   [50] Atiyah, op. cit., 3.

combination of legal, philosophical, and economic analysis. This kind of inter-disciplinary approach does not typically involve an articulate, 'scientific' methodology. It is relatively pragmatic and intuitive and this, for better or worse, has been characteristic of most contextual work by lawyers in recent years. This is a matter which both scientific and ideological purists regard with suspicion.[51]

One may conclude from this analysis that the conception of *Accidents, Compensation and the Law* conformed almost exactly to the ideal type of a 'Law in context' book, before that ideal type was fully formulated. It was also one of the more systematic, as well as the most brilliant, in respect of execution. One reason why other contextual works differ significantly in conception, however well or badly they are executed, is just because that ideal type is open-ended in so many respects. Atiyah's *Accidents, Compensation and the Law* provides a model of excellence within a genre which accommodates a variety of standpoints, ideologies, perspectives, and methods. 'Law in Context' is neither a distinctive theory of or about law, nor an academic orthodoxy.

[51] e.g., C. M. Campbell and P. Wiles 'The Study of Law in Society in Britain', 10 *Law and Society Rev.* 547 (1976).

4

Pericles and the Plumber

Prolegomena to a working theory for lawyer education*

MIRANDA. O brave new world,
That has such people in't!
PROSPERO. 'Tis new to thee.

(*Tempest*, Act V, scene I.)

To begin by clarifying some terms: the subtitle of this lecture is 'Prolegomena to a working theory for lawyer education.' 'Education' is used here to cover the whole area that is sometimes divided into 'education' and 'training'. The term 'lawyer education', though ungainly, has the merit of separating off those aspects of legal education which are concerned with preparation for a career as a professional lawyer from those which have other objectives. The term 'legal education' is retained in contexts where the distinction is blurred. This lecture is concerned first and foremost with the question: what is a desirable education for the prospective lawyer? Thus, for example, in this context it is a secondary consideration that a significant proportion of undergraduate law students do not plan to or will not in fact take up the practice of law and that this proportion may well be increasing. Because most university law faculties do in practice try to make their undergraduate courses serve several objectives, such considerations are not irrelevant; but there are grounds for believing that a widespread ambivalence as regards objectives has been a fertile source of confusion of thought and of unsatisfactory compromises in our present system. If this is so, then it may be a sensible intellectual procedure to start by trying to develop separate theories for lawyer education and for education in law for non-lawyers, and only after this has been done, to examine to what extent their objectives and the best methods of attaining them are compatible. This lecture, then, proceeds on the basis that the problems of lawyer education are sufficiently complex in themselves to merit separate attention.

As an academic jurist I am primarily concerned with that portion of lawyer education that does or might take place within universities. But these matters cannot be coherently treated in isolation from the context of the total process of

* This is an abbreviated version of an inaugural lecture delivered as Professor of Jurisprudence at the Queen's University, Belfast on 18 Jan. 1967. The full text was published in 'The New Lecture Series' of the Queen's University. A shorter version was published in 83 *LQR* 396 (1967).

preparation for practice. Accordingly I shall have to venture beyond the confines of the university campus, but I shall do so with the qualified diffidence of a theatre critic who is not a professional actor. Finally, what is here offered is prolegomena, not a complete theory, still less a blueprint. That is to say, what is here offered is a collection of interrelated observations which, it is suggested, should be taken into account by any working theory of lawyer education purporting to give a coherent answer to the Lasswellian question: For what purposes should what be taught to whom by whom using what methods in what milieux with what resources?

The first step in developing such a theory is to clarify objectives. Just as our legal literature is peopled by such symbolic characters as John Doe and the 'man on the Clapham omnibus', so the literature of legal education is dominated by a fictitious character, 'the lawyer', who is used to symbolize the objectives, assumed or stated, of legal education. He seems to be even more Protean and elusive than the reasonable man; the only characteristic on which there appears to be general agreement is that he is a good fellow, not to be confused with the grasping shyster of the world of fiction.

Despite the bewildering variety of these images, generally speaking, they tend to approximate more or less to one of two polar images which, for the sake of alliteration, may be called respectively Pericles and the plumber. The image of the lawyer as a plumber is a simple one. 'The lawyer' is essentially someone who is master of certain specialized knowledge, 'the law', and certain technical skills. What he needs is a no-nonsense specialized training to make him a competent technician. A 'liberal' education in law for such a functionary is at best wasteful; at worst it can be dangerous. Imagine the effect, it might be argued, on our drains and central heating systems if our plumbers had been made to study the history and philosophy of plumbing, the aesthetics of drains, housing policy, Roman baths, comparative plumbing, and a special subject in the water supply of the Houses of Parliament. When practitioners emphasize the value of a broad education for intending lawyers, they frequently also indicate that it is of secondary importance whether or not it is in law. Some go so far as to say that a subject other than law is to be preferred for university study. If plumbers are to study philosophy, it should not be the philosophy of plumbing.[1]

At the other extreme is the image of the lawyer as Pericles—the lawgiver, the enlightened policy-maker, the wise judge. The Periclean image of 'the lawyer' is not so distinct; this is perhaps due in no small part to the influence of our ideas of liberal education. In England three characters have regularly jostled for first

---

[1] The Wilson Report ('A Survey of Legal Education in the United Kingdom', by J. F. Wilson 9 *JSPTL* (*NS*) 1 (1966), at 55–7) records 73.3% of barristers and 64% of solicitors as expressing a preference for graduates: 'While the majority of practitioners, therefore, were in favour of the graduate entrant, views were more divided on the merits of a law degree' (62% of solicitors, but only 38% of barristers, definitely preferring law graduates to graduates in other subjects). It would be interesting to know how far these figures reflect a recent shift in opinion in favour of law degrees.

position as the appropriate image of the liberally educated man: the cultured gentleman (education for leisure), the wise ruler (education for leadership), and the scholar researcher (education for scholarship).[2] Sometimes they are fused into a composite image, sometimes they are quite clearly differentiated; the differences between them reflect different strands within the liberal tradition; they tend, at least, to share a few attributes: intellectual discipline, detachment, breadth of perspective, an interest in human nature, and a capacity for independent and critical thought. Although the three characters are most closely associated with the liberal arts, the pure scientist has been accommodated with relative ease in the guise of the scholar researcher. The social scientist, one suspects, has found it less easy to fit in. In recent times a fourth character, the applied scientist, sometimes in the guise of technocrat, sometimes more humbly as a technologist, has, in Sir Eric Ashby's words, been 'tolerated, but not assimilated'.[3] From outside the ivory tower there has nearly always been pressure, varying in intensity at different periods, to make university education more obviously useful and vocational. The 'practical man', sometimes in the form of 'business executive', sometimes as professional man, sometimes, more seductively, as 'practical reformer', clamours for admission. He has often been resisted. Sometimes his demands have been ridiculed as being philistine, myopic, narrow-minded or trivial. He is most effectively repulsed when he is shown to have misconceived his own needs. Sometimes the line of resistance has verged on obscurantism: 'a university education needs no justification', 'a university has no purpose', or, as I heard someone assert recently, 'we should take a pride in being useless'. Insofar as such statements express a fear that concern with the vocational or the practical almost certainly involves a sacrifice of 'liberal' values, they deserve to be taken seriously, though sceptically. Insofar as they tend to glorify aimlessness, they are unacceptable, for one assumption upon which my argument is based is that education should as far as possible be treated as a purposive activity, at least at the level of discussions of strategy.

How to reconcile the liberal tradition with the demands of the world of affairs is one of the perennial problems of university education. Possibly of all university subjects law faces the basic dilemma in its most acute form. Other 'professional' subjects such as medicine and engineering seem to an outsider to have been relatively uninhibited in their response to 'vocational' pressures, perhaps because they have been relatively isolated from the liberal arts tradition. Our literature of legal education shows an almost pathological concern with trying to please our colleagues in the arts faculties and our brethren in the legal profession at the same time. It is small wonder that the Periclean image of the lawyer is something of a hybrid.

It is not here suggested that either the Periclean or the plumbing image bears

---

[2] See Ashby, *Technology and the Academics* (London, 1963), *passim*.
[3] Ashby, op. cit., at 66.

much relationship to real lawyers, nor for that matter to the historical Pericles or real plumbers. Nor, when people articulate what they consider to be the proper objectives of legal education, are they often so modest as to equate lawyers with plumbers or so immodest as to suggest that every lawyer should aspire to be a Pericles. But much of our theory and practice about legal education proceeds on the basis of assumptions, hidden or only half-articulated, that are strongly influenced by these images.

While the plumbing image tends to identify 'the lawyer' with a relatively humble small-town solicitor, the image of the lawyer as Pericles tends to identify him with a Law Commissioner or an appellate judge. In a delightfully revealing passage the Wilson Report tells us that 'The general view of university teachers and practitioners alike was that law degree courses should be designed to provide the student with a liberal education and *to train him to think like a lawyer rather than to give him a vocational training.*'[4] It is amusing to speculate on the implications of this contrast between 'thinking like a lawyer' and 'vocational training', but it is perhaps more revealing to substitute 'Lord of Appeal' or even 'Lord Chancellor' for 'lawyer' in this context. Insofar as university students, in the process of learning to think, are served appellate judgments as their staple diet, they are being taught to reason in a manner more suited to the work of appellate judges than to that of private practitioners, especially solicitors. When they are called on to evaluate the existing system, they are usually asked to adopt the posture of leaders of the profession. Our university curricula rarely, if ever, even descend to the level of courts of first instance to concern themselves with such matters as the reasoning processes involved in drawing inferences from evidence or the intellectual problems of sentencing, to take but two examples.[5] Even more rarely do they venture into processes that take place outside the courts. This surely is not because such topics are not suitable for teaching in a university, for many of them are as susceptible to 'liberal' and rigorous treatment as many of the subjects included in conventional curricula. It can hardly be denied that the image of the lawyer that dominates law teaching in our universities is an elevated one.

Some of the complexities of the Periclean image may be explained in terms of the multiple objectives of university legal education and the consequent refusal to distinguish clearly between lawyer education and education in law for

---

[4] Op. cit., at 92 (emphasis added).

[5] A good example of distortion is the attention paid in books and courses on 'criminal law' to such matters as 'insanity' and 'diminished responsibility', which, as Dr. Nigel Walker has pointed out, 'account for only an atypical minority of the detected offenders whose mental abnormality is recognized and taken into account'. ('The Mentally Abnormal Offender in the English Penal System', in *Sociological Studies in the British Penal Services* (ed., Halmos, 1965), at 133. To what extent in our law courses is attention paid, for example, to mental abnormality in relation to post-conviction procedures under the Mental Health Act? To justify the exclusion of discussion of such topics on the ground that such procedures are not part of 'the substantive criminal law', would merely raise the further question: 'Why are students expected to restrict themselves to "criminal law", so defined?' I am grateful to Kevin Boyle for drawing my attention to this point.

non-lawyers. But, it is suggested, more fundamental than this is a lack of consensus or clarity about what kind of end-product is required. This is confirmed if one looks to the United States, where for well over 100 years their university law schools have unabashedly been concerned with lawyer education, yet similar strains between the Periclean and plumbing images have been apparent. The ways in which the Americans have tried to resolve these strains deserve consideration, for they have a close connection with some of the reasons for the high regard that many people have for the upper reaches of the American system. The development of their leading law schools may hold some clues for the future of ours.

The history of legal education in the United States still awaits a Rashdall or an Ashby. If there is any truth in the suggestion that its law schools have made the greatest contribution of the United States to the general field of education,[6] then their story deserves an adequately equipped historian. There are some useful preliminary sketches; a wealth of detailed information and analysis is to be found in histories of individual law schools, in legal biographies and autobiographies, and in periodicals;[7] since the Second World War there has been a striking rise in the level of sophistication of discussions of legal education in the English-speaking world; in this development American law teachers have taken the lead. But two important ingredients still seem to be missing from most of the existing literature: first, a refined set of concepts adequate for the satisfactory discussion of complex issues and phenomena; and, secondly, the professionalism and the breadth of perspective that would be gained by setting the study of legal education firmly in the context of education as a whole. Even in the United States the literature of legal education is still in a relatively undeveloped state.

In the circumstances and in the course of a single lecture all that can be done is to draw a few brief sketches which may at least suggest potentially fruitful lines for further investigation and thought. In order to suggest some of the kinds of lessons that we in this country might learn from the American experience let us consider five phases in the development of their university law schools. The first two sketches are based largely on secondary accounts,[8] which tend to accept Carlyle's view of history as being but the biography of great men, and to tell the tale largely in terms of a few leading personalities and events. From this simplified treatment emerges a relatively simple picture of a long-drawn-out progress

---

[6] Hurst, *The Growth of American Law* (Boston, 1950), at 275.

[7] Two useful bibliographies are Klein, *Judicial Administration and the Legal Profession* (New York, 1963), and Sullivan, *A Bibliography of Materials on Legal Education* (New York, 1961). [Since this was written there has been a quite extensive literature on the history of legal education in the US—the outstanding example being Robert Stevens, *Law School* (Chapel Hill, 1983).]

[8] Notably, *The Centennial History of the Harvard Law School, 1817–1917* (Cambridge, Ma., 1918); Brown, *Lawyers and the Promotion of Justice* (New York, 1938); Harno, *Legal Education in the United States* (San Francisco, 1953); Hurst, *The Growth of American Law: The Law Makers* (Boston, 1950); Currie, 'The Materials of Law Study' 3 *Jo. Leg. Ed.* 331 (1951); 8 *Jo. Leg. Ed.* 1 (1955); Reed, *Training for the Public Profession of the Law* (Carnegie, 1921).

from haphazard apprenticeship and self-education to increasingly sophisticated instruction by full-time professional teachers in educational institutions.

STORY

The first stage of this progress is commonly associated with the acceptance by Judge Joseph Story of the Dane Professorship of Law at Harvard in 1829. Up to that time nearly all professional training had taken place outside the universities, most commonly taking the form of apprenticeship supplemented by reading on one's own. Story's appointment to the Dane Professorship was a remarkable event. In the twelve years since its inception Harvard Law School had achieved very little and had a poor reputation. In 1828 there had been only four students. Story, by contrast, was one of the greatest judges to have graced the Supreme Court of the United States and his prestige was immense. Merely by accepting the appointment Story enhanced the status of law teaching. But he did much more than this. His mission was to assist in the establishment of an alternative system of legal training to the apprenticeship that had been his lot.[9] He was largely successful in his objective and by the time of his death Harvard Law School had been transformed. The school had achieved a national reputation, there were over 150 students, many of them attracted from outside Massachusetts, and Story had set an outstanding example to legal scholars by producing a remarkable series of eight treatises on different branches of law.

So great was Story's achievement that it may seem strange to hear that his influence on legal education has not always been regarded as salutary by his successors. When one bears in mind that Story was a man with lofty ideals and a high-minded attitude towards the profession of law, it seems almost paradoxical that he should be charged with fathering a narrow legalistic approach to legal education. The fact remains, however, that while his concept of the lawyer tended towards the Periclean, his educational ideas were in many respects better suited to the production of legal plumbers.

Story's conception of the vocation of the lawyer was noble and idealistic; he proclaimed it often, including in his inaugural lecture as Dane Professor.[10] Perhaps the most explicit statement is to be found in a letter to his son:

A lawyer, above all men, should seek to have various knowledge, for there is no department of human learning or human art which will not aid his powers of illustration and reasoning, and be useful in the discharge of his professional duties. It has been the

---

[9] 'The old mode of solitary, unassisted studies in the Inns of Court, or in the dry and uninviting drudgery of an office, is utterly inadequate to lay a just foundation for accurate knowledge in the learning of the law. It is for the most part a waste of time and effort, at once discouraging and repulsive.' Letter to Principal of Dublin Law Institute, quoted by Harno, op. cit., at 43.

[10] 'Value and Importance of Legal Studies', in *Miscellaneous Writings of Joseph Story* (Boston, 1852), at 503, discussed by Harno, at 43 ff.

reproach of our profession in former ages, and is, perhaps, true to a great extent in our own times, that lawyers know little or nothing but the law, and that, not in its philosophy, but merely and exclusively in its details. There have been striking exceptions, such as Lord Hardwicke, Lord Mansfield, Lord Stowell, Lord Brougham and Mr. Justice Blackstone. But these are rare examples; and too few to do more than to establish the general reproach.[11]

Story's approach to legal education seems hard to reconcile with his picture of the good lawyer. He included in the curriculum only that which was solid law. 'What we propose,' he said, 'is no more than plain, direct, familiar instruction',[12] and this is what his students got. It was highly desirable for the good lawyer to have studied philosophy, rhetoric, history, and human nature, but it was not the function of the law professor to teach it to him. Liberal studies were an important part of the education of the lawyer, but they were separate from legal education. The study of law was essentially the study of established legal doctrines. When and how this liberal education was to be acquired is not clear, unless one takes at its face value Story's claim that 'in the elementary education, everywhere passed through before entering upon juridical studies, they were usually taught with sufficient fullness and accuracy'.[13] This is a strange claim when one bears in mind that in Story's time there were no formal entry requirements for Harvard Law School and by no means all students had a college degree.

Story also appears to have accepted a fairly clear-cut distinction between 'academic' and 'practical' training. This does not mean that he saw the university study of law as having no vocational significance, far from it, but rather he saw its main function as being the learning of the general doctrines of the common law and little else. The development of the skills and arts of the practitioner was left to be acquired as an apprentice and in the early years of practice.

Thus in Story's educational programme one finds sharp distinctions between law and other disciplines and between legal doctrine and legal practice. Given the opportunity to lengthen the time spent in study and better resources generally, Story might have challenged this rigid segregation; perhaps it is not his fault that distinctions which were partly forced on him by circumstances should have persisted as gospel after the circumstances changed.[14]

This double isolation of the subject-matter of legal studies is, of course, very common indeed. In our own tradition, even today, rigid distinctions are often drawn between 'law' and 'not law' and between 'academic' and 'practical' legal studies. Criticism of these distinctions is at the base of the modern American

---

[11] Letter to W. W. Story, 27 Jan. 1839; *Life and Letters of Joseph Story*, Vol. 2 (ed., William W. Story, 1851), at 311–12.

[12] Op. cit., n. 10, at 532.   [13] Op. cit., at 536.

[14] Cf. Harno: 'Our criticism perhaps should be directed against those who followed Story for their tardiness, when circumstances were more favorable for the schools, in broadening the foundations he had laid': op. cit., at 50.

rejection of Story's ideas; insofar as our ideas on legal education are similar to Story's, a study of the reaction against him may be suggestive.

LANGDELL

The appointment to Harvard Law School of Christopher Columbus Langdell in 1870 marks the next important development. Langdell, at the time of his appointment, was an obscure and somewhat retiring New York practitioner. What he brought to Harvard was a coherent theory of law teaching and a determination to apply it with consistency and rigour. A well-known passage from *A Selection of Cases on the Law of Contracts* (1871) is the classic formulation:

Law, considered as a science, consists of certain principles or doctrines. To have such a mastery of these as to be able to apply them with constant facility and certainty to the ever-tangled skein of human affairs is what constitutes a true lawyer; and hence to acquire that mastery should be the business of every earnest student of law. Each of these doctrines has arrived at its present state by slow degrees; in other words, it is a growth, extending in many cases through centuries. This growth is to be traced in the main through a series of cases; and much the shortest and best, if not the only way of mastering the doctrine effectually is by studying the cases in which it is embodied.[15]

Several points are worth making about Langdell's theory. He considered law to be capable of systematic study as a science, and if this were not so, 'a university will best consult its own dignity in declining to teach it. If it be not a science, it is a species of handicraft, and may best be learned by serving an apprenticeship to one who practices it.'[16] A university is not a trade school for the production of plumbers. Yet Langdell's image of the lawyer is too narrow to be Periclean; 'the true lawyer' is someone who has a mastery of legal doctrine and an ability to apply it; the law student must be fed on a strictly regulated diet of law, which for Langdell meant cases; non-legal matter was to be kept out of the curriculum. Since law was to be treated as a science, the most suitable kind of teacher was not necessarily an experienced practitioner. One of Langdell's innovations was to secure the appointment to a full-time teaching post of James Barr Ames, a young graduate with no experience of legal practice. The appointment was criticized, and Langdell's apology is revealing:

I wish to emphasize the fact that a teacher of law should be a person who accompanies his pupils on a road which is new to them, but with which he is well acquainted from having travelled it before. What qualifies a person, therefore, to teach law is not experience in the work of a lawyer's office, not experience in dealing with men, not experience in the trial or argument of cases—not experience, in short, in using law, but experience

---

[15] Christopher C. Langdell, Preface to *A Selection of Cases on the Law of Contracts* (Birmingham, 1871), at viii.   [16] Address of 1886, quoted by Harno, op. cit., at 58.

in learning law; not the experience of the Roman advocate or of the Roman praetor, still less of the Roman procurator, but the experience of the juris consult.[17]

In time Ames fully justified Langdell's faith in him and he became a noted legal historian. His appointment was significant, not only because of his qualifications, but also because, in the words of Hurst, it 'inaugurated, as a new branch of the legal profession in the United States, the career of the scholar-teacher of law'.[18] Up to that time nearly all law teaching had been done on a part-time basis; even Story had continued to serve on the Supreme Court after accepting the Dane Professorship. The histories of Harvard, Yale, and Columbia law schools and many others tell the same tale: the rise to eminence of a law school is associated almost inevitably with the achievement of a strong faculty of full-time teachers.[19] Teaching, research, educational administration, and intellectual leadership are functions that are nearly always best performed by people who are free to devote nearly all their time, energies, and loyalties to them. The growth of this 'other branch' of the legal profession was accompanied by repeated expressions of concern that a gulf was growing up between the academic and the practising lawyer. The Wilson Report reveals a similar concern at current trends in this country.[20] It has been one of the greatest achievements of American legal education that this danger has, on the whole, been averted. It is part of my thesis that this has been due not only to such obvious factors as the relative mobility of the American lawyer, who moves in and out of full-time teaching more easily than his UK counterpart, but also because of the predominance of a type of legal theory that has promoted a much healthier relationship between theory and practice than has been the case with English jurisprudence.

Langdell's contributions to Harvard were numerous: under his leadership the intellectual standards and the resources of the school improved immeasurably and a scholarly atmosphere was established which, *inter alia*, fostered a great series of legal treatises by Beale, Williston, Gray, and Thayer. Langdell is, of course, best known for his introduction of a method of teaching—'the case method'—which was the main vehicle for implementing his theory of legal education. Langdell was not the first to emphasize the value of making students read cases in the original; nor was he the first American law teacher to employ the Socratic method; nor was he a born teacher—in fact his first efforts at Harvard provoked more opposition than support from his students.[21] His main contribution was to provide a rationale and a stimulus for introducing this method

---

[17] Quoted by Hurst, op. cit., n. 8, at 263.   [18] Op. cit., at 264.

[19] Two important differences between present patterns in the US and the UK are that in the US almost all law teachers have had a substantial period in practice before they take up teaching.

[20] *Passim.* A well-known critique of relations between academic and practising lawyers is to be found in Gower, 'English Legal Training' 13 *MLR* 137 (1950), at 199–202; this is echoed by Abel-Smith and Stevens, *Lawyers and the Courts* (London, 1967), at 183–4, 367, 375.

[21] A vivid account is given by Fessenden, 'The Rebirth of Harvard Law School' 33 *Harv. L Rev.* 493 (1930).

of teaching throughout the curriculum and, by producing a new style of teaching tool, his casebook on contracts, to provide a model vehicle for the method.

In the course of time with the help of brilliant teachers such as Ames and Keener the case method became established as the main method of instruction, first at Harvard, and later at nearly all leading law schools. It was not seriously challenged until the rise of the Realist Movement. In Langdell's version it had several obvious strengths: first, he insisted on the study of primary sources; secondly, he substituted participation for passivity on the part of students; and, thirdly, he established a tradition of scepticism, liveliness, and rigour in lieu of dogmatic, dreary parrot learning. The introduction of the case method also involved a crucial switch from emphasis on knowledge to emphasis on skill.

For the most part the mainstream of American legal education has been built upon these strengths. Langdell was later to become the target of criticism by Holmes,[22] Frank,[23] Llewellyn,[24] and a number of others. But even his most virulent critics have not challenged these aspects of his contribution. What then was the weakness of his approach? Langdell, like Story, made a clear-cut distinction between law and other disciplines. Unlike Story he did not make a similar distinction between academic and practical training, but his picture of the 'true lawyer' and his picture of the law teacher tended to produce the same sort of remoteness from life and from legal practice that the insistence on such rigid distinctions tends to promote in our system.

THE REALIST CONTRIBUTION

Langdell and his disciples set the pattern for nearly all the major law schools for the next fifty years. There were pockets of resistance from traditionalists in the law schools (for instance, at Yale), and his ideas were for some time viewed with scepticism on the part of practitioners. However, the most telling attack came from a different quarter. First Holmes and then Pound set the lead in advocating a jurisprudence that was broader in approach and closer to everyday life. The sceptical temper of the times, the philosophy of pragmatism, and above all the extraordinarily rapid rate of economic and social change were some of the factors that drew increasing attention to what Pound termed the divorce between law in books and law in action.[25] But neither Holmes nor Pound really

---

[22] Esp. Holmes, 14 *American L Rev.* 233 (a review of Langdell's casebook). *Inter alia* Holmes said: 'Mr. Langdell's ideal in the law, the end of all his striving, is the *elegantia juris* or logical integrity of the system as a system. He is, perhaps, the greatest living legal theologian. But as a theologian he is less concerned with his postulates than to show that the conclusions from them hang together.'

[23] Esp. Frank, 'Why not a Clinical Lawyer-School?' 81 *U Pa. L Rev.* 907 (1933), *passim*; 'A Plea for Lawyer-Schools' 56 *Yale LJ* 1303 (1947), at 1313.

[24] e.g., Llewellyn, *The Common Law Tradition* (Boston, 1960), at 38 ff., at 360.

[25] Pound, 44 *Am. L Rev.* 12 (1910).

translated their jurisprudential ideas into concrete educational patterns.[26] Despite the fact that Harvard was the academic base of these two great pioneers of sociological jurisprudence, it did not become the headquarters of the movement for further reforms of legal education. The lead was taken in this respect first at Yale by Corbin, Hohfeld, and Cook in the second decade of this century, and then during the 1920s by an extraordinarily brilliant group of young men of whom Herman Oliphant, Underhill Moore, and Karl Llewellyn were the most prominent. Columbia in the 1920s was the headquarters of a concerted attempt to work out in detail the implications of sociological jurisprudence for legal research and legal education.

One of the most striking features of this ferment was the two year-long study of the curriculum which took place at Columbia under the chairmanship of Leon C. Marshall, an economist. It has been rightly said by Brainerd Currie that these studies 'constituted the most comprehensive and searching investigation of law school objectives and methods that has ever been undertaken'.[27] It is worth quoting Currie's appraisal of their significance:

A drastic retooling would be required to convert the facilities of legal education to such an effort. Two basic requirements were announced to the law school world with seismic effect: First, the formal categories of the law, shaped by tradition and by accident, tend to obscure the social problems with which law deals, the purpose which is the vital element of principle, and the actual working of legal processes; they constitute a framework which forces artificiality in perspective and development; they must be revised along lines of correspondence with the types of human activity involved. Second, an understanding of the social structure in which law operates can no longer be taken for granted or regarded as irrelevant; law students—and hence law teachers—must acquire that understanding, and must somehow learn to take into account the contributions which other disciplines and sciences can make to the solution of social problems.[28]

Developments at Columbia in legal education preceded the rather unsatisfactory jurisprudential polemics of the early 1930s that have come to be known as the 'Realist Controversy'. A few provocative passages of a rather general nature have unfortunately given people in the United Kingdom a seriously distorted image of what these young scholars at Columbia and Yale were really trying to do.

Perhaps we can understand something of the significance of the Realist Movement for legal education if we compare the ideas of one of their number, Karl Llewellyn, with those of Langdell.

Langdell, says Llewellyn, saw three deep truths. The first was that a university training in law, indeed a liberal arts study of anything . . . must be technically solid, technically reliable, in a word, craftsmanlike . . . The second thing that Langdell saw was that history,

---

[26] Llewellyn, *Jurisprudence: Realism in Theory and Practice* (Chicago, 1962), at 378.
[27] Brainerd Currie, 'The Materials of Law Study', 3 *Jo. Leg. Ed.* (1951), at 333–4.
[28] Op. cit., at 334–5.

carefully studied, is one good road to understanding. Depth is of the essence, and the time-dimension is one main road to depth.

And, thirdly, as was mentioned above, Langdell shifted the emphasis from acquisition of knowledge to development of proficiency in 'legal analysis, legal reasoning, legal argument and legal synthesis'.[29]

Llewellyn accepted these ideas, but he felt that as a theory for lawyer education Langdell's did not go nearly far enough. Llewellyn agreed with Langdell in putting considerable emphasis on training in legal method: 'Technical skill is not a foundation only. It is *the necessary* foundation.'[30] But whereas Langdell saw the group of skills that could be developed by his version of case analysis as being *the* skill that a university legal education should seek to develop, Llewellyn's conception of technical proficiency in this context was very much broader. For him the practice of law in a fused profession was the practice of a set of crafts.[31] Knowledge of legal rules and ability to extract doctrine from cases form only a part of these crafts. Lawyers in practice have to employ other skills, many of which are teachable, some of which are teachable in a university. Llewellyn was chairman of a committee which in 1944 produced an influential report on the place of skills in legal education in which it was recommended that law schools should seek to foster not only the case skills of the Langdell method, but also such matters as skill in interpretation of statutes, appellate advocacy, simple drafting, and counselling (i.e., the giving of advice), and the making of intelligent policy decisions.[32] Llewellyn himself pioneered a course in 'Legal Argument' and in recent years a variety of other 'skills courses' have been offered by American law schools, some of them making a relatively sophist-icated use of clinical experience and simulation techniques. Llewellyn emphasized technical proficiency, but he was equally emphatic that technical proficiency was not enough. Langdell's skills, he said, 'though sharp and well instilled, were narrow. The wherewithal for vision was not given.'[33]

Llewellyn is best known as the exponent of a jurisprudential approach that emphasizes the importance of observing the ordinary processes of the law in action in their social context. Doctrine must be seen in the context of legal process and legal processes must be seen in the context of the totality of social processes. Any lawyer, in this view, however humble, must be equipped to understand his environment; his perspective must be a broad one, preferably that of society as a whole. The message repeated again and again is that for practic-ally any purpose law cannot be treated in isolation, and that any attempt to do

---

[29] Llewellyn, 'The Study of Law as a Liberal Art' (1960), reprinted in *Jurisprudence: Realism in Theory and Practice*, op. cit., at 375, 377.   [30] Ibid.

[31] This theme is developed at length by Llewellyn in some unpublished teaching materials: *Law in Our Society: A Horse Sense Theory of the Institution of Law* (1950), 13–20. [Parts of this are reproduced in *KLRM*, App. C.]

[32] *Handbook of the American Association of Law Schools* (1944), 159–201; 75 *Col. Law. Rev.* (1945), at 345–91.   [33] Op. cit., n. 29, at 377.

so prejudices both understanding and efficiency. By concentrating on legal doctrine and by trying to set up an autonomous science of law, Langdell committed the cardinal sin from this point of view and he was branded as an apostle of formalism.[34]

This is not the place to give detailed consideration to the advantages and dangers of a contextual approach to law. The arguments will be familiar to many of you. Of course, Llewellyn and his fellow realists were by no means unique in advocating this kind of approach. Perhaps their greatest contribution was in the direction of working out the implications of a sociological jurisprudence for detailed work of various kinds. The Uniform Commercial Code, the modern types of casebook, empirical research projects, such as the Chicago jury study— these and many other concrete achievements are the real monuments to the contribution of Llewellyn and his fellow realists.[35]

Against this background it may be useful to consider Llewellyn's image of the end-product of lawyer education. From what has already been said, it should be clear that some of his ideas are compatible with the plumbing image. First, in discussions of legal education he nearly always identifies 'the lawyer' with the private practitioner of law.[36] This, as we have seen, is closer to the plumbing pole than to the Periclean. Secondly, he emphasizes the need for basic technical proficiency. But the lawyer, both to be effective and, more important in his view, to fulfil his responsibilities to his clients and to society, must be more than a competent technician, he must be more than a plumber. And if the plumbing image implies that broad or liberal education is unnecessary for lawyers, then it must be rejected. In an address in Chicago he made the point with characteristic vigour:

The truth, the truth which cries out, is that the good work, the most effective work, of the lawyer in practice roots in and depends on vision, range, depth, balance and rich humanity—those things which it is the function, and frequently the fortune, of the liberal arts to introduce and indeed to induce. The truth is, therefore, that the best practical training a university can give to any lawyer who is not by choice or by unendowment doomed to be a hack or a shyster—the best *practical* training, along with the best human training—is the study of law, within the professional school itself, as a liberal art.[37]

Llewellyn's picture of the end-product of lawyer education shares something with both the plumbing and the Periclean images, but it is much more sophisticated and complex than either of them. It is, indeed, far too complex to receive full justice here. Before we leave Llewellyn, however, it is worth noting four points about his ideas that fit in with the themes of this lecture. First, he was one

---

[34] Llewellyn, *The Common Law Tradition*, at 38–9.

[35] See generally *KLRM*. For a critique of the contribution of realism to the development of legal research, see Hurst, 'Research Responsibilities of University Law Schools' 10 *Jo. Leg. Ed.* 147 (1957).

[36] See especially Llewellyn, *The Bramble Bush*, 2nd edn. (New York, 1951). On the distorting effect of the private practitioner image in some contexts, see Twining, 'Legal Education within East Africa', *East African Law Today* (London, 1966), at 139 ff.   [37] Op. cit., n. 29 at 376.

of the pioneers of the development of a systematic sociology of the legal profession, a subject that is currently receiving much attention in the United States.[38] Secondly, he was actively concerned with the problem of providing legal services to all classes of the population.[39] He was *inter alia* associated with law school legal aid clinics, those admirable institutions that marry clinical training and social service. These concerns of his were associated with the view that one function of lawyer education is to foster social consciousness, perhaps even a social conscience, in intending lawyers. Thirdly, shortly before his death he gave active encouragement to the individual who has made the most systematic attempt so far to relate a detailed job analysis of lawyers' operations to problems of law teaching.[40] Finally, and perhaps most important, is the point that Llewellyn's jurisprudential themes and his ideas on legal education are so bound up together as to be almost indistinguishable; a concern with problems of legal education was a most important stimulus to the early development of his general juristic ideas, which ideas in turn had important implications for legal education. Many of those ideas had deep roots in the social sciences, notably anthropology, sociology, economics, and psychology. In all of them lawyers' work was a central focus and it is fair to say that one of Llewellyn's achievements was to graft onto the traditional law-oriented jurisprudence a lawyer-oriented jurisprudence.

THE LASSWELL-MCDOUGAL PLAN

In 1943 Harold Lasswell and Myres McDougal published a notable paper entitled 'Legal Education and Public Policy: Professional Training in the Public Interest',[41] which remains the nearest approach to date to a comprehensive theory for lawyer education. It is significant that the paper was also the vehicle for the first important statement of the Lasswell-McDougal intellectual system, which is commonly referred to as 'Law, Science and Policy' or LSP for short.[42] LSP is currently the jurisprudential counterpart of LSD: its effects on individuals vary from exhilaration, to deep depression, to indifference and nobody is quite sure to what extent it is habit-forming. There are some who would make it the basis of a religion. Bold, visionary, comprehensive, encased in a petrifying terminology, this neo-Benthamite theory has received in the United Kingdom far less attention than it deserves. The intellectual difficulties of the theory need not concern us here; for present purposes the paper is significant as representing the

[38] Op. cit., n. 36, Ch. II.   [39] Ibid.
[40] Irwin Rutter of the University of Cincinnati. See especially Rutter, 'A Jurisprudence of Lawyers' Operations' 13 *Jo. Leg. Ed.* 301 (1961).
[41] Harold Lasswell and Myres McDougal, 'Legal Education and Public Policy: Professional Training in the Public Interest' 52 *Yale LJ* 203 (1943), reprinted in McDougal, et al., *Studies in World Public Order* (New Haven, 1960).
[42] The fullest treatment of 'Law, Science and Policy' is to be found in a set of mimeographed materials used by the authors in a number of courses at Yale Law School.

American viewpoint which goes furthest in the direction of the Periclean model. The authors take as their starting-point a bold statement of aim: 'We submit this basic proposition: if legal education in the contemporary world is adequately to serve the needs of a free and productive commonwealth, it must be conscious, efficient, and systematic *training for policy-making.*'[43]

Lasswell and McDougal justify this rather startling statement in terms of an image of 'the lawyer' which even some American lawyers tend to find somewhat grandiose:

It should need no emphasis that the lawyer is today, even when not himself a maker of policy, the one indispensable adviser of every responsible policy-maker of our society— whether we speak of the head of a government department or agency, of the executive of a corporation or labor union, of the secretary of a trade or other private association, or even of the humble independent enterpriser or professional man. As such an adviser the lawyer, when informing his policy-maker of what he can or cannot *legally* do, is, as policy-makers often complain, in an unassailably strategic position to influence, if not create, policy.[44]

'Policy' in this context is defined as 'the making of important decisions which affect the distribution of values'.[45] In this usage the lawyer advising a potential petitioner for divorce, or a testator, is involved in 'policy-making' almost as much as the participant in the decisions of appellate courts, administrative tribunals or legislatures. Nevertheless a perusal of the detailed proposals for the reform of lawyer education put forward by Lasswell and McDougal suggests that 'the aggrandisement effect'[46] has been at work, for great stress is put on the higher levels of policy-making in the national (and the world) arenas and the operative images of their end-product seem to be the senior partner in the Wall Street law firm, the maker of American foreign policy, and the world statesman. In short the Lasswell-McDougal plan for legal education seems to me to be a thinly disguised élitist programme for the training of national leaders, the sort of thing that might emerge if, in 1984, Plato's Academy were taken over by MIT with Jeremy Bentham as director.

Apart from reservations that some people would have about the general theory of LSP, the specific proposals for lawyer education are open to criticism that they place far too little emphasis on the plumbing aspects of lawyers' work and that they are based on a serious underestimation of the difficulty of attaining minimum technical competence. However, insofar as nearly everyone's views of legal education aspire to some extent towards the Periclean image, the Lasswell-McDougal thesis is stimulating in its proposals for producing national leaders and devastating in its criticisms of traditional approaches and even of the piecemeal innovations that followed the Realist 'revolution'.[47]

---

[43] Op. cit., at 206.   [44] Op. cit., n. 41, at 208–9.   [45] Op. cit., at 207.
[46] See Berelson and Steiner, *Human Behavior* (New York, 1964), 279.
[47] For Llewellyn's assessment, see 43 *Col. L Rev.* 476 (1943).

It is not surprising that this extraordinarily stimulating exercise has been
viewed somewhat sceptically by those whose ideas of lawyer education have
been governed by a more humble image of the lawyer. Relatively few people
have accepted the Las-Mac system *in toto*, and even at Yale, their headquarters,
their ideas do not seem to have made as fundamental an impact on curriculum
planning or teaching methods as might have been expected. Nevertheless there
are signs that thinking similar to theirs is becoming increasingly influential. It
is worth noting that in this analysis of the development of American legal
education in terms of rough stages, each stage is marked by one or more notable
departures in forms of student legal literature. The Story period is represented
by Story's famous treatises; the Langdellian reforms by Langdell's casebook on
contracts; the Realist 'revolution' was launched by the publication of a series of
casebooks at Columbia Law School, of which Llewellyn's *Cases and Materials
on the Law of Sales* is the outstanding representative;[48] the Asheville Conference, which will be discussed later, took place in the same year as the publication of Kelso's *Programmed Introduction to the Study of Law*, I,[49] a work which
is notable both as being the first major application of programmed learning in
legal education to have been published,[50] and also as being one of the most
rigorous attempts to develop teaching of basic skills in a systematic manner;
recently two books of materials[51] emanating from Yale Law School have been
widely acclaimed as an important new departure in student legal literature; both
show unmistakable signs of LSP-type thinking. Do they mark the arrival of a
Lasswellian era in some American law schools?

ASHEVILLE, 1965

So far in this brief tour of some highlights of the history of American legal
education we have glanced at a few of the operative ideas of leading thinkers

[48] Llewellyn, *Cases and Materials on the Law of Sales* (Chicago, 1930); others include Berle,
Cases and Materials on Corporation Finance (St. Paul, 1930); Goebel, *Cases and Materials on the
Development of Legal Institutions* (New York, 1931); Magill and Maguire, *Cases and Materials on
Taxation* (Mineola, NY, 1931); Hanna, *Cases and Materials on Creditors' Rights* (Mineola, NY,
1931); Hanna, *Cases and Materials on Security* (Mineola, NY, 1932); Magill, *Cases on Civil Pro-
cedure* (Mineola, NY, 1932); Patterson, *Cases and Materials on Insurance* (Mineola, NY, 1932);
Jacobs, *Cases and Materials on Landlord and Tenant* (St. Paul, 1932); Powell, *Cases and Materials
on Trusts and Estates*, 2 vols. (St. Paul, 1933); Powell, *Cases and Materials on Possessory Estates*
(St. Paul, 1933); Handler, *Cases and Materials on Vendor and Purchaser* (St. Paul, 1933); Jacobs,
Cases and Materials on Domestic Relations (Mineola, NY, 1933); Magill and Hamilton, *Cases and
Materials on Business Organisation*, Vol. I (St. Paul, 1933), (Report of Dean Young B. Smith, 1933,
at 12–13).
[49] Kelso, *Programmed Introduction to the Study of Law*, I, (Indianapolis, 1965).
[50] In the UK one of the first programmes for law was developed, significantly, by the Army
Education Corps: Meyrick, *Military Law* (1964).
[51] Donnelly, Goldstein, and Schwartz, *Criminal Law* (New York, 1962); Goldstein and Katz, *The
Family and the Law* (New York, 1965); cf. Katz, Goldstein, and Dershowitz, *Psychoanalysis, Psychiatry and Law* (New York, 1967).

—Story, Langdell, Llewellyn, and Lasswell and McDougal. The last sketch is different: it is a conference rather than a thinker. I wish to treat it in personal terms, because it symbolizes much of what to me, at least, is most admirable in American legal education. In September 1965 I was privileged to attend, as an observer, a conference of law school deans at Asheville, Tennessee. The purpose of this conference was to consider reports on some twenty experimental projects in a general area designed as 'Education for Professional Responsibility',[52] a title which, when I first heard it, carried associations of high-minded and vague sermons on professional ethics. The reality was quite different. In this context the term 'professional responsibility' was used to cover not only matters relating to professional ethics, but also other aspects of the individual practitioner's relationship to his client (expressed in terms of 'helping the whole client') and the public responsibilities of individual lawyers and of the organized Bar. The projects ranged from variations on the well-known legal aid clinic to courses dealing with such matters as counselling in family law, to summer internships in correctional institutions or with organizations connected with the legal problems of the underprivileged.

In most of the projects class work was combined with firsthand experience of the law in action. In many of them there was a research element. All of them were done under the auspices of university law schools acting in co-operation with practitioners, judges, and officials. Although many of the experiments were interesting in themselves, what struck me more was the general atmosphere of the conference. The stimulus behind this series of experiments and the spirit in which they were conducted was a deep and searching concern about the actual and potential role of lawyers in society. One could not but be impressed by the willingness to experiment, the fertility of ideas, the sophistication of the level of discussion, and the hard-headed way in which experiments were evaluated. Academics and practitioners were talking on the same wavelength in a manner which presupposed a developing sociology of the legal profession and a shared professionalism about problems of education and training. It was also pleasing to an academic lawyer to find practitioners and judges looking to the law schools for intellectual leadership and to find the law schools responding.

One example may help to convey some sense of the occasion. During a discussion of the problems of teaching professional ethics there was a lively debate about a number of related issues. How far ought a teacher to go beyond posing for his students in as illuminating a way as possible some of the ethical dilemmas that confront practitioners? Should he abdicate all responsibility for moral propaganda? Are problems of professional responsibility best considered in a single course or are they more satisfactorily raised in the context of a large

[52] See 'Education for Professional Responsibility', *Summaries of Law School Projects Supported by the National Council on Legal Clinics* (Sept. 1965); the recently published *Proceedings of the Asheville Conference of Law School Deans on Education for Professional Responsibility* was not available at the time of writing.

number of courses by what is known as 'the pervasive approach'?[53] Can the
ethical dilemmas of lawyers be discussed meaningfully without consideration of
problems of professional loneliness and disillusionment and the whole psychology of lawyer-client relations? And so on. Some of these questions may be new
to some of you, as they were to me; some raise perennial issues in a new context. In the course of discussion a fascinating range of methods of treating the
subject was considered and a number of interesting ideas was aired. But even
more striking was the amount of common ground that was taken for granted by
people who were taking different stands on some of these issues. They assumed
first of all that professional ethics is a suitable subject for discussion in a university course and that it poses problems that are as intellectually demanding as
standard legal issues; they assumed that classroom time need not be expended
on imparting elementary information about the content of canons of ethics,
because such information could easily be acquired by a student on his own;
furthermore, they assumed that, even if indoctrination was a legitimate aim,
sermonizing would at the very least be an inefficient method of achieving this
aim and it might well have an effect opposite to the intended one. Sometimes
assumptions of this kind are indicative of shallow and thoughtless jumping to
conclusions. But in this instance they appeared to represent a consensus that had
been reached over a long period of trial and error and thoughtful discussion.
This epitomizes what I mean by sophistication in legal education.

THE RELEVANCE OF THE AMERICAN EXPERIENCE

The suggestion that there is much to be learned from American experience is not
intended to carry with it the implication that the American system is wholly
admirable or that there is nothing worthy of preservation in our own tradition.
Nor is it suggested that the many significant differences between our respective
situations should be ignored. Moreover, the ideas of Story, Langdell, Llewellyn,
and Lasswell and McDougal are, of course, the ideas of some intellectual leaders
of a few élite institutions on the eastern seaboard—notably Harvard, Yale, and
Columbia. We have, in other words, been concentrating on only one small part
of the total picture of American legal education; much of value was initiated in
other places and in recent years the general excellence of the leading law schools
has spread downwards to a large number of smaller and less well-known institutions. The fact that nearly all of the experimental projects under discussion at
Asheville were based on smaller law schools is indicative of this. Nevertheless
many thoughtful Americans are justifiably worried at the state of affairs in the
lower reaches of the system. Carlin's notable study on *Lawyers on their Own*[54]

---

[53] See esp. Smedley, 'The Pervasive Approach on a Larger Scale—"The Vanderbilt Experiment"'
15 *Jo. Leg. Ed.* 435 (1963).   [54] Op. cit., n. 58.

in Chicago brings out in striking fashion how remote is the world of the national law school and the big law firm from that of the low-standard, despised, struggling, and sometimes corrupt solo practitioner. It prompts the thought that perhaps the Americans might learn something from the British about the preservation of *minimum* standards of competence and ethicality.

Granted these caveats, I still firmly believe that we have much to learn from the Americans both in respect of general ideas and of specific techniques. At this stage in our development the American experience of the 1920s and thirties seems to be particularly pertinent. Historically the American Realist Movement was as much as anything a response to the joint stimuli of rapid change and increasing complexity in American life. There is perhaps something in the suggestion that there are quite remarkable parallels in the legal sphere between trends in the United Kingdom in the 1960s and trends in the United States in the 1920s and thirties; these parallels might be explained to some extent in terms of pressures resulting from social and technological change. If Professor Goldstein of Yale is correct in suggesting that we are due for 'a realist revolution',[55] it can be expected to be less dramatic and less turbulent than the American one, not least because our problems of change and complexity are less acute. In a relatively homogeneous group of societies addicted to gradualism we may expect the 'r' in 'revolution' to be muted. Nevertheless, is it not fair to say that the pace of change is one of the most fertile sources of problems in our time and that, in the sphere of education, perhaps the most pressing problem is how to prepare students to cope with rapidly changing situations? Our legal system having lagged behind other institutions in adapting itself to modern conditions, the coming generation of lawyers may have to make extra adjustments. In short, adaptability must become a key concept of lawyer education for the future. Now it happens that circumstances have combined to make adaptability a central characteristic of the products of the national law schools in the United States. With students drawn from a large number of jurisdictions, it is practically impossible to concentrate on the law of any single jurisdiction, except in federal matters; the dominant place of law and lawyers in American society and, related to this, the great variety of types of lawyer within the legal profession; the ethnic and social heterogeneity; and the rapid pace of technological and economic

---

[55] The context is a discussion of the prospects for development of empirical research into legal processes in the UK. The passage reads: 'Though brave efforts are being made in a handful of places, it seems quite clear to me that research in the legal process of the kind and quality I have described can only come after the ideological spade-work has first been done. There must first be an extended period of inter-disciplinary fumbling; and that is likely to come only when English law teaching, and the conception of law which animates it, has had its "legal realist" revolution.' A. L. Goldstein, 'Research into the Administration of Criminal Law: A report from the United States', 6 *Brit. Jo. Criminology* 27 (1966), at 37. Compare the plea by G. P. Wilson of Cambridge for 'a vigorous philosophy of law that will tie together the leading influences and motives behind the new developments and at the same time point the way to the future', [1966] *CLJ*, at 148–9. The interdependence of legal theory, legal education, legal research, and legal literature is discussed briefly in the full version of this lecture.

advance are among the factors that have produced a concerted pressure to make legal education above all an investment in certain ideas and skills of wide application. In trying to produce adaptable lawyers, whose stock-in-trade, it is sometimes said, is a creative problem-solving approach,[56] there have been two main shifts from the patterns of the Joseph Story tradition: first, a switch from emphasis on knowledge of rules of law to emphasis on the acquisition of skills;[57] secondly, a broadening of the focus of attention, so that legal doctrines are rarely studied without reference to the social situations, the problems, the policies, and the processes which constitute the context of their operation.

American law schools have not had a monopoly of education for adaptability. Any contemporary institution concerned with the study of science or technology is faced with the same basic problem in a particularly acute form. Furthermore, it should not be forgotten that the notion of 'transferability' has also been an important part of the 'liberal' idea. Many would agree that the leading American law schools have recaptured much of what is worthy of preservation in the liberal tradition. Those who feel that the frenetic atmosphere of their law schools is inimical to quiet contemplation may also feel that the wine of Jowett and Newman (and of German vintage) was diluted while crossing the Atlantic. The bouquet was lost, perhaps, but fizz was added. Nevertheless, Llewellyn's perception that the liberal and the vocational could be wedded in a single institution was a sound one.

FOUR THEMES IN NEED OF DEVELOPMENT

Given time, many themes could be developed. Perhaps four should be singled out for brief treatment as having special potential significance:

1. A systematic approach to the problems of lawyer education needs as a foundation a developed sociology of the legal profession. Before it is possible to formulate sound detailed objectives there is a need for a clear and differentiated picture of the kind of end-product desired. The simplistic images of 'the lawyer' that have so often been hidden in people's

---

[56] The idea has also reached Australia: 'The essential task of the lawyer is problem-solving': Preface to Maher, Waller, and Derham, *Cases and Materials on the Legal Process* (Sydney, 1966).

[57] There are those who would contend that the switch from acquisition of information has been carried too far in the US, even having regard to the special conditions there; in the UK there would be considerable opposition, some of it justified, to the scrapping of all memory work (e.g., see the Wilson Report at 52). My own position is that even in relatively stable times too much emphasis was put on 'knowing the law', and in the present situation of enormous complexity and relatively rapid change, it is a poor investment to devote a great deal of effort to storing information in one's head. Nevertheless it is possible to carry this too far. In African contexts I have found myself disagreeing with compatriots who considered that there should be little or no time devoted to skills teaching in a university, whilst chiding those American teachers (not by any means all of them) who considered that the imparting of information was not included in their functions.

assumptions about legal education have been a fertile source of confused and confusing controversy. Both the Periclean and the plumbing images are quite inadequate: they are crude, over-simplified, and unrealistic.

In order to arrive at an adequate formulation of objectives there is a need to ask and re-ask the questions: What are lawyers for? What could lawyers be for? What should lawyers be for? A necessary foundation is a job analysis of what lawyers do, a skills analysis of the operations involved, and some reliable studies of the economics of the profession, the psychology of professionalism, and the many other fields of inquiry that fall under the general rubric 'the sociology of the legal profession'.[58] Of course, empirical research by itself will not provide all the answers. There will always be plenty of scope for variety and for disagreement about values, priorities, and methods. Also, being concerned with the future, education must always involve a large element of faith, especially for the enlightened educator who looks on it as a long-term investment. Other ineffables will always be with us. Nevertheless much can be gained by starting from a solid base of reliable information about the present situation and current trends.

2. There is a need to break free from the extraordinarily rigid stereotyped thinking that has come to dominate most discussions of legal education: that the cosmos is irrevocably divided into fields of law such as contract and torts; that the only mode of classification to be used in curriculum planning is that of fields of law; that examinations must be three hours in length; that examinations can only test knowledge of legal doctrines and ability to apply rules to hypothetical fact situations; that all courses must be given equal weight; that every course must have a textbook; that every textbook must conform to a standard pattern; that legal doctrine is *the* subject-matter of legal studies; that every lawyer is a private practitioner of law; that there should be a uniform pattern of qualifications for law teachers; that there are accepted and fixed criteria of the suitability of a subject for study in a university—and so on.[59] Such assumptions all need to be questioned. In particular some general working distinctions, which are admittedly useful in some contexts, have become frozen into rigid

---

[58] Following on the heels of the pioneering Survey of the Legal Profession summarized in Blaustein and Porter, *The American Lawyer* (Chicago, 1954), there have been some notable recent studies, especially Carlin, *Lawyers on Their Own* (New Brunswick, 1962) and *Lawyers' Ethics* (New York, 1966); Smigel, *The Wall Street Lawyer* (Bloomington, 1964); Weyrauch, *The Personality of Lawyers* (New Haven, 1964). Abel-Smith and Stevens, *Lawyers and the Courts*, op. cit. provide a most useful historical foundation for the development of the subject in England. Johnstone and Hopson, *Lawyers and Their Work* (Indianapolis, 1967) promises to mark the rise of the comparative sociology of legal professions. The subject has potentially far-reaching implications for several areas of legal theory.

[59] Several of these assumptions are to be found in the Wilson Report; examples of the others will almost inevitably be discoverable by anyone who cares to listen for a few hours to discussions of curriculum among academic lawyers.

dichotomies; 'education' and 'training';[60] 'academic' and 'practical';[61] 'theory' and 'practice'; 'liberal' and 'vocational';[62] 'law' and 'other disciplines'. Over-reliance on such distinctions, it is suggested, has been the Achilles' heel of our present patterns of lawyer education. One suspects that some of them have been functionally important in the power struggle between the universities and the legal profession. If *rapprochement* is not practicable, then they may continue to serve a function. But are academics justified in assuming that the legal professions are doomed to perpetual and incurable unenlightenment in their attitudes to lawyer education? Are practitioners for ever to look on academics as inevitably destined either for effete and starry-eyed irrelevance or for the subservient status of plumbers' mates? If so, these distinctions will continue to be functionally important as artificial boundaries between spheres of influence.[63] There are signs, however, that the situation has become comparatively fluid recently and

[60] For a recent defence of the distinction between 'professional education and vocational training', see Professor Kahn-Freund's stimulating lecture 'Reflections on Legal Education', 29 *MLR* 121 (1966). Contrast documents relating to industrial training: Central Training Council Memorandum No. 1, 'Industrial Training and Further Education', Ministry of Labour (London, 1965); cf. City and Guilds of London Institute, First Year Certificate in Engineering Crafts, Regulations and Syllabuses Valid for Examinations to be Held in 1967 (London, 1966), at 7.

[61] The worst example of this has been the division of fields of law into 'academic' and 'practical' subjects. Whereas torts, contract, equity, and land law have been considered 'academic', whatever that means in this context, civil and criminal procedure, conveyancing, company law, even interpretation of statues, and to a lesser extent evidence, have often been treated as 'practical' subjects to be studied outside the universities or to be included within undergraduate curricula only grudgingly, as a concession to the profession. Analytically the distinction is difficult, if not impossible, to defend, except perhaps in terms of a question-begging differentiation between subjects suitable and unsuitable for undergraduate study. Two rules of thumb in determining suitability seem to have been that case-law should be preferred to statute law and substantive law should take precedence over procedure. Dead or dying, both rules deserve burial. We have to a large extent rejected the old idea that legislation is not a fit study for gentlemen; we have yet to accept fully that it is unrealistic and often intellectually indefensible to study substantive law subjects in isolation from their procedural context. I would go further and say that civil and criminal procedure and the interpretation of statutes, cases, and documents should be given a prominent place as foundation subjects in our university curricula. On this theme generally, see Abel-Smith and Stevens, op. cit., Ch. XIII.

[62] American law schools have tended to adopt an openly vocational approach, yet the intellectual atmosphere of schools of my acquaintance compares very favourably indeed with that of their counterparts in other countries. This gives support to the view that there is no necessary incompatibility between a vocational approach and such values as free enquiry, intellectual rigour, independence of thought, and breadth of perspective. In short, there is a false antithesis between 'vocational' and 'liberal' in this context. There is also no necessary incompatibility between a contextual approach to the study of law and a vocational approach to legal education. To contrast them is to make another false antithesis. Indeed, if the lawyer to be aimed for is to be a technologist rather than a technician, there is a high degree of compatibility between the two approaches; as Sir Eric Ashby says: 'A student who can weave his technology into the fabric of society can claim to have a liberal education; a student who cannot weave his technology into the fabric of society cannot claim even to be a good technologist': *Technology and the Academics* (London, 1958), at 85. On false antitheses that have permeated our ideas on university education, see id., at 71–88.

[63] Gower, op. cit., n. 20, at 151–62, while acknowledging that the distinction between education and training can be pressed too far, favoured a clear separation between theoretical and practical training on the grounds of political expediency.

that there is an opportunity for a *rapprochement*. In particular the current dissatisfaction among practitioners about the provisions for lawyer education gives ground for optimism.[64] It is to be hoped that they will not be satisfied with what Reisman called 'the reverent modification of small particulars'.[65] If *rapprochement* is to be more than an uneasy patched-up affair it must be based on a measure of agreement about fundamentals at the level of theory. Otherwise the self-confirming element in these mutually hostile attitudes allied to other divisive factors (notably the growing tendency to recruit law teachers immediately on graduation and the increasing number of undergraduates who have little or no prospect of practising) will tend to widen the existing gap between the academic and practising branches of the profession.

3. So far little has been said about method, because discussion of method is usually best done after the clarification of objectives. Much could be said. Clearly there is enormous scope for extension of the use of simulators, clinics, programmed learning, and other devices. Perhaps the Asheville Conference marks the start of an era of systematic development of such techniques. A precondition for this is a faith in teachability. We may smile smugly, sometimes with justification, at the American tendency to believe that one can learn anything by taking a course in it; but in so far as this is occasioned by a persistent urge to make more communicable what man has had the opportunity to learn by experience, the impulse has much to commend it. An almost essential precondition for educational progress is a willingness to ask such questions as: Is it teachable? How might it be taught? Would expenditure of time and resources on teaching it be justified? What priority should it be given? The discipline of having to define 'it' in this context can in itself be a substantial stimulus to thought and understanding.

In the United Kingdom a major obstacle to progress is likely to be the idea that the successful practice of law involves mastery of a mystical art that cannot be studied systematically, but can be picked up in the course of practice. The Pick-it-up Theory of Training has a sound core of sense in it; but it is odd to find it still so predominant in law when in most other occupations haphazard apprenticeship and the cult of the gentleman amateur are both fast disappearing. Almost any sensible scheme of lawyer education would give a significant role to experience, especially planned experience, as a teacher; but there are almost certainly things at present left

---

[64] According to a poll conducted by Wilson, only 22.5% of barristers and 29.5% of solicitors at that time considered that provisions were adequate; even more striking were the figures for practitioners of under five years' standing: 82.5% of barristers in this category and 68% of solicitors considered the provisions to be inadequate; op. cit., at 73 and 83. Since then some changes have been introduced by the Council of Legal Education.

[65] 'Law and Social Science' 50 *Yale LJ* 636 (1941), at 637.

to be picked up which could be learned more efficiently or more economically or both by other methods; there are also instances in which it would be appropriate to try to capitalize on the lessons of experience by post-mortem discussions or more formal kinds of follow-up. Experience is often potentially the best teacher, but unaided the man of action is not always an equally good learner. In respect of such matters legal educators could probably learn much from the Armed Forces, from the medical schools, and from those involved in industrial training, perhaps even from those connected with the training of real plumbers.

Of the various matters which might be treated under the heading of 'method' there is one which deserves to be given very high priority indeed. There is surely an urgent need for a fundamental and rigorous re-examination of the whole system of law examinations. This exercise should be concerned not only with such obvious matters as defining with precision what is being tested and extending the range of techniques of testing, but also with some questions which may be of greater social importance: what are the effects of our present examination system on the behaviour of students, teachers, authors, publishers, curriculum planners, and the products of the process of legal education? To what extent are these effects compatible with desired objectives of the process? To what extent are these effects desirable and undesirable in other ways? It is a plausible hypothesis that the formal examination is the device which has more influence than any other on participants in the educational process, creating expectations, forming attitudes, and channelling energies.[66] If this is so, those who are depressed by nutshells, parrot learning, cram courses, stereotyped thinking, and other features of the present scene would do well to ask some searching questions about the extent to which those who have most power over the examination system have been exercising their power with perception, enlightenment or responsibility. As a university examiner who has had a minute share of such power I confess that my conscience is troubled; it is a source of comfort that my responsibility has not been wider.

4. A comprehensive working theory, based on a systematic study of the profession and using a developed terminology, would serve many purposes. One of the most important gains for lawyer education might be that proposals based on hard fact and systematic analysis might possibly make the most conservative of professions a little more amenable to innovation and experiment. The way might then be open for the belated injection of some educational professionalism into professional education. This will probably

---

[66] R. Megarry: 'Under modern conditions, it is the examination that is the master of both the teacher and the author. If there are examinations on a subject, it will be taught, and books will be written on it; if there are no examinations on a subject, then probably, though not inevitably, there will be neither teaching nor students books': *Lawyer and Litigant in England* (London, 1962), at 96.

take a long time; while waiting, those who ought to be professional legal educators, we academic lawyers, might set an example by putting our own house in order. One suspects that our own educational amateurism has been a major factor in the ineffectiveness of criticisms of the traditional 'system' of professional training. For surely many of its weaknesses have been primarily educational weaknesses: in formulation of objectives, in planning of syllabuses, in teaching methods, in examinations, in administration, in the concepts and the thought patterns that have been dominant, and, in other respects, what has been lacking has been a willingness to learn from those who know something and care about education and training.

ENVOI

These prolegomena fall far short of a comprehensive working theory. If the tone of this lecture has seemed in places to be radical, please remember that few, if any, of the ideas put forward are new. In fact my present position, as far as I am able to define it, seems to me to be somewhat conservative, or at least liberal-conservative. It would be good to see our idea of liberal education refurbished a little—in particular its associations with social and intellectual snobbery need to go, together with its proneness to defensive obscurantism—but the central values, such as free inquiry, interest in human nature, breadth of perspective, intellectual discipline, independence of thought and judgment, and love of truth need to be preserved, indeed in legal education some need to be recaptured. This is hardly the creed of a revolutionary. Impatience with pre-Langdellian ideas is surely forgivable, if one remembers that in three years' time the centenary of Langdell's appointment to Harvard will be celebrated. Is there indecent haste in the suggestion that the lag behind the United States might be reduced to a decent thirty or thirty-five years? The Lasswell-McDougal plan for legal education, published in 1943, is still rather too avant-garde for my taste. Let us by all means wait another ten or twenty years before introducing the first Lasswellian social planetarium into the United Kingdom. Is this hot-headed radicalism?

One final point: when this lecture was in a fairly advanced state of preparation it became apparent that it would bring together at least three potentially unpopular themes: I frequently encounter people who expect me to apologize for being a theorist; 'legal education' is often sneered at as being a subject unworthy of the serious attention of legal educators; there are people who may think it unpatriotic to suggest that we might learn from the experience of others. Yet I have dared to suggest that we need a theory for lawyer education based in part on foreign ideas. I am unrepentant; and I hope at least to have communicated the idea that legal education as a subject is socially important and intellectually exacting and that as such it is worthy of sustained reflection, dispassionate inquiry, and creative thought. Today I have merely flicked at a few cobwebs. A more disciplined treatment would require another medium and a better equipped exponent. As was recently suggested at a notable conference of younger law teachers, legal education is too serious a topic to be left to inaugural lectures.[67]

[67] J. P. W. B. McAuslan, 'The Proper Relation between University Law Teaching and Training for the Legal Profession in England: Some Thoughts on our Present Discontents': paper read at Conference on 'The Concept of a Law Degree', (Cambridge, September 1966).

5

*Taking Facts Seriously**

Once upon a time, on the eastern seaboard of Xanadu, a brand-new law school was established. An innovative, forward-looking, dynamic young dean was appointed, and he quickly recruited a team of innovative, forward-looking, dynamic young colleagues in his own image. At the first faculty meeting—there were as yet no students to complicate matters—the only item on the agenda was, naturally, curriculum. The dean opened the proceedings: 'Persons,' he said, 'there is only one question facing us today: What can we do that is new, creative, innovative, path breaking . . .?' His colleagues nodded assent; being young and forward-looking they had not yet learned that even in legal education there is nothing new under the sun. Suggestions followed quickly: law and the social sciences, a clinical programme, psycho-legal studies, eco-law, computer-based instruction, law and development, and many of the fads, fashions, follies, and frolics of the 1970s and 1960s, and even some from the 1950s (for how far back does the history of legal education stretch?) were all quickly rejected as old hat. They were, in Brainerd Currie's phrase, 'trite symbols of frustration'.[1] For our subject is governed by a paradox: In general education there is no reported example of an experiment that has ended in failure; in academic law no movement or programme has ever achieved success.

Eventually the Oldest Member spoke up. He had actually looked backward into past numbers of the *Journal of Legal Education* and other forgotten sources:

It was once suggested that 90 per cent of lawyers spend 90 per cent of their time handling facts and that this ought to be reflected in their training.[2] If 81 per cent of lawyer time is spent on one thing, it follows that 81 per cent of legal education ought to be devoted to it. There have been some isolated courses on fact finding and the like, but no institution has had a whole programme in which the main emphasis was on facts. I propose that we base our curriculum on this principle and that we call our degree a Bachelor of Facts.

Opposition to this proposal was immediate and predictable.

---

* This chapter, a revised version of an address delivered at the ceremonies celebrating the opening of the Begbie Building, Faculty of Law, University of Victoria, BC, in November 1980, was published in *Essays on Legal Education* (ed., Neil Gold, Toronto, 1982). A slightly different version was published in 34 *J Legal Educ.* 22 (1989). The informal style of an address has been retained.

[1] Brainerd Currie, 'The Materials of Law Study', 8 *J Legal Educ.* 1 (1955), at 4.

[2] Recent research suggests that the Oldest Member may have been exaggerating. A particularly suggestive study which has a bearing on several issues in this paper is Frances K. Zemans, 'Preparation for the Practice of Law in the United States: The Views of Practitioners', a paper delivered at the Conference on Legal Services in the 1980s (Cardiff, March 1980). See further, Frances K. Zemans & Victor G. Rosenblum, *The Making of a Public Profession* (Chicago, 1981).

We do it already.

Illiberal!

It's only common sense, therefore it is unteachable.

Fact finding can only be learned by experience.

None of us is competent to teach it.

There are no books.

You cannot study facts in isolation from law.

Law schools should only teach law.

The students would not find it interesting or easy.

The concept of a fact is a crude positivist fiction.

Who would want to go through life labeled a BF?

The Oldest Member was an experienced academic politician; he had studied not only the *Journal of Legal Education* but also Cornford's *Microcosmographia Academica* which, as you know, is our special supplement to Machiavelli's *The Prince*. Adapting the tactic of the Irrelevant Rebuttal, he seized on the objection to the title of the degree and made a crucial concession: 'It need not be a bachelor's degree,' he said, 'there are good American precedents for calling the undergraduate law degree a doctorate. To call our graduates Doctors of Facts will not only attract students and attention, it will also signal that we are well aware that reality is a social construction and not something out there waiting to be found.'

The opposition having been routed, a curriculum committee was set up to work out the details. To their surprise they learned that the range of potential courses was virtually limitless and, what is more, that there already existed an enormous, if scattered, literature. They submitted a detailed plan for the curriculum, including a full range of options, and added a recommendation that the length of the degree should be increased to five years.

This fantasy was concocted for a seminar on legal education, with two objectives in mind. Readers of the *Journal of Legal Education*, as professional educators, should have no difficulty in satisfying the first objective, that is spotting the dozen (or more) standard educational fallacies illustrated by this hypothetical example. The second objective was to underline the point that the study of evidence, broadly conceived, is potentially a rather large subject. My purpose is to explore some aspects of this latter suggestion and to examine why it has been relatively neglected in most programmes of legal education.

The problem might be stated as follows: At least since the time of Jerome Frank it has been widely acknowledged that an imbalance exists between the amount of attention devoted to disputed questions of law in upper courts and the amount devoted to disputed questions of fact in trials at first instance, in other tribunals, and in legal processes generally. Frank might be interpreted as suggesting that the amount of intellectual energy devoted to a subject varies inversely with its practical importance. His thesis was not restricted to legal education, but covered legal discourse generally: legal research, legal literature, debates about law reform and lawyers' perceptions of the law, and their underlying assumptions about it. He was inclined to overstatement and used some vulnerable arguments to bolster his case; but it is now very widely accepted that his central thesis was sound.[3]

Frank's crusade is by no means unique; it is the most sustained polemic in what has been an almost continuous tradition: this includes the German scholar Hugo Münsterberg's campaign for scientific experimental psychology;[4] Albert Osborn's proposal for a Chair of Facts;[5] and numerous pleas from leading judges, practitioners, and committees. The Ormrod Committee on Legal Education in England explicitly included as one major objective of the first or academic stage: 'The intellectual training necessary to enable [the student] to handle facts and apply abstract concepts to them.'[6] In addition to such general prescriptions, there have been numerous calls for more attention to be paid to specific aspects of fact handling: recently, for example, Eggleston, Finkelstein, Barnes, and others[7] have echoed Holmes's argument that 'the man of the future is the man of statistics'[8] and that the calculus of chances, Bayes' Theorem, and a general ability to spot fallacies and abuses in statistical argument should be part of the basic training of every lawyer. Similarly, numerous specific suggestions are to be found in the literature on clinical legal education[9] and the recent debates in the United States on lawyer competence.[10] Thus, even before Frank, attempts had been made to right the imbalance that he pinpointed; such attempts have continued, but they do not seem to have caught on in the sense that Evidence, Proof, and Factfinding (hereafter EPF) does not seem to be generally accepted as an integral and central part of the core curriculum nor of legal discourse generally.

Before considering some specific attempts to deal with the problem, we might at least provisionally indicate the potential scope of the subject. Jerome Michael, who is one of the heroes of our story, summarized his view of the theoretical bases of the arts of controversy as follows:

[3] See generally Jerome N. Frank, *Law and the Modern Mind* (New York, 1930); *Courts on Trial* (Princeton, 1949); 'Why Not a Clinical Lawyer-School?', 81 *U Pa. L Rev.* 907 (1933).

[4] Hugo Münsterberg, *On the Witness Stand* (New York, 1908).

[5] Albert S. Osborn, *The Problem of Proof* (New York, 1922) 21.

[6] *Report of the Committee on Legal Education*, HMSO Cmnd. 4595 (1971) at 94; for other examples see Robert S. Marx, 'Shall Law Schools Establish a Course on "Facts"?', 5 *J Legal Educ.* 524 (1953).

[7] Richard M. Eggleston, *Evidence, Proof and Probability*, 2nd edn. (London, 1983); Michael O. Finkelstein, *Quantitative Methods of Law* (New York, 1978); Alan D. Cullison, 'Identification by Probabilities and Trial by Arithmetic', 6 *Houston L Rev.* 471 (1969); David W. Barnes, *Statistics as Proof* (Boston, 1983). For a critique of 'mathematicist' approaches, see L. Jonathan Cohen, *The Probable and the Provable* (Oxford, 1977).

[8] Oliver W. Holmes, Jr., 'The Path of the Law', 10 *Harv. L Rev.* 457 (1896), 469.

[9] See the useful bibliography by P. C. A. Snyman in 30 *J Legal Educ.* (1979), at 56–66.

[10] See, e.g., 'Lawyer Competency: The Role of the Law Schools'. Report and Recommendations of a Task Force of the ABA Section of Legal Education and Admission to the Bar (1979).

since legal controversy is conducted by means of words, you need some knowledge about the use of words as symbols, that is, some grammatical knowledge. Since issues of fact are constituted of contradictory propositions, are formed by the assertion and denial of propositions, and are tried by the proof and disproof of propositions, you need some knowledge of the nature of propositions and of the relationships which can obtain among them, and of the character of issues of fact and of proof and disproof, that is, some logical knowledge. Since the propositions which are material to legal controversy can never be proved to be true or false but only to be probable to some degree and since issues of fact are resolved by the calculation of the relative probabilities of the contradictory propositions of which they are composed, you need some knowledge of the distinction between truth or falsity and probability and of the logic of probability. Since propositions are actual or potential knowledge, since proof or disproof is an affair of knowledge, since, if they are truthful, the parties to legal controversy assert, and witnesses report, their knowledge, and since knowledge is of various sorts, you need some knowledge about knowledge, such, for instance, as knowledge of the distinction between direct or perceptual and indirect or inferential knowledge. Since there are intrinsic and essential differences between law and fact, between propositions about matters of fact and statements about matters of law, and between issues of fact and issues of law and the ways in which they are respectively tried and resolved, you need some knowledge about these matters. Since litigants and all those who participate in the conduct and resolution of their controversies are men and since many of the procedural rules are based upon presuppositions about human nature and behavior, you need some psychological knowledge. Finally, of course, you need such knowledge as is necessary to enable you to understand the tangential ends which are served by procedural law and to criticize the rules which are designed to serve them.[11]

Michael's list is impressive: it includes the classic trivium of logic, grammar, and rhetoric; epistemology; forensic psychology; the detailed exploration of probabilities; the interconnections between law and fact; and the basic concepts, doctrines, and policies of the law of evidence. Other pioneers in the field have outlined similar schemes which differ in detail and emphasis. Indeed, there is a continuous intellectual tradition from Bentham, through Wills, Best, Stephen, Thayer, Gulson, Wigmore, Michael and Adler to Leo Levin, Irvin Rutter, and contemporary teachers of law who have treated EPF as an important focus of attention.[12]

When one contemplates the history of this particular tradition, however, one

---

[11] Jerome Michael, *The Elements of Legal Controversy* (Brooklyn, 1948).

[12] On Bentham see n. 14 below; on Wigmore, Michael, Levin, and Rutter see below. Classic works in the Anglo-American tradition include: William Wills, *An Essay on the Principles of Circumstantial Evidence*, 1st edn. (London, 1838); William M. Best, *A Treatise on the Principles of Evidence*, 1st edn. (London, 1849); J. Fitzjames Stephen, *The Indian Evidence Act with an Introduction on the Principles of Judicial Evidence* (Calcutta, 1872); J. R. Gulson, *The Philosophy of Proof*, 1st edn. (London, 1905). For a useful historical survey see 1 Wigmore *Treatise*, Sect. 8. Almost without exception these concentrate on disputed questions of fact in litigation ('legal controversy') on the basis of a number of largely shared assumptions about the nature of adjudication and of what is involved in 'rational' fact determination. This shared perspective can be characterized as 'optimistic rationalism', see *RE*, Ch. 3.

sometimes wonders whether it has been the subject of some peculiar curse. For it reads like the story of Sisyphus who was condemned forever to roll a heavy boulder up a hill, only to see it roll down just before he reached the top.[13] The study of rhetoric, which had its origins in forensic situations, has been the inspiration of important developments in several disciplines—inductive logic, literary criticism, semantics, even parts of psychology, for example—but it has been forgotten by the discipline of law. James Mill edited Bentham's *Introductory View of Judicial Evidence* and one-third of the work was in proof when the printer took fright because of Bentham's views on jury packing (and possibly his potentially blasphemous critique of oaths), with the result that publication was delayed by some thirty years.[14] Immediately after the young John Stuart Mill had completed the Herculean feat of editing Bentham's *magnum opus*, the *Rationale of Judicial Evidence*, he suffered his famous breakdown and substituted Wordsworth's poetry for Bentham's relentlessly intellectual pushpin.[15] Most of Bentham's concepts and basic theoretical analysis have been thoroughly absorbed into the Anglo-American tradition of evidence scholarship, but his main argument—that all exclusionary rules should be abolished and that fact finding should be treated as a quintessentially rational process—has gained only limited acceptance.

In 1908, Hugo Münsterberg trumpeted a new era for forensic psychology,[16] only for John Henry Wigmore, the rising star of evidence, to write a satire, laced with most un-Wigmorean wit, which was so effective that it helped to dampen the budding enthusiasm of psychologists—and forensic psychology went to sleep for several decades.[17] Ironically Wigmore himself then moved into the field,[18] but more in the mode of a dilettante anthologist, drawing almost as heavily on writings by lawyers and the work of a member of the Indian Civil service,

---

[13] A similar pattern in law and the social sciences is discussed by Harry Kalven, Jr., 'Some Comments on the Law and Behavioral Science Project at the University of Pennsylvania', 11 *J Legal Educ.* (1958), at 94–6.

[14] *The Works of Jeremy Bentham* (ed. J. Bowring, Edinburgh, 1838–43) 6. The proof of the unpublished printing of 1812 of approximately the first third of *An Introductory View* survives in the Bentham manuscripts at University College, London. A sheet dated 1822 states that the printing was stopped 'owing to the disappearance of some papers which have since been recovered'. James Mill's biographer suggests that booksellers feared prosecution because of Bentham's critique of jury packing (Alexander Bain, *James Mill: A Biography* (New York, 1882) 120); Bentham's famous discussion of oaths, *Swear Not at All*, was originally written as part of the *Introductory View*. It was separately printed in 1813, but publication was postponed until 1817. For Bentham's account, see *Works*, vol. 5, (ed., J. Bowring), at 189.

[15] Jeremy Bentham, *Rationale of Judicial Evidence*, (ed. John Stuart Mill, London, 1827); John Stuart Mill, *Autobiography* (London, 1873).　　　　　　　　　　　　　[16] Op. cit.

[17] John Henry Wigmore, 'Professor Münsterberg and the Psychology of Testimony, Being a Report of the Case of COKESTONE V. MÜNSTERBERG', 3 *Ill. L Rev.* 399 (1909). See also Charles C. Moore, 'Yellow Psychology', 11 *Law Notes* 125 (1907); Moore, a practitioner, was himself author of a remarkable work, *A Treatise on Facts* (Northport, NY, 1908). Wigmore, while praising the work in general terms, criticized Moore for suggesting that rules of law can determine the weight or credibility of testimony: 3 *Ill. L Rev.* 441 (1909).

[18] John Henry Wigmore, *The Principles of Judicial Proof*, 1st edn. (Boston, 1913); 2nd edn., (Boston, 1931); 3rd edn., *sub nom The Science of Judicial Proof* (Boston, 1937).

G. F. Arnold, who was neither a lawyer nor a psychologist, as he did on serious empirical research.[19] During the heyday of the Realist Movement, the young Robert Maynard Hutchins collaborated with a psychologist, Donald Slesinger, for a number of years;[20] but after he had been translated precociously to the presidency of the University of Chicago, Hutchins recanted, suggesting in a remarkable paper entitled 'The Autobiography of an Ex-Law Student' that he had been wasting his time.[21] In the 1930s Jerome Michael and Mortimer Adler prepared the most elaborate account of the logical and analytical aspects of EPF, entitled *The Nature of Judicial Proof*.[22] This actually reached the stage of being privately printed for limited circulation, but the full version never received full publication, perhaps because commentators, including Wigmore, dismissed it as being of no practical value.[23] Wigmore's own *Principles of Judicial Proof* suffered a rather more bizarre fate. For many years he taught a course on proof at Northwestern University which remains the most systematic and intellectually sophisticated attempt of its kind to deal with the analytical and psychological dimensions of proof in forensic contexts. While Wigmore was dean, his course on proof was a regular part of the curriculum, first as a required course and latterly as an option; after he ceased to be dean, it was relegated to the summer programme. The book of the course was first published in 1913. It was well received critically, but so far as I have been able to discover it was never adopted more than once in any other law school during Wigmore's lifetime. The reason why it went into three editions appears to have been that his publishers, Little, Brown, valued their relationship with Wigmore (for good reason) and Little, Brown salesmen found a modest market among practitioners who treated it as good bedside reading.

Since the 1930s the pattern has continued. For example, in the late 1950s Leo Levin of the University of Pennsylvania Law School prepared an excellent set of materials, *Evidence and the Behavioral Sciences*, but this too was never

---

[19] G. F. Arnold, *Psychology Applied to Legal Evidence and Other Constructions of Law*, 1st edn. (Calcutta, 1906; 2nd edn., 1913).

[20] Robert Hutchins & Donald Slesinger, 'Some Observations on the Law of Evidence', 28 *Colum. L Rev.* 432 (1928); 'Some Observations on the Law of Evidence—The Competency of Witnesses', 37 *Yale LJ* 1017 (1928); 'Some Observations on the Law of Evidence—Consciousness of Guilt', 77 *U Pa. L Rev.* 725 (1929); and 'Some Observations on the Law of Evidence—Family Relations', 13 *Minn. L Rev.* 675 (1929). These articles are discussed in John H. Schlegel, 'American Legal Realism and Empirical Social Science: From the Yale Experience', 28 *Buffalo L Rev.* at 480 ff. (1979).

[21] Robert M. Hutchins, 'The Autobiography of an Ex-Law Student', 1 *U Chi. L Rev.* 511 (1934).

[22] Jerome Michael & Mortimer Adler, *The Nature of Judicial Proof* (New York, 1931). The Foreword states: 'This is not a book. It is merely galley proof, which after considerable revision and elaboration will become a book, and it is being put forth in this form so that the authors can use it in classes which they are now conducting. It is not intended for wider circulation.' Some of the material was later used in articles and other writings by the two authors; see especially Jerome Michael & Mortimer Adler, 'The Trial of an Issue of Fact', 34 *Col. L Rev.* 1224 (1934), at 1462; 'Real Proof', 5 *Vanderbilt L Rev.* 334 (1952); and Jerome Michael, *Elements of Legal Controversy* (Brooklyn, 1948). [23] Wigmore (1937), op. cit., at 6, n. 1.

published as a book.[24] In the 1970s an ambitious project to produce a definitive edition of Bentham's very extensive writings on evidence—in the eyes of some, one of the most important and least known aspects of his work—was frozen *sine die* for lack of funds.[25]

So far as legal education is concerned, a similar, less dramatic, pattern is to be discerned. Before 1960, there were some attempts to establish courses on fact finding and the like in law schools, particularly in America. Almost without exception, like all educational experiments, these have been reported as successes; Jerome Michael at Columbia, Jerome Frank at Yale, Wigmore at Northwestern, Judge Marx and Irvin Rutter at Cincinnati, Marshall Houts at UCLA, and Leo Levin at Pennsylvania are among those who have attempted to develop courses on fact finding.[26] These are fascinating in their diversity, but the more striking fact is that they did not become established; almost without exception they stand as monuments to the ephemeral contributions of individual teachers. They did not become institutionalized, nor did the lessons of experience cumulate. The pattern was perhaps symbolized by staged witness 'experiments'. The literature abounds with reports along the following lines: A student dressed in a top hat and tails, with a monocle in his left eye, a bottle of champagne on a silver-plated salver in the right hand and a gun in the left hand, rushes into the classroom, shouting 'You bounder, I have got you at last'; he shoots the teacher and rushes out again, still carrying the champagne. The teacher then rises from the dead and asks the class to write down an account of what they have just witnessed. Almost invariably they put the monocle in the wrong eye, forget about the champagne, and substitute some other word for 'bounder'. No doubt these so-called eyewitness experiments taught a simple lesson vividly, but even in respect of the method of staging them, knowledge did not *accumulate* on the basis of experience. They remained idiosyncratic, spasmodic, and essentially amateur.[27]

---

[24] A. Leo Levin, *Evidence and the Behavioral Sciences* (mimeo, edn. 1956), discussed in Levin's article, 'The Law and Behavioral Science Project at the University of Pennsylvania: Evidence', 11 *J Legal Educ.* 87 (1958).

[25] On the Bentham Project see John R. Dinwiddy in *The Bentham Newsletter*, May 1978 and May 1980. The project on adjective law will shortly be revived.

[26] Marx, op. cit.; Marshall Houts, 'A Course on Proof', 7 *J Legal Educ.* 418 (1955); see also *From Evidence to Proof* (Springfield, 1956); Michael, op. cit.; Irvin Rutter, 'A Jurisprudence of Lawyers' Operations', 13 *J Legal Educ.* 301 (1961); Levin, op. cit. The coverage of Frank's course at Yale approximated to the topics dealt with in *Courts on Trial*, op. cit.

[27] For published accounts of demonstrations and 'experiments' in the classroom, see e.g. Wigmore (1931) op. cit. (2nd edn.), at 532 ff.; Marshall Houts, *From Evidence to Proof* (Springfield, 1956), Ch. 1; John G. Merrills, 'Fact and Fancy', 11 *JSPTL (NS)* 155 (1971). On research in this area see especially Arne Trankell, *Reliability of Evidence* (Stockholm, 1972); Mirjan Damaska, 'Presentation of Evidence and Factfinding Precision', 123 *U Pa. L Rev.* 1083 (1975); Brian R. Clifford & Ray H. C. Bull, *The Psychology of Person Identification* (London, 1978); Elizabeth Loftus, *Eyewitness Testimony* (Cambridge, Ma., 1979); Sally Lloyd-Bostock & Brian Clifford (edd.), *Evaluating Witness Evidence* (Chichester, 1983). Recent research has made traditional classroom 'experiments' look rather naïve.

Some years ago I suggested that legal education had been strongly influenced by two sharply contrasting images of the lawyer: on the one hand, the lofty image of Pericles, the lawgiver, the enlightened policy-maker, the wise judge; on the other hand, the image of the lawyer as plumber, a no-nonsense, down-to-earth technician.[28] My argument, which has sometimes been misunderstood, was that neither image was suitable as a model for the end-products of a sane system of legal education and training and that the influence of these two images, typically in the form of unstated assumptions, has contributed to unnecessary controversy and tensions within legal education. In a nutshell: the academics have often been too lofty, but practitioners have tended to be too mundane. Understanding and practising law are more difficult, more varied, and more interesting than the plumbing image implies; but legal education has no special claim to be suited to the mass production of statesmen.

In respect of EPF there may be something in the view that the plumbing image has been too influential on attempts to respond to calls to take facts more seriously. At least some of the courses described in the literature seem to have concentrated more on specific techniques than on basic, transferable skills and to have tried to instil skills without an adequate theoretical base. Some have also tried to cover too much ground in a very limited time. Insofar as this has been the case, it is hardly surprising. Much of the pressure for teaching courses on fact handling and the like has come from the practitioners and judges who typically, but by no means universally, express the need in terms of securing minimum competence in respect of immediately usable techniques. The standard academic response to such requests is that formal legal education should concentrate on matters that represent a long-term investment, on understanding as well as skill, on transferable skills rather than narrowly focused techniques.[29]

Let us consider briefly one of the more carefully worked out courses from this perspective—Wigmore's course on proof. His starting-point is a sharp distinction between the rules of admissibility and proof—what he termed 'the ratiocinative process of contentious persuasion'.[30] He adopts the standpoint of the trial advocate at the point when the questions of admissibility have been dealt with and the evidence is all in and 'the counsel sets himself to the ultimate and crucial task, i.e., that of persuading the jury that they should or should not believe the fact alleged in issue'.[31] Stated like this, it sounds as if Wigmore is reviving the ancient art of forensic oratory; in fact his primary educational aim was quite different: it was to develop '*skill in thinking about evidence*'[32] and, in particular, of mastering a limited number of types of mental process which bear on systematically analysing a mixed mass of evidence in order to come to a judgement about its probative force for the case as a whole. To this end Wigmore developed a particular method which is designed, in his words, 'to enable us to

---

[28] See Ch. 4 above.
[29] On the distinction between 'skills' and 'techniques', see Rutter, op. cit.
[30] Wigmore (1937) op. cit., at 5.   [31] Id., at 6.   [32] Id., at 7.

lift into consciousness and to state in words the reasons why a total mass of evidence does or should persuade us to a given conclusion and why our conclusion would or should have been different or identical if some part of the total mass had been different'.[33]

The basis of this method is inductive logic, as expounded by John Stuart Mill, Alfred Sidgwick, and Stanley Jevons. The core of the course was a series of exercises in applied inductive logic. The initial exercises deal with analysing examples of different kinds of evidence according to this method, in the course of which Wigmore introduces a considerable amount of psychological and scientific material. All these particular sections are only preliminaries to the finale—an elaborate exercise of analysing a mixed mass of evidence, using records of famous trials as examples. Put simply, a two-stage process is involved: first, all the evidence which the student considers to be potentially relevant, directly or indirectly, to a fact in issue has to be expressed in the form of simple propositions of fact. Each proposition is given a number and becomes part of a 'key list of evidence' for the case. The second stage is to map, using a limited number of symbols, all the significant relationships between all the propositions, and to indicate the author's *belief* about the probative force (or otherwise) of each proposition in relation to its immediate *probandum*. The final result should represent a rational reconstruction of the chart-maker's belief about the significance of each item of evidence and its bearing on the case as a whole.

For several years past I have set undergraduates exercises based on a modified and somewhat diluted version of Wigmorean analysis. Typically selected *causes célèbres* have provided the raw material—Sacco and Vanzetti, Alger Hiss, Tichborne, Hanratty, and, above all, Bywaters and Thompson, have turned out to be reasonably suitable for this kind of exercise.[34] To keep matters under control I have had to lay down a set of artificial ground rules, for example, that no key list should contain fewer than 250 or more than 500 propositions and (after receiving a chart that extended for thirty-seven feet) that no chart should be more than ten feet long.

This is not the place to give a full account of my impressions of the value and the limitations of such exercises. Suffice to say that although they are extremely time-consuming and are clearly both artificial and academic (in non-pejorative senses), I am convinced that they are an excellent pedagogical device for a number of purposes: doing such exercises should drive home the lesson that analysis of evidence involves careful exploration of *relations between propositions*; it

---

[33] Id., at 8.

[34] Wigmore provides a list of trials useful for study in the appendices of the 2nd and 3rd editions of the *Principles of Proof*, together with a list of historical problems susceptible to the same kind of analysis. Professor Terence Anderson of the University of Miami Law School has used National Trial Competition problems and other such materials as the basis for exercises in Wigmorean analysis from the standpoint of a lawyer preparing for trial. Although Wigmore *claimed* to be adopting the standpoint of the trial attorney during trials, by using inert records he often switched to the standpoint of a historian.

should help to make the student aware of the complexity of such relations and of the many possibilities of logical jumps and of fallacious reasoning when a mass of evidence is involved. Wigmore's method lays a foundation for a systematic approach to analysing disputed questions of fact; it sets forth a disciplined approach to charting the overall structure of a case, to digging out unstated, often dubious propositions, and to mapping all the relations between all the relevant evidence. It is not merely a vehicle for giving a grounding in some elementary techniques of analysis, for it also provides a perspective—a way of looking at evidence and at complex cases which does not come naturally to most students. My impression of student reactions to Wigmore exercises is that many either groaned while they were sweating it out or became obsessed with their particular cases, but that nearly all have been glad to have been through the process and have learned a great deal from it.[35]

In the present context, Wigmore's *Principles* is significant for a number of reasons. First, it represents the most concrete and developed version of an analytical, non-mathematical, approach to problems of forensic proof. Second, it purports to integrate logic, forensic psychology, and forensic science into a single coherent scheme. Some of the psychological and scientific material looks rather dated and, to a lesser extent, the same may be said of the logic. But that does not undermine the validity of the general approach. Third, Wigmore's educational objectives are unashamedly vocational, but the main lessons that can be learned from such a study would satisfy the criteria of most liberal educators. There is no conflict. However, Wigmore's approach is narrowly focused—it concentrates on one standpoint, the trial advocate, at one moment of time. It concentrates on one point in the totality of legal processes. Wigmore filters out many questions and factors that the process school and sceptical students of legal processes would consider to be very important.[36] This, I think, signals a limitation, but does not undermine the validity or the value of the enterprise. Fourth, it provides a coherent, if not fully argued, theory within a central intellectual tradition—English empiricism—which can be compared and contrasted with perspectives and ideas that fit more easily with other philosophical traditions, such as neo-Kantian, Hegelian, or Marxian approaches.[37] This last point deserves emphasis: for Wigmore's 'science' provides as good a starting-point as any for exploring a wide range of theoretical issues which he did not himself

---

[35] Lord Wright, in an enthusiastic review of *Wigmore's The Science of Proof*, wrote: 'I have asked myself whether I should have done my work any better if I had studied the book in earlier days, not merely for information, but for living mastery of the principles so as to apply and use them. I think the answer should be in the affirmative. Rule of thumb is all very well, especially in a subject like legal proof . . . But all the same, the logic is there. A workman is all the better if he knows and understands his tools as scientifically as he can.' 24 *ABAJ* 478 (1938).

[36] Almost all of the writings discussed in this paper, with the possible exception of some of the works of Jerome Frank, fall within what might be termed 'the rationalist tradition of evidence scholarship'. Some possible implications for EPF of various sceptical and relativist approaches are explored in *RE*, Ch. 4.   [37] *RE*, Ch. 4.

explore, such as the nature of probabilistic reasoning in forensic contexts, how judgements about the weight of different items of evidence are to be combined, 'holistic' versus 'atomistic' approaches, how 'reality' is constructed in the courtroom, and the nature and purposes of different kinds of legal processes.[38]

Wigmore's science is only one—but indubitably the most important—example of an attempt to deal with factual questions seriously and systematically within legal education. Other precedents, of course, are worthy of attention—though none, in my view, are sufficiently comprehensive to go beyond showing what can be done by a systematic approach to one or two particular aspects of this broad field. We do not yet have a blueprint for a comprehensive approach to EPF within legal education, but in the courses and writings of Wigmore, Michael, Levin, Rutter,[39] Eggleston, Anderson, Schum, and others we have a valuable heritage of relatively sophisticated and diverse precedents. One lesson to be learned from this past experience is that it is unwise to expect to be able to tackle even the basics of all that is encompassed by EPF satisfactorily within the confines of one of two courses.[40]

Given the quality of much of the thinking and the avowed success of a number of individual courses, why has EPF not been more firmly entrenched in the law schools? I shall address this question, without attempting to give a comprehensive answer, by looking first at some arguments which are sometimes advanced against extending the study of EPF and then at some other factors in the intellectual climate of law schools that may have contributed to the neglect of an important dimension of academic law.

In the hypothetical example of the Xanadu Law School I implied that the objections that were raised against the proposal for a BF degree were all either fallacious or seriously defective. If we put forward a more modest proposal— that the systematic study of facts in law should have a central, but not dominating, place in undergraduate legal education, for example, there are some rational objections that at least deserve a response. The main arguments can be divided into three categories: (1) the subject is dealt with adequately already; (2) the subject is important, but is not dealt with extensively in most law schools because it is unnecessary to devote valuable class time to it; (3) in theory one should devote more time to it, but there are severe difficulties in doing so. Let

---

[38] For a general evaluation of Wigmore's chart method, see The Uses and Limitations of Wigmore's Chart Method in *ANALYSIS* at 117–31.

[39] The earlier version of this paper contained a comment on Irvin Rutter's course at Cincinnati, as described in his well-known paper, cited above.

[40] In addition to those already mentioned, contemporary precedents include Sir Richard Eggleston's courses at Monash University, Terence Anderson's Evidence Workshop at the University of Miami, David Schum's work at Rice University (see David Schum & Anne Martin, 17 *Law & Society Review* 105 [1983], and my own course on Advanced Legal System at Warwick, 1973–82.) These are just a sample of university-based courses. Anderson, Schum, and Twining all build on Wigmore's 'Science of proof'. Some relatively new types of vocational training courses that developed during the 1970s in many common law jurisdictions devote a substantial amount of time to aspects of 'fact management', typically without resort to such terms.

us call these respectively: the 'we do it already', the 'too soft', and the 'too hard' arguments. Finally, questions also arise about the ethics of some aspects of 'fact-handling'.

The first argument, that enough is done already to teach students the fundamentals of handling facts, was cogently put by Jack B. Weinstein in commenting on issues raised by Jerome Frank and Judge Marx.[41] Speaking of Columbia in the 1950s, but by implication more generally, he argued that three fundamental 'fact skills' were already being taught and that was all that could be expected in a three-year degree. First, students are taught 'to differentiate between facts which are and which are not materially significant'.[42] The main vehicle for this was the case method which, claimed Weinstein, 'is uniquely conceived and designed to build a foundation for an understanding of the relationship of facts to law and for skillful handling of facts'.[43] This was supplemented at Columbia by Jerome Michael's more theoretical approach which, alas, has since been largely forgotten.[44] The second skill, 'knowledge of how courses of conduct may be planned to shape the material facts', is dealt with in courses on contracts, tax, trusts and estates, and the like. The third skill, 'an awareness of how evidence of the facts may be gathered and used in litigation', is adequately dealt with in courses on procedure and evidence and reinforced by such electives as legal aid work, mock trials, moots, and specialized seminars. Beyond that, instruction in fact handling is unnecessary or else is best left to be learned in practice.[45]

Even in this simplified version (he makes a number of other points), Weinstein's argument deserves respect. At the very least it suggests that Jerome Frank had exaggerated the extent of the imbalance and that, in its turn, Columbia in the 1950s had implemented at least some of Frank's suggestions.

A modern successor to Weinstein could with some justification claim that in many law schools his argument could be put with even greater force today: in particular, clinical programmes and trial practice courses have since become more sophisticated and more widespread, and the post-Realist 'process school' has stimulated a much greater academic awareness and attention to pretrial aspects of civil and criminal litigation and to such matters as sentencing, parole, and arbitration.

I can make only a peremptory reply here to this line of argument. One can readily concede both that Jerome Frank overstated his case and that the situation has improved significantly since his day. But it is just not true that the pleas of Frank and others have been met in a systematic and satisfactory manner. First, Weinstein's conception of the field is narrowly vocational. It is confined to the fundamental 'fact skills' of private practitioners and omits nearly all of the broad or theoretical dimensions outlined by his colleague Jerome Michael. He

---

[41] Jack B. Weinstein, 'The Teaching of Facts Skills in Courses Presently in the Curriculum', 7 *J Legal Educ.* 463 (1955), discussing Marx and Frank's thesis op. cit.
[42] Weinstein, op. cit., at 464.   [43] Id., at 465.   [44] Ibid.   [45] Id., at 464.

concentrates on techniques and says almost nothing of more general understanding and criticism.

Second, even in respect of the unashamedly vocational teaching of elementary skills, his account of what is involved is too simple. If one takes as the baseline for the claim 'we do it already' a more systematic job analysis of what is involved in 'fact handling' by private practitioners, such as that by Irvin Rutter, few programmes of legal education and training can claim systematically to deal even at an elementary level with the whole range of basic skills of private practitioners—let alone at a more advanced level or with other skills or with the concerns of other participants. It is difficult to generalize, of course, for both programmes and the experience of individual students within a programme vary considerably. What I wish to suggest in general terms is that by and large fact-handling skills, insofar as they are taught directly, are taught less systematically and at a more elementary level than rule-handling skills, and that there is anyway more to legal education than the inculcation of basic skills.

Third, Weinstein was writing about Columbia in 1954, which may in some respects have been exceptionally well off. In particular, Jerome Michael's courses on procedure and analytical aspects of proof represent one of the clear cases of a model that did not catch on. At best his ideas were accepted in a watered-down form, without the rigorous analytical approach on which he insisted; on the whole they have been largely ignored or forgotten.

Weinstein also raises one important issue: How far is it sensible to isolate the study of fact finding from other substantive and procedural issues? His answer is clear: 'It ought to be distributed throughout the curriculum so that students begin to think of a case in the many different ways that a lawyer might.' This raises a familiar issue over which first-year teachers regularly disagree: the 'direct' versus the 'pick-it-up' approaches to the study of legal method. Suffice to say here that I am as committed to the direct approach in respect of EPF as I am in respect of orthodox legal analysis and interpretation.[46] The 'pick-it-up' approach to basic skills typically confuses laying a foundation for mastery of a skill and reinforcing it through practice. Moreover, picking things up tends to proceed in a theoretical vacuum.

The second argument against direct and extensive teaching of EPF is that it is neither necessary nor appropriate for law schools to undertake to teach it. There are several versions of this argument. One is that fact handling is largely a matter of clear thinking and general knowledge, which should have been adequately developed before law school by general education. Law schools, so

---

[46] See Preface to *HDTWR*. In respect of skills, a direct approach postulates the need to allocate time (a substantial part of a course on legal method would, in some contexts, be adequate) and to isolate relevant aspects of EPF for study. This is not inconsistent with advocating 'a pervasive approach' in other courses for purposes of reinforcing and extending such basic skills. A strong case can be made for direct study of several aspects of EPF, in addition to what is already done in curricula of the kind postulated by Weinstein.

the argument goes, should not take on the mantle of general education, but should confine themselves to law. Accordingly they should deal only with matters which are peculiar to law or which involve special problems of application.

A variant of this argument is more fundamental: we are told that the logic appropriate to reasoning about evidentiary issues is the ordinary inductive reasoning used in everyday practical affairs; that judgements about relevance and about probabilities are based on common sense and the common course of experience;[47] after all, we entrust some of our most important fact-finding decisions to jurors, ordinary citizens who are without any training—indeed, perhaps because they are untrained. You cannot teach common sense and you should not try to do so.

Some support for this view is to be found in Bentham, who apologized for the obviousness of much of his *Rationale of Judicial Evidence* in the following terms:

So obvious are most of the considerations above presented, so much in the way of everybody's observation, that, under the name of instruction, they have scarce any pretension to be of any use. But, what a man has had in his mind, he has not always at hand at the very moment at which it is wanted: what conveys no instruction, may serve for reminiscence.[48]

Another variant is that some aspects of EPF may be considered to be soft options, less intellectually demanding or stimulating than traditional law courses. This is a criticism, often implicit rather than explicit, that has sometimes been made about courses on forensic science and forensic psychology in American law schools and about largely descriptive courses on institutions generally. The argument might be stated as follows: much of the material central to fact finding is undoubtedly important, but one does not need a course in it to learn the main lessons. It is of course important to be aware, for example, that memory is unreliable, perception is unreliable and is subject to distortion through bias, inattention, and lapse of time, that interrogation can be intrinsically coercive, and that decision makers are likely to have unconscious biases. Do we need to spend scarce and expensive time and resources in a law school to create such awareness? Even when it is not just a matter of common sense, can it not be done just as efficiently through self-education? Provide the student or lawyer with a list of recommended reading—Frank's *Courts on Trial*, Wellman's *The Art of Cross-Examination*, some manuals of advocacy, and standard works on forensic science and forensic psychology—and let him get on with it.

---

[47] A sophisticated statement of this view is to be found in Cohen, op. cit., at 274–5.

[48] Bentham, Book 1, Ch. 10, at 182; cf. *Bentham's Treatise on Judicial Evidence* (ed. Dumont, trans. anon., London, 1825) at 269: 'There would be no absurdity in inserting in a course of law, and, above all, in a treatise on the judicial art, a summary of the laws of nature, as applicable to different questions which may arise before judges; but it ought to be presumed, that the men who are elevated to high judicial functions, have passed through the schools of philosophy.'

Perhaps the most important objection to direct teaching of basic skills of fact handling is an ethical one. Many techniques of the effective advocate are inimical to the traditional values of a university, for they involve the undermining of rational argument rather than its promotion: they include techniques for keeping relevant information out, for trapping and confusing witnesses, for 'laundering' the facts, for diverting attention or interrupting the flow of argument, and for exploiting means of non-rational persuasion. The teacher of advocacy within the academy has an ethical dilemma: it may be appropriate to discuss the ethics of such techniques in class, but is it compatible with his calling to train students in the skills of a non-rational or anti-rational means of persuasion which are a part of *effective* advocacy? Or, for the university teacher, is this a form of *trahison des clercs?*

The argument may be restated as follows:

1. Insofar as certain skills and knowledge of a general kind need to be taught at all, they should be made a prerequisite for entry to law school.
2. Insofar as much of what is involved in fact finding is based on common sense, it is unnecessary to teach it.
3. Insofar as some relevant knowledge and awareness is easily acquired through general reading or experience, valuable law school time should not be devoted to it.
4. Insofar as effective fact handling involves unethical, non-rational, or anti-intellectual skills and techniques and perspectives, it is inappropriate for these to be taught in the academy.

These arguments are powerful and need to be taken into account in planning a sensible programme of education and training and in assessing priorities. But they are by no means dispositive. First, some aspects of clear thinking and general knowledge need to be developed to an especially high standard. To put the same point differently: one of the main claims of case method teaching and of analytical jurisprudence is that they develop *general* powers of reasoning and analysis—distinguishing the relevant from the irrelevant, handling abstract concepts, constructing and sustaining an argument, drawing precise distinctions. Much of the Langdellian tradition depends on the dual claim that lawyers need to be trained to think clearly and that legal materials are a particularly good vehicle for this purpose. Similar claims can be made for the analytical aspects of EPF, but the skills and techniques are not identical. Elucidating the concepts of 'fact' or 'proof' or 'relevance' poses somewhat different problems from elucidating basic legal concepts, such as 'right' or 'cause' or 'intention' or 'justice' or 'law'; and different lessons may be learned in analysing a mixed mass of evidence from analysing a series of reported cases.

Similarly, while some aspects of EPF are indeed quite easily understood and could provide the basis for 'soft options', many of its analytical and theoretical dimensions are at least as demanding as anything to be found in the expository

and Langdellian traditions of legal education. Furthermore, the problems of understanding the special applications to legal contexts of general principles of clear
thinking or general concepts affect questions of fact as well as questions of law.

Nor is it realistic to throw the burden back on general education and law
school entrance requirements. To take but one example: most law students and
lawyers readily confess to being innumerate; some even boast of it. Yet the
mathematicists claim that in arguing about disputed issues of fact one is reasoning about probabilities and that this kind of reasoning is always in principle
mathematical and requires at least an elementary command of basic statistical
and related techniques.[49] I am not concerned here about the validity of the
mathematicist thesis; but I would suggest that the serious study of reasoning in
regard to disputed matters of fact is at least as important and can be at least as
intellectually demanding as the study of reasoning in respect of disputed questions of law. In short, the answer to the 'too soft' argument is that the claims
of EPF, far from diluting the rigorous core of traditional legal education, would
involve a broadening of the scope of analytical studies and, if done well, would
make legal education more rather than less demanding.

This also provides at least a partial response to the ethical objection. No
doubt, in dealing with advocacy and other aspects of lawyering, teachers as well
as practitioners are regularly faced with moral dilemmas, as is illustrated by
some of the classic debates in the history of rhetoric. But if one believes that an
intellectually sound argument is often the most persuasive argument or even that
good advocacy involves a subtle combination of rational and non-rational means
of persuasion, then one has at least a partial answer to the objection. A rigorously intellectual approach to the skills of fact handling may help to further the
cause of promoting rationality in legal processes. A direct approach to the analysis of evidence (and related matters) may also help to illuminate the relations
between rational and non-rational factors and different conceptions of rationality. Such an approach belongs to the mainstream of Western university education, for fact handling is as much a basic human skill as rule handling. That
some such skills may be amoral, immoral, or open to abuse is not a sufficient
reason for not dealing with them in the academy. All skills give rise to ethical
problems; how to cope with such problems is an issue facing every educator.

The next, and converse objection—is that the systematic study of fact finding
is not too soft, but that it is too hard. This argument is more commonly expressed in terms of feasibility rather than of intellectual toughness.[50] Let us put

---

[49] On the debate between 'mathematicists' and Baconians see the articles and correspondence by
Glanville Williams, Jonathan Cohen, Sir Richard Eggleston, and others in successive issues of *The
Criminal Law Review* during 1979–80; see further the bibliography in *RE*.

[50] In conversation with teachers of evidence in the UK, the US, and Canada I have found that the
two most commonly articulated objections to extending the study of evidence and proof beyond the
rules of evidence are that (1) professional examinations concentrate on the rules and (2) law teachers
are not competent to teach the logical, psychological, and other aspects of a broadened conception
of EPF. In respect of (1), one object of this paper is to make the case for change in the long term;

on one side perennial questions of priorities and of teacher competence, which are best discussed in the context of specific programmes. Two robust maxims will suffice here: 'Questions of priorities should be debated on the merits' and 'If competent teachers cannot be found, they must be made.' Let us rather consider two different versions of the argument about feasibility—the 'no literature' argument and the 'Pandora's Box' argument.

In a rational and orderly world one might expect the natural sequence of development in education to be, first, some initial theorizing; then, research into and a new understanding of narrow areas leading to the publication of specialized studies; next, the publication of general books based on these particular studies; then, the establishment of courses based on the general books. In legal education the process is sometimes reversed: courses precede research and theorizing; general educational books grow out of the courses; detailed particular research follows the general studies. This need not be the case today in respect to EPF, for there is an extraordinarily rich literature—from Aristotle's *Rhetoric* to Perelman's *The New Rhetoric*; from Bentham's great *Rationale* to Wigmore's marvellously entertaining and instructive *Principles of Proof*; from Mill's *Logic* to Jonathan Cohen's *The Probable and the Provable*. Forensic science is reasonably well served and there is a burgeoning literature on forensic psychology, on legal process, and on particular topics such as probabilities, identification evidence, and the ethics of advocacy. It may be that manuals on cross-examination and some other aspects of trial practice have not evolved much beyond the cookbook stage,[51] but there is an enormous and varied secondary legal literature. Orthodox evidence scholarship, although it has tended to be rather narrowly focused, has often been of outstandingly high quality, and there is, of course, the vast heritage of relevant literature from the humanities and social sciences—on epistemology, on logic, on historiography, on the sociology of knowledge, for example.

In addition to the secondary literature, a body of primary material remains to an extraordinary degree under-exploited from the point of view of legal research and education—trial records and accounts of *causes célèbres*. It is a striking fact of our intellectual life that these are seen more as a source of entertainment (note, for example, the fate of Wigmore's *Principles*) than as raw material for systematic study and analysis. The law teacher's relatively well-developed expertise in using appellate cases as rich, stimulating, and demanding educational material has not been extended to records of trials. The potential uses of this kind of source, the criteria for selection, and the kinds of skills and awareness

meanwhile professional requirements need not so directly limit the extension of the study of EPF within law schools. In respect of (2) my impression is that lack of confidence is more of an obstacle than lack of competence. Several reviewers of Wigmore's *Principles/Science* attributed its neglect to 'the real or imagined incompetence' of law teachers to deal with the subject; see, e.g., 30 *Mich. L Rev.* 1354, (1932).

[51] See Rutter, op. cit., at 312–16.

it can help to develop are, in some respects, significantly different from the law reports. The human element is more clearly displayed in trial records, for example; the law reports are more compact and have special status as authorities. But, from a pedagogical point of view, they are quite closely related species of the same genus—case-studies; they are concrete, often dramatic, dialectical examples, which can be analysed in numerous ways. They can be used to illustrate general ideas, but they are anecdotal and as such they can be almost systematically misleading. The most interesting cases are typically atypical and, as has often been pointed out, the case-trained lawyer is in danger of having a distorted picture of the world in which the pathological and the exotic obscure the healthy and the routine.

Thus it is just not true that there is not an adequate literature on which to base a significantly expanded study of EPF within a broadened conception of academic law. It is nearer the mark to say that a potentially rich body of literature has been almost systematically neglected. It is symptomatic of this neglect that some of the most significant works in the field have either gone out of print or were never even published.[52] It is also symptomatic of neglect that, by and large, law teachers have so far failed to develop anything like the same level of pedagogical sophistication in selecting, presenting, and using trial records as they have done in respect of the law reports. The literature is there, but it has yet to be exploited.

But, it will be objected, you are opening Pandora's box. Pursue this line and all knowledge becomes your province: epistemology, logic, statistics, historiography, psychology, all the behavioural sciences, and heaven knows what else will escape and swamp us. Let us stick to what we can do well; let us keep the clamp down on the lid or we shall be assaulted by reality. Maybe I dismissed too summarily the notion that the gods are angry. Could it be that the sad story of the publishing history of theorizing about evidence by lawyers, of all those aborted projects and culs-de-sac, were small thunderbolts from heaven, shots across the bows warning academic lawyers to keep off? There is after all the precedent of Prometheus who stole fire from Olympus and opened the eyes of humankind by asking a lot of awkward questions. Is not taking a serious interest in facts rather like that? What is truth? What is proof? What part can reason play in adjudication? Is judicial process really concerned with truth? All the endless concerns of the humanities with knowledge, reality, and reason are threatening to break in. Start opening up these questions and you are lost.

Back to earth. There are no gods to anger, but the fears are not groundless: it is the case that the potential ramifications of EPF are endless and taking facts

---

[52] However, Bentham's *Rationale of Judicial Evidence* has been reprinted in a facsimile edition as part of *Classics of English Legal History in the Modern Era* (New York, 1978); *Wigmore's Science* (3rd edn.) is available in photocopy or microfilm from University Microfilms International. Michael & Adler's work is not so accessible, except in their excellent series of articles op. cit., Levin's mimeographed materials are to be found in a number of law libraries in the US.

seriously is a daunting prospect. Jerome Frank's position on this is quite clear: The elusiveness and complexity of the world of facts is a central part of the lawyer's world. One can either duck or confront reality. Frank is a confronter *par excellence*, his recipe the American equivalent of the stiff upper lip, a Freudian notion of maturity.[53] The completely adult jurist acknowledges the difficulties and gets on with the job. In this view the main objection to the orthodox tradition of evidence scholarship is that it evades the difficult problems. It is a tradition of relatively complacent common sense empiricism that concentrates on the most formal and most public part of judicial processes and has devoted far more attention to the rules of admissibility than to questions about the collection, processing, presentation, and weighing of information that reaches the decision makers. The rationality of the process is by and large assumed; the elusiveness of reality is barely acknowledged. There is again a good precedent in jesting Pilate. What is truth? asked the evidence scholars, and would not stay for an answer.

Let me restate my response to the four main arguments against a modest version of the Frank thesis. To the claim 'we do it already', my reply is that this is only partly true and that rarely is fact finding as such directly studied in a systematic, comprehensive, and rigorous manner. To the 'too soft' or 'unnecessary' argument, my reply is that this is also partly true, but that there are important aspects of EPF for which almost identical claims can be made as for those aspects of traditional legal education, which are considered to be both practically important and intellectually demanding. To the 'unethical' argument, my reply is much the same: the problem is not peculiar to fact studies. To the 'too hard' argument, my response is that insofar as these are arguments about feasibility they are unconvincing; insofar as they are objections on grounds of intellectual difficulty they are despicable; and insofar as they are objections on grounds of absence of a suitable literature they are incorrect. The strongest response to 'it can't be done' is to point out that it has been done—often rather well. Insofar as the argument is one about priorities—for example, that there is not time to fit this extra material in—I merely wish to suggest that the claims of EPF should be considered on the merits. It is not self-evident that the study of the rules of evidence deserves a higher priority than the principles of proof or that appellate cases are *ipso facto* better pedagogical material than trial records.

While there is some force in the objections so far considered, I do not accept them as satisfactory justifications for the *status quo*. Nor on their own do they provide a plausible explanation for the relative failure of responses to the repeated pleas for righting the imbalance. Nor do I think that academic conservatism and inertia, no doubt potent factors, provide the missing link. Without claiming to be exhaustive, I wish to consider briefly two further related contributory factors: the gravitational pull of the rule-centered tradition of academic

---

[53] See especially Jerome N. Frank, *Law and the Modern Mind* (New York, 1930).

law and the failure of its critics to construct a *coherent* theoretical alternative in respect of EPF.

One interpretation of the American Realist Movement, of which Frank is generally regarded as a leading member, is that it represented a rather diverse and loosely co-ordinated series of reactions against rule-dominated notions of academic law, exemplified by Langdellism in the United States and the expository orthodoxy in the United Kingdom. According to this view the Realists were reacting against an orthodoxy, but their grounds for criticizing or rejecting that orthodoxy were diverse. On the positive side they shared one single idea, which can be expressed as a truism: there is more to the study of law than the study of rules. It is a caricature of almost all Realists to attribute to them the view that rules are a myth or are merely predictions or are unimportant, just as it is a caricature of many expositors to suggest that they seriously deny the central truism that united Realists. The reasons for the dissatisfaction of the Realists with the orthodoxy were diverse in crucial respects—one basic concern was practitioner oriented: how to narrow the gap between academic law and the day-to-day realities of legal practice? Another was scientistic: how to develop an empirical, research-oriented science of law quite far removed from the day-to-day concerns of practitioners? Some Realists were concerned to criticize existing legal institutions, rules, and practices with a view to reform. Failure to perceive this diversity of concerns obscured the crucial point that a corresponding diversity of alternative solutions or programmes was indicated. Constructing a more enlightened system of vocational training is a very different enterprise from developing an empirical science of law or a basis for a reformist or radical critique of the legal order.[54]

Part of the toughness of the expository orthodoxy was that it had a strong internal coherence; law is a system of rules and the study of law involves the exposition, the analysis, and occasionally the evaluation of those rules. The raw material for this study is primary sources of law; the central questions were disputed questions of law. Concessions could be, and were, made to demands to raise wider issues, to include non-legal materials and so on, but it was clear that these belonged to the periphery rather than the centre. In respect of the core curriculum the starting-point and the main subject of study were rules. It was accordingly natural that the study of evidence was equated with reasoning about questions of law. The toughness of the tradition was due in large part to its coherence.

When such Realists as Holmes, Frank, and Llewellyn opened Pandora's box they seemed to be letting loose an almost limitless number of possible avenues of enquiry. If the study of rules alone is not enough, what is enough? The danger was that nothing was to be excluded, everything was relevant. In order to cope, this problem had to be confronted and new coherences had to be developed.

---

[54] See generally, *KLRM*.

Unfortunately some of the leaders, such as Holmes and Frank, were stronger on diagnosis than they were on prescription—neither of them ever worked out the full implications of their position in terms of coherent programmes for legal education, legal research, or law reform.[55] Karl Llewellyn, it has been suggested, retreated in his later years to the relatively safe ground of the Uniform Commercial Code and the study of appellate courts. Scientists such as Cook and Moore underestimated the magnitude and difficulty of the tasks they had set themselves. There were some notable particular achievements, but they were fragmented and diverse. No new core or cores were established.

One reason for this failure was a failure of theory. For one major function of theorizing is to provide coherence—to map connections and to develop a systematic, internally consistent overview. But, by and large, the Realists failed to do this. They pursued some of the particular hares (and other creatures) that they had let loose when they lifted the lid, but they failed to marshall these diverse creatures into any sort of order.

In respect of this kind of organizing theory, evidence has been better served than most. Bentham's theory of evidence purports to integrate the logic, psychology, and philosophy of evidence and makes the case for having no binding exclusionary rules. Moreover, Bentham's theory of evidence is subsumed under a theory of adjudication which in turn has its place within the Constitutional Code as part of his general theory of law.[56] Wigmore's theory of proof, although more narrowly focused, integrates the study of the logic and psychology of proof and forensic science with evidence doctrine. Both belong to a tradition of rather optimistic rationalism about legal process, are unduly court-minded, and, as one would expect, are outdated in a number of ways. Nevertheless the legacy of Bentham and Wigmore (and of other theorists) provides an impressive foundation from which to start to develop a systematic mapping theory of EPF as part of a broadened conception of academic law. Such a theory may help to provide the coherence that is needed if alternatives to the rule-dominated tradition are to have much staying power. Such a theory needs to be conceived, in first instance, independently of its educational implications—for over-concern with the day-to-day realities and constraints of academic life can have a distorting effect on theory construction. But some of the basic foundations exist for the development of a coherent theory of EPF within the framework of a broad approach to academic law.[57] When such a theory is developed, then it may be that Jerome Frank's vision—in its saner aspects—will be realized in practice.

[55] On Holmes, see William Twining, 'The Bad Man Revisited', 58 *Cornell L Rev.* 275. Frank's prescriptions are to be found in *Courts on Trial*, op. cit., Ch. 16, and at 422–3; and 'A Plea for Lawyer-Schools', 56 *Yale LJ* 1303 (1947).

[56] See especially Elie Halévy, *The Growth of Philosophic Radicalism*, (ed., Beacon, London, 1955), 373 ff.; and Gerald J. Postema, 'The Principle of Utility and the Theory of Procedure: Bentham's Theory of Adjudication', 11 *Ga. L Rev.* 1393 (1977).

[57] Cf. Kalven, op. cit., on the odd and mistaken view 'that the only test of relevance of research in the law school world is whether you can teach it'.

6

Evidence and Legal Theory*

One way of looking at jurisprudence is as the theoretical part of law as a discipline. In this sense, it is synonymous with legal theory, but it is broader than legal philosophy. One's view of the nature and role of legal theory depends upon one's view of the discipline of law. In this context general definitions are not very helpful. Just as law as a social institution shades off and overlaps with other social phenomena in extraordinarily complex ways, so law as a subject cannot and should not have rigid boundaries that segregate it from other disciplines. For certain purposes, in some contexts, lines have to be drawn; but as often as not precise definitions and sharp boundaries do more harm than good. In relation to other disciplines, the study of law is a complex, varied, and amorphous part of a general intellectual enterprise, the direct end of which is the advancement of knowledge and understanding. As a practical matter there has to be a rough division of intellectual labour; there need to be specialized institutions, and individual specialists. But when these artificial boundaries become institutionalized or rigidified, the theorist has a much more important role to play in subverting divisions and building intellectual bridges than in settling lines of demarcation.

Academic law can also be seen as the intellectual and scholarly branch of law-related activities in the real world—whether it is related to the concerns of professional lawyers or of other specialized participants in legal and law-related social processes; or to the unspecialized and enormously diverse concerns of non-specialists who become involved in such processes. Here again specialization has its uses; one does not expect, for example, many judges or solicitors or policemen or plaintiffs to be academic experts in jurisprudence or indeed in

* This is an abbreviated version of an inaugural lecture, delivered at University College, London on 2 June 1983 and published in (1984) 47 *MLR* 261. The intention is to restate and develop in general terms a number of themes that have been explored at greater length in a series of writings over 12 years. The view of legal theory and its place in the discipline of law is advanced in (1) 'Some Jobs for Jurisprudence' (1974) *Brit. J Law and Society* 149 and (2) 'Academic Law and Legal Philosophy: The Significance of Herbert Hart' 95 *Law Quarterly Rev.* 557 (1979) and (3) 'The Great Juristic Bazaar' (1978) *J Society of Public Teachers of Law* (*NS*) 185. A programmatic statement of the need for rethinking the field of evidence is set out in (4) 'Good-bye to Lewis Eliot' (1980) *J Society of Public Teachers of Law* (*NS*) 9; for ease of reference these works will be cited hereafter in the following form: op. cit., n. *, no. 3. The lecture also drew on a number of papers which were subsequently collected in *Rethinking Evidence* (Oxford, 1990; Chicago and London, 1994) (*RE*). The approach to evidence was developed in two further books, *Theories of Evidence: Bentham and Wigmore* (London and Stanford, 1985) (*TEBW*) and *Analysis of Evidence* (with Terence Anderson, Boston and London, 1991) (*ANALYSIS*).

most fields of law. But one function of legal theorizing is to break down institutional barriers, habits of action, or ways of thought that divide off the academic from the applied, theory from practice, the law in books from the law in action.

Law is a fascinating, complex, important, and pervasive phenomenon in society. Professional legal practice is a quite varied and influential form of specialized activity which is by no means coextensive with the law in action. The discipline of law is also wide-ranging, varied, amorphous, and important. It is potentially enormously interesting, even if in practice it is sometimes made unforgivably boring.

If one looks at law as a discipline in these terms, it is hardly surprising that its relationship both with other disciplines and with the world of affairs is perennially problematic. Such problems are close to the core of the concerns of many legal theorists—whether they proceed by agonized introspection, overconfident assertion (usually reading one part as the whole), eye-catching polemics, grand theorizing or patient reflection about quite small questions. The primary task of the jurist is to study the assumptions underlying legal discourse; many of those assumptions lie at key points of contact between the world of learning and the worlds of practical affairs.

This kind of perspective on law as a discipline may seem almost banal, yet it has many implications and ramifications. Here let me just pick out a few quite simple points for brief comment. First, on this view, the notion of an autonomous discipline or a pure science has, at most, a very limited place. Understanding law is dependent on understanding much else besides. If there are general aspects of legal discourse or action that are characteristic or unique, they are a relatively small part of the enormously complex phenomena, practices, and ideas that make up the subject of law. For example, many legal skills such as interpreting rules or determining facts or negotiating or justifying decisions in legal processes involve practical reasoning and basic human skills that are of enormously wide application. Everyone interprets rules; everyone weighs evidence; everyone is involved in negotiations; everyone applies rules to facts. Lawyers and jurists sometimes speak as if they are the only people who do such things. To concentrate on the characteristic or the peculiar or the unique—to treat such elements as 'the core' in a strong sense—involves not only leaving out much that is equally important to understanding; it also involves risks of distortion— as is clearly illustrated by approaches to evidence that concentrate on the artificial rules. If the direct end of any discipline is understanding, isolating the peculiarly legal or treating law as a subject apart is very often inimical to that end. In this view, the study of law is dependent on other disciplines; such notions as a pure science of law or law as an autonomous discipline are dangerous, even if in a very few narrow contexts they might be defensible.

Because of its intimate connections with the world of affairs—with legal practice and the law in action in a broad sense—nearly all legal discourse is strongly participant-oriented. This is true, even in its theoretical aspects. Its main audiences are actual or intending participants with concerns related directly or indirectly to their own activities. These participants are very varied and so are their concerns. Legislators, judges, barristers, solicitors, bailiffs, caterers, prostitutes, bureaucrats, bandits, tenants, pressure groups, and revolutionaries are all producers and consumers of legal discourse. The activities and products of academic law as an enterprise—teaching, research, writing, and theorizing—are inevitably influenced by these varied concerns. The response is often *ad hoc* and unsystematic—witness the biases and imbalances in legal literature. But the gravitational pull is persistent and strong. This is a fact of considerable significance in interpreting our received heritage of legal theorizing. For many of our leading jurists have treated one kind of participant as their primary audience or target: for example, Bentham addresses his model legislator; Holmes's bad man is an ordinary office lawyer thinly disguised; much of Karl Llewellyn's work and Ronald Dworkin's universe have appellate court judges as their main focus; much critical legal theory is primarily directed at dissentient insiders and outsiders.

This view of law is pluralistic in a descriptive sense. Here pluralism is not some indecisive form of evasion or fence-sitting; it is quite compatible with strong commitment to particular values, positions, postures or strategies. Rather it is an acknowledgement of the variety and richness of our subject, the multiplicity of perspectives and levels at which it can be approached, and the limited capacity of any of us to obtain more than an occasional glimpse of the whole.

So much for law as a discipline. Jurisprudence can be viewed as the theoretical aspect of that discipline—that is, it is concerned with general questions about and assumptions underlying all kinds of legal discourse, including both law talk and talk about law. One way of looking at legal theorizing is as an activity directed to a variety of tasks all of which are directly concerned with understanding. These tasks occur at various levels and require different kinds of knowledge, skills, and aptitudes. They can be characterized in various ways and the list could be quite long. For present purposes—with particular reference to problems of theorizing about evidence—a brief restatement of the tasks might go as follows:

1. Intellectual history, that is the systematic study and criticism of the heritage of legal thought and critical study of the work of individual thinkers.
2. High theory, that is to say the exploration of fundamental general questions related to the subject-matter of law as a discipline, such as questions about the nature and functions of law, the relations between law and justice, or the epistemological foundations of different kinds of legal discourse. This is the particular sphere of legal philosophy.
3. Middle-order theorizing, prescriptive as well as descriptive; in particular:
   (*a*) the development of general hypotheses about legal or law-related phenomena capable of being tested by empirical methods; and

(*b*) the development of prescriptive working theories for various kinds of participants in legal processes, such as prescriptive theories of legislation, adjudication, and legal reasoning.

4. The conduit function, that is to say the systematic exploration at a general level of the relationship between law and at least the more general aspects of all other disciplines relevant to law. This is approximately equivalent to Julius Stone's view of jurisprudence as 'the lawyer's extraversion'.[1]

5. The integrative or synthesizing function, that is to say, the task of exploring and articulating frames of reference which provide a *coherent* basis for law as a discipline, for legal discourse generally, and for particular parts of it.[2]

The list is incomplete and there are many overlaps. But this formulation helps to bring out a number of points that are worth stressing in the present context.

First, legal theory in this broad sense encompasses a great diversity of questions. These questions arise from quite different concerns at different levels in varied contexts; appropriate responses to such questions are correspondingly diverse. Confusion of levels and conflation of questions foster the kind of artificial polemics to which jurisprudence is particularly prone. This way of mapping legal theory is, I think, more helpful and far less misleading than classifications in terms of 'schools' and 'isms' and 'ists'.

Secondly, this kind of map is a safeguard against the error of treating one part as if it were the whole. The most common version of this error today is the tendency to treat legal philosophy as coextensive with legal theory. It is unduly narrow, and impoverishes the discipline of law, to equate jurisprudence with legal philosophy or to treat philosophical questions as being the only, or the primary, worthwhile concern of every serious jurist. Questions which one kind of philosopher or another would treat as philosophical questions occupy a special place in legal theorizing. These are questions about the most general and, in a loose sense, the most fundamental assumptions of legal discourse. Such questions stand at the centre of legal theory; they also represent a critical point where boundaries between disciplines break down. For questions about justice or the nature of law or rights or reasonings, for example, are shared by philosophers, political theorists, social scientists, and jurists on an almost equal footing. However, there are many general questions about law which also deserve to be treated as theoretical questions, but which are not peculiarly or exclusively philosophical. Prescriptive working theories for participants (for example a theory of appellate advocacy or judging); middle-order theories about legal phenomena (for example, a cross-cultural theory of litigation or dispute settlement); or a theoretical framework for a particular field of law or an area of legal discourse (such as a theory of contract or of criminal law) are examples of theorizing and

---

[1] Julius Stone, *Legal System and Lawyers' Reasonings* (1964) 16.
[2] See further, op. cit., n. *, no. 3.

theories which belong to jurisprudence, but fall outside, or at least go beyond legal philosophy—though they all, of course, have philosophical dimensions.

This view is not anti-philosophical. But it does strongly suggest that over concentration on legal philosophy—on the more abstract problems of legal theory—may lead to the neglect of some other functions of legal theorizing, such as the construction and criticism of middle-order theories, of working theories for participants, and the devising of mapping theories, that is coherent frames of reference for law-as-a-discipline and for particular sectors thereof.

The theory of evidence provides a concrete illustration of this general view of law-as-a-discipline, and of the role of theorizing within it. It highlights one kind of theorizing which is particularly important at a time when established conceptions of academic law are being challenged and attempts are being made to construct or develop coherent alternatives. The emphasis will be on the integrative function—that is on mapping connections between different lines of enquiry and constructing coherent frames of reference; but the other main tasks of legal theorizing are also involved. Evidence scholarship has a rich, but extraordinarily homogeneous, intellectual heritage; there are numerous and rather complex connections with other disciplines, notably logic, epistemology, historiography, psychology, forensic science, and forensic medicine. Much of our stock of existing theories takes the form of advice to particular participants, notably triers of fact, trial lawyers, detectives, and, of course, Bentham's legislator. Some fundamental philosophical questions, not conventionally seen as having jurisprudential relevance, are central. And, I shall suggest, a theory of evidence and proof needs to be set in the context of—indeed it almost necessarily presupposes —a middle-order theory of litigation and like processes.

What follows then is a brief sketch of what might be involved in attempting to develop a coherent approach to the study of evidence and related matters within a conception of law as a discipline that is much broader than the orthodox rule-dominated, expository tradition of academic law. It is a case-study of one way of trying to broaden the study of law from within in respect of a particular field or topic.

THE PROBLEM STATED

In the orthodox view, evidence is the means of proving or disproving facts, or of testing the truth of allegations of fact, in situations in which the triers of fact have no firsthand knowledge of the events or situations about which they have to decide what happened. Typically, decisions on disputed questions of fact are decisions to be taken in situations of uncertainty. In a broader view, that I shall develop later, 'evidence' is *information* from which further information is derived or inferred in a variety of contexts for a variety of purposes. Most legal discourse about the subject of evidence is centred on the rules of evidence. The leading textbooks and treatises expound the rules and explore their rationales; public debate has tended to concentrate on the reform or conservation or codification of the rules—although there have been some significant moves away from this narrow perspective in recent years.[3] Most specialized writing about evidence by lawyers for lawyers reveals the same rather narrow range of questions and concerns. Nearly all courses on evidence are devoted almost exclusively to the rules; they are based almost entirely on appellate cases, statutes, and secondary writings based on these sources. The most important arena in which problems of evidence and proof arise in practice is in the contested trial, but records and reports of trials are hardly ever looked at in courses on evidence—let alone made the object of systematic study. Yet the cases of Alger Hiss or Sacco and Vanzetti or Roger Tichborne or Alfred Dreyfus are potentially rich materials for law study, as important and as susceptible to disciplined analysis as HADLEY V. BAXENDALE or DONOGHUE V. STEVENSON or D V. NSPCC.[4] There is relatively little empirical research on the operation and impact of the rules. In short, the predominant conception of the field of evidence, by judges and practitioners as well as by scholars, teachers, and students, is a rather clear case of the dominance of the expository or black-letter tradition. The subject of evidence is typically treated as being coextensive with the law of evidence.

This is strange for a number of reasons. First, the scope and practical importance of the rules of evidence have generally declined over the years. If Bentham had had his way there would have been no rules of evidence to study, but the subject would surely have remained an important part of the study of law. Secondly, the dominant academic view, of the law of evidence is that it is but a series of not very coherent exceptions to a general presumption of freedom of proof—that is an absence of formal rules. A variant of this view, often attributed to Thayer, was recently expressed by Professor Heydon as follows:

The rules of evidence state what matters may be considered in proving facts and what weight they have. They are largely ununified and scattered, existing for disparate and sometimes conflicting reasons: they are a mixture of astonishing judicial achievements and sterile, inconvenient disasters. There is a law of contract, and perhaps to some extent a law of tort, but only a group of laws of evidence.[5]

Thirdly, there are quite well-established enclaves of study of problems of proof and proving in forensic contexts that have not been assimilated into the study of evidence within the discipline of law. The whole field of forensic science, psychological studies of eyewitness identification, and the recent debate about probabilities are obvious examples. They are well-established lines of enquiry that have no settled place within the study of law. They float fragmented in a

---

[3] e.g., Report of the *Royal Commission on Criminal Process* (1981; Cmnd. 8092).
[4] See ANALYSIS, *passim*.
[5] J. D. Heydon, *Cases and Materials on Evidence* (London, 2nd edn.; 1984) 3.

void, detached from any larger subject and from each other, randomly colliding or sailing past each other like meteorites.

Fourthly, there is a remarkable series of abortive attempts from Bentham through Wigmore to the present day to produce general theories of evidence that integrate the logical and the other aspects into a coherent whole. Almost without exception, they have failed to become established as standard ways of approaching the subject. There is a legacy of broad theories, but they have been largely forgotten.[6]

Fifthly, even within the expository tradition, it has been recognized as very dangerous to isolate evidence from procedure and from substantive law. Yet evidence scholarship has done just that—quite systematically. The motives for this separation have quite often been worthy—to search for underlying principles, for example, or to simplify and to codify the rules of evidence. The result has been an extreme form of isolation that has left much evidence discourse largely unaffected by intellectual developments elsewhere.

This critique of the predominant mode of evidence discourse provides a basis for a preliminary statement of the problem of rethinking the field: if current treatments tend to be narrow, fragmented, artificially isolated from contiguous fields, unempirical, and, above all, incoherent, then an adequate alternative needs to be comprehensive, coherent, realistic, empirical, contextual, and sufficiently well integrated that the relations between different lines of enquiry are clearly mapped. This suggests that there is a need for a broad synthesizing or mapping theory that meets these standards.

INTELLECTUAL HISTORY

This general formulation of the problem will do as a start; but it requires refinement through more detailed probing. One way of doing this is through intellectual history—one of the standard tasks of the theorist.

There are, of course, many ways of approaching and justifying intellectual history. In the enterprise of rethinking a field, at least three perspectives are particularly helpful. One can look at past writings as a resource—as a treasury of particular questions, answers, concepts, arguments, errors, and so on. By reviewing the heritage of past work in the field as a whole, one can form some judgement of its strengths and weaknesses, spot imbalances and distortions, false trails and non-questions, as well as acceptable answers and other achievements. One can, in short, take stock and map out the current state of our collective knowledge, ignorance, and disagreements. Communing with one's predecessors—at least those who seem worthy of attention—is also one of the

---

[6] *RE*, Chs. 2 and 3.

most fruitful ways of clarifying one's own views. Criticism is, *inter alia*, a mode of self-definition. Such communion is also a powerful antidote to hubris—not least in the field of evidence, which is peopled by giants: Bentham, James and John Mill, Fitzjames Stephen, Thayer, Wigmore, and a host of substantial figures who might have been treated as stars in a less rich tradition.

The stock of literature about or relevant to judicial evidence is vast. It includes not only the primary and secondary specialized legal literature of many jurisdictions, but also a wealth of spasmodically interacting writings from other disciplines. A full-scale intellectual history of this heritage would have to deal with classical, medieval, and modern rhetoric; with the emergence of probability; with developments in psychology, forensic science, and forensic medicine. These are all central. One also needs to identify possible parallels and connections with such fields as decision theory, information science, historiography, and the sociology of knowledge.

Here I shall confine my remarks to something much narrower; specialized literature on judicial evidence in the Anglo-American tradition. This includes a mass of cases scattered throughout the law reports; an equally bulky and almost totally neglected accumulation of trial records and secondary accounts of such proceedings—a potentially rich source both for studying the law of evidence in action and of raw material for exercises in analysing mixed masses of evidence; in England, an unruly jungle of statutory bits and pieces; in other common law jurisdictions, a series of interesting attempts at codification—from the Indian Evidence Act 1872; various American codes, of which the most important is the Federal Rules of Evidence; and, looking to the future, a draft Canadian Code of Evidence that the late Sir Rupert Cross praised as being the best of the lot.[7] These statutory fragments and codes have almost all been preceded by public debates which have at least two notable characteristics: one is their repetitiveness—for example, the points of disagreement and arguments advanced in recent debates in England about the Criminal Law Revision Committee Report of 1972 and the Police and Criminal Evidence Act 1984 have many familiar echoes in the pages of *The Edinburgh Review* and other journals as far back as the 1820s.[8] A second characteristic has been that apart from a few hiccups, the trend has been almost entirely in the direction of the reduction of the scope and importance of the exclusionary rules—a stumbling trek in the direction indicated by Bentham, who favoured their total elimination. The trend is clear; whether it represents the march of progress towards rationality is much more debatable. In this instance, it is typically conservative proponents of law and order who claim to have reason on their side.

The secondary literature on evidence—despite its extent—represents only a tiny portion of this vast heritage. My own researches have been largely confined to this sector, which is more than enough for one individual. It is extraordinarily

---

[7] R. Cross, *Evidence* (5th edn., London, 1979).   [8] See further, *TEBW*.

rich and has attracted some of the best legal minds, of whom Bentham, Wigmore, and Thayer are the outstanding figures.[9]

All five functions of legal theorizing are amply represented in the specialized secondary literature on evidence. Bentham, Wigmore, and others addressed directly fundamental philosophical problems of epistemology and logic. Bentham and Wigmore again tried to provide broad synthesizing theories which, *inter alia*, indicated important points of connection with other disciplines. Wigmore's *The Science of Judicial Proof* represents the most systematic attempt to integrate the logical, psychological, and scientific dimensions of proof within a single conceptual framework.[10] This was sufficiently flexible to accommodate at least some specific advances in those subjects over a period of some forty years. The central concern of both writers was to advance largely middle-order working theories for participants—but different participants. Bentham's *Rationale* is consistently addressed to the legislator and, only indirectly through him, to the trier of fact. Wigmore's *Science* purports to adopt the standpoint of the trial attorney in court. The historical development of the law of evidence and of writings about it was treated at length by Thayer, Wigmore, and Holdsworth. Rather surprisingly, not much detailed history of this kind has been done since.[11]

The weakest part of this heritage is on the empirical side: there is very little sustained work either at the level of empirical middle-order theorizing or in respect of detailed factual research. I shall return to this later. The relevant point here is that most of the functions of theorizing have been attended to in the past in respect of evidence, but almost no work of significance was done in the fifty years before the late 1970s. Thus it is not true that we have no tradition of theorizing about evidence; rather it is the case that this tradition has been almost entirely forgotten, at least until recently. Few evidence scholars have drawn on Bentham's *Rationale* or Wigmore's *The Science of Judicial Proof* or the heritage of classical and modern rhetoric. Thus *Cross on Evidence,* the most influential contemporary English work in the field, contains only one citation of a theorist (Gulson), the most casual of references to Bentham, and no references to Wigmore's *Science* or even to his general theory of proof.

The most striking feature of this received tradition of evidence scholarship is how homogeneous it is. Nearly all of the Anglo-American writers from Gilbert to Cross have shared essentially the same basic assumptions about the nature and ends of adjudication and about what is involved in proving facts in this context.[12] There is undoubtedly a dominant underlying theory of evidence in

---

[9] For a historical overview, see *RE*, Ch. 3.

[10] J. H. Wigmore, *Principles of Judicial Proof* (1913, 1931); the third edition was entitled *The Science of Judicial Proof* (1937), but this change was of no intellectual significance.

[11] For references to historical writings on evidence since Wigmore, see Wigmore 1, *Treatise* (Tillers rev., 1983) § 8.

[12] *RE*, Ch. 3. The most notable exception is the Scottish writer James Glassford, whose *An essay on the Principles of Evidence and their Application to Subjects of Judicial Inquiry* (Edinburgh, 1820) adopted a holistic rather than an 'atomistic' approach to the evaluation of evidence. Glassford's

adjudication, in which the central notions are truth, reason, and justice under the law. It can be restated simply in some such terms as these: the primary end of adjudication is rectitude of decision, that is the correct application of rules of substantive law to facts that have been proved to an agreed standard of truth or probability. The pursuit of truth in adjudication must at times give way to other values and purposes, such as the preservation of state security or of family confidences; disagreements may arise as to what priority to give to rectitude of decision as a social value and to the nature and scope of certain competing values—for example, whether it makes sense to talk of procedural rights or to recognize a privilege against self-incrimination. But the end of the enterprise is clear: the establishment of truth.

There is also a broad consensus about means. Proving is seen as essentially a rational process, involving the weighing of the probative force of evidence relevant to specific allegations of fact. The primary difficulties involved are seen as practical rather than theoretical: it may be difficult to find or manufacture evidence; it may be difficult to get it before the trier of fact; it may be difficult to assess its reliability or to know how to decide when the evidence is incomplete or unreliable—hence the elaborate apparatus of burdens, presumptions, and standards of proof which are essentially rules for or aids to decision in situations of uncertainty. But, by and large, the underlying assumptions as to what is involved are treated as if they are unproblematic. There is a world of fact independent of our beliefs about it; experience is the basis of belief; making inferences from evidence and reasoning about disputed questions of fact involve a straightforward application of ordinary common sense or practical reasoning; this in turn assumes a shared stock of knowledge in society—a sort of cognitive consensus—and a general ability on the part of most adult members of society to make rational judgements about issues of fact on the basis of their general experience—what Jonathan Cohen calls a general cognitive competence.[13]

In short, nearly all Anglo-American writers seem by and large to have adopted, either explicitly or by implication, a particular ontology, epistemology, and theory of logic. All of these are closely identified with a particular philosophical tradition, that is English empiricism, as exemplified by Locke, Bentham, and John Stuart Mill. Evidence scholarship and theorizing have been characterized by a series of long-running debates and disagreements—for example, about the scope and justifications of exclusionary rules of evidence. These have almost invariably taken place within a framework of shared philosophical assumptions or by the almost systematic ducking or begging of difficult philosophical questions.[14]

work is discussed by M. A. Abu Hareira 'A Holistic Approach to the Analysis and Examination of Evidence in Anglo-American Judicial Trials', (1984), unpublished doctoral thesis, University of Warwick.

[13] L. Jonathan Cohen, 'Freedom of Proof' in *Facts in Law* (ed. W. Twining, Wiesbaden, 1983) 1, 6 ff. Cohen also uses the terms 'cognitive capacity' and 'cognitive ability' in this context.

[14] *RE*, Ch. 3.

Thus most disagreements have not been seen as stemming from philosophical differences, except perhaps in relation to defenders and opponents of utilitarianism. The dominant tradition of evidence discourse has largely taken for granted a set of assumptions that bear the hallmark of the eighteenth-century enlightenment, what may be termed optimistic rationalism: one seeks the truth by observation and reason and if one seeks long enough the truth will out most of the time.

Thus a stocktaking of our heritage of specialized scholarship and theorizing about evidence suggests the following: a clear and straightforward theory of proof integrated with a rather simplistic normative truth theory of adjudication. A collection of relatively sophisticated concepts and distinctions in respect of such matters as rationality, relevance, standards of proof, and presumptions. A broad consensus among specialists that any deviation from a presumption in favour of freedom of proof requires justification; a lack of consensus about what constitute good justifications, with the result that there is a rich, but confusing body of literature on the rationales and practical utility of those particular deviations that make up the surviving laws of evidence in a given jurisdiction.

The great bulk of this heritage of specialized evidence scholarship has been normative rather than empirical. We have little systematic knowledge about the psychological processes of weighing evidence, about the actual operation and impact of the rules of evidence, about the probative value of most kinds of evidence in respect of particular kinds of probanda, or about how information is actually processed and used at different stages of litigation and like processes. Moreover, much of this specialized tradition is uncontextual—the tendency has been to concentrate on events in the courtroom in contested jury trials, rather than on what happens to information at every stage in a great variety of different processes and arenas. The Rationalist Tradition is simplistic; much of specialized evidence discourse postulates one law of evidence, one type of process, one kind of enquiry, and a single purpose or end to litigation. There is, moreover, no sustained concern to explore the implications of adopting more sceptical postures or a different conception of rationality.

Obviously, these sweeping generalizations are subject to exceptions and caveats. Here I want to develop the last point briefly: the essentially unsceptical nature of the Rationalist Tradition of evidence scholarship seems to contrast rather sharply with the tone of much contemporary writing on judicial processes.[15] This other body of literature is much more varied than the literature on evidence. It includes attempts to develop some middle-order empirical theories of dispute-settlement or litigation (for example Black, Abel, Griffiths);[16] it includes

---

[15] Id.

[16] See esp. J. Griffiths and D. Black (edd.), *Toward a General Theory of Social Control* (Orlando, 1984) and R. Abel, 'A Comparative Theory of Dispute Institutions in Society' 8 *Law and Society Rev.* 217 (1973); cf. Griffiths, 'The general theory of litigation—a first step' (1983) 5 *Zeitschrift für Rechtssoziologie*, Heft 2.5.145.

normative design theories of adjudication (for example Bentham); participant working theories (such as Llewellyn's Grand Style of Judging or Fuller's theory of rational adjudication);[17] and a vast agglomeration of contributions, written from a variety of perspectives, at different levels of generality by people from a wide range of disciplines. There is a strain of scepticism that runs through much of the literature that is strikingly absent from writings on evidence. Rabelais's Judge Bridlegoose throws dice to decide cases (a precedent followed in 1983 by Judge Alan Friess in New York);[18] trials are referred to as forensic lotteries or degradation ceremonies or licensed battles or conveyor belts. Some of the main survivals of the law of evidence, such as technical safeguards for the accused, have been attacked from the right as sacred cows[19] and from the left as harmful or useless obfuscating devices.[20]

This is not the place to examine these different kinds of scepticism in all their rich variety. What is striking is the extent to which we have two contrasting intellectual traditions that have developed largely in isolation from each other, although they deal with extensively overlapping subject-matter. The one is homogeneous, isolated, normative, and optimistically rationalistic. The other is diverse and interdisciplinary; some of it is based on empirical research and much of the writing is sceptical, at least in tone. The aspirational rationalism of the evidence scholars is rooted in assumptions that belong to the eighteenth-century enlightenment; the more sceptical or realistic writers on judicial processes seem to be more the heirs of late-nineteenth-century and early-twentieth-century thought—of Croce, Collingwood, Freud, Mannheim, Marx, and Weber.[21] Yet the potential incompatibilities between the two traditions may not be quite as fundamental as might at first sight appear; the rationalism of evidence writers is modified by some important caveats: for example, the pursuit of truth in adjudication is often subordinated to other values; their concern is with approximations to truth, with standards of proof expressed in terms of probabilities, rather than certainties; and the kind of reasoning involved is the 'soft logic' of open-system reasoning with regular acknowledgement that deductive reasoning and strict mathematical reasoning have limited scope in practice. Similarly, few, if any, of the iconoclastic writers about judicial processes prove, on examination, to be genuine philosophical sceptics; many explicitly deny that they are 'extreme relativists'; in criticizing particular institutions the same writers often invoke the very standards of aspirational rationalism; and few, except in moments of rhetorical exaggeration, deny that truth, reason, and justice are core concepts in any plausible prescriptive theory of adjudication.

[17] K. N. Llewellyn, *The Common Law Tradition: Deciding Appeals* (Boston, 1960); L. Fuller, *The Principles of Social Order* (ed. K. Winston, Durham, NC, 1981) 86 ff.; R. Summers *Lon. L Fuller* (Stanford and London, 1984). [18] *New York Law Journal* 17 Apr. 1983.

[19] e.g., Cross, 'The Right to Silence and the Presumption of Innocence—Sacred Cows or Safeguards of Liberty?' 11 *J Society of Public Teachers of Law* (NS) 66 (1970).

[20] e.g., D. McBarnet, *Conviction* (London, 1981).

[21] See generally H. Stuart Hughes, *Consciousness and Society* (London, 1959).

The Rationalist Tradition of evidence scholarship has also been very largely isolated from other relevant but diverse fields, such as forensic medicine, forensic psychology, probability theory, epistemology, and decision theory. In each case, the extent of interaction and the nature of the relationship is rather different. For example, psychologists working on eyewitness identification have tended to accept rather uncritically some of the unsceptical assumptions of the Rationalist Tradition, even though the general tendency of much psychological work in this area is sceptical of the reliability of eyewitness testimony.[22]

PHILOSOPHICAL DIMENSIONS

A theory of evidence has to confront a number of questions that are clearly philosophical and so belong to a philosophy of law in a narrow or strict sense. As Bentham saw more clearly than most, questions about proving the truth of allegations about past facts are directly related to fundamental issues of ontology and epistemology. Is there a world of fact independent of our beliefs about it? Are warranted judgements about the truth of allegations of fact about objects and events in the real world possible in principle? What is the basis for such judgements? Professor Postema has recently shown that there is an intimate historical and analytical connection between Bentham's theory of fictions and his theory of evidence.[23] Bentham's ideas on evidence are founded on his epistemology and ontology; and his work on evidence may well have stimulated some of his later thoughts on logic and fictions. Closely related to these concerns is the persistent tradition of scepticism and relativism in philosophy; but as I have already indicated, just as few legal theorists are either fully fledged or solely specialist philosophers, similarly few legal sceptics are genuine philosophical sceptics.

A significant recent development has been a resurgence of interest in philosophical problems of probabilities and proof. This has been stimulated by Jonathan Cohen's work in the logic of induction and the series of lively controversies that this has provoked.[24]

These examples by no means exhaust the connections between philosophy and the theory of forensic evidence. A striking feature of these particular examples is that the points of contact are with areas of philosophy that are not commonly perceived as being central to jurisprudence. In recent years the most sustained connections between jurisprudence and philosophy have related to ethical, political, and conceptual problems and to the nature of reasoning about disputed questions of law. The theory of evidence is also concerned with practical

[22] *RE*, Ch. 5.
[23] G. Postema, 'Facts, Fictions and Law: Bentham on the Foundations of Evidence' in *Facts in Law*, op. cit., 37.
[24] Esp. L. Jonathan Cohen, *The Probable and the Provable* (Oxford, 1977).

reasoning—mainly about disputed questions of fact; its links with probability theory, epistemology, historiography, and the philosophy of science are relatively unfamiliar to lawyers.[25] Thus the resurgence of interest in this area involves extending the range of questions that may properly be regarded as central to the philosophical sector of jurisprudence. It is particularly welcome that there is a growing recognition that it really does not make much sense to confine the study of 'legal reasoning' or 'lawyers' reasonings' to disputed questions of law —another example of the narrowing influence of the expository tradition. Out of this may develop a much broader and richer perspective on questions about the nature of practical reasoning in legal discourse. Justifying, arguing towards and appraising decisions on questions of fact, questions of sentencing, assessment of damages, parole, and many other important decisions in legal processes involve a complex mixture of philosophical issues about the nature of practical reasoning and of other kinds of questions about the nature of legal processes; these in turn raise interesting and relatively neglected questions about the interrelationship between forms and styles of reasoning and different kinds of practical decisions. For example, to what extent do modes of reasoning accepted to be appropriate to questions of law, questions of fact, and questions of sentencing exhibit the same logical structure? To what extent do contextual factors generate different criteria of relevance and of appropriateness?—and so on.

MIDDLE-ORDER THEORY

If the appropriateness of modes of reasoning about questions of fact or other important reasonings in legal processes is to a greater or lesser extent dependent on the contexts of the decisions involved, we need to try to understand something about these contexts. Here I should make an admission. When I started on my work on the theory of evidence I defined the topic as 'theoretical aspects of evidence and proof in adjudication'. The reference to 'adjudication' signalled that I was mainly concerned with decisions on disputed questions of fact by adjudicators, that is judges, juries, and other third-party triers of fact. I realized, although not clearly enough, that there must be an intimate relationship between a theory of legal evidence and a theory of adjudication—that adjudicative decisions on questions of fact take place in the context of what are commonly referred to as adjudicative or judicial processes and that the notion of these processes is problematic. As my work progressed, this organizing category came to seem less and less satisfactory. The reasons for this are too complex to retail here, but one can put the matter in simplified form as follows:[26] terms like 'adjudicative process' and 'judicial process' are misleading insofar as they distract

---

[25] This is less true of continental Europe where there is considerable interest in questions of epistemology and the philosophy of science.   [26] See further *RE*, Ch. 11.

attention from the truism that adjudicative decisions are always preceded and succeeded by a series of other decisions—such as decisions to prosecute or to sue; not to settle; to plead not guilty; to appeal; and so on. It is an accepted part of the study of so-called judicial processes that adjudicative decisions cannot be understood in a vacuum. They need to be seen as one stage, which is usually not reached in practice, in a complex form of social process that we know as legal process or litigation. The interaction between adjudicative decisions and events that precede and succeed them is so complex and so intimate that it is perilous to study them in isolation. Strictly speaking it is misleading to speak of adjudicative or judicial *processes*, as if these are something other than *stages* in some longer process. Similarly the same bit of information may start as a clue (or lead) in the process of detection, be transmuted, possibly transformed, into potential evidence (for example in the form of a deposition or a written confession), and play a role in a whole variety of decisions, before it is presented—perhaps in a new form, if at all—directly to the trier of fact as evidence. The same bit of information may subsequently have a role to play at later stages, for example, in sentencing and parole; again it may appear in different forms at these stages.[27] A theory of evidence, in this view, needs to give an account of how information is or may be processed and used at all the important stages in the process, and not just at the adjudicative stage. In short, a contextual approach pushes one to substitute for evidence and proof in adjudication as an organizing concept, something like the processing and use of information in litigation.[28] The prospect of thus broadening the scope of the enquiry is rather daunting; but it may be the best way of avoiding some of the distortions, omissions, and artificialities of the more traditional modes of discourse.

One can elaborate this point briefly by returning to Bentham. One of the strengths of his theory of evidence, as with so much of his jurisprudence, is that it is closely integrated with many other aspects of his thought, and the connections are pretty clearly indicated. Thus his theory of evidence is part of his general theory of adjective law (including procedure and judicial organization) which in turn fits into the framework of the constitutional code. This in turn is but one part of his 'pannomion'—or complete body of laws—which in turn is founded on utility. Within his theory of evidence the interconnections between procedure, substantive law, and the logical, psychological, epistemological, and scientific aspects of proof are all fairly clearly sketched. Their place in his grand design is also clearly mapped. Bentham's theory of adjective law is *par excellence* an example of a design theory, that is to say it is an integrated body of recommendations addressed to the ideal legislator for the design of a body of institutions, procedures, and laws in accordance with utility. His *Rationale of*

[27] The question how far information and evidence can be appropriately individuated into 'bits' and how far it is safe to talk of 'the same bit' at different stages in a process are issues that need further exploration.
[28] On the use of 'litigation' as an organizing category see Griffiths, op. cit. and *RE* 353–6.

Judicial Evidence has, with some justification, been called his masterpiece.[29] It is remarkable that it has been almost forgotten in this century. It still repays careful study. But, for my purposes, it has proved to be seriously deficient. Setting aside particular points where it is outdated or Bentham's judgements were idiosyncratic or distorted by his passions, one can single out three main limitations. First, it involves a direct and all-too-consistent application of the principle of utility in a way which reveals both the intellectual power and the unacceptable consequences of unmodified utilitarianism. He is dismissive of the presumption of innocence and other safeguards, he places too much faith in publicity as the main safeguard against the abuse of power, and he is even prepared to condone a limited use of institutionalized torture.[30] While his analysis reveals very clearly the intellectual weaknesses of some of the arguments that have traditionally been advanced by civil libertarians and his lack of concern for the protection of the innocent, his dismissal of central ideas of due process as mere sentimentality cannot, I think, be explained away merely as miscalculations that can be adjusted within utilitarianism. My personal attitude is one of respectful ambivalence and, on some issues, Bentham seems to me to be best regarded as a worthy enemy.

Secondly, Bentham's theory is, in essence, very simple. The direct end of procedure is the correct application of substantive law to true facts in accordance with utility, subject to preponderant vexation, expense, and delay. The truth of allegations of fact is to be tested by ordinary methods of common-sense reasoning within a framework of free proof. The simplicity and coherence of the theory give it enormous clarity and persuasive force—but it is too simple. Even in his day, I think that it was unrealistic to try to postulate a set of institutions designed simply to serve a single direct end. His model of the Natural System of Procedure, despite its attractions, smacks more of Rousseau than Bentham.

In any society and especially in modern industrial society, institutionalized litigation has to cope with a variety of types of problems, involving in respect of evidence, proof of many different kinds of fact by a multiplicity of means. For example, I do not think that straightforward implementation of law and enforcement of rights are the only desired or desirable outcomes of litigation. Compromise, termination of conflict, redistribution of goods, focusing of public attention, political or legal change, and many other ends for which litigation is in fact used are sometimes justifiable ends and need to be accommodated in institutional design.[31] At best, Bentham's theory is one possible ideal type for certain kinds of standard cases.

---

[29] Mary Mack, *Jeremy Bentham: An Odyssey of Ideas* (London, 1962) 3. See generally, *TEBW*, Ch. 2.

[30] See further W. and P. Twining, 'Bentham on Torture' in *Bentham and Legal Theory* (ed. M. Jomes, Belfast, 1973) 39;' W. Twining, 'Why Bentham?' (1984) 8 *The Bentham Newsletter* 34.

[31] In *Scotch Reform* Bentham said: 'Another mode of termination is by what is called a *compromise: which*, being interpreted, is denial *of justice*.' 5 *Works* 35 (ed. Bowring) discussed *TEBW* 94–5. The nature of litigation has, of course, changed radically since Bentham's day: e.g., trials have

Thirdly, Bentham's theory is solely an aspirational, prescriptive—in some aspects Utopian—theory.[32] It is part of a tradition that has made almost no attempt to advance knowledge and understanding of the actual operation and effects of legal processes empirically. Even an adequate design needs to be based not only on a clear normative theory, but also on a realistic and differentiated appreciation of how things work in practice and of what is feasible. A middle-order empirical theory of litigation, and of the processing and uses of information within it, may contribute not only to better designs, but also to a better understanding of social processes and phenomena, including law. The study of evidence needs to be empiricized and here Bentham's work is of only limited value. In this respect we are likely to obtain more help from elsewhere.

PARTICIPANT WORKING THEORIES

Bentham's prescriptions were addressed to the legislator and through him to the judge in the form of instructions about the weighing of evidence. Some of his advice is also relevant to others; but there are clearer examples of participant working theories. The most prominent of these is Wigmore's *Science of Judicial Proof*, which is directly relevant to the trial lawyer in court and almost equally valuable for him in preparing for trial and for all who are involved at the stages of investigation or in the processes of collecting, recording, and manufacturing evidence.[33] Wigmore provides a framework for accommodating the findings of forensic science and psychology as they bear on assessing the probative force of various kinds of evidence in respect of different probanda—ranging from the probative force of fingerprints in proving identity to what the 'science' of his day had to tell us about the influence of gender, race, and age on the veracity of witnesses—almost nothing. This aspect of his work seems to the modern reader to be both old-fashioned and naïve, but his application of some simple methods of logic to the analysis and organization of complex, mixed masses of evidence is of lasting value and deserves to be better known. In my own teaching, I have been getting students to undertake detailed analysis of complex trial records using a modified version of Wigmore's method; Professors Anderson and Ewald of the University of Miami have been using the same scheme for injecting an element of analytical rigour into teaching the elements of trial court practice and Professor David Schum, a psychologist, has used Wigmore's theory

become much longer and more complex than in 1800; much more emphasis is put on documentary evidence; techniques of preserving evidence and the rules of discovery have changed beyond recognition; various kinds of discretions of adjudicators have been much enlarged. Bentham would have approved of some, but not all, of these developments. But his simple model of the adjective law as being directed solely to the efficient enforcement of substantive law does not fit the varied purposes, functions, and types of modern litigation in its broadest sense.

[32] See however, H. L. A. Hart, *Essays on Bentham* (Oxford, 1983) 37 n.
[33] Op. cit., n. 11, discussed *TEBW*, Ch. 3.

as the basis for some impressive theoretical and empirical work about how triers of fact actually reason from evidence in simulated trials.[34]

Nearly ninety years ago Oliver Wendell Holmes said: 'For the rational study of the law the black-letter man may be the man of the present, but the man of the future is the man of statistics and the master of economics'.[35] It is only relatively recently that this theme has been taken up by Sir Richard Eggleston and a number of others, who have emphasized how a basic grasp of elementary mathematics and statistics is an essential part of the equipment of the practitioner in handling evidentiary matters even in contexts in which formal statistical analysis cannot be openly or directly applied.[36] The trial lawyer may be able to pick up without formal training some of the general lessons that psychologists have to teach or what he needs to know about forensic science and medicine; but ability to analyse and evaluate evidence is as important and fundamental a part of the intellectual discipline of law as ability to analyse and argue about rules.[37]

So far I have reported to you a few, highly selective impressions and conclusions arising from some research into the history of specialized writings on evidence. The main conclusions that emerge from this part is that there is a vast range of different kinds of questions that are worth asking in respect of evidence; that our stock of answers to these questions is fragmented and uneven; and that perhaps the first need is for a broad coherent framework that would map the relations between a range of different lines of enquiry that seem to converge and interact in complex ways in the context of the study of what Bentham called 'judicial evidence'. In short, what is needed is a synthesizing or mapping theory. One possible perspective, to which I am personally attracted, is to look at questions about evidence and proof as questions about the processing and uses of information in the context of the total process of litigation, broadly conceived. This, I think, would at least provide the prospect of mapping and co-ordinating different approaches and specialized lines of enquiry in a way that would meet at least some of the criticisms of the underlying theory of the Rationalist Tradition, while preserving such notions as truth, reason, and justice as core concepts. Many standard topics would look quite different from that perspective. To take but one example, the problem of eyewitness identification. In the orthodox

[34] See especially David Schum and Anne Martin, 'Formal and Empirical Research on Cascaded Inference' 17 *Law and Society Rev.* 105 (1982) and references there. In my view, the work of Schum and his associates represents one of the most significant contributions both to the theory of evidence and to empirical research in the field in recent years. David Schum has subsequently developed his ideas in three substantial works: *Evidence and Inference for The Intelligence Analyst*, 2 vols. (Lanham, Md., 1987); *Evidential Foundations of Probabilistic Reasoning* (New York and Chichester, 1994); and (with Joseph B. Kadane) *The Sacco and Vanzetti Evidence: A Probabilistic Analysis* (New York and Chichester, 1996). Further important work on fact investigation with Peter Tillers is in progress, see P. Tillers and D. Schum, 'A theory of preliminary fact investigation', 24 *UC Davis Law Rev.* 931 (1991).   [35] 'The Path of the Law' 10 *Harvard Law Rev.* 457, 469 (1897).
[36] R. Eggleston, *Evidence, Proof and Probability* (2nd edn., London, 1983); David W. Barnes, *Statistics as Proof* (Boston, 1983).   [37] See Ch. 5 above.

view, as exemplified by the Devlin Report and notorious cases such as George Davis, Luke Dougherty, and Oscar Slater, the problem of misidentification is perceived as a problem of *unreliable evidence in* contested jury trials. The perceived evil is that there is a risk of wrongful conviction and imprisonment of a few persons accused of serious crime—perhaps six to a dozen a year in England. If, however, one adopts a total process model of litigation, one is concerned with the processing and uses of information at every stage in criminal and other proceedings. From this perspective the problem of misidentification has to be redefined quite radically. Identification statements are seen not merely as *evidence* presented to a jury, but as *information* that performs a variety of functions in a series of *decisions*: decisions to investigate, to arrest, to interrogate, to hold an identification parade, to confess or to plead guilty—to mention the most obvious criminal examples. In criminal proceedings, the *mischiefs* of misidentification are all of the substantial harms suffered by victims (i.e., objects of false identification statements). They extend beyond wrongful conviction to include all the vexations and expenses of being subjected to legal proceedings —the financial, psychological, and other evils of being suspected, harassed, interrogated, arrested, threatened with prosecution, cautioned, or even tried and acquitted. The category of victims of misidentification statements is correspondingly enlarged. Vandals, demonstrators, football supporters, and juveniles are likely to outnumber the alleged murderers, professional thieves, and robbers who have occupied centre stage in the traditional debates. Problems of misidentification are seen to arise in other proceedings and arenas; and the nature of the problem, as well as its scale, looks rather different.[38]

All of this has implications for research as well as reform. For example, most psychologists have by and large accepted rather uncritically the orthodox definition of the problem—as concerning unreliable evidence in contested jury trials. As a result they have concentrated on a rather narrow range of issues and, in particular, on that ungainly device, the identification parade—often with a distorted view of its importance and its actual functions in practice: they tend to see it solely as an evidence-manufacturing device, overlooking the fact that it may serve to eliminate suspects, to lead to closing a case for lack of evidence or to securing the co-operation of a suspect by persuading him that the game is up.[39]

The example of misidentification suggests that a mapping theory can do more than merely provide a coherent framework for charting relations between traditional questions and established lines of enquiry; it may also identify new or neglected questions or suggest that old ones were misposed. And this may lead both to different lines of enquiry and to new perceptions of connections with established enclaves of knowledge that had not previously been seen to be relevant. However, suggesting that a different perspective may provide a more

[38] *RE*, Ch. 5.   [39] Ibid.

coherent and suggestive framework for approaching a field such as evidence falls far short of advancing a general theory of evidence. A mapping theory charts relations between lines of enquiry and raises questions; a general theory purports to provide answers to such questions.

Here I wish to sound a note of caution. In an epiphanic moment in my adolescence my father, quite matter of factly, asked me: 'What are flowers for?'; he hardly paused for an answer. If I were asked today, 'What is a theory of evidence for?', it would be tempting to make some grand utilitarian claims: to organize a mass of divergent material; to guide practice; to generate hypotheses; to restructure courses; to devise new institutions; to reorient or update public debate; to provide a rationale for conservation, reform or radical action. A fully worked-out theory of evidence might modestly or immodestly contribute to all these ends. But I am reminded of a famous introductory lecture at University College by A. E. Housman in 1892, in which he effectively mocked short-sighted and mundane justifications of science as missing the point. He concluded that 'the true aim of science is something other than utility. . . . Men who have risen, if you call it rising, from barge boys to millionaires have not risen by their knowledge of science.'[40]

I am much of Housman's mind. I would also carry his scepticism a little further. Jurisprudence is often presented—especially to students—as a bewilder-ing and diverse collection of refined products called 'theories' as if it were a sort of motley exhibition of mud pies or sandcastles—of alleged 'schools' and 'isms'—which they are invited to peruse, evaluate, admire or destroy. Of the many fallacies involved in this mud-pie image of theorizing two need to be laughed out of court: the first is the fallacy of treating all theories of or about law as comparables and rivals—indeed to treat them as more or less solid things like mud pies. The second is to assume that the only positive outcome of theorizing is the manufacture of theories. The activity of theorizing is much more varied than that. Some jurists do produce collections of answers that are tangible enough to be praised for their elegance or their explanatory power or to be used for target practice. But that is only one of many ways of advancing understanding.

It is tempting to move from a critique of past theories to a bold clarion call proclaiming the need for a new theory. My remarks on evidence could be inter-preted as a call for a Brand New Theory of Evidence for the Modern Age. But this is also too neat and too simple. In sketching one possible way of developing a different perspective on evidence and information in litigation, I have been suggesting that legal theorists have a constructive role to play in building bridges, sculpting syntheses or hatching theories. The study of evidence also reminds us that all such structures are built on shifting sands. We may have to wait many years for a new theory of evidence to emerge, probably as the work of many minds; if it does, however useful or illuminating it may be, it will not be difficult

---

[40] A. E. Housman, 'Introductory Lecture', University College, 1892 (1933 reprint) 8.

to show up the flimsiness of its foundations, whatever its particular form and content. Meanwhile, there is one further job for the jurist to undertake in his daily work—to examine critically the underlying assumptions of all legal discourse and to question established ways of thought, especially those that are becoming entrenched. One task of the theorist is to pick away at all assumptions, including his own. Whether he adopts the role of court jester or the Innocent in *Boris Godunov* or the child in the story of the Emperor's clothes or any other form of hired subversive—his first job is to ask questions and, with the greatest respect to the greatest of our gurus, to let the consequences take care of themselves.

7

Theory in the Law Curriculum*
(with Neil MacCormick)

To be sure, there are lawyers, judges and even law professors who tell us
that they have no legal philosophy. In law, as in other things, we shall find
that the only difference between a person 'without a philosophy' and someone with a philosophy is that the latter knows what his philosophy is.

Filmer Northrop[1]

Once upon a time the School of Law in Xanadu celebrated its fifth anniversary
by holding a curriculum discussion. Having decided not to take facts seriously,[2]
they had salved their consciences with a compulsory final year course in jurisprudence, while making most other courses optional. On this occasion, uncertain
where to start, they decided to open the proceedings by debating whether jurisprudence should remain compulsory. Opinion was divided almost equally, as
appears from the following passage from the debate:

Why should intending lawyers be coerced into studying philosophy?
Do we really want our graduates to leave us unreflective, uncritical, and unaware?
Students should have complete freedom of choice.
Students are not the best judges of what is good for them.
What relevance has Kelsen to drafting a conveyance?
Can someone who has not done Kelsen claim to be a member of a learned profession?
How embarrassing for learned counsel or a learned judge to have to ask: 'Who is Ronald
Dworkin?'
Legal theory is too hard for undergraduates.
Jurisprudence is a soft option, too vague and woolly to compete with hard law.
Our aim should be to train our students to think like lawyers, not philosophers.
How can anyone learn to think like a lawyer without studying legal reasoning?
There is no need for a specialized course in jurisprudence; we teach theory in every
course already.
There is no need for a specialized course in jurisprudence; law is a practical art.
Jurisprudence is the most practical course in the whole curriculum.

---

* This essay was originally published in *Legal Theory and Common Law* (*LTCL*). This was a
collection of essays in most of which British law teachers explored the relationship between 'theory'
and particular fields of law.
[1] F. Northrop, *The Complexity of Legal and Ethical Experience* (Boston, 1959), at 6.
[2] On the first curriculum discussion in Xanadu, see Ch. 5, above.

Eventually the Oldest Member spoke up: 'All of your arguments are fallacious. It is important that we should not do the right deed for the wrong reason. Therefore let us consult some experts.' His colleagues disliked his premise, but liked his conclusion. So they decided to invite two teachers of jurisprudence of seemingly divergent views to justify their way of life. To the surprise of all, including the authors, they produced an almost unanimous report, from which the following extracts are taken:

INTRODUCTION

The question put to us was: 'Should we continue to have a compulsory course on jurisprudence in our curriculum?' We suggest that it is appropriate to restate the issue as follows: 'What learning objectives might be served by making the direct study of legal theory an integral part of an undergraduate degree pro-gramme in law?' There are two different kinds of reasons for this reformulation. First, the issue is posed in general terms, because any specific decisions on a particular curriculum inevitably involve local factors such as the interests (vested and intellectual), expertise, personalities, and prejudices of the existing faculty and the educational background, attitudes, and predominant motives of its stu-dents. Specific decisions about whether, when, how much, and how legal theory should be directly studied have to be made in a particular context. Our task is to intellectualize the issue; it is for the locals to contextualize it.

Secondly, this kind of educational question deserves to be framed with a reasonable degree of precision. Our formulation is preferred for the following reasons: an educational question of this kind is better expressed in terms of learning objectives rather than courses and teaching; similarly 'programme' is preferred to 'curriculum' because the latter too often tends to be conceived largely in terms of coverage of particular subject-matters by teachers rather than in terms of a programme of study directed to a range of learning objectives. 'Direct study' is contrasted with incidental or pervasive or pick-it-up approaches in which the objectives or subject-matters in question are not the primary focus of attention: for example, when 'legal method' is left to be picked up or mas-tered while studying courses on torts or contracts or revenue law. Our phrasing also leaves open for consideration the question whether the relevant learning objectives should be pursued mainly or exclusively in a single course.

The phrase 'integral part' is less emotive than 'compulsory'. Both of us fa-vour educational programmes that give wide scope to students to choose to pursue a range of objectives by diverse means in respect of a variety of subject-matters; but we also believe that, in first degrees in law, such choices are usually best made within a coherent structure with sufficient common ground as to objectives, subject-matter, and methods to allow for integration of different parts of the programme, for sequencing of study, and for a reasonably coherent and balanced educational experience for each student. A law school, especially one that seeks to develop a distinctive educational ethos, should aspire to be more like a restaurant than a cafeteria.

Thus as educators we tend to favour structured choice. In order to present a coherent argument about the educational values of studying legal theory we also have to make some further general assumptions about undergraduate legal education in this country as an educational enterprise, but at a more general level than that of a particular law school or programme. The issue cannot be totally decontextualized. However, before considering possible rationales for theory courses here, we propose to explore in general terms the nature of legal theory and some general claims that are sometimes made for theoretical studies.

THEORY WHAT?

Invite a dozen specialists in particular areas of law to discuss the relationship between legal theory and their area of expertise and they are likely to interpret the task in a number of different ways. This is rather clearly illustrated by the essays in *Legal Theory and Common Law*. Some contributors have treated it as an invitation to explore critically assumptions underlying orthodox or traditional modes of discourse in the relevant field; Veljanovski conceives the task of theory as giving a general empirical explanation of particular phenomena (in this case judicial decisions); Twining emphasizes the value of constructing coherent frames of reference; Simpson explores the relationship between the common law and a selection from the existing stock of theories of law; Cotterrell asks what kind of theory can provide a means of identifying and interpreting legal doctrine in the property field and general contemporary problems underlying analysis of such doctrine. Stokes attempts to show that a great deal of company law 'can be understood as a response to the problem of the legitimacy of corporate managerial power'.[3] Collins critically examines the claim that 'liberalism' provides a coherent basis for the law of contract. O'Donovan casts doubt on all attempts to explain family law solely in instrumental terms.

This diversity is perhaps not as great as it seems. All the contributors to this symposium have been selective; but they have all interpreted the invitation to look at their subject in general terms; some have explored underlying assumptions; some have related specialized discourses, such as contract or property talk, to standard bodies of inherited theory; they have chosen somewhat varied levels of generality, although all have been concerned with what Austin called 'particular Jurisprudence'.[4] But, we suggest, these seemingly different views of theory and theorizing are all intimately related.

---

[3] *LTCL*, at 155.
[4] J. Austin, 'The Uses of the Study of Jurisprudence' in *The Province of Jurisprudence Determined* (ed. H. L. A. Hart, London, 1954), at 366.

Let us briefly consider four different perspectives on legal theorizing and legal theory. First, theorizing can be viewed as an activity directed to reflecting on, reasoning about, and trying to answer general questions about laws, legal practices, legal institutions, and processes and about the nature of law as a social phenomenon and as a subject of study.[5] Secondly, theorizing can be a matter of articulating, refining, and critically examining important underlying assumptions and presuppositions of legal discourse. Thirdly, there is a received heritage or tradition of ideas about and approaches to the first two sets of topics, and theorizing involves critical appraisal, selection, and exploitation of these ideas and approaches independently of their historical provenance. But, fourthly, the propounding and development of these ideas and approaches has a history of its own. Legal theory can be perceived as a vast body of literature, a heritage of texts and texts about texts, emanating from individuals and groups of thinkers who lived and worked and debated in particular contexts. Accordingly, theorizing may involve reading, interpreting, and criticizing at least some of those texts in their historical settings. All of these perspectives are intimately related, but each merits special consideration.

Theorizing as Abstraction

Talk of theory is sometimes associated with mystery or pretentiousness. One can avoid this by looking on theorizing as nothing more than the business of asking and tackling general or abstract questions. Typically such questions have somehow or other come to be matters of interest or concern at a more or less particular or concrete level. Theorizing involves trying to get a better understanding of particulars by seeing them in a more abstract and general way. In this, the movement of our thought is nearly always towards the establishment of links or connections of things such that we in some measure see the reasons of things

---

[5] To look on theorizing as an activity enables us to locate examples of that activity in specific historical contexts; for actual people theorize in particular times and places. From the perspective of what might be called the ethnography of knowledge it is possible to make meaningful statements about the nature and state of this kind of activity, and trends relating to it, in a given legal culture. Twining was adopting this kind of perspective when he suggested that one way of looking at legal theorizing is as an activity directed to a variety of tasks within the discipline of law, itself an intellectual enterprise involving a variety of activities: 'Evidence and Legal Theory', Ch. 6 above. In a paper on 'Property and Legal Theory' (*LTCL*, Ch. 5), Roger Cotterrell suggests that Twining contradicts himself by asserting that there is a distinct discipline of law, but giving only a very limited place to the notion of 'law as an autonomous discipline'. To view legal research, legal education, and legal theorizing as activities that are carried out in the context of a distinctive legal culture ('the culture' of law schools in England, e.g., is markedly different from the culture of medical schools or history departments) involves no commitment to any particular view on the autonomy of disciplines. Ethnographic statements about intellectual cultures belong to a different sphere of discourse from epistemological claims about the 'autonomy' of particular kinds of knowledge. It is not possible to pursue this complex issue here, but it seems that Twining and Cotterrell differ rather than disagree on this matter, as they have adopted different perspectives in pursuit of rather different concerns.

or the reasons for things. Sometimes the connections found are causal, sometimes statistical or probabilistic. Sometimes they are conceptual, and sometimes
they are normative, evaluative or justificatory. So our theorizing may lead us
towards causal or probabilistic generalizations, or to analytical understandings
or to critical or justificatory accounts of things. As many as are the illuminating
kinds of general connections we can make between things-in-particular, so many
are the kinds of theorizing there are.

Not all theorizing involves constructing or proposing full-blown theories, in
the sense of a relatively articulated, coherent, and complete set of answers to one
or more general questions.[6] Indeed, it would not be a sign of a discipline being
in good health if everybody theoretically interested in it were always proposing
their own new theoretical account of it. Much theoretical work goes forward
within or in the shadow of some already proposed theory. One's focus may be
on *improving* or refining an ongoing theory, whether in general or for some
particular range of topics, as Mill tried to do for Bentham's principle of utility,
or many of his followers have done for Marx and, more recently, MacCormick
has attempted to do for Hart.[7] Or one may be applying a theory with a view to
explaining, accounting for or justifying some position, as Richard Posner purports to do for much of the common law; or one can use a theory as the basis
of a *critique* of some received understanding in a field, as several contributors
to *Legal Theory and Common Law* have set out to do. Or one's application of
a theory to a topic may have the special purpose of testing the theory, or testing
a whole range of theories sharing some common hypothesis. An excellent example of this is Brian Simpson's essay 'Common Law and Legal Theory',
which tests against a historical view of the common law the theoretical proposition that legal systems are 'systems of rules'.[8] The thesis that one cannot
account for the common law in those terms deals a devastating blow to any
theory of law which depends on that proposition. Such a theory will have to be
refined or abandoned—or Simpson's evidence reconsidered—in order to defend
a 'rules' theory of law.

Among the most general and abstract questions that we can pursue in our
theorizing are included a range of questions which Neil MacCormick has recently suggested to be foundational for any philosophical approach to law.[9] The
suggested list ran to six:

1. He begins with ontological questions, questions about what there is, in the
   sense of demanding an account of the kinds of things that there are and
   that go to making up our world—questions which at a fairly concrete level
   keep cropping up, as Roger Cotterrell's essay shows, in a law of property.

[6] *LTCL*, at 78.   [7] D. N. MacCormick, *H. L. A. Hart* (London and Stanford, 1981).
[8] *LTCL*, Ch. 2.
[9] MacCormick, 'The Democratic Intellect and the Law', Presidential Address, Society of Public
Teachers of Law, 5 *Legal Studies* 172 (1985).

We can make a 'law of things' intelligible only through some reflections on the quality of 'a thing'.

2. Then there are questions of structure—how do different modes and levels of existence interrelate? How, for example, do we connect together law and legal relations with economic relations, socio-political power with ideology? The problem of these interrelationships in various ways pre-occupies many of the contributors to *Legal Theory and Common Law*. They are by no means in agreement as to the answers—but none doubts the importance of trying to address the question with critical reference to other possible answers.

3. There are also epistemological questions, questions about how we know and about how knowledge is possible as to some or any subject-matter. Local and particular variants crop up in William Twining's discussion of evidence and proof, i.e., of the lawyer's modes of apprehending 'facts' and also in Richard Tur's invocation of the Kelsenian approach to an epistemo-logy of law.

4. Closely related are methodological questions, here perhaps best represented by David Miers's reflections on methods of interpretation of statutory materials and David Sugarman's critique of traditional approaches to legal exposition.

5. Then there are questions about the relationships of humans as rational agents to each other and to whatever else there is, and for present purposes this encompasses all the sociological aspects and elements of theoretical studies of law.

6. Finally there are the questions of how people ought to live and conduct themselves; here belong all aspects of practical reason and critical or jus-tificatory theory, such as one finds, for example, in Katherine O'Donovan's discussion of the part which law can and should (not) play in domestic and familial relations or Ronald Dworkin's accounts of what constitute valid and cogent legal arguments.

The conception of 'legal philosophy' which this range of questions defines is plainly a broad one, and (as indicated) one which does not exclude the pursuit of enquiries at a quite low level of abstraction as well as at the high level represented by the 'six questions' in their more general statement. Such a con-ception of philosophical theorizing about law is thus probably safe from Twin-ing's caveat against equating all legal theory with philosophy and thus opening up a gap between the middle-range theorizing of some jurists and 'high' or 'grand' theory.[10] Whether or not that is so, it remains quite obvious that, even

---

[10] In the past we, the two authors, have expressed somewhat different opinions about the relation-ship between legal philosophy and jurisprudence and we are still inclined to express our conclusions differently. But what divides us is more a difference of terminology and expression that a disagree-ment of substance. William Twining treats 'jurisprudence' and 'legal theory' as synonymous; he has

given so broad and generous a conception of the sphere of the philosophical, there would remain areas of theoretical enquiry about law which lie beyond its scope, for example, the kind of positive economic theorizing discussed by Veljanovski. The activity of theorizing as a search for general and abstract explanations or connections includes philosophical activity at its most fundamental level, but goes beyond it too. It is primarily an activity, not an end-product; though when it goes well it may yield more or less satisfying and relatively comprehensive theory or theories.

Presuppositions and Assumptions

A particular kind of theoretical investigation is that which tries to dig out and expose underlying presuppositions and assumptions of taken-for-granted ways of explaining things and deeming them intelligible. Here, as it were, there is implicit theory in the way we account for things. But not until it is articulated and made explicit are we able to check it and criticize it. All exposition and explanation presupposes some explanatory framework, some abstract connectedness of things which makes particular connections meaningful. In this sense all expository or explanatory or justificatory discourse has theoretical assumptions which are usually, but not always, implicit. Thus, underlying any expository textbook, however modest its intellectual pretensions, lurks a series of assumptions, which may be more or less coherent and consistent, about the nature of

suggested that jurisprudence is much wider than legal philosophy and that the term 'philosophy' should in this context be confined to the most general or abstract questions of legal theory (High Theory). Behind this point lie several interrelated concerns: first, that there has been a tendency to treat jurisprudence and legal philosophy as coextensive, with the result that many other theoretical questions have tended to be neglected; secondly, that if there is to be a continuing and fruitful interaction between the general and the particular in legal discourse, it is important to explore and to make explicit the relations between different levels of generality. A third concern is that there is a tendency to treat all legal theories as rival answers to the same questions and to interpret and criticize all jurists at the level of philosophy. By no means all questions in legal theory are in first instance philosophical questions and not all jurists are philosophers. Finally, there has been a tendency in English analytical philosophy to emphasize analysis and to be suspicious of grand synthesizing theories or even of more modest attempts to construct coherent frames of reference. Yet one of the primary jobs of jurisprudence is to perform this synthesizing function for law as a whole and for particular branches, fields or topics. Whether this activity is considered 'philosophical' is a secondary matter.

Neil MacCormick, on the other hand, following the broad usages of the enlightenment writers of the 18th c., is more disposed to use the term 'philosophy' to include any abstract or general thought or talk about law. This usage serves to make the point that professionals and specialists in departments of philosophy have no monopoly rights in the concept of 'philosophy'. More important, it sets up no artificial barriers between the multiple levels of generality at which nearly all theorizing takes place. In this view, the absence of discontinuity between different levels of theorizing could justify treating the whole range of theoretical work as 'philosophical' in the broad sense of the term. But this broad sense is one in which lawyers are as fully entitled to have 'philosophies' as any others; indeed, according the Northrop, all who engage in legal discourse are committed to having 'legal philosophies' in this sense.

the enterprise of legal exposition and methods appropriate to it.[11] Similarly any
argument about a disputed question of law by a barrister or a judge or a legal
commentator involves assumptions about what constitute valid and cogent justifications in the kind of context in which the argument is advanced. More
generally, assumptions and presuppositions involving MacCormick's six questions abound in all our thought and talk about law and other things. We all
have—perhaps have to have—implicit assumptions about what there is, about
how we know and how we should explain, and on what basis we recommend
or criticize or make evaluations. The six questions represent an attempt to flesh
out the idea, adopted from Northrop, that all lawyers have some philosophy, but
only some have developed awareness of what that philosophy is.[12] Only in
making ontological, epistemological, methodological, and evaluative assumptions explicit can we begin to check, refine, and test them, by 'theorizing' them,
rather than assuming them unreflectively. Analytical work can often have this
character, as when we try to explain or elucidate the implicit ideas about possession or ownership which lie behind, for example, parts of the law of property;
or when we try to work out the values which must be presupposed in order to
make justificatory sense of contract or company law.

Exploiting the Inheritance

All that has been said so far might conjure up a picture of us going forward with
theorizing and with digging out theoretical assumptions as though we had to do
so completely from scratch. But of course this is not the case. It is not a theoretical vacuum but an embarrassment of theoretical riches that we actually face
in the field of law. Others have been at the explanatory, justificatory, and analytical tasks long before us, and a broad sweep of ideas about and approaches
to the understandings, analysis, and justification (or critique) of law exists, often
at the most ambitious and comprehensive levels of generalization. As foolish as
reinventing the wheel generation by generation would it be to ignore this inheritance of ideas and approaches. Our theorizing is not to be tackled *ab initio*, but
standing on the shoulders of our predecessors, as likely as not working within
some particular intellectual and ideological tradition. There one is not merely
advancing one's own explanations and justifications and testing one's own assumptions. Just as likely one is testing and repruning or rejecting some body of
theoretical ideas or some leading idea which is already given in the voluminous
literature of jurisprudence. For example, many contributions to jurisprudence
have centred around the idea of law as in some way or sense a system of rules
of a relatively coherent and ordered kind. Again, as Brian Simpson's 'Common
Law and Legal Theory' shows, even so cherished an idea is challengeable.[13]

[11] See *LTCL*, at 26–7, 48–54 (Sugarman), and Twining, 'Treatises and Textbooks' 12 *JSPTL (NS)*
267 (1973).
[12] Op. cit., n. 1.   [13] *LTCL*, Ch. 2.

Tested against the common law, it seems inadequate to explain it historically or at the present. Faced with the anomaly, what becomes of this idea? Do we abandon it, or do we refine it and adjust it, perhaps in some wider theoretical framework, in order to develop a more coherent and intelligible account of the common law? Or do we challenge the evidence on methodological or other grounds so as to reject the claim that common law is more muddle than system, hence perhaps saving the idea of law as a system of rules? A latter-day Benthamite, a Kelsenian, a disciple of Llewellyn or Dworkin, or an economic analyst could all be expected to adopt different strategies in tackling these questions. Each would be drawing on part of the existing stock of ideas and approaches that are already available to us in tackling almost any theoretical question.

Dialogues With Past Thinkers

Ideas, theories, methods, arguments, even questions are human constructs, stimulated, articulated, promulgated, disseminated, debated, revised, refined, and distorted by actual people in particular situations. To describe the heritage of legal theory as a body of literature, as a collection of texts, is no more than a convenient simplification. Our subject conspicuously lacks any counterpart to the encyclopaedic guides that exist for English literature or music or political thought. Jurisprudence has no Grove or Kobbe or even a Quentin Skinner or a Margaret Drabble. If such a work were to exist its subject-matter would resemble not so much the tip of an iceberg, as a motley collection of flotsam and treasures fished out of a turbulent and murky ocean of discourse and debate.

Why should undergraduates devote time to studying the works of leading thinkers? A jurist may be significant because of his place in intellectual history, because he originated, developed or promulgated ideas that became widely adopted or otherwise important, or a jurist may be thought to have been more or less directly influential on historical events—as historians debate how far certain nineteenth-century reforms are attributable to the 'influence' of Jeremy Bentham. Or a jurist's work may be worth reading because it addresses in a worthwhile way issues that are of contemporary significance. Both of us welcome recent developments in the history of ideas[14] and are emphatic that juristic texts should be read in context.[15] But, in our view, the main intellectual value of studying juristic texts is as an aid to addressing important contemporary issues in legal theory. Any worthwhile text raises and attempts to answer one or more questions. Studying a text involves a form of dialogue between the author and the reader about such questions. Thus it is the study of issues-via-texts, not intellectual history or the study of texts for their own sake, that provides the main educational justification for paying attention to our intellectual heritage.

[14] e.g., Q. Skinner, *The Foundations of Modern Political Thought* (Cambridge, 1978); S. Collini, D. Winch, and J. Burrow, *The Noble Science of Politics* (Cambridge, 1983).
[15] This theme is developed in TAR and RB.

Because we are fortunate to live in a period of great liveliness in jurisprudence a remarkably high proportion of the texts that are currently studied are by modern authors, many of whom are still alive and battling. Reading jurisprudence need not be a form of ritual obeisance to dead ancestors.

LEGAL THEORY—WHY?

Three general types of justification are commonly advanced for compulsory courses on legal theory or jurisprudence. Firstly, such courses are sometimes claimed to have a symbolic function. In its crudest version this is little more than a cynical kind of window-dressing: a law degree needs to be seen to include one or two 'cultural' subjects in order to be accepted as belonging in a university. To argue thus is no more respectable nor more plausible than maintaining that lawyers need to be able to drop the names of at least ten famous jurists in order to be able to pass themselves off as members of a learned profession.

A more interesting symbolic argument is that unless a law degree contains a required course on jurisprudence students will not believe any claims made for it as a serious intellectual or academic enterprise.[16] At first sight this argument is appealing; for it is difficult to take seriously the intellectual claims of a degree programme that does not contain a substantial theoretical element. However, direct study of theory does not take place only in courses labelled 'Jurisprudence'; and to require any course merely or mainly for symbolic or window-dressing reasons hardly counts as a justification either for such courses or for the programme as a whole.

A second kind of argument stresses the vocational relevance of theory courses. Concentration on analytical jurisprudence, for example, has sometimes been justified as a kind of gymnastic exercise in clear thinking—a particularly demanding assault course in the enterprise of teaching people 'to think like lawyers'.[17] Similar utilitarian or instrumental justifications are made for particular topics. Such arguments need to be treated with caution, not because they are fallacious, but because typically they are not the main or the strongest reasons for studying theory. Furthermore instrumental justifications may have a distorting effect on what is studied. And jurisprudence courses may not be the only or the best means of achieving such ends. It would be as absurd to claim that all theoretical study is of direct practical value as it would be to claim that all theorizing is useless. Working at a high level of abstraction may be of great

[16] This argument was put eloquently and persuasively to one of us recently by student representatives in an Australian university. In the context the argument was cogent, as it was in essence a plea for a coherent educational philosophy for a law degree of the kind advocated in this paper. This does not vitiate the point, made in the text, that required courses need to be justified in terms of their educational rather than their symbolic value.

[17] E. G. Hart, 'Analytical Jurisprudence in Mid-Twentieth Century: A Reply to Professor Bodenheimer' 105 *U Penn. L Rev.* 953 (1957).

utility for some particular purpose, for example, because it is more economical or opens up possibilities or makes illuminating connections or helps to destroy the arguments of an opponent. But the purposes for which theory may be of immediate practical value are many and varied and do not provide a general or a coherent rationale for whole courses on jurisprudence. Practical training can undoubtedly benefit from injections of theory;[18] but the most urgent reasons for theoretical study are independent of its immediate utility.

The vocational relevance of some kinds of jurisprudence course is sometimes advanced in general terms. Perhaps the most eloquent exponent of this view was Karl Llewellyn.[19] His argument can be restated as follows: a liberal education in law is the best practical training that a university law school can offer to intending lawyers. A compulsory course on jurisprudence can play a central role in such a liberal education by helping students to integrate their study of law with their knowledge of other subjects, with their own firsthand experiences, and with their beliefs concerning religion, morals, politics, and life. Llewellyn's fullest statement of this is set out in a paper written in 1940.[20] It is an eloquent plea for a particular kind of course directed to the objective of helping each student, in Northrop's words, 'to know what his legal philosophy is'. It is the best statement we know of the vocational relevance of our subject.

We agree with Llewellyn's emphasis on understanding law, on the integrative role of legal theory, and on the value of clarifying connections between one's 'life work' and one's general beliefs—of integrating one's legal philosophy and one's general philosophy, in Northrop's sense. We are personally quite sympathetic with the notion of 'the good lawyer' that underlies his argument and with the claim that the kind of jurisprudence course that he advocated could have immediate practical utility as well as helping to serve this noble aspiration. However, not everyone accepts his notion of 'the good lawyer'[21] and, more important, our case for direct study of legal theory has to be made in a rather different educational context: Xanadu and British law students tend to be younger and less extensively educated than their American counterparts; many law graduates either do not seek, or fail to obtain, professional qualifications; many who qualify do not practise law for a substantial period, if at all; many undergraduate law students have not yet decided whether to qualify or to practise and many who think they have decided one way or the other are destined to change their minds. Within our structure of preparation for practice the law degree represents

[18] It is beyond the scope of this paper to consider the role of theory in formal training in professional legal skills and in continuing legal education. One implication of our argument is that specific theoretical inputs can be valuable, sometimes necessary, in such courses. In recent years there has been a strong trend, especially in the US, in this direction in the teaching of negotiation, advocacy, analysis of evidence, and professional responsibility. See, e.g., Ch. 5 above.

[19] K. Llewellyn, 'The Study of Law as a Liberal Art' in *Jurisprudence: Realism in Theory and Practice* (Chicago, 1962) Ch. 17, and 'A Required Course in Jurisprudence', *LTCL*, Ch. 14.

[20] This was first published in full in *LTCL*, Ch. 13.

[21] On ideas of 'the good lawyer', see below Ch. 16.

only the first, explicitly 'academic' stage of a process that continues for a substantial period after graduation.

Because law degrees are multifunctional and have been explicitly given the role of satisfying the 'academic' stage in the four-stage structure of preparation for legal practice (academic, professional, apprenticeship, continuing legal education), the task of making the case for courses on jurisprudence within law degrees is easier; on the other hand, because our students tend to be less mature and less broadly educated than their American counterparts, our expectations of what can realistically be achieved by a single course may have to be lower. We propose to argue that in this context the 'why?' of studying jurisprudence is essentially the same as Llewellyn put forward, but the which?, when?, and how? have to take account of the characteristics of our system of legal education and of particular degree programmes.

In the present context the general case for direct study of theory can be summarized as follows: a serious understanding of law is an intellectual objective of plain and obvious intrinsic value. In the context of the United Kingdom, and anywhere else that similar conditions apply, if law degrees are to have a coherent rationale, the primary objective of legal education through some kind of academic course of study is nowadays properly demanded as a precondition of entry into the professional practice of law. So whether a student takes a law degree with a view to legal practice or takes one as a general educational qualification, perhaps before he or she has decided on a career, it seems safe to say that the course for a law degree ought to be geared, so far as it can be, to the aim of generating a serious understanding of law, and that the condition for award of a law degree should be proof that the student has pursued such an understanding with a tolerable or hopefully even a substantial measure of success. It is accordingly neither necessary nor desirable to construct the rationale for law degrees, and for theory courses, in narrowly vocational terms, that is to say in terms of direct relevance to particular practical or professional goals. The strongest vocational justification for the study of legal theory is that it promotes understanding of law.

That understanding law requires a real and considerable element of theory in the curriculum is a point which the other contributors to *Legal Theory and Common Law* have saved us the trouble of having to argue at any length. Each of the essays which is dedicated to a particular 'branch' of legal study demonstrates the integral involvement of theoretical considerations in any valid understanding of the subject in view. Each of the authors interprets the special relevance of theory to his or her part of the discipline of law in an individual way; there is no single theory-monolith upon which each inscribes or from which each transcribes the unitary wisdom for the legal enterprise. For theorizing is not the kind of activity which postulates or generates a single all-encompassing body of doctrine upon the authority of which laws are expounded subject by subject and branch by branch. It is much more exciting and challenging because it is a much more pluralistic and dialectical business than that.

Thus the task of explicating the role of theory in the law curriculum has its job half done for it already. Asked whether there is a place for theory in an undergraduate law degree, we are able to say in the light of our colleagues' papers that theory has to be omnipresent in the law curriculum. In all the various ways that they describe and argue for, and doubtless in many others besides, theory must penetrate and infuse all that is taught and studied in legal education. There could be some kind of rote learning otherwise; but no serious understanding. This is not mere dogma—it is a claim needing proof. But the proof is already given. We rest this part of the case on our colleagues' arguments.

Theory is necessary to understanding law. But are separate courses of study on 'Jurisprudence' or 'Legal Philosophy' or 'Sociology of Law' necessary for this purpose or at least sufficiently important to justify giving them space in an already crowded programme? The very success of arguments for injection of theoretical elements with all else that is taught as law may ostensibly weaken the case for independent treatment; and, indeed, some law teachers argue that separate theory courses are unnecessary precisely because 'we all do it already'. We are sceptical that this last claim is true of the actual practice of most law teachers; but assuming, for the sake of argument, that this were the case, it suggests a number of questions: if other courses contain a proper measure of theoretical study, what is left for a special course on 'theory'? If they do not, of what help will a discrete 'theory course' be? And following on from there: is there not even a risk that specialized theory courses will impoverish the curriculum by encouraging teachers and students in the other courses to suppose that all the theory they need is covered there?

Let us start from this last question. For we do think that there is such a risk. We are aware that theory can be thought of as something special and apart. So theoretical elements may tend to drop out of the contract class or the constitutional or family law class, while on the other hand the theorizing that goes on in the theory class does, or seems to, say little or nothing which connects up with the content of contract, constitutional or family law or indeed anything much else in the law syllabus. As William Twining warns in 'Evidence and Legal Theory',[22] a jurisprudence course can become too much a matter of high theory, a purely philosophical (or sociological, for that matter, adds MacCormick) discoursing about some rather vague and undifferentiated 'law' in its relations to the political, the social, the moral or the economic or in its character as a special topic for analytical reflection. An always present, and in itself laudable, ambition to draw from and contribute to philosophy and sociology can nevertheless lure the theorist away from the ordinary discourse of the discipline or disciplines of law; and the jurist in the 'straight law' class loses touch with theorists' theory and may even lose sight of the essential theoretical element in his or her own branch of legal study. So there is always some risk of a gap

---

[22] *LTCL*, at 65.

opening between law and theory, or, rather, between law courses and theory courses. A large part of the point of *Legal Theory and Common Law* as a collaborative work was to do a bit of gap-closing. But the movement must be a two-way one; if law must keep open to theory so must theory keep open to law and, in teaching jurisprudence, one of the most pressing problems is to prevent it from becoming, or from being perceived to be, remote or redundant. Jurisprudence should not be a subject apart.

What special role is left for separate theory courses in a curriculum that is generally informed by theory? In our view the answer is quite simple. Of course, much depends on context—on what is adequately dealt with in other courses and what are the main learning objectives that are proposed for the specific theory course or courses in question. Nevertheless, it seems likely that none of Twining's five functions of legal theory can be done as economically or as efficiently by means of a 'pervasive approach'.[23] It is difficult to see how intellectual history or central questions of legal philosophy can be dealt with systematically or in depth other than by direct study. Certain kinds of middle-order theorizing can no doubt be accommodated in other courses; for example, it may be possible to accommodate theories of adjudication or legislation, or even some aspects of the sociology of the legal profession, within courses on legal institutions or legal process or legal method. But, insofar as such courses deal adequately with those topics they become in effect 'theory courses'. Furthermore, it is not easy to get to grips with, for example, Ronald Dworkin's theory of adjudication or the nature of legal reasoning if one is divorced from the context of broader theoretical debates. Similarly, while a broad approach to family law or criminal law or constitutional law inevitably involves drawing on material from other disciplines, a more systematic exploration of the relationships between law and these other disciplines requires attention to be focused directly on such relationships at a higher level of generality than would be appropriate for most standard law courses. Most important of all is the integrative function. One role of 'theory' within a course on contract or torts or constitutional law is to provide a coherent view of the subject as a whole. But it is difficult to see how a coherent view of law as a whole or, more mundanely, of all the subjects studied by an individual student within his or her degree course can be achieved other than by direct study. Whatever other educational objectives are served by separate theory courses, perhaps their most important function is to provide an opportunity to students to stand back from the detailed study of particular topics and to look at their subject as a whole at a higher level of generality and from a variety of perspectives. Such a course, whatever it is called, which draws on and feeds into all other courses in the curriculum and thereby helps to provide the basis for an integrated educational experience, is performing one of the main jobs of jurisprudence.

[23] *LTCL*, at 64.

WHICH THEORY?

The picture that we have painted of the nature and scope of legal theory is rather daunting. It includes many basic issues of philosophy and much else besides. The heritage of juristic texts, if not quite as extensive as English literature, is vast, rich, and amorphous. As anyone who has been involved in curriculum planning should know, many of the sharpest disagreements in legal education relate to priorities. It is not enough just to make a general case for the desirability of a particular subject. Reasons have to be advanced for giving it priority over other desirable subjects; when it is claimed that the subject should be a required or integral part of a degree programme the reasons have to be even more cogent. In the case of vast subjects like international law or legal history, selection and ordering of priorities *within* the subject are also required. One must then take care to ensure that the rationale for including the subject within the curriculum fits the aspects of the subject that have been selected for inclusion.

This is especially important in the case of jurisprudence. It is hardly plausible to claim that studying jurisprudence provides an excellent form of training in analytical skills or helps to integrate all the other subjects in the curriculum, if what is in fact involved is a superficial and inaccurate Cook's tour of so-called 'schools'. Similarly rigorous in-depth study of one or two major texts may serve some valuable educational objectives, but is less likely to sustain claims that the jurisprudence course provides a map of our intellectual heritage. Accordingly general justifications for the study of legal theory need to be treated with caution; what learning objectives are likely to be served in fact depends on which from a range of possible objectives have been selected. However, this caution can easily be exaggerated for two reasons: first, the most cogent justifications for giving direct study of theoretical issues a high priority all relate to MacCormick's six basic questions of legal philosophy. These, we would suggest, can reasonably be treated as the core of the subject, provided it is recognized that each of them is open to consideration in a variety of contexts at a number of levels of generality. Secondly, the heritage of attempted answers is much more extensive than the range of questions. The corpus of juristic texts can be seen as a series of more or less ambitious attempts to provide answers to one or more of a less extensive number of interrelated questions. Juristic debate is notoriously repetitive, often involving false polemics and the ritual exaggeration of minute differences. If the main purpose of direct study of legal theory is for students to reflect critically about important issues, it is of secondary importance which theories or theorists they use to assist this enterprise. In order to confront questions about justice it is not necessary for an undergraduate to consider more than two or three from the vast stock of attempted answers to such questions. If, as we shall argue, students should be exposed to a reasonably wide range of important *issues* in legal theory, the problem of selection becomes less acute. One should not be too selective about fundamental questions, but one can be ruthless about coverage of texts, theorists, and theories, for these are mainly to be treated as aids to confronting the questions.

THEORY—WHEN?

If the primary objective of a law degree is to promote understanding of law, and if wrestling with abstract questions, answers, and concepts is a necessary part of that enterprise, then theorizing should not only be an integral part of the programme, it should also pervade it. At the very outset of their studies, and at every stage, students will be helped by maps which establish connections both within and between particular areas of study. From the start they need to be persuaded that understanding law involves continuous movement through different levels of abstraction; they need to be acclimatized to the atmosphere of abstract discourse and to the problems of moving from the general to the particular and vice versa. Most will almost certainly benefit from direct instruction in some of the specific techniques of theoretical analysis, such as elucidating abstract concepts, digging out hidden assumptions, constructing logical arguments, and spotting common kinds of fallacy. Much of this is as much a matter of confidence as competence, for in our experience student resistance to theorizing is grounded as much in unfamiliarity, fear, and indolence as in anti-intellectualism. Generally speaking law teachers are more likely to differ about the means of achieving these ends than about the ends themselves.

A more controversial question is *when* space should be made for direct study of theoretical questions. In particular, in law degrees in which one or more theory courses are an integral part of the programme, what is the best place for such courses? In most, but by no means all, undergraduate degrees in the United Kingdom jurisprudence courses have traditionally been postponed until the final year. Similarly Llewellyn argued that a required course on jurisprudence in an American law school should come at the end, building on all that has gone before and bringing it together into a coherent whole.[24] Without claiming that there is a single right answer to this question, we would venture a different opinion. The thrust of the foregoing analysis, backed by our practical experience as teachers, is that jurisprudence courses work best towards the middle of the programme. They should feed into other courses as well as feed off them. The implications of general ideas and approaches for particular fields of study can be more readily perceived and understood after these ideas have been assimilated and when the opportunity is given to apply them in an academic context. It is our impression that student resistance to theory tends to be less entrenched in the second year (of a three- or four-year degree) than it is later, partly because by their third year many students have been socialized into habits and attitudes that

[24] *LTCL*, at 255.

are inimical to theoretical study. This is due not only to crude anti-intellectualism, but also to the particularizing tendency of much legal education. Moreover, the tendency to perceive theory courses as separate and irrelevant to other courses is fortified by postponing them until last, by which time most students are beginning to think about the next stage of their career, whatever that may be. Finally, one practical reason for favouring placing jurisprudence in the second year is that it can serve as a building block for more advanced theory courses. There are obvious limits to what can be achieved by a single course and teachers of jurisprudence are no less imperialistic about their subject than their colleagues, though (if our argument is valid) with better justification.

JURISPRUDENCE—HOW?

There are, of course, almost as many different jurisprudence courses as there are jurisprudence teachers. And given the conception presented here as to the why, the which, and the when of such courses it is plain that there are many possible ways of dealing with the range of subject-matters which a theory class should address. We are certainly opposed to the idea that there could or should be any single prescription for every self-respecting course in jurisprudence. Indeed, it has been part of the point of this paper to exhibit the multiplicity of valuable possibilities in the way of jurisprudence teaching.

To one style of approach to this multiplicity of possibilities we are firmly opposed—viz. that of the comprehensive survey of all the possibilities. Any attempt at total comprehensiveness in a single course can lead only to a kind of second- or third-hand rehashing through lectures or textbooks of bundles of ideas ascribed—with almost inevitable distortions—to given authors or to 'schools' of thought. Such an approach replicates some of the more problematic and indeed undesirable features of teaching and learning in a certain style of 'black-letter' approach to substantive law subjects. Even if (which we doubt) such concern for 'coverage' is necessary in the study of most branches of substantive law, it is totally stultifying if applied to legal theory, the chief point of which is to help students to think out and articulate their own philosophy of law (in the wide sense of 'philosophy' favoured by Northrop and MacCormick) or some aspects of it.

What is perhaps most damaging about the potted-theories approach is that it actually obscures to students both the difficulties and the fascinations of working out a careful theoretical position on law or on anything else. For students to experience that it is as important for them to study primary sources as in 'case-law subjects' it is important that they actually read cases. That is they must read some text or texts of legal theory or philosophy at least in very substantial extract and preferably *in toto*. They should confront some theorizing in the raw, and develop their own critique of it.

Certainly, whatever texts are prescribed in a course—and the range of reasonable possibilities to be read is enormous—it is necessary for course teachers to help with filling in context and background. And for context and background a good general text can be helpful. But even at the risk of some selectivity in concentration both as to topics and as to approaches, the encouragement of students to engage seriously with serious texts is of the first importance in jurisprudence. It is also of value as an input into a law-degree course as an educational experience. For law students in other courses are unlikely ever to find themselves reading and assessing whole books as wholes. Most legal texts are hardly written to be read in that way.

Against that background of inevitable selectivity, fairness of mind does require some breadth of coverage, if only to keep students fully aware of the controversial quality of the subject and the range of positions among which they can reasonably seek to find their own point of view. MacCormick, at least, would be unhappy with any general legal theory course which did not expose students to some version of legal positivism, some statement of the natural law view, and some variant on liberal and on socialist thought in the sociology of law or applied political theory. He also believes that some work or works on the nature of reasoning about law and about facts has to be included in any serious course; and this should involve confrontation with legal realist or sociological versions of scepticism about legal processes, as well as some statement, for example Ronald Dworkin's, of a more rationalistic view on these matters.[25]

These are only bare-bones suggestions anyway; to go further would compromise our stated view that there are many reasonable possibilities. What line is taken depends on many variables—on the relationship of the theory class to other classes in a degree curriculum, and, in particular, on the extent to which a general course on jurisprudence may be followed up by more specialized courses in special aspects of philosophy and sociology of law and in studies of legal processes, as is common in at least the Scottish universities and in Northern Ireland. At this point in the discussion, we therefore return to the proposition that while it is for locals (that is, for each of us as a local of some locality) to contextualize the teaching of legal theory, the task of the present authors is to intellectualize it.

Here ended the report to the Law Faculty of Xanadu. History does not record the reception it was given by the faculty. However, one of us heard a rumour (or was it a dream?) that over-expenditure on prestige building led to such pressure on public funds in Xanadu that the university was closed down and training for the professions reverted to a system of pure apprenticeship. It is not thought that this had enhanced the quality of either legal practice or legal understanding in Xanadu.

---

[25] Twining would be rather more cautious about making general prescriptions here; cf. Llewellyn, *LTCL*, at 256–7.

8

General and Particular Jurisprudence:
Three Chapters in a Story*

GLOBALIZATION

We are now living in a global neighbourhood, which is not yet a global village.[1] The term 'globalization' refers to those processes which tend to create and consolidate a unified world economy, a single ecosystem, and a complex network of communications that covers the whole globe, even if it does not penetrate to every part of it. It is difficult to interpret these trends and it is easy to underestimate them; but it is also easy to exaggerate the extent and the speed of the process, to oversimplify its dynamics, to foreshorten history by treating a story that stretches over several centuries as if it is a recent development, to assume some inevitable, teleological progress in a single direction, and to ignore the countervailing processes of fragmentation and localization.[2]

Recognition of these processes has stimulated a new academic industry, 'globalization theory'. In most disciplines in the humanities, social sciences, and physical sciences the implications of globalization are firmly on the agenda.[3] The discipline of law has become distinctly more cosmopolitan in recent years, but its theoretical branch, jurisprudence, seems to have lagged behind. In the English-speaking world traditional positivism, normative legal philosophy, critical legal studies, post-modernism, and even economic analysis of law seem to have been going through a somewhat parochial or inward-looking phase, although there are some notable exceptions. The time may be ripe for a revival of a more general jurisprudence.

---

* This is a revised version of an essay published in Stephen Guest (ed.), *Positivism Today* (Aldershot, 1996).

[1] e.g., *Our Global Neighbourhood*, The Report of the Commission on Global Governance (Ingvar Carlsson and Shridath Ramphal, Co-Chairmen) (Oxford, 1995).

[2] See generally, Fred Halliday, *Rethinking International Relations* (Basingstoke, 1994).

[3] A fairly typical summary reads as follows: 'in social science there are as many conceptualizations of globalization as there are disciplines. In economics globalization refers to economic internationalization and the spread of capitalist market relations . . . In international relations, the focus is on the increasing density of interstate relations and the development of global politics. In sociology, the concern is with increasing world-wide social densities and the emergence of "world society". In cultural studies, the focus is on global communications and world-wide standardization, as in CocaColonization and McDonaldization, and on the post-colonial culture. In history, the concern is with conceptualizing "global history" . . .' Jan Nederveen Pieterse 'Globalization as Hybridization' in M. Featherstone, S. Lash and R. Robertson, *Global Modernities* (London, 1995). Equally typically, there is no mention of law.

The literature on globalization has already sparked a series of debates, some familiar, some relatively new. Here it is sufficient to make three preliminary points that are directly relevant to my argument and about which there is widespread agreement. First, globalization needs to be considered on at least three levels: relations between states (international relations); non-state relations across frontiers (transnational relations); and the operation of the global system(s) as a whole (global relations).[4] Global relations at all three levels involve a multiplicity of actors, but this does not necessarily spell the end of the independent nation-state as one of the most important.[5] It does, however, put the concept of sovereignty back on the agenda, along with a number of conceptual questions about the relations between such notions as sovereign states, governments, peoples, nations, societies, communities, and classes.

Secondly, and related to this, the significance of territorial boundaries has been radically changed by globalization. This presents a challenge to all 'black box theories' which treat nation-states or geographically bounded 'societies' or legal systems as discrete entities that can be studied in isolation either internally or at the international level. Rawls's theory of justice and any legal theory which treats municipal legal systems as discrete entities are vulnerable to this challenge.[6]

Finally, the process of globalization changes the agenda of issues with which any field of study is concerned: it revives and recasts old issues such as those surrounding sovereignty and war; it makes familiar problems more urgent, such as environmental control and the regulation of multinational corporations; and it creates new ones such as those connected with developments in technology and communication, such as Internet and CNN World News. What are problems, what should be the agenda, what are priorities depends on a whole raft of ideological and other assumptions. But it is clear that if legal theory is to engage seriously with globalization and its consequences a critical re-examination of its agenda, its heritage of ideas, and its conceptual tools is called for.

This essay is one of a series exploring the implications for legal theory and the discipline of law of globalization and globalization theory. It deals with one narrow topic: three distinct phases of the history of the distinction between 'general' and 'particular' jurisprudence within the tradition of English legal

---

[4] Halliday at 1.

[5] 'A wide range of actors may be involved in any one area of governance. To cite just one example, those with a role in bringing order to international trade in sugar and sweeteners include transnational firms, national and international authorities in charge of competition policy, a global group (The International Sugar Council) with specific responsibility for trade, and a host of smaller private associations, including plantation workers, beet farmers, and dieticians. An international organization may easily develop an interest in a local issue, as when the World Bank finances an agricultural project in a country. A local voluntary association may just as easily become a participant in an international regime.' *Our Global Neighbourhood*, op. cit., n. 1, at 3.

[6] This theme will be developed in a later paper. For a general critique of Rawls along these lines see Thomas W. Pogge, *Realizing Rawls* (Ithaca, 1989). Pogge states: 'In the modern world there are no self-contained national societies; a closed background system exists only at the global level. The question, therefore, is whether Rawls's conception, if it applies at all, applies to open national societies (as Rawls seems to prefer) or to the closed social system of humanity at large (as I maintain in Part Three).' (id., 7–8). See further, Halliday, op. cit., 78–81.

positivism: first, the place and significance of the distinction in the thought of Jeremy Bentham and John Austin; second, the fifty-year long debate surrounding Professor T. E. Holland's idea of a 'formal science of law' and his denial of the possibility of 'particular jurisprudence'; and, third, the recent revival of the distinction as a basis for arguing that H. L. A. Hart and Ronald Dworkin were involved in quite different enterprises, rather than disagreeing: Hart doing general jurisprudence, Dworkin confining himself to a particular, participatory theory of adjudication. The essay concludes with a brief consideration of the implications of this story for reflecting on globalization and law.

JEREMY BENTHAM AND JOHN AUSTIN

J. B.'s frame of mind.
J. B. the most ambitious of the ambitious. His empire—the empire he aspires to—extending to, and comprehending the whole human race, in all places.—in all habitable places of the earth, at all future time.
J. B. the most philanthropic of the philanthropic; philanthropy the end and instrument of his ambition.
Limits it has no other than those of the earth.[7]

Bentham wrote this in his Memorandum-book the day after his eighty-third birthday. This was not just an old man's private musings. From *A Fragment on Government* and other early writings until the end of his life Bentham often explicitly adopted the standpoint of a (or the) 'citizen of the world'.[8] This standpoint was based on utility as a universal principle which extended to humankind in general, sometimes going further to include all sentient beings. It formed the cornerstone of his jurisprudence, which was in key respects truly global.[9]

As is well known, Bentham's project was to extend the experimental method of reasoning from the physical sciences to the moral sciences, especially legislation:

What Bacon was to the physical world, Helvetius was to the moral. The moral world has had its Bacon, but its Newton is yet to come.[10]

Underpinning Bentham's perspective was a quite elaborate series of distinctions, which have been succinctly summarized by Philip Schofield:

Bentham's conception of jurisprudence had two branches: the first, expository, the second censorial, or the art of legislation. 'To the province of the *Expositor* it belongs

---

[7] *Works*, vol. xi, 72.

[8] *A Fragment on Government*, ed. Burns and Hart (CW, London, 1977) 397–8; cf. *Introduction to the Principles of Morals and Legislation (IPML)* ed. Burns and Hart (CW, London, 1970) 294–5.

[9] See further, RB, 129 ff. It is pertinent to note that Bentham claimed to be doing *universal* jurisprudence, Austin '*general*', Buckland and Gray favoured '*particular*' and '*comparative*', and Bentham allowed for '*local*' (i.e., sub-national). See further, below n. 19. This point is not to be conflated with the debate about whether Bentham's utilitarianism was 'parochial' or 'universal'—see, e.g., David Lyons, *In the Interests of the Governed* (Oxford, 1973, rev. edn. 1993) and F. Rosen, *Jeremy Bentham and Representative Democracy* (Oxford, 1983) at 203–6.

[10] *Jeremy Bentham's Economic Writings*, ed. W. Stark (London, 1952–4), vol. 1, 100–1.

to explain to us what, as he supposes, the Law *is*: to that of the *Censor*, to observe what he thinks it *ought to be*.'[11] He divided jurisprudence into authoritative, when it was the product of the legislator himself, and unauthoritative, the work of any other person. He then made a further distinction between local jurisprudence, concerned with the laws of one nation or a particular group of nations, and universal jurisprudence, concerned with laws of all nations. Though in substance no two nations had exactly the same laws, while others possibly had none in common, there were certain words corresponding to concepts, for instance power, right, obligation, liberty, which could be found in all.[12] It followed that universal expository jurisprudence had very narrow limits: it could not apply to the substance of laws, but 'must confine itself to terminology'. Censorial jurisprudence on the other hand, considering both substance and terminology, was much wider in scope: there were 'leading points'[13] which it would be advantageous for all nations to introduce into their laws.[14]

Here, three points deserve emphasis: first, the distinction between general (or universal) and local (or internal) jurisprudence was subordinate to the more fundamental distinction between expository and censorial jurisprudence. 'The expositor was to be the servant of the censor, who in turn would be the adviser of the legislator.'[15] Bentham distinguished the is and the ought for the sake of the ought.[16]

Secondly, the distinction between universal and local jurisprudence is not coextensive with the distinction between the censor and the expositor. In *A Fragment on Government*, it is suggested that 'the *Expositor* . . . is always the citizen of this or that particular country: the *Censor* is, or ought to be the citizen of the world'.[17] Elsewhere, Bentham modified this by including analysis of some fundamental concepts as part of universal expository jurisprudence, but as Schofield notes, this was very limited in scope.[18] However, this became the starting-point of Austin's conception of General Jurisprudence.

[11] *Fragment*, op. cit., at 397.

[12] In *IPML* 295 Bentham ends this list of examples with the significant words 'and many others'. Earlier, in the same work, he talked of 'the short list of terms, the exposition of which contains all that can be said with propriety to belong to the head of *universal jurisprudence*'. He listed as examples 'obligation, right, power, possession, title, exemption, immunity, franchise, privilege, nullity, validity, and the like', id., at 6; cf. *Works*, iii, 217.

[13] 'Points' here refers to the substance of laws. *IPML*, 293–5.

[14] Philip Schofield, 'Jeremy Bentham and Nineteenth-Century English Jurisprudence', 12 *Jo. Legal History*, (1991) 58, 59.

[15] Id., 61. Bentham was quite explicit about his lack of interest in simple exposition: 'The business of simple exposition is a harvest in which there seemed no likelihood of there being any want of labourers: and into which therefore I had little ambition to thrust my sickle.' *Fragment*, Preface, 404. The context of this statement is a passage in which he justifies his attack on Blackstone in the character of Expositor, because 'the imbecility' of his treatment of the censorial infected his exposition of English Law.

[16] Oren Ben Dor has pointed out to me that the is/ought distinction for Bentham operates at different levels; here I am concerned with the distinction between law as it is and law as it ought to be.   [17] *Fragment*, 398.

[18] 'To be susceptible of an universal application, all that a book of an expository kind can have to treat of, is the import of words: to be, strictly speaking universal, it must confine itself to terminology.' *IPML*, 295.

Thirdly, Bentham coined the term international jurisprudence to apply to relations between sovereigns and contrasted it with internal jurisprudence, which he subdivided into national, provincial, and local. The latter term applied to small districts, such as towns, parishes, and manors, which he acknowledged could have laws of their own.[19] He observed that: 'It is evident enough, that international jurisprudence may, as well as internal, be censorial as well as expository, unauthoritative as well as authoritative.'[20] Thus Bentham at least made provision for jurisprudence to operate at a number of different levels from the global to the very local, but he restricted the term 'international' to relations between sovereigns.

Bentham's distinction between universal and local was in part developed in connection with his critiques of Blackstone. However, it was more important in connection with his constructive project for a pannomion. He was a forerunner of the modern constitution-monger and legal 'expert' who offer their services to foreign governments.[21] Anyone involved in this trade has a vested interest in claiming that their expertise is of general application. Bentham was no exception. He was acutely aware that there was a tension between the claims of universality of the Censor and the need to be sensitive to local exigencies. He returned to this theme again and again.

At first sight Bentham did not appear to maintain an entirely consistent stance on the extent to which the censor needed to take account of local circumstances in proposing legislation. In some passages he appears to assume that the pannomion would have wide applicability in respect of substance as well as form. In *A Fragment on Government* he suggested 'That which is Law, is, in different countries, widely different, while that which ought to be, is in all countries to a great degree the same.'[22] Similarly, in offering his services as a codifier to James Madison, the President of the United States, he played down the amount to which his draft codes would need to be adjusted to local conditions in respect of either form or substance.[23] He even went so far as to suggest:

[19] *IPML*, 296–7. He suggested that 'particular' might be substituted for local, but in the present context I shall confine the term particular jurisprudence to what he called 'internal' in this passage, but which he referred to at different times as 'local' and 'national'. He criticized Blackstone's use of 'municipal' to apply to national law and the term 'law of nations' to apply to international jurisprudence rather than internal (laws of nations). The terminology is unimportant; but Bentham's willingness to recognize a multiplicity of levels is significant.   [20] Ibid.

[21] e.g., J. Bentham, *Constitutional Writings for Greece and Tripoli*, ed. P. Schofield (CW, Oxford, 1990) and below n. 24. See further, W. Twining, 'Some Aspects of Reception' (1957) *Sudan Law Jo. and Reports* 229, and 'Constitutions, Constitutionalism and Constitution-mongering', in Irwin P. Stotzky, *Transition to Democracy in Latin America: The Role of the Judiciary* (Boulder, 1993), Ch. 25. A less sceptical view, closer to Bentham's position on the transferability of laws, is developed by Alan Watson in *Legal Transplants* (Edinburgh, 1974).

[22] *Fragment*, 397–8; cf. *IPML*, 295.

[23] Letter to Madison, 30 Oct. 1811, 8 *Correspondence* 182–215, ed. S. Conway (CW, Oxford, 1988). A version of this long letter was published as part of *Papers Relative to Codification and Public Instruction* (1817) and was partly reprinted in the Bowring edition, *Works*, vol. iv, 453–67. It can be read as an example of sustained special pleading, but is consistent with his general position.

that, upon a closer scrutiny, the points, which present a demand for local knowledge, would not, it is supposed be found to cover, in the field of law, so great an extent, nor yet to be so difficult to discriminate beforehand, as upon a transient glance, general notions might lead any person to imagine.[24]

On the other hand, he usually maintained a sharp distinction between form (especially terminology) which should in most respects be universal,[25] and substance in which he was often rather cautious in recommending change. In considering directly the influence of time and place in matters of legislation, Bentham was prepared to give some weight to local customs and circumstances. And, as Michael Lobban has suggested, he acknowledged that even the common law was a rich source of raw materials for the censor, that his objections to it related much more to form than to substance, and that he was in respect of reform of substantive law remarkably cautious.[26]

Although there are differences of emphasis, Bentham's general position can be interpreted as being quite consistent: existing laws of different nations vary considerably in respect of both form and substance.[27] However, the principle of utility and the form of laws in the pannomion are of universal application; but caution needs to be exercised in legislating for a particular country in case expectations based on local customs and circumstances should be disappointed— for the non-disappointment principle is an important principle subordinate to utility. Thus Bentham's project was to develop a science of legislation which was both 'censorial' and universal; the *construction* of precise conceptual tools—

The central argument is that only in a few areas would the preparatory work he had already done (on penal law, civil law, judicial establishment, procedure, evidence, and constitutional law) require extensive amendment to fit local conditions. For example: 'Thus in the case of Penal Law. Of the *genera* of Offences, as distinguished or distinguishable by their generic names—Murder, Defamation, Theft, Robbery and so forth—definitions for the most part are the same all the world over. But for particular species, occasion may be afforded, by particular local circumstances: and so in regard to causes of aggravation, extenuation, justification, or exemption, with demand for corresponding varieties in respect of *satisfaction* or punishment. And so in regard to *contracts*.' (id., 203).

[24] Id., 202. This general statement needs to be read in context: Bentham was making the case for employing an Englishman as legislative adviser to a political leader whose legal system was historically and culturally closely related to English Law, but who had to be wary of local nationalist sentiment. Bentham was careful to show his familiarity with American legal developments and to pronounce them to represent 'prodigious improvements' on English Law (at 211). Local knowledge could be supplied by locals, who in any event would have the final say.

[25] e.g., *Of Laws in General*, ed. H. L. A. Hart (CW, London, 1970) (*OLIG*) 233–4, discussed by Hart in his *Essays on Bentham* (Oxford, 1982) Ch. 5, esp. 125.

[26] See M. Lobban, *The Common Law and English Jurisprudence 1760–1850* (Oxford, 1991) 179–84 which contains a useful discussion based on a variety of published works and unpublished manuscripts from different periods.

[27] e.g., *IPML*, 295. The distinction between form and substance in the thought of Bentham and other writers discussed below deserves further exploration. Professor Robert Summers is currently working on a major project on 'the formal character of law', which, *inter alia*, reminds us that the description of the form and structure of legal systems and of laws is not solely a matter of elucidation of concepts. For preliminary reports see Summers, 'The Formal Character of Law', 51 *Cambridge Law Jo.* 242 (1992) and 'The Formal Character of Law III', 25 *Rechtstheorie* 125 (1994).

what Mary Mack called 'a legislative dictionary'—[28] was one narrow, subordinate, but important, part of the science or art of legislation.

Austin

John Austin is the prototype of a disciple who subverts his master. Recent scholarship has convincingly shown that Bentham had a broader vision, a more subtle and flexible mind, and a much more radical programme than his tortured follower. Austin did follow his master in three important respects that are relevant to this paper: the sharp distinction between law as it is and law as it ought to be; a subordinate distinction between the study of one particular legal system and legal systems or law(s) in general; and the identification of analysis of concepts that transcend particular legal systems as a distinct field of study. However, Austin's enterprise was quite different from Bentham's and he used these distinctions, and to some extent altered them, for his own purposes.

Bentham's objective was to develop a politically radical science of legislation. Austin's enterprise was to establish the study of positive law as an autonomous scientific discipline quite separate from censorial jurisprudence or the science of legislation. Bentham distinguished the is and the ought for the sake of the ought; Austin made the same distinction for the sake of isolating law as it is for detached study.

Both thinkers are subject to multiple interpretations. There may be several Benthams and at least two Austins.[29] However, in the present context some points are reasonably clear. The most important is that Austin confined jurisprudence to the analysis and description of positive law. The science or philosophy of legislation[30] was not part of jurisprudence, but constituted a separate discipline. This was no mere semantic point: Austin wished his science to be apolitical; although he himself treated the philosophy of legislation to be important, his distinction paved the way for a conception and practice of the discipline of law that were avowedly uncritical.[31] Nothing could have been further from the spirit of Bentham.

Like Bentham, Austin distinguished between general and particular jurisprudence and explicitly concentrated on the former. Both treated the laws of individual sovereign states as the main subject of particular jurisprudence and state

[28] Mary Mack, *Jeremy Bentham: An Odyssey of Ideas 1748–1792* (London, 1962); cf. Douglas Long, 'Censorial Jurisprudence and Political Radicalism: A Reconsideration of the Early Bentham', 12 *The Bentham Newsletter* 4 (1988), arguing that 'Bentham was a radical *about* political terms.'

[29] Lobban, op. cit., 256. On the general theme of 'Benthamic ambiguity' see William Twining, 'Hot Air in the Redwoods', 86 *Michigan L Rev.* (1988) 1523, 1536–9 and 'Why Bentham?' 8 *The Bentham Newsletter* 34 (1984).

[30] In several places Austin used the terms 'science' and 'philosophy' interchangeably, e.g., J. Austin, 'The Uses of the Study of Jurisprudence' (1863, ed. Hart, 1954) 365 (hereafter *Uses*).

[31] Austin included Legislation among the subjects that should be studied as a preparation for legal practice or politics, *Uses* 387–8. He stressed the need for law to be based on ethics, but his interpretation of utility was more conservative than Bentham's.

legal systems as the primary units of law; both emphasized the importance of studying basic legal concepts that transcended particular legal systems. Following Hobbes, Austin declared that his aim was 'to show, *not what is law here or there, but what is law*'.[32]

Austin devoted much more space than Bentham to the distinction between general and particular jurisprudence.[33] In an important passage he specified the scope of general jurisprudence:

I mean then by 'General Jurisprudence', the science concerned with the principles, notions, and distinctions which are common to systems of law: understanding by systems of law, the ampler and maturer systems which, by reason of their amplitude and maturity, are pre-eminently pregnant with instruction.

Of the principles, notions and distinctions which are the subjects of general jurisprudence, some may be esteemed necessary. For we cannot imagine coherently a system of law (or a system of law evolved in a refined community), without conceiving them as constituent parts of it. . . . Of the principles, notions, and distinctions which are the subjects of General jurisprudence, others are not necessary (in the sense which I have given the expression). We may imagine coherently an expanded system of law, without conceiving them as constituent parts of it. But as they rest upon grounds of utility which extend through all communities, they in fact occur very generally in matured systems of law; and therefore may be ranked properly with the general principles which are the subjects of general jurisprudence.[34]

Austin's list of examples of necessary notions is quite long. It includes the notions of Duty, Right, Liberty, Injury, Punishment, Redress; Law; Sovereignty, and Independent Political Society; the distinctions between written and unwritten law; rights *in rem* and rights *in personam*; obligations arising from contracts, injuries, and '*quasi ex contractu*'; and so on. It is a longer list than Bentham's and it is not entirely clear what he meant by 'necessary' in this context.[35] By

---

[32] *Lectures on Jurisprudence* (*LJ*) 32 (Austin's italics). Rumble has pointed out that Austin slightly misquoted Hobbes. W. Rumble, Introduction to Austin, *The Province of Jurisprudence Determined* (Cambridge, 1995).

[33] At least in print. Bentham's early manuscripts, on which Douglas Long has done pioneering work, contain some further discussions of the distinction.

[34] *Uses*, 367–9. This passage is almost identical to a passage in Lecture XI of *LJ*, which contains a longer analysis of the distinction between general and particular jurisprudence. This is one of the passages which has led to controversy about the interpretation of Austin. Did his reference to utility here and his lengthy treatment of it in his lectures undermine his positivism? Indeed, some later critics suggested that he was a closet natural lawyer. And was Austin's conception of General Jurisprudence 'formal' (as Moles and Lobban suggest) or 'empirical', as is argued by W. L. Morison, *John Austin* (London and Stanford, 1982)? My own view is that there are passages in which Austin's references to utility did threaten to undermine his strict positivism; it seems to me to be clear that he considered concepts to be *tools for empirical description*, that these were to some extent constructed from real life examples, but that his general jurisprudence did not claim to be empirical in the sense that it could be falsified by evidence, and so in that sense it was analytical or formal. See further, Lobban at 223–7. On Hart's claim to be describing 'the form, structure and content' of legal systems in general see below at n. 100.

[35] If it means 'logically necessary', Austin's list should have been confined to a few meta-concepts, such as sovereign, command, sanction, and a very small number of legal concepts, of

including additional 'common' concepts and by focusing mainly on shared features of 'maturer' systems he may have extended the scope of his concept of General Jurisprudence a bit beyond Bentham's universal expository jurisprudence, but overall his conception of law and of its study is much narrower than Bentham's.

Austin emphasized the distinction between general and particular jurisprudence because he wished to lay a foundation for an autonomous discipline distinct from the Science of Legislation and from historical and empirical enquiries. General jurisprudence was anterior to and the necessary foundation for the systematic study of both particular jurisprudence and the science of legislation.[36] It was the theoretical part of law as a discipline.

Austin did not advocate the study of jurisprudence for its own sake. In his lecture on 'The Uses of the Study of Jurisprudence' he emphasized its pedagogical value as the basis for the 'theoretico-practical' study of English law. By providing a map of the whole and making clear the rationale of law in general and of its practice, it would contribute to more efficient vocational training for legal practice and public life. It would also be of value in understanding foreign legal systems, in daily legal practice, in adjudication, in law reform, and in the development of 'a juridical literature worthy of the English Bar'.[37] Austin's vision was of an institutionalized, autonomous discipline of law which would at once be as systematic as that of Prussia, but without the 'secluded habits' of German Professors. 'In England, theory would be moulded to practice.'[38] Significantly, he asserted: 'The only practical jurisprudence is particular.'[39]

David Sugarman and Philip Schofield have sketched the story of the rise of analytical jurisprudence (not Austin's term) and 'the expository tradition' of academic law in the late nineteenth century.[40] The outlines are familiar: Austin sterilized and narrowed Bentham's jurisprudence; the followers of Austin further narrowed down Austin, by excluding his discussions of utility and by shifting the focus to particular jurisprudence. Bentham was rendered impotent by a combination of misunderstanding, misinterpretation, and neglect. It was claimed that Bentham was essentially a destructive thinker, whereas Austin was constructive and that Austin's theory of law was an improvement on Bentham's.[41] Such claims are specious. A more plausible interpretation is that the pioneering full-time academic lawyers were concerned to establish their credentials with both the practising profession and the scholarly community. Bentham's radicalism and antipathy to the common law would antagonize the former; Austin's

---

which duty or obligation and legal persons may be almost the only ones. In theory, one could envisage a legal system which prescribed only absolute duties, backed by sanctions that did not include punishments. If, as seems more plausible, by 'necessary' Austin meant important or basic or salient, then the distinction between necessary and common is vague and not very significant.

[36] e.g., *Uses*, 372.   [37] *Uses*, 390.   [38] Id., 372.   [39] Ibid.

[40] D. Sugarman, 'Legal Theory, the Common Law Mind, and the Making of the Textbook Tradition', in *LTCL* at 26; Schofield, op. cit.

[41] J. S. Mill, 'Austin on Jurisprudence', cxviii, *The Edinburgh Review* (1863), 439–41, discussed by Schofield, op. cit., 70–1.

rigorously 'scientific' approach might persuade the latter of the intellectual respectability of this new discipline. This story is broadly correct. But, in the present context, it requires to be' modified in at least two respects. Austin was never accepted uncritically even within English positivism and, as we shall see in the next section, the distinction between general and particular jurisprudence was the focus for a long-running and rather sterile debate that was symptomatic of a wider unease about the development of academic law.

Poor John Austin! A public and a private failure in his lifetime, after his death he was elevated to the status of 'Father of English Jurisprudence' to be used for purposes quite different from what he had intended and to serve as a whipping-boy until he was decently buried by Herbert Hart. It was Austinian Jurisprudence that was said to stink in the nostrils of the practising barrister;[42] Austin provided the main target for attack by Henry Maine, James Bryce, and other proponents of historical jurisprudence; some of his closest disciples, Clark, Holland, and Salmond, carped and criticized him; by 1945 Buckland could say: 'He was a religion; to-day he seems to be regarded rather as a disease.'[43] In recent years scholars have usually treated Austin as a lesser figure than Bentham. In 1961 Herbert Hart secured his own reputation by destroying Austin's, only for a series of well-intentioned scholars to disinter him—in one case to use him as a launching pad for a virulent and largely irrelevant attack on Hart.[44] These 'debates' can mostly be read as a series of family squabbles with strong Oedipal overtones within English legal positivism. Since World War II the most persistent attacks on analytical jurisprudence have been from without: on the one hand, the attack on the alleged amoralism of positivism exemplified by the criticisms of Hart by Devlin, Fuller, and Dworkin—a line of criticism that largely ignores the significance of Bentham's distinction between expository and censorial jurisprudence; on the other hand, the broader critique of formalism and the expository tradition, most recently exemplified by Morton Horwitz's categorization of the English analytical tradition as being unhistorical, unempirical, uncritical, and based on an outdated hermeneutics.[45]

It was Austin's intention to develop and disseminate Bentham's ideas, not to dethrone him. He can hardly be blamed for the uses to which he was put after his death. His originality as a thinker and his influence have often been greatly exaggerated, except perhaps in his role as someone to react against.[46] A charit-

---

[42] The phrase is attributed to Dicey; cf. Buckland below at n. 43.

[43] W. W. Buckland, *Some Reflections on Jurisprudence* (Cambridge, 1945) 2.

[44] Robert Moles, *Definition and Rule in Legal Theory: A Reassessment of H. L. A. Hart and the Positivist Tradition* (Oxford, 1987). Moles makes some interesting points, but his criticism of Hart rests on the secondary, and by no means uncontroversial, claim that Hart misread Austin; in his own interpretation of Austin he eccentrically pays almost no attention to his relationship to Bentham.

[45] Morton J. Horwitz, 'Why is Anglo-American Jurisprudence Unhistorical?', H. L. A. Hart Memorial Lecture, May 1995 (forthcoming).

[46] Apart from Bentham, the influence of Hobbes on later English positivists, such as Pollock, is often underestimated.

able interpretation suggests that he struggled valiantly, but unsuccessfully, with some intractable problems;[47] a less kind view is that he was hopelessly confused. He deserves to be reburied and allowed to rest in peace.

HOLLAND AND HIS CRITICS

From 1863, when Austin's lectures first became available, until the 1890s there is a case for saying that his doctrines 'dominated the teaching of Jurisprudence in England and the Commonwealth'.[48] Several factors explain this: Austin's positivism and his antipathy to Natural Law; the apolitical and 'scientific' nature of his analytical jurisprudence; his relative sympathy with the common law tradition compared to Bentham; and, above all, the absence of rivals.[49]

However, such claims to Austin's 'dominance' should be taken with a large pinch of salt. First, university legal education in this period was new and very small in scale. Second, it took some time for jurisprudence to become firmly established in the curriculum. In London, Austin's successors in the Chair in the subject were more notable for their rapid turnover, their lack of students, and their interest in other subjects than for their productivity—the major exception being Sheldon Amos.[50] In the older universities for a long time jurisprudence was almost 'unheard of'.[51] Furthermore, Austin was the subject of persistent criticism after the publication of his lectures, and for a time the Historical School, led by Sir Henry Maine, threatened to become a serious rival.[52]

In the 1880s Jurisprudence began to be recognized as an important element in legal education, even by the Inns of Court.[53] But it was felt that there was no satisfactory student text on the subject. Thomas Erskine Holland decided to fill the gap.[54] His *The Elements of Jurisprudence* was first published in 1880. At one level it was a success; it went through thirteen editions in his lifetime, and was

---

[47] Holland see below at n. 59.

[48] H. L. A. Hart, 'John Austin' in A. W. B. Simpson, *Biographical Dictionary of the Common Law* (London, 1984) 23.

[49] The first generation of university law teachers believed that the production of students' works was a high priority in the struggle to establish law as an academic discipline. Works by Foster, Amos, and Markby did not meet the felt need for an accessible text on jurisprudence; nor did the full version of Austin's lectures, but students' works based on them, such as those by Campbell (1874) and Clark (1883) were produced to fill the gap. See further Schofield, op. cit., at 72–3.

[50] Id., 69.   [51] Ibid.

[52] It is significant that most of the leading pioneers of English university law teaching in this period, Bryce, Maitland, Dicey, to a lesser extent Pollock, and later Vinogradoff, distanced themselves from analytical jurisprudence. The main exception was Holland. However, nearly all went out of their way to stress the potential compatibility of these distinct enterprises.

[53] Pollock, *Essays on Jurisprudence and Ethics* (London, 1882) 1.

[54] Sir T. E. Holland (1835–1926) was Chichele Professor of International Law at Oxford from 1874–1910. The page citations used here are from the 10th edn. (1906). Holland had earlier published *Essays on the Forms of Law* (1870). This was concerned with legislation and codification in England and could, ironically, be interpreted as a contribution to particular jurisprudence.

reprinted several times after his death in 1926; it was pirated in the United States and for almost fifty years it was the most widely used textbook on jurisprudence in England—but again one should bear in mind the relatively small scale of academic law throughout that period.[55]

Holland was a quite suitable person to follow in Austin's footsteps. He was a strong positivist, a lucid writer, and 'the whole bent of his mind was towards orderliness and simplification'.[56] He was impervious to criticism, precise to the point of pedantry, and well-read in Roman Law and English Law as well as International Law and History. Above all he was a good expositor. As Pollock said, compared to Austin's work, 'Professor Holland's is concise without abruptness, flowing without tediousness, and distinct without wearisome repetitions.'[57]

Holland considered himself to be a pioneer. Bentham and Austin had helped to highlight the need for a formal science, but Bentham had muddied the waters by his distinctions between expository and censorial and authoritative and unauthoritative jurisprudence. Censorial Jurisprudence, Bentham's main interest, referred to the Art of Legislation rather than the Science of Law; 'authoritative' jurisprudence is nothing more than a body of law; 'unauthoritative local jurisprudence' is mere commentary; only 'unauthoritative general jurisprudence' is scientific and Bentham contributed little to this.[58] Austin made a significant contribution, presenting, in Holland's words, 'the spectacle of a powerful and conscientious mind struggling with an intractable and rarely handled material'.[59] Unfortunately, 'the defects of the work are even more widely recognized than its merits'.[60] Austin's work was fragmentary, repetitive, neglecting large tracts of his subject, while devoting too much space 'to digressions upon questions, such as the psychology of the will, codification and utilitarianism'.[61] Holland found little in modern civil law scholarship, except among pandectists, that bore directly on analytical jurisprudence as he conceived it.[62]

The way was therefore open for the first systematic work on the formal science of law. Holland followed Austin and Clark in concentrating on general analytical jurisprudence. However, he went one step further in refusing to recognize particular jurisprudence as a serious or even a proper pursuit. For him,

---

[55] Holland's *Jurisprudence* was seen as the main vehicle of Austinian analytical jurisprudence. It was more systematic and more readable than Austin. By and large, it was treated with respect in Holland's lifetime, but it did not stand the test of time. In later writings in the tradition it was almost never cited with approval and it was used as a target for criticism by Kocourek, Stone, Dias, and others. It has been almost completely ignored by writers as diverse as Friedmann, Hart, and Dworkin. Today, it seems seriously flawed in respect of both conception and execution—an elementary textbook on a subject not suited to textbook treatment. Cf. W. Twining, 'Is your textbook really necessary?' XI *JSPTL* (*NS*) 81 (1970).

[56] J. L. Brierley, Obituary, 42 *LQR* 475 (1926).   [57] F. Pollock, op. cit. (1882) 9.

[58] This is a misjudgement based on ignorance of some of Bentham's less well-known published writings as well as his unpublished work.

[59] Id., Preface, vii.   [60] Ibid.   [61] Ibid.

[62] Holland suggests that this is because 'that continental jurists find in Roman law a ready-made terminology and a typical method, upon which they are little inclined to innovate'. (Preface, viii.)

the issue was not just one of semantics, a loose extension of the term 'jurisprudence' to the study of particular municipal legal systems. Jurisprudence is 'the formal science of positive law'[63] and science must be general. 'Particular jurisprudence' might mean either of two things: it might be a general science derived from observation of the laws of one country, in which case the particularity applies to the sources from which the science is derived, rather than to the science. Thus, one might start to build up a science of geology by observing strata in England, but the outcome would not be 'English geology', for the findings would only be scientific if the generalizations would hold good everywhere, 'insofar as the same substances and forces are everywhere present'.[64] Alternatively, particular jurisprudence may mean acquaintance with the laws of a particular people; 'but it is improper to apply the term "science" to such merely practical and empirical knowledge'.[65]

Holland argued that a better analogy was with Grammar—'the science of those ideas of relation which, in greater or less perfection, and often in most dissimilar ways, are expressed in all the languages of mankind'.[66] There is a fundamental difference between learning a particular language and studying the scientific principles of grammar. The formal science of law is concerned with 'those few and simple ideas which underlie the infinite variety of legal rules' (in all systems).[67]

Here we are only concerned with Holland's idea of a formal science of positive law. Holland was a rigid positivist and a severe formalist and, as such, open to attack by critics of such positions. But his conception of analytical jurisprudence was also criticized from within legal positivism by Pollock, Buckland, and Gray among others. Holland stood his ground and only made passing reference to his critics.

Frederick Pollock was the first critic of consequence. In a review article on

[63] Id., 13.
[64] Id., 10–11; cf. Maine's use of the analogy with geology in *Ancient Law* (London, 1861), Ch. 1.   [65] Id., 11.
[66] Id., 7. On the link between Bentham's Universal Jurisprudence and his idea of a Universal Grammar see D. Long, op. cit., 16–18.
[67] Holland sought to explain his idea of a 'formal science' by an example. If a scholar accumulated knowledge of every European system of law and found each to be entirely unlike the rest, there would be no basis for constructing a science; there would just be a heterogeneous body of information. 'Suppose however, *as is the case*, that the laws of every country contain a common element; that they have been constructed in order to effect similar objects, and involve the assumption of similar moral phenomena as everywhere existing; then such a person might proceed to frame out of his accumulated materials a scheme of the purposes, methods, and ideas common to every system of law. Such a scheme would be a formal science of law; presenting many analogies to Grammar . . .' (id., 7, italics added). This passage is vulnerable to criticism on several grounds: first, what he describes is an empirical rather than a formal science; secondly, he lacked the evidence to support his assertion that the laws of every country contain a common element; he merely asserted what his science set out to prove; third, he includes purposes, assumed moral phenomena, and methods as well as ideas. But elsewhere his formal science is presented as dealing only with analysis of concepts. This is the gravamen of Buckland's criticism. Compare the recent debate about whether Austin's jurisprudence was formal or empirical, above n. 34 and below n. 87.

'some recent contributions to Legal Science',[68] he criticized Holland's conception of a formal science on educational grounds. The analogy with Grammar was 'felicitous, and only too felicitous', for there is little demand for books on the science of grammar. One learns grammar through learning one concrete language and not vice versa. The saving grace of Holland's book is that the author, while denying its possibility, in fact practises particular jurisprudence concisely and intelligibly. However, jurisprudence of this abstract kind is doomed to vacillate between two unsatisfactory alternatives: a pure theory of legal classification ('a catalogue of blank forms') or partial exposition of a particular system. An institutional work on English Law, a successor to Blackstone's *Commentaries* or analogous to the German *Pandekten* would serve the needs of students and practitioners better than a purely abstract study of legal ideas.[69]

John Chipman Gray of Harvard challenged Holland's conception of Jurisprudence, also mainly on grounds of practicality. There are three kinds of Jurisprudence: Particular; Comparative; and General. All are scientific, in the sense that they involve systematic study. Particular Jurisprudence is more than the particular law of a particular people—'It means the scientific knowledge of the law of a particular people.' Particular Jurisprudence is of much more utility to intending practitioners than Comparative or General Jurisprudence.[70]

One particularly harsh critic, Albert Kocourek, criticized Holland for not staying loyal to his conception of an abstract science.[71] But Kocourek's own contribution to abstract jurisprudence was dismissed or ignored as being totally impractical and useless. This supports the hypothesis that Holland's *Jurisprudence* survived in spite of rather than because of his commitment to a formal science.[72]

The most interesting criticism of Holland's 'formal science' came from W. W. Buckland of Cambridge. This took the form of one of the longest-running non-debates in the history of Anglo-American jurisprudence. In 1890, Buckland published an article in *The Law Quarterly Review* on 'The Difficulties of Abstract Jurisprudence', in which he attacked Holland's conception of general jurisprudence as misconceived.[73] Whereas Holland had denied the possibility of particular jurisprudence, Buckland doubted the feasibility of general jurisprudence. Holland, who was not one to change his mind, ignored the criticism in

---

[68] F. Pollock, op. cit. (1882).

[69] Pollock, in his *First Book of Jurisprudence* (London, 1896) Preface, explicitly distanced himself from the analytical school.

[70] J. C. Gray, *The Nature and Sources of Law* (New York, 1909) Ch. 7.

[71] A. Kocourek, *Jural Relations* (1st ed., Indianapolis, 1928).

[72] F. H. Lawson wrote of Holland's *Elements of Jurisprudence* that it resembled Markby's *Elements of Law* 'in containing quite a good deal of what is not so much jurisprudence as law' and quoted Lord Birkenhead as saying that it was 'one of a number of books which appeared in Oxford in the eighties which made sense of English law'. *The Oxford Law School, 1850–1965* (Oxford, 1968) at 75.

[73] W. W. Buckland, 'Difficulties of Abstract Jurisprudence', 24 *LQR* 436 (1890).

successive editions. Fifty-five years later, Buckland renewed the attack in almost identical terms, claiming that he saw nothing to alter in what he had said.[74]

Buckland followed Pollock in doubting the utility of abstract jurisprudence, while praising Holland for improving on Austin in respect of his exposition and arrangement. But he launched a more substantial attack on his conception of the subject. Holland defined jurisprudence as 'the formal science of those relations of mankind which are generally recognized as having consequences'. This assumes that there are legal concepts that are widely shared among systems of law: to what extent that is true, even of Western systems, is an empirical question to be determined by detailed comparative study of actual bodies of law.

If jurisprudence is a formal science like grammar, it is of very limited utility. If it is an empirical science, the analogy with geology is inappropriate: one may start to build up a picture of geological strata because they are subject to physical laws which are everywhere the same; but law is dependent on its social context. The extent to which there are shared legal concepts is an empirical question requiring proof by comparative study of many systems. But where is the evidence? Holland either assumes what he set out to prove or else was relying on a priori axioms reminiscent of German transcendentalism; in that case, like John Austin, he may be suspected of being a closet natural lawyer.[75] In fact, Buckland as a comparatist and Roman lawyer, knows of some evidence which suggests that there are a few common notions, such as duty, but their bulk is not great and a 'science' based on these alone would be meagre at best.[76] The fundamental notions of law are not everywhere the same, for law is 'to a great degree the product of the milieu in which it has developed'.[77] Holland's analogy with grammar might be apt, but it suggests at most the limited scope and utility of such a science; on the other hand, the analogy with geology was misleading because geology is subject to universal physical laws, whereas law is culturally relative.

For Buckland, general jurisprudence is either empirical and speculative or else it is formal, in which case it is both narrow and useless. On the other hand, particular jurisprudence, as the study of the underlying notions of one system of law is both feasible and useful. The method is scientific, but the subject is empirical. Its aim, to show 'the underlying principles and broadest generalizations' of a given system as a foundation for the study of domestic law.

In several respects the differences between Holland and his critics were not very great.

First, Holland, Pollock, and Buckland, and in different ways, Gray and Kocourek, were all committed legal positivists who maintained a sharp distinction between law and morals and sought to establish the study of positive law as a distinct discipline, separate from politics, ethics, and sociology. Holland,

---

[74] W. W. Buckland, *Some Reflections on Jurisprudence*, op. cit., Ch. VI, at 68. This work is fairly typical of Buckland's style: succinct, perceptive, astringent, and strongly positivist.
[75] e.g., *Reflections*, 68. [76] Id., 70. [77] *Reflections*, 69.

Pollock, and Buckland all criticized Austin for treating utilitarianism as part of Jurisprudence.[78] For example, Pollock referred to it as 'irrelevant and mostly bad moral philosophy'[79]—a far cry from Bentham. Buckland insisted that Jurisprudence was 'Austin's real subject. This was the analysis of legal concepts.'[80]

Secondly, they shared a conception of law that treated municipal legal systems as the primary subject of the study of law. Each was sympathetic to the idea of viewing Public International Law as analogous to municipal law; and they treated it as dealing almost entirely with relations between sovereign states.[81] In short, they all held similar, strong versions of a 'black box' theory of law.

Thirdly, Holland and Buckland wished to confine Jurisprudence to the analysis of concepts; Pollock was more circumspect. All placed the study of legal doctrine at the centre of legal education. The fact that all three fought hard for this admittedly narrow enterprise does not mean that they were narrow-minded as men or as scholars. Pollock is well-known for the breadth of his interests. Buckland was a Roman lawyer and linguist who was familiar with German and French legal literature. Holland wrote extensively on the history of International Law and, largely through frequent letters to *The Times*, participated in many contemporary public debates, while maintaining a rigidly positivistic stance on the interpretation and application of principles of International Law.

Fourthly, Pollock doubted whether discussions of uses of the word 'law' and the theory of sovereignty—the subject of the first two chapters of Holland's *Elements*—were properly within the scope of jurisprudence, but rather should be treated as prolegomena. Buckland agreed, but took a stronger line:

Jurisprudence has no independent existence. Its formulae are meaningless except in relation to concrete legal rules. It is a part of the law. That the same jurisprudence is a part of all law is a point to be proven not assumed.[82]

This was a crucial part of his argument that analytical jurisprudence is in first instance particular. Its primary task is analysis of the basic legal concepts of a single municipal legal system. It is an empirical question to what extent, if at all, even advanced legal systems have common concepts. This is a matter for comparative legal research. Buckland, on the basis of his knowledge of Roman Law

[78] e.g., Holland at vii; Buckland, *Reflections*, 2 and 42–3.
[79] F. Pollock, *Introduction to the History of the Science of Politics* (London, 1890) 67.
[80] *Reflections*, 2.
[81] e.g., Holland, Ch. xvii; Pollock (1896); Buckland, *Reflections*, Ch. 2. Holland referred to International law as 'law by courtesy' (id., 127) and its study as 'the vanishing point of jurisprudence' (380).
[82] (1890) at 438; cf. *Reflections* at 3: 'Law and sovereignty are not legal conceptions; they are presuppositions.' This is reminiscent of Thayer's treatment of 'relevance' as being a presupposition of the law of evidence, rather than part of it. (J. B. Thayer, *A Preliminary Treatise on Evidence at Common Law* (Boston, 1898) 264–5.) For both Buckland and Thayer the distinction between presuppositions and legal rules was logically, but not pedagogically, important. Buckland acknowledged that his *Some Reflections on Jurisprudence* was a misnomer as much of it dealt with what he considered to be prolegomena to Jurisprudence (Preface).

and some contemporary civilian systems, was inclined to scepticism. He suspected that the universalism of Bentham, Austin, and even Holland undermined
the distinction between the is and the ought and opened the way for natural law
to re-enter by the back door. Buckland it seems was a relativist in respect of both
ethics and culture. However, he was as committed as any to the systematic study
of legal doctrine.

What was at stake in these debates? It was not a merely or mainly a semantic
question about the meaning of the term 'jurisprudence'. The main concerns were
pedagogical: the search for a suitable underpinning for the detailed study of
English Law. It is striking that Buckland's article of 1890 begins with reference
to the attitude of 'disgust and scarcely veiled contempt' of practical lawyers
towards Jurisprudence as a subject. In the context 'abstract' is used pejoratively.
The article assumes that most undergraduate law students are intending barristers.
This fits the thesis, convincingly developed by David Sugarman, that the establishment of a narrow expository orthodoxy by legal scholars, who were themselves far from narrow-minded, represents a compromise aimed at establishing
the study of English Law in universities as being at once scientific and of clear
practical value. In the present context the primary reference group was the practising Bar. This required that Jurisprudence should be simultaneously rigorous,
uncritical, and in tune with the legal culture of the common law. This in turn
necessitated a distinct shift of emphasis from general jurisprudence to a form of
particular jurisprudence that was closely integrated with the study of substantive
doctrine—the basic concepts of common law talk rather than of talk about law.

On revisiting these largely forgotten texts, one is struck by the modesty of
their intellectual ambitions. Unlike Bentham, Austin, and Maine, who were serious theorists, Pollock, Holland, and Buckland were competent legal scholars
who were suspicious of philosophy. The debate between universalists and
particularists took place in the context of the preparation of elementary student
texts by lawyers, for whom jurisprudence was an avocation. Over time the
particularists won the day and by 1945 Buckland could write: 'Most English
writers deal with Particular Jurisprudence.'[83] Bentham was ignored, Austin was
bowdlerized, and Maine was marginalized. Holland was at first treated as a
particularist *malgré soi* and was in due course superseded.

HART AND DWORKIN[84]

I began my study of law in Oxford in 1952, the year in which Herbert Hart was
elected to the Corpus Chair of Jurisprudence in succession to A. L. Goodhart.
So when I embarked on the study of jurisprudence towards the end of my second

[83] *Reflections*, 71.

[84] Except where it is indicated otherwise, this section focuses on two texts: Hart's *The Concept
of Law* (2nd ed., Oxford, 1994), including his posthumous Postscript, and Ronald Dworkin's *Law's
Empire* (London, 1986) (hereafter, *LE*).

year, I found myself at the cusp of two traditions of English legal positivism. I experienced both versions.

By the early 1950s taught jurisprudence had become rather eclectic, exemplified by the main textbooks, Paton and Salmond. Some cursory attention was paid to 'schools', such as Natural Law, the Historical School, and Sociological Jurisprudence. More emphasis was placed on particular analytical jurisprudence, which fell into two parts: the sources of English Law as they were treated, for example, in C. K. Allen's *Law in the Making*, and analysis of concepts, including law, sovereignty, legal personality, ownership, possession, *ratio decidendi*, rights and duties. A typical essay topic was: 'Does English Law have a theory of possession? Does it need one?' One approached such questions by reading a mixture of cases and secondary writings. These were interpreted as '*Num*-questions', that is questions expecting the answer 'No'. So in dealing with possession one compared the use of the term in cases on larceny, bailment, sale of goods, trespass to land and goods and concluded that it had a slightly different definition in each context, thereby confirming 'the pragmatism' and distrust of abstraction of English legal culture.

Such exercises were particularistic in two ways: the focus was on concepts of English law and they were studied at a relatively low level of generality. However, the approach was not entirely parochial. One might read (or read about) Savigny on possession, German theories of corporate personality, and American writers on rights. One made regular comparisons with Roman Private Law, possibly referring to Buckland and McNair.[85] Buckland's argument about the possibility and value of particular analytical jurisprudence was fully vindicated. It was clearly relevant to other subjects that we were studying; it served to break down the artificial boundaries between fields of law and to make a number of connections; and it helped one to see the common law—especially private law—as a whole, if not quite as a system.[86] For the degree I took two papers in Roman Law (having also done Roman Law for the preliminary examination, 'Mods.') and one in Legal History. When I revised for my Finals, I studied the English and Roman law of contract, the history of English contract doctrine, and Hohfeld's analysis of rights simultaneously. It made a lot of sense. This kind of 'particular analytical jurisprudence' has virtually disappeared. From an educational point of view, something of real value was lost as these exercises in applied jurisprudence were replaced by more abstract enquiries.

Of course, this kind of study had distinct limitations. It was narrowly focused; it was somewhat uncritical;[87] it bore little relationship to law in action in society;

---

[85] W. W. Buckland and A. D. McNair, *Roman Law and Common Law* (1936).

[86] The standard justification for studying Roman law was that it enabled one to study a legal system as a whole. In fact, one focused almost entirely on the rules and concepts of Roman Private Law.

[87] Horwitz, op. cit., characterizes English Analytical Jurisprudence as ahistorical; unempirical; apolitical; and uncritical. This is only partially correct in respect of the version I encountered as an undergraduate at Oxford: everything one studied was suffused with history, albeit of a rather narrow

and it was strikingly atheoretical, especially in respect of method. The subject, as Buckland had suggested, was part of English law; one *did* it as one did any other subject: one read secondary writings and some cases and one wrote an essay.

In his inaugural lecture on 'Definition and Theory in Jurisprudence', Hart seized on the methodological weaknesses of traditional or classical jurisprudence.[88] Questions framed in such terms as 'What is law?', 'What is a right?', 'What is a legal person?' were misposed. They invited answers in the form of definitions of single words *per genus et differentiam*; this was inappropriate for elucidating familiar abstract terms and it failed to dissolve the puzzlements underlying the questions. While theory in law was welcome, the growth of theory on the back of definition was not. In one seminal lecture Hart re-established links with philosophy and provided some powerful tools of analysis of potentially wide application. Significantly, he explicitly gave the credit to Bentham for the main tool, *paraphrasis*, by implication dismissing the methods of all of the intervening jurists in the analytical tradition, including Austin.

In his lectures, which culminated in *The Concept of Law* in 1961, Hart focused mainly on those concepts which particularists like Pollock and Buckland treated as prolegomena to jurisprudence—law, legal system, command, rule, sovereignty, sanction, and the like. However, he drew no sharp distinction between general and particular jurisprudence and some of his best later work—on causation, intention, responsibility, and rights—could reasonably be interpreted as contributions to particular jurisprudence. For much of his life, such categorizations were unimportant.

The main challengers to Hart, such as Fuller, Dworkin, and Devlin, and defenders, such as Raz and MacCormick, have generally concentrated on issues relating to his positivism and modified utilitarianism. The approach has been philosophical and the debates have normally taken place at a rather abstract level, often quite far removed from the particularities of English law.[89] There has, of course, been criticism from a variety of other perspectives. In considering the distinction between general and particular jurisprudence it is worth referring briefly to two of these. First, Brian Simpson, drawing on his deep knowledge of English legal history, has argued that Hart's concept of a legal system just does not fit the 'muddle' of the English common law.[90] This can be interpreted as

kind—the tracing of the development of doctrines of English private law largely through the cases. The predominating approach was doctrinal-empirical rather than social-empirical. We were not discouraged from criticism (*de lege ferenda*), but we were not equipped to do this in an intellectual way. The predominant approach was apolitical, except that some of us drew inspiration from the writings of Wolfgang Friedmann.

[88] H. L. A. Hart, 'Definition and Theory in Jurisprudence', 70 *LQR* 37 (1953).

[89] The problem of building bridges between abstract theorizing and the study of specialized fields of law is explored in *LTCL*, the central theme of which is that, for purposes of legal education and legal scholarship, 'Jurisprudence should not be a subject apart'.

[90] A. W. B. Simpson, 'The Common Law and Legal Theory' in Simpson (ed.), *Oxford Essays in Jurisprudence*, 2nd series (Oxford, 1973); reprinted in *LTCL*, Ch. 2.

turning on its head Bentham's argument that the common law is not law.[91] Simpson's argument is that a theory of law which excludes the common law must be defective. Subsequently, Charles Sampford has argued at a more general level that it is fundamentally misleading to think of law anywhere as 'systematic'.[92] His picture of law as being part of a 'social mêlée' at both national and international levels is very much in tune with the thrust of those aspects of globalization theory, and of legal pluralism, which challenge all 'black box' conceptions of law. At first sight Simpson's thesis looks particularistic, Sampford's general. But both represent important challenges to theories of law that treat legal systems as self-contained and 'systematic' in a strong sense. As such they are contributions to general rather than particular jurisprudence, if the distinction has any value.

A second challenge to Hart took the position that his kind of analytical jurisprudence, by focusing on lawyers' talk, divorced law from its social context and diverted attention from sociological enquiries that are essential to understanding legal phenomena. One of the first versions of this line of criticism, by Edgar Bodenheimer, was made before the publication of *The Concept of Law*.[93] It provoked an immediate response from Hart, who argued that his form of conceptual elucidation was as important for sociology as for law and that sociologists could do well to put their own house in order. For jurists clarity begins at home. It may be that the exchange with Bodenheimer was behind the famous claim in the Preface that *The Concept of Law* 'may also be regarded as an essay in descriptive sociology'. This statement has provoked hoots of derision from the sociologically inclined, but little analysis.

My own view, as one who is committed to developing broader approaches to law, has been that Hart 'won' the battle with Bodenheimer, but by not following through in making the case for the importance of conceptual elucidation in *any* approach to the understanding of law, he missed an opportunity to extend the scope of analytical jurisprudence. In short, he exposed the naïvety of traditional analytical jurisprudence in respect of *method* (Bentham excepted), but accepted uncritically its *agenda* .[94] One implication of this argument is that, if legal theory

---

[91] e.g., *OLIG*, Ch. xvi.

[92] Charles Sampford, *The Disorder of Law* (Oxford, 1989).

[93] Edgar Bodenheimer, 'Modern Analytical Jurisprudence and the Limits of its Usefulness', 104 Univ. of *Pennsylvania Law Rev.* 1680 (1955–6); H. L. A. Hart, 'Analytical Jurisprudence at Mid-Twentieth Century: A Reply to Professor Bodenheimer', 105 id., 953 (1957).

[94] 'Hart has not in a systematic way attempted to proceed beyond the confines of Bentham's expository and censorial jurisprudence into the kind of broader perspective that is encompassed by phrases such as "sociology of law". He has not, for example, devoted sustained attention to analysis of key terms in the vocabulary of sociological theories about law such as society, group, class, function, process, dispute, social problem, institution or decision. He has clarified concepts, such as rule, habit, and sanction, which are important in social theory as well as analytical jurisprudence; but he has, on the whole, been content to reformulate and refine issues posed by a fairly narrow tradition of academic law, rather than to raise in a sustained way the kinds of questions which a broader social perspective is likely to treat as central or significant.' William Twining, 'Academic Law and Legal Philosophy: The Significance of Herbert Hart', 95 *LQR* 557, (1979) at 578–9.

is to respond adequately to the challenges of 'globalization', it needs, *inter alia*, to develop a sophisticated conceptual apparatus for the task. That is a theme for another occasion. Here, however, it is pertinent to note that the generalists as well as the particularists in the analytical tradition are equally open to the charge of 'narrowness', insofar as they concentrated almost exclusively on legal concepts (with a few 'prolegomena'), that is on 'law talk' to the almost total exclusion of 'talk about law'.

It is sometimes suggested that Hart's *The Concept of Law* is solely concerned with 'linguistic analysis' and in this sense is semantic. Buckland, as we have seen, equated analytical jurisprudence with 'analysis of legal concepts'.[95] However, Hart's conception of a descriptive jurisprudence goes far beyond this: it includes both elucidating concepts and *using* them;[96] concepts and models (such as the model of law as a system of rules) are tools of description; *The Concept of Law*, and general descriptive jurisprudence, go beyond conceptual clarification to describing common features of the form, structure, and content of legal systems.[97]

The distinction between general and particular jurisprudence was for a long time treated as of little significance and the debates surrounding it were usually treated as trivial logomachy. However, the distinction was revived in a symposium based on a conference in Jerusalem held in honour of Hart. Commenting on some draft chapters of Dworkin's *Law's Empire*, shortly before it was published, Ruth Gavison wrote:

Dworkin's analysis of law as an interpretive concept, under his own model of interpretation, makes classical legal theory impossible. In other words, Dworkin is challenging here the possibility and the value of 'general jurisprudence', the attempt to analyse societies at their most general (like the attempt to analyse human nature) and identify those features common to all social organizations which might lead to the need for similar institutions and practices. Law is one such social institution found in all societies and exhibiting a core of similar features.[98]

Hart made a similar point in the same volume, but developed it much further in his Postscript to *The Concept of Law*, which was published posthumously in 1994. Here he defended his views largely in terms of two propositions: that Dworkin has misrepresented his position on a number of key issues and that he and Dworkin were involved in two different, not necessarily incompatible, enterprises, the one general, the other particular.

---

[95] Above, n. 80.

[96] e.g., Postscript at 240: 'As a means of carrying out this descriptive enterprise my book makes repeated use of a number of concepts . . .'.   [97] See the passage quoted below at n. 100.

[98] Ruth Gavison, Comment in Gavison (ed.), *Issues in Contemporary Legal Philosophy: The Influence of H. L. A. Hart* (Oxford, 1987) 28. Later Gavison continues: 'I shall risk being called a "semantic scholar" and say that for these comparative lessons to be drawn we need some universal conceptual scheme, in terms of such basic legal functions such as dispute resolution, which may help us both to understand the similarities and highlight the differences between societies.' (id., 29).

Hart claimed that he and Dworkin have very different conceptions of legal theory. Hart's is *general* 'in the sense that it is not tied to any particular legal system or legal culture';[99] and it is *descriptive* 'in that it is morally neutral and has no justificatory aims'.[100] Dworkin's jurisprudence is in large part evaluative and justificatory and 'is addressed to a particular legal culture', which is typically the theorist's own. [101] Dworkin is concerned to interpret the settled law and legal practices of a particular system and to provide the best moral justification for them.[102] Hart considers that these two enterprises are so different as not to involve any substantial joinder of issue that need constitute a disagreement.

The Concept of Law deals with the nature of law in general rather than the law of a given society. Hart's work is clearly in the tradition of general jurisprudence, occasionally concretized by particular applications to English or to Anglo-American law. But can we say that Dworkin is doing particular jurisprudence? At first sight it looks absurd to confine Dworkin's ideas in this way. For example, the idea that interpretation of a social practice involves 'showing it in its best light'[103] or the distinction between semantic and interpretative theories are not ideas that are linked to any given legal system. Are not Dworkin's ideas on democracy, equality, and liberty founded on some idea of universalizability? Hercules clearly has roots in American legal tradition. He may not be a citizen of the world, but does he not provide one model for judging in any liberal democracy both in respect of his conception of his role and his method of interpretation? Does not Dworkin advance a prescriptive theory of adjudication that is general, if not universal? And, surely, Dworkin's criticisms of legal positivism are not confined to England and the United States.

One possible interpretation of the claim that Hart and Dworkin are involved in significantly different enterprises is that they are addressing different questions. Jurisprudence is a wasteland of false polemics and one way of disposing of such squabbles is to show that the best interpretation of two apparently

---

[99] *The Concept of Law*, Postscript, 239.

[100] Id., 240. In his response to Dworkin in the Jerusalem symposium, Hart states: 'there is a standing need for a form of legal theory or jurisprudence that is descriptive or general in scope, the perspective of which is not that of a judge deciding "what the law is", that is, what the law requires in particular cases . . . but is that of an external observer of a form of social institution with a normative aspect, which in its recurrence in different societies and periods exhibits many common features of form, structure and content.': 'Legal Theory and the Problem of Sense', in Ruth Gavison (ed.), op. cit., 36. Hart goes on to state that descriptive analytical jurisprudence is preliminary to the articulation of a justificatory theory of a community's legal practices (id., 37). I am grateful to Robert Summers for reminding me of this important passage. The main point of difference between Hart and Dworkin here is that Dworkin does not accept that description can be neutral nor that it is preliminary to interpretation (e.g., *LE* 13–14). It is not clear why Hart excludes the interpretation that Dworkin may be offering a general prescriptive theory of adjudication (including legal reasoning) or that his justificatory theory need not be limited to a particular community rather than, as with Rawls's theory of justice, any constitutional democracy. On the claim that descriptive general jurisprudence can describe the content of legal systems, compare Buckland's cautionary admonitions (above) and the 'jurisprudential relativism' of Atiyah and Summers (below).

[101] Id., citing *LE*, 102.   [102] Id., 241.   [103] *LE*, 90.

conflicting positions is that they provide answers to different questions rather than rival answers to shared questions. Prima facie this looks attractive in the present context. In *The Concept of Law* Hart's explicit agenda was to consider three recurrent issues: (1) How does law differ from and how is it related to orders backed by threats? (2) How does legal obligation differ from and how is it related to moral obligation? (3) What are rules and to what extent is law an affair of rules?[104] Dworkin claims that *Law's Empire* is centrally concerned with the problem of sense, that is the truth conditions for correct interpretation of propositions of law. Here, one needs to distinguish between a general theory of legal interpretation or of legal reasoning and what constitutes the best interpretation of a particular rule in a given system. One might render this in the form: 'Under what conditions is it true to say that "rule X means this" or that "this is the correct interpretation of rule X"?' This is a different question from those listed by Hart, but it is in similar form at the same level of generality as Hart-type questions, such as: 'Under what conditions is it true to say that a legal system exists?' or 'Under what conditions is it true to say that X has a right?' *All* of these questions are general in that they are not confined to or derived from a single legal system and they can be asked of many, if not all, legal systems. Similarly, for both Dworkin and Hart, questions such as 'Is this the best interpretation of rule X?' or 'Does Y have a right to delivery of goods from the seller?' require local knowledge of a particular legal system as well as a general theory guiding the answer. Here, the distinction between general and particular jurisprudence provides no basis for distinguishing between the theories of Dworkin and Hart.

It is also doubtful whether the technique of attributing different questions to different positions will take us very far. Hart and Dworkin have different, but overlapping agendas. For example, Dworkin is interested in Hart's questions (2) and (3) and Hart acknowledges that his theory has implications for adjudication and interpretation. He also acknowledges that they do have some substantial differences of view.[105] There are some grey areas, for example where Hart claims that Dworkin has misinterpreted or caricatured his position, but insofar as Dworkin does not accept this, they are disagreeing about the best interpretation of Hart.[106] What is significant in the present context is that Dworkin's criticisms of Hart and Hart's reply are almost without exception pitched at a higher level of generality than any particular legal system. Neither is claiming that they are solely or even mainly arguing about English law or some American jurisdiction or even the common law family. So, again the distinction between general and particular jurisprudence explains almost nothing about the exchanges between Hart and Dworkin.

However, it is Dworkin who insists that: 'interpretive theories are by their

---

[104] *CL*, 13; cf. Postscript, 240.   [105] e.g., Postscript, 248, 261, 264–7.
[106] e.g., id., 244–8; at the time of writing Dworkin has not yet replied in print to Hart's Postscript.

nature addressed to a particular legal culture, generally the culture to which their
authors belong'.[107] In the same passage he draws a distinction between 'the very
detailed and concrete legal theories lawyers and judges construct for a particular
jurisdiction' and the abstract conceptions of law that philosophers build, which
are not so confined.[108] He argues that an abstract philosophical conception of
law, still less a justificatory theory for a given system (or, *semble*, a family of
systems belonging to one legal culture), will probably not fit 'foreign legal
systems developing in and reflecting political ideologies of a sharply different
character'. His main point is that one can only determine whether a given proposition of law is true for a given system by participating in that system, because
this activity involves interpreting and choosing between contested meanings and
that necessitates taking sides. For Dworkin there is no such thing as neutral
interpretation.[109] However, in making these caveats, Dworkin may be being
unduly cautious about the general significance of his theory.

A charitable interpretation of Dworkin's emphasis on the particularity of
interpretation may include two points which we have already encountered. He
may draw almost exclusively on Anglo-American materials and he may leave
open the scope of the applicability of his ideas to civilian and other systems on
the grounds of limited expertise, but so did Austin, Maine, and Holland, all of
whom claimed to be doing general jurisprudence. This seems rather like Holland's example of a geologist who has only studied English strata and who is
cautious about generalizing beyond his data base.[110]

Secondly, in emphasizing the importance of local knowledge, Dworkin seems
to be making a similar point to that made by Buckland in his critique of Holland.
If general jurisprudence is confined to describing the features that are common
to all or nearly all legal systems, the description will almost certainly be rather
thin because in fact legal systems are quite diverse and the interest of a legal
system lies typically in its detail. General jurisprudence on its own will be too
abstract to be useful or interesting. Insofar as Dworkin is concerned with interpretation, argumentation, and justification by legal practitioners and judges, he
would agree with Austin that jurisprudence to be practical has to be local and
particular. But that does not mean that the core elements in his theory only apply
to one system.

Moreover, only by studying all legal systems in detail can one identify which
features are universal or common. Dworkin's variant on this argument is that

---

[107] *LE*, 102.   [108] Id., 102–3.

[109] Dworkin agrees with Hart that one can report a debate about the meaning of a legal rule or
the content of the rule of recognition from the outside, but as soon as one purports to say what any
law means one is involved in interpretation and hence is participating and, in any actual or potential
contest, taking sides.

[110] This is analogous to Raz writing about Rawls: 'The writer's theory must, to be successful,
apply to his society at the time of writing, but there is no general answer as to which societies and
what other times it applies to. The applicability of the theory to different societies must be examined
on a case-by-case basis.' Joseph Raz, *Ethics in the Public Domain* (Oxford, 1994) 63 n.

general jurisprudence cannot deal with the problem of sense, that is the attribution of truth values to propositions of law.[111] This seems to conflate a general theory of adjudication or legal interpretation with its application in a local context. The former may be lean, but that does not mean that it is not important. *Law's Empire* advances a general theory of law, or at least of adjudication; it contains very few concrete examples of interpretation and those are mainly illustrative; some of Dworkin's other writings are more local, but these can be interpreted as applications of his general approach.[112]

A less charitable interpretation of Hart and Dworkin is suggested by Atiyah and Summers, who advocate 'jurisprudential relativism' in the interpretation of legal cultures:

In our view, then, the primary subject-matter of jurisprudence is not a single universal subject-matter, abstracted from the variant phenomena of law in all societies. It should, rather, consist of relevant features of the phenomena of law in one or more particular societies.[113]

Atiyah and Summers were comparing and contrasting the legal cultures of England and the United States which are closely related by history, language, and continuing links. Interestingly they suggest that the two cultures even have different conceptions of some concepts which are usually allocated to the metalanguage of general jurisprudence, such as 'law' and 'rule' and 'legal validity'. In their view, both Hart and Dworkin are best interpreted as contributing to, or as being most useful at the level of, particular jurisprudence. Dworkin's theory is both derived from American intellectual tradition and fits American culture better than English. Conversely Hart is recognizably English in respect of the derivation of his ideas and their application. For example, the ideal role for judges and legislators is dependent on context, for political institutions are fashioned by history, tradition, and culture:

What is the practical utility of a theory which postulates how Hercules J. ought to behave on the bench, if appointing authorities insist on nominating judges who do not even want to emulate Hercules?[114]

This ethnographic perspective raises many intriguing questions that cannot be pursued here. Atiyah and Summers acknowledge that it may be possible to identify some features and concepts which are common to the phenomena of law in all societies, but the list is likely to be short and its explanatory value meagre. This is very like Buckland's view that law is culturally relative and that jurisprudence must in the main be particular. I have some sympathy with this position,

---

[111] Dworkin concedes that there are other questions for general legal theory—historical, sociological, etc. which may produce illuminating propositions *about* law—but maintains that such enquiries have to build on interpretive theories about the meaning of propositions *of* law. *LE*, 13–14.

[112] e.g., 'How to Read the Civil Rights Act', *New York Review of Books*, 20 Dec. 1979, 37.

[113] P. S. Atiyah and R. S. Summers, *Form and Substance in Anglo-American Law* (Oxford, 1987) 418. [114] Id., 420, cf. 264–6.

but I do not think that this is an interpretation that makes Hart's and Dworkin's theories the best they can be. I would rather suggest that both theories largely stand or fall on an assessment of their value as contributions to general jurisprudence.

Dworkin is not a strong cultural relativist.[115] It is one thing to claim that a thick description of any society or culture or social practice must depend on local knowledge and hence be particular; it is another to claim that a society or culture or practice can only be described, interpreted or explained solely in its own terms. Most writing by historians and social anthropologists is particular and local, because they tend to study events and phenomena that are unique in important respects; but those writings are based on theories, methods, and concepts that have some claim to generality—and some may be unknown locally. Conversely, it is a truism, accepted by both Hart and Dworkin, that to give an adequate account of a particular social practice or legal system typically involves taking into account the internal point of view of participants in that practice or system, including their concepts and language. One cannot give a 'thick' account of English or Tiv or Barotse law either solely in terms of some foreign or metalanguage, which does not capture the ways of thought of the participants, nor solely in terms of the folk concepts of the participants themselves.[116] Hart is not committed to ignoring or discounting the internal point of view; Dworkin is not committed to treating local concepts as exclusive for purposes of justification or description. For example, in the standard example of a foreign anthropologist describing and interpreting a rain-making ceremony, the external observer needs to take into account the belief of some or all participants that it does indeed make rain, but s/he could explain and possibly justify the practice in terms of social solidarity: 'Whether or not it makes rain, it serves a useful purpose for them'.

What colour is Hercules' passport? He may be of American origin, have a slight American accent, and possibly some deep-rooted American cultural biases.[117] But clearly he is offered, and deserves attention, as a possible role model

---

[115] Gavison comes close to accusing Dworkin of this: she asserts that Dworkin's theory challenges the possibility and the value of 'general jurisprudence' (above). She argues that one implication of Dworkin's subversion of the distinction between law and a theory of law 'is that a theory of law is no more than the general assumptions about law in a given community, i.e., theories of law are time- and community-dependent' (id., 26–7). My own view is that Dworkin need not be so confined: he may be right in maintaining that to give a precise meaning to a particular provision of the US Constitution or some aspect of English doctrine is participatory, but what is interesting about Dworkin is his general perspective and approach which has wide potential application, whether right or wrong.

[116] Cf. the debate in legal anthropology between Gluckman and Bohannan about the relative importance of 'folk concepts' and metalanguage for giving an account of customary law, Max Gluckman, *The Judicial Process among the Barotse of Northern Rhodesia* (Manchester, 1957); Paul Bohannan, *Justice and Judgment among the Tiv of Nigeria* (London, 1957). This reflected a wider debate about 'emics' and 'etics' in social anthropology, on which see Ward Goodenough, *Description and Comparison in Social Anthropology* (Chicago, 1970). It is now widely accepted that both 'folk concepts' and metalanguages are necessary tools, but that metalanguages are themselves culturally relative social constructs.   [117] Atiyah and Summers, 264–6.

for judges in many systems—certainly the common law family, almost certainly Western civilian systems, possibly the European Union and judges of international tribunals, perhaps even the judiciary in an Islamic state. The reason for this is obvious: the basic ideas underlying Hercules' approach are not derived from nor confined to any one legal system or culture: law as integrity; interpretation as making a system the best it can be; reasoning by the two-stage process of fit and justification; justification in terms of institutionally embedded principles of political morality. All of these concepts are not system-specific. Hercules has strong claims to be a citizen at least of the West, and possibly of the World.

Let us consider some possible objections to this. First, it might be argued that these ideas are not sufficient conditions for appointing Hercules as a judge in any jurisdiction. Of course, that is correct. In order to be able to perform the role of a judge well one needs a number of other qualifications, including a good deal of local knowledge about, for example, the general prescriptions of the legal system concerning authoritative sources of law, including any rules of priority and interpretation; and about other factors subsumed under the idea of 'fit'.[118] Similarly in interpreting the law in a hard case, Hercules' duty is to resolve difficulties by reference to fundamental principles of political morality which give *this* system integrity. These will typically be contested, but in Dworkin's theory this does not mean that Hercules should merely resort to his personal opinions; rather he should seek for the 'best' solution in the system's own terms. Such justificatory principles are not purely local, but form part of a coherent theory of political morality which, one assumes, makes some claim to generality. Dworkin makes clear his commitment to a particular version of liberal democratic theory of wide application, but he recognizes that Hercules may serve in a system based on a different moral theory. Presumably that moral theory is basically compatible with Hercules' own values, for he could not otherwise in good conscience have taken the judicial oath.[119] Hercules' characteristics are not sufficient conditions for judicial appointment; they are presented as desirable, ideal, perhaps even necessary, standards for good judging.

A second objection, suggested by Atiyah and Summers, is that Hercules just does not fit most actual legal systems. If he were a candidate for judicial appointment in England, he would probably not be appointed. Dworkin has two possible answers to that: first, if a system does not subscribe to his aspirational standards for judging, more's the pity. His is 'the best theory' prescribing an

---

[118] The amount of 'local knowledge' required of some judges may not be very great. For example, the British Colonial Legal Service, whose members could be posted and transferred relatively freely from jurisdiction to jurisdiction, was an example of how a legal culture can operate relatively detached from local social contexts. Whether, many judges in that tradition emulated Hercules is another question.

[119] My personal view is that Dworkin's theory is at its most persuasive when applied to the judicial oath (and all that it symbolizes), for this represents an undertaking to be loyal to the system and to try to make it 'the best it can be'. For a more sceptical view of his idea of 'interpretation' in other contexts, see *HDTWR*, 383–5.

ideal. Secondly, Dworkin—more controversially—claims that his theory describes good practice in the Anglo-American system. In this view, Atiyah and Summers misrepresent English practice.

A third objection is that Dworkin advances a general theory of adjudication, but courts and judges are institutionalized in different ways in different societies and so have different roles, methods, and so on. Even in modern Western societies third party adjudication is only one of several modes of dispute-processing and, in terms of frequency and accessibility, it is often one of the least important in practice. What precisely is the role of courts in a given society varies considerably according to time and place. This argument can be extended in two ways: first, as any comparative lawyer knows, even terms like 'court', 'judge', 'lawyer', 'case', and 'trial' are culture-specific. Second, some societies do not have any institutionalized third-party adjudication at all.[120]

This is a powerful argument that needs to be taken into account by any legal theory that claims to be even minimally sensitive to 'social realities'. It is particularly pertinent in considering globalization, given the relative unimportance of 'courts' in international, transnational, and other global relations. Here I think that Dworkin may have done himself a disservice by claiming to advance a theory of adjudication. What he is really advancing is a theory of correct interpretation of legal norms. Hercules is not just a role model for actual judges; rather he is a symbol for the Upright Interpreter, who is loyal to the system— that is for anyone who is concerned to reach the correct or 'best' or 'right' interpretation of the law.[121] This includes upright officials, good citizens, and other participants who wish to make decisions based at least in part on clear understandings of what the law prescribes. One doubts whether labelling Dworkin's theory as 'a theory of adjudication' is making it the best it can be. It has a much wider reach than that.

Finally, Atiyah and Summers draw a distinction between their 'jurisprudential relativism' and moral (or ethical) relativism, which they reject. They also express scepticism about Utopian universalism in the field of law and, as we have seen, dismiss Hercules as representing a Utopian ideal with regard to the role of judges. It seems that they are more sympathetic to Hart's concern to develop a descriptive theory that fits the facts of actual legal phenomena, but they place more emphasis on cultural or local specificity than Hart does.[122] Here, there is a more fundamental difference with Dworkin; for although he makes some allowance for cultural diversity, he considers that law and its interpretation are a moral and an argumentative enterprise, founded on a moral theory that is a general theory of political morality and a theory of rationality that is similarly

---

[120] e.g., P. Gulliver, *Social Control in an African Society* (London, 1963) (an account of the Arusha of Northern Tanzania).

[121] On other kinds of interpreters, see *HDTWR*, *passim*, especially 69–74, 184–92.

[122] Atiyah and Summers, as well as Hart, are interested in 'ideal interpretive method', but as a distinct enterprise.

based on general principles of valid reasoning. Thus, at its core, Dworkin's seemingly particularistic theory is at least as general as its positivistic rivals.

Hart's Postscript and the mutual courtesies of the two friendly protagonists suggest that the differences between them can easily be exaggerated. They come from a shared philosophical tradition, but from somewhat different legal cultures. Neither has drawn much inspiration from anthropology, sociology or history. They both present a picture of law in terms of monistic unity: law as a system of rules and law as integrity treat the laws of independent nation states as units of analysis in ways that approximate to the ideal type of 'black box' theories. Even at what many consider to be the key point of differentiation between positivist and anti-positivist positions, many would argue that they may not be very different. On the one hand, some would interpret Dworkin as a 'positivist' in that Hercules must look for underlying principles that are institutionally embedded in an existing system; conversely, Hart's insistence on a sharp distinction between the is and the ought has sometimes been interpreted as a conservative attempt to legitimate legal systems—conservatism masquerading as neutrality. A more plausible reading is that for Hart, as for Bentham and Holmes, separating the 'is' and the 'ought' serves clarity of thought, which in turn is based on a moral concern: one needs a vocabulary for depicting actual legal institutions and systems in terms than can depict the true awfulness of many such exercises of power—like *The Bonfire of the Vanities* writ large. I am personally more sympathetic to this last interpretation, but in the present context the main point is that the distinction between general and particular jurisprudence does little or nothing to illuminate the similarities and differences between Hart and Dworkin.

SOME CONCLUDING OBSERVATIONS

This paper is one of a series of essays exploring the implications of globalization for legal theory. It suggests that sharp distinctions between general and particular jurisprudence are of limited value. Its starting-point was the suggestion that some Anglo-American jurisprudence seems to have been going through a somewhat parochial phase and continues to be dominated by theories which treat societies, nation states, and legal systems as largely self-contained units. In this context, 'parochialism' can relate to focus, or to sources, or to perspectives. Jurisprudence, can be inward looking in respect of its agenda, ethnocentric in respect of its perspective, or limited in respect of its sources and inspiration. Globalization brings to the fore a wide range of issues at transnational, international, and global levels and is rapidly changing the significance of national boundaries. As such it challenges 'black box theories', it is inimical to ethnocentric perspectives on transnational issues, but it does not minimize the importance of the local. 'The citizen of the world' may still be a rooted cosmopolitan, in Bruce Ackerman's phrase,[123] setting the study of local issues and phenomena in a broad geographical context.

This preliminary study of one aspect of the vast heritage of jurisprudence suggests that the English positivist tradition has tended to emphasize general more than particular jurisprudence; it has been quite cosmopolitan in outlook, but over time it increasingly narrowed its focus to a relatively narrow range of concepts and issues relating mainly, but not exclusively, to English or Anglo-American legal doctrine. Of the individuals studied, Bentham was the one who was most consistently committed to the viewpoint of 'the citizen of the world' and, although he did not develop his ideas very far in this respect, he was more sensitive than most of his successors to the limitations of 'black box' theories of national or municipal legal systems.[124]

It is worth commenting briefly on each of these points. First, English legal positivism since Bentham has usually placed more emphasis on general than on particular jurisprudence. Bentham, Austin, Maine, Holland, and Hart all fit this category, as do many others. Holland's English critics, such as Pollock and Buckland, were not being parochial or ethnocentric in respect of perspective. They were mainly concerned that an over-abstract approach to the teaching of Jurisprudence would be less useful than the systematic study of the basic concepts and principles of English Law and would reinforce the resistance of the practising profession to the academic study of law and especially to legal theory. I have argued that the differences between Hart and Dworkin cannot be usefully explained in terms of a distinction between general and particular jurisprudence and that Dworkin's central ideas, both explicitly and implicitly have general, if not universal, significance.

Secondly, the English tradition of academic law has generally been quite cosmopolitan. Historically, the study of Roman Law, Canon Law, Public International Law, and, to a lesser extent, Comparative Law have been an important part of our intellectual tradition. The British Empire, the Commonwealth, the European Union, and the strong networks within the extended family of common law jurisdictions have usually kept in check any tendencies to confine legal studies to English domestic law. Even the advocates of particular jurisprudence such as Buckland and Pollock were hardly Little Englanders. They were familiar with Roman Law and contemporary European legal thought. Like them, generalists such as Austin and Maine, drew most of their examples from Roman and English Law. The recent decline in the study of Romanist systems, the confining of 'core subjects' to domestic law, and the general parochialism of modern professional examinations, will almost certainly prove to have been a relatively short historical phase. The European Union, the internationalization of much legal practice, and the broader processes of globalization will ensure that.

Thirdly, analytical positivism was, however, narrow in a different sense. The

---

[123] Bruce Ackerman, 'Rooted Cosmopolitanism', 104 *Ethics* (1994) 516.   [124] RB, 134–6.

sharp distinction between the is and the ought and between law and other disciplines supported a tendency to confine the study of law to the exposition and analysis of legal doctrine. The expository tradition tended to become ahistorical, decontextualised, and uncritical.[125] Despite a series of challenges it remains the dominant force in our academic legal culture.[126] This is clearly illustrated in the work of our most influential modern jurist, Herbert Hart: his method was of potentially very wide application, his commitment was to general jurisprudence, but his focus and agenda for jurisprudence were quite narrow. Conceptual clarification and formal description are as important for broader approaches to law as for legal dogmatics, but Hart neither applied his great analytical skills to the basic concepts needed for such approaches nor did he encourage others to do so. Similarly, Ronald Dworkin's agenda for Legal Philosophy is really quite narrow. Insofar as his main interest is adjudication, he confines his focus to questions of law in hard cases, ignoring almost entirely the whole range of problems of interpretation and justification involved in other important decisions in legal contexts.[127]

Another limitation of the tradition has been to treat societies and municipal legal systems as self-contained units and to pay scant attention to transnational and global relations and to legal pluralism. Even in respect of traditional Public International Law, theorists as different as Hart, Rawls, and Dworkin share the tendency to treat 'legal systems' and societies as isolated and self-contained phenomena, and as a result they tend be at their least convincing at the international and transnational levels. How far their central ideas can be rescued from such criticism requires further exploration.

Finally, the distinction between general and particular jurisprudence has a function, but it has been and is likely to be of limited value in setting an agenda for the discipline of law and for jurisprudence as its theoretical part. I, for one, benefited as a student from exposure to particular analytical jurisprudence and regret its passing. But 'general' and 'particular' are relative matters and the distinction cannot bear much weight. In considering the implications of globalization for legal theory, it will be necessary to be concerned with a wide range of questions at different levels of generality. 'Thick description' of local particulars set in broad geographical contexts will be as important as ever in the development of a healthy discipline of law in a more integrated world.

---

[125] Twining, 'Academic Law and Legal Philosophy', op. cit.; cf. Horwitz, op. cit., n. 45.
[126] See *BT*, Ch. 6.   [127] This theme is developed in Ch. 17, below.

9

*Legal Skills and Legal Education**

In 1985 I delivered a paper entitled 'Taking Skills Seriously',[1] as part of the American Bar Association Conference in London; the audience was largely American practitioners and academic lawyers interested in the legal profession. My subject on that occasion was professional legal skills—('lawyering skills' in American)—and I argued that what is involved in teaching, learning, and assessing such skills is under-theorized and under-researched. Despite twenty-five years of practical experience by institutions which are, in theory, devoted to direct teaching of professional skills, almost nothing is known about how effective, efficient or worthwhile such teaching is. The paper was in essence a plea for the institutionalization of research and development in this area on an international and interdisciplinary basis.

In September 1987, I attended the first workshop sponsored by the Commonwealth Institute for Legal Education and Training (CILET) now established in Windsor, Ontario. The main, but not the sole, emphasis of CILET's initial programme is research and development into legal skills. Support is also growing for the revival of a forgotten recommendation of the Ormrod Committee that there should be a national Institute of Professional Legal Studies in this country.[2] Such an institute should also be primarily concerned with research and development into, rather than delivering, practical training. It could provide an important arena for the academic legal community to make a more substantial contribution to post-degree legal education and training than it does at present in respect of basic training, specialization, continuing and advanced education, retraining, and the development and assessment of aptitude and competence. These are all matters requiring educational professionalism. Where is such expertise to come from if it is not provided in large part and on a regular basis by those who have made their career in full-time legal education?

The purpose of this paper is to take the argument one step further. Again my

---

* This paper is based on the text of an address given at the CNAA Conference on 'Innovation in Legal Education' in London on 6 Oct. 1987 and was first published in 22 *The Law Teacher* 4 (1988).

[1] Twining, 'Taking Skills Seriously' *Commonwealth Legal Education Association Newsletter*, No. 43 (Oct. 1985), reprinted in *Journal of Professional Legal Education* and *LLS*, Ch. 1.

[2] Twining, 'Legal Education and Training: Some Lessons of History', paper presented to the Annual Conference of the Bar Council of England and Wales in Sept. 1987 and published as an appendix to The Commonwealth Legal Education Association *Newsletter* No. 52 (Jan. 1988) at 36–41. [Since then some steps have been taken in this direction at the Institute of Advanced Legal Studies first by the formation of a Legal Skills Research Group and later by the establishment of the Woolf Chair in Legal Education.]

thesis is simple: it is that the time is ripe for academic lawyers to take the lead in making direct learning of 'skills' a central component of every stage of legal education and training. Such a change will involve not only shifts of emphasis in curriculum but, more importantly, changes in attitudes and competencies of law teachers, as well as new institutional and collective arrangements. This paper concentrates on undergraduate and postgraduate legal education in academic institutions. But the general argument applies *pari passu* to all sectors of legal education and training; it includes the thesis that there is a need for more theorizing, research, and development in respect of skills relevant to both the discipline and the practice of law. It is opportune to concentrate on law degrees for two further reasons: first, it is worth restating the case for the view that the notion of 'skills' is as central to the discipline of law and academic legal education as it is to professional training and practice; secondly, there is a danger that the law teaching profession will be further marginalized within the total system of legal education and training unless one kind of attitude is confronted directly: that is the view that emphasis on skills in legal education is necessarily illiberal, amoral, narrow, reactionary, anti-intellectual, impractical, or unnecessary ('we do it already'). Let us call this diffused resistance to talk of 'skills' 'the Luddite fallacy'.

SOME PRELIMINARY ISSUES

For the sake of brevity let us take some potentially controversial assumptions for granted. First, the current structure of legal education and training in this country —academic, vocational, apprenticeship, and continuing—was established more for reasons of political convenience than on sound theoretical or educational grounds. It more or less conveniently divided up spheres of influence between different interest groups—notably the Bar, the Solicitors, the law teaching profession, and the Treasury (which was thereby relieved of pressure to provide large-scale funding for the last stages). Secondly, the current structure is likely to stay for the foreseeable future; the best that we can hope for is to mitigate some of the worst effects of these artificially sharp divisions. Thirdly, some of the standard dichotomies in discourse about legal education—liberal/vocational; theory/practice; book learning/experience; academic/practical; education/training; clinical/intellectual; skills/understanding—are at the very least too sharp. Often they represent mischievous nonsense. Finally, while law degrees serve as multi-purpose feeders to a variety of occupations, their primary *educational* function within our system is and should be to provide a good general education in the discipline of law. On this issue I am content to nail my flag to the mast of classical liberal values in legal education.

All of these propositions are complex and controversial, but they have been extensively explored and argued on other occasions. Here they are taken as given, except insofar as some of their implications have a direct bearing on the argument.

As a preliminary to developing the central thesis of this paper, it is useful to bear in mind two working distinctions, both of which relate to learning objectives: the distinction between learning about and learning how; and the distinction between direct and indirect pursuit of particular learning objectives.

In educational theory it is widely recognized that the concept of 'skill' is problematic. There is also increasing recognition within legal education that 'legal skills' and associated notions are badly in need of both theoretical and empirical development. However, for present purposes, it is sufficient to equate the concept of 'skill' with learning objectives that are formulated in terms of a student's ability to behave in specified ways, to perform certain operations to a defined standard, and so on. This kind of 'learning how' can be roughly (but not too sharply) contrasted with 'learning about', in which the learning objectives are stated in terms of recalling information or exhibiting understanding. It would be pedantic in this context to categorize ability to recall or to regurgitate information as a skill. To take some examples from Legal Theory; if in a Jurisprudence course students are expected to study critically Dworkin's or MacCormick's theory of legal reasoning they are learning *about* legal reasoning. A student will do well in an examination if she can accurately state Dworkin's position on the question 'what constitutes a valid and cogent argument on a disputed question of law?' and can rehearse alternative views and evaluate the merits and weaknesses of each theory. This is, I believe, a valuable educational enterprise; but it is different from developing the skill of *constructing* a legal argument on Dworkinian lines. There is a difference between describing Hercules and seeking to emulate him.

Again, there is a very considerable difference between studying the recent debates between Pascalians and Inductivists about probabilities and proof and learning how to apply Bayes's theorem to particular legal examples. In my experience, students who are capable of producing an excellent defence or critique of Bayesianism in this context are often incapable (largely because of terror of numbers) of *using* Bayes's theorem. Of course, learning about and learning how are very often intimately related. One cannot apply Dworkin's theory or Bayes's theorem without at least a minimal knowledge of what those theories are; conversely the experience of applying such theories may be very helpful in learning about their validity and utility. In practice the difference is one of emphasis. Recently, my colleagues and I have decided to shift the emphasis of our undergraduate jurisprudence course explicitly from learning *about* legal theories to *doing* legal theory—learning how to theorize. I, for one, have found it quite difficult in practice to make the transition cleanly.

The second working distinction is intimately related to the first. That is the distinction between direct and indirect pursuit of particular learning objectives. This is depressingly familiar in the context of arguments about 'Legal Method' so-called. Some law teachers maintain that students learn orthodox legal method (how to read cases, how to construct and criticize arguments about questions of law, how to interpret statutes, and so on) in courses on Torts and Contracts and Property. Some even claim that the main objective of such courses is to teach Legal Method ('thinking like a lawyer'). Others, including myself, doubt such claims. Often they are implausible as an account both of the objectives of the teachers and of what students, in fact, learn. So we advocate (usually unsuccessfully) devotion of substantially more time to direct study of such basic skills on the ground that this is more efficient and more effective than 'pick-it-up' strategies. I shall have to return briefly to this well-worn controversy when I consider the claim that 'we do it already' in relation to skills; here the point is that there is a difference between direct and indirect learning. My thesis concerns direct learning of skills.

SKILLS

So much for preliminaries. Let me restate the thesis: the time is ripe for legal educators to take the lead in making direct learning of skills a central component at every stage of legal education and training, including the academic stage. I shall elaborate this under three heads: Why Now? Why skills? Which skills?

(1) Timing

Satirists from Bentham to Cornford have attacked the Principle of Unripe Time as a delaying tactic, sometimes quite unfairly. In arguing for the converse I am aware that my readers are unlikely to have universally shared criteria of Ripeness. So let me try to please all of you.

For those who take a long view, one can point to the revival of interest in Rhetorical studies in law after a gap of about 150 years.

For those who think that the intellectual lag behind the United States should be kept to a decent 100 years, one can point out that the historic switch from emphasis on information to emphasis on skills was taken at Harvard in 1870. This is not to glorify the Kingsfield interpretation of Langdellism as a form of narrow-minded bullying in the pursuit of an absurd view of what 'thinking like a lawyer' involves—on which more later. Rather it is a reminder that what liberated American law schools from the worst aspects of the tyranny of coverage was the move away from studying about law of a single jurisdiction to studying how to handle legal issues, problems, concepts, and principles in relation to a largely fictitious entity, 'American Law'. Holmes predicted that 'The man of the future is the man of statistics and the master of economics.' 1987 is the ninetieth birthday of 'The Path of the Law'.

For those who take a shorter view of history, one can point to the fact that the network of professional law schools in the Commonwealth, set up largely under the influence of Jim Gower, to remedy the deficiencies of *both* apprentice-ship and undergraduate legal education, in respect of skills training for the profession has now been going for nearly thirty years (the Lagos Law School was established by Gower in 1961). In recent years there has been a steady increase in self-monitoring and sophistication of such programmes. There is also a growing sense that the professional law schools in England have got left behind by some of their sister institutions in Australia, Canada, Hong Kong, and Northern Ireland, especially in respect of systematic and wholehearted imple-mentation of the Gower-Ormrod philosophy that full-time vocational training should be mainly skills-oriented. The Ormrod Committee reported in 1971. For those who regret that some of its main recommendations have yet to be fully implemented, some may think that sixteen years represents a decent, or indecent, delay.

For those who are concerned with the present, there are several straws in the wind to suggest that the climate of professional opinion is changing, stimulated in part by the Marre Committee. Both the Law Society and Council of Legal Education (CLE) courses have been criticized for placing too much emphasis on substance and too little on skills and competence; the warm welcome given to CILET by teachers in professional schools around the Commonwealth; the conference on Professional Legal Skills in December 1986; the establishment of a CLE Working Party to review the vocational course for the Bar; and recent trends in continuing legal education all suggest that there has been a general shift in the climate of professional opinion in the direction of taking skills seriously.

There are several reasons why academic lawyers should pay attention to these developments. I shall mention just two. First, if direct teaching of skills at the vocational and continuing stages is to develop more systematically and quickly than in the past, there will be both a need and an opportunity for academics to contribute their expertise both as educators and researchers to these developments.

Secondly, the effect of switching emphasis from substance to skill at the vocational stage could have an impact on the academic stage. On the one hand, pressure on law degrees could increase by shifting greater responsibility for 'coverage' to them either through extension of the number of core subjects or by indirect means relating to optional subjects that intending recruits to either branch may be encouraged to study at undergraduate level. On the other hand, that pressure could be avoided and a new *rapprochement* might be achieved, if we could persuade those concerned that, to put it simply: 'We are in the skills business too—and rightly so.' It is significant that at the professional legal skills conference in December 1986, several leading figures in professional training schools, from the United Kingdom and other parts of the Commonwealth, were critical of law graduates, not on the ground that they were ignorant, but because of their alleged inability to express themselves in writing and orally, to analyse, to construct arguments, and to conduct research; a tendency towards intellectual immaturity also worried some critics. Significantly, one of them compared law graduates unfavourably to non-law graduates in History and Philosophy in this respect. This has been repeated in several recent public statements.

In short, many employers and at least some leading professional trainers want law graduates with developed intellectual and linguistic skills. There is, in one sense, nothing new about this—witness the 'look-at-me' syndrome that we associate with judges of an earlier generation who boasted that they had had no legal education. But, if that is what the professional schools and other consumers of our 'products' want of our graduates and if that is what we want our students to learn (or part of it), then surely we should recruit the former as public allies rather than treat them as unfriendly foreign powers.

(2) Why skills?

For many people, it may seem self-evident that development of 'skills' associated with clear thinking and problem-solving is desirable as an end in itself or as a means to relatively uncontroversial ends. Many of the standard 'intellectual skills' associated with legal education are of this kind: ability to be discerning about 'relevance'; to construct and to criticize legal and moral and policy arguments; to spot fallacies; to analyse, interpret, and apply rules to facts and so on. So why the need to justify a concern with skills? In the light of the recent report by Julie Macfarlane and others about law teachers' priorities for learning objectives, this may be preaching to the converted.[3]

I have much sympathy with such views and do not wish to belabour the obvious. However, there is considerable resistance to direct teaching of skills by many law teachers. Some of the reasons and motives behind the resistance need to be probed. Many law teachers either do not practice what they preach or preach to unconverted students. Furthermore, I would personally argue for giving attention to a number of skills that have not traditionally been emphasized in legal education and the case for this needs to be made.

One possible source of concern can be dealt with briskly. I am not arguing for concentration on skills to the exclusion of all else—whether that 'else' be labelled as 'perspectives', 'grasp of principle' or 'consciousness raising', for example. It is trite that most disagreements within legal education are differences about priorities. Making space for a substantial amount of direct skills teaching would inevitably involve sacrificing other worthwhile and not-so-worthwhile enterprises. But, if for the sake of simplicity, one stipulates that what one is arguing for would involve no more than say twenty-five to thirty per cent of a standard three- or four-year degree, that leaves room for other valued learning objectives. That will do for the moment.

---

[3] J. Macfarlane, M. Jeeves, and A. Boone: 'Education for Life or Work?' *New Law Journal*, (4 Sept. 1987), at 835–6.

Further grounds for resistance are to be found lurking in what I characterized as 'the Luddite fallacy': that is that emphasis on skills in undergraduate education is necessarily illiberal, amoral, narrow, reactionary, anti-intellectual, impractical or unnecessary. Before unpacking this fallacy, it can be acknowledged that some genuine fears and concerns can lie behind resistance which is expressed in such terms—hence the insertion of 'necessarily'. But I hope to show, by example as much as precept, that opposition to skills *as such*—as opposed to aberrations sometimes associated with them—is profoundly mistaken. Subject to that caveat let us consider each of these interrelated grounds for resistance in turn:

(a) Illiberal

The simplest way of demolishing this blanket smear is to appeal to history. If by 'illiberal' is meant incompatible with the values associated with traditional 'liberal' education, this just does not fit the facts. Historically, the core subjects of liberal education have all had a large component of 'learning how' in them. The classic 'trivium'—Logic, Grammar, and Rhetoric—was mainly devoted to method. A traditional classical education was as much concerned with construing, translating, composing, and parsing as with learning about classical literature and ancient history. The same applies to Languages—English and Foreign—Mathematics and History, and a great deal of study in the pure Sciences. Such subjects were sometimes studied in 'illiberal' ways, as when the study of Latin was confined to learning vocabulary and rules of grammar or History became mainly a matter of memorizing facts. Once, when arguing for Four-Year Degrees in Law, I foolishly invoked the argument that 'there is more Law than there used to be' in the presence of a historian. 'Are you suggesting that there is less History?' he asked. I came away thinking that Law is one of the most primitive disciplines in its response to the information explosion.

(b) 'Teaching skills is amoral'

This objection may be interpreted to mean that skills and techniques are means to ends and in that sense are 'instrumental'. So is mathematics, logic, typing, driving a car, shooting, and information processing. The fact that skills may be used for bad as well as good purposes is not in itself a ground for not teaching them. Or the objection may be interpreted to mean that no legal argumentation and analysis can be isolated from political and moral values. Insofar as this is so, these concerns surely relate more to fundamental questions about the whole enterprise of legal education and to *how* particular skills should be presented within that enterprise (if it is morally and politically justifiable), rather than to whether skills deserve to be given a high priority within the enterprise. Perhaps underlying this objection is a traditional concern about the ethics of argumentation and persuasion. This was, of course, also a central concern of classical rhetoric: the issue then as now was not *whether* people should be taught how to argue, but *how* this should be done.

(c) 'Teaching skills is narrow'

There are two versions of this objection: the first is the classic complaint against Langdellism: that the Langdellian case method at its best developed one set of analytical skills and thereby reinforced the natural tendency of the legal mind towards tunnel vision. A standard version of this critique was Karl Llewellyn's: 'The resulting technical skills, though sharp and well instilled, were narrow, and they remained so. The wherewithal for vision was not given.'[4] His proposed remedy was first to extend the list of skills from one to six and second to insist that 'the wherewithal for vision' should be provided by what have variously been labelled 'perspectives', 'contextual approaches' or 'thinking in terms of total pictures'.[5]

A second version of this objection is most often expressed in terms of 'the trade school' image. 'Skills' sometimes conjures up a vision of the banausic: low level techniques that are beneath the dignity of an institution of higher learning. There are two standard responses to this. First, one can point to the social and intellectual snobbery inherent in such attitudes, a snobbery exemplified as much by refusal of degree-level teachers to correct the spelling and grammar of their pupils as by misplaced conceptions of the dignity of intellectual labour. A second response is to make a distinction between highly transferable skills—such as those connected with clear thinking—and particular techniques associated with mundane tasks such as routine form filling and letter writing. The issues involved are too complex to pursue here—I personally think that charges of snobbery bite uncomfortably deep, but it should be reasonably clear that, on both interpretations, the charge of narrowness relates to the question 'Which skills are worth learning when?' rather than to the question 'Should we be concerned with skills at all?'

(d) 'Teaching skills is reactionary'

This can be interpreted to mean that emphasis on learning 'how' can, and often does, result in producing efficient, uncritical servants of the *status quo*. There is no doubt an important element of truth in this, illustrated not only by familiar images of the Eichman-like bureaucrat, but also by those who teach economic analysis of law solely as a technique without being willing to question its theoretical and ideological underpinnings. But this objection again goes to questions about 'Which skills?' and 'How should they be taught?' and 'What else?' rather

---

[4] K. N. Llewellyn, *Jurisprudence* (Chicago, 1962), at 365.   [5] TAR, at 367–78.

than the question of whether. It is tempting to suggest that some skills teaching is radical—for instance 'deconstruction' and 'immanent critique' involve *techniques* associated with critical legal studies; but that is to fall into the error of confusing means with ends. These same techniques are available to reactionaries and reformists as well as radicals and revolutionaries.

(e) 'Teaching skills is anti-intellectual'

What then of so-called 'intellectual skills'? Insofar as one can extract any sense out of this objection, which I have heard advanced on numerous occasions, it can either be subsumed under one or more of the previous heads or it requires clarification. Meanwhile, look at the *Reading Law Cookbook*.[6]

(f) 'Teaching skills is unnecessary'

There are at least three versions of this that are worth considering. The first is that some skills and techniques are more efficiently and effectively learned by doing on the job than through simulated instruction in the classroom. Intuitively one feels that this must be partly true, but is often presented in an exaggerated form. One of the areas in most urgent need of theoretical analysis and empirical research relates precisely to questions about the efficiency, effectiveness, timing, and duration of the lessons of simulated and real experience. Such enquiries may produce some surprises and stimulate some fundamental rethinking. Meanwhile, we have to act on a combination of faith and good sense and such basic equipment as we have, such as distinctions between learned technique and individual flair, between minimum competence and excellence, between direct and 'pick-it-up' strategies, and between laying a foundation and reinforcement. These elementary distinctions are often ignored in our discourse and in our practice— witness, for example, the primitive level of current talk and action about the fashionable idea of 'communication skills'.

A second version of the objection is that skill is often a matter of 'natural flair' or 'talent' or 'aptitude' and that increasing one or other pool of competence is more a matter of selection than instruction. 'Good advocates/teachers/ scholars are born and not made.' Such half-truths are also in need of sustained research and analysis.

The third interpretation of the objection that 'teaching of skills is unnecessary' relates to the specific context of our current educational practices. The claim is that 'we do it already' or 'students in fact pick up the important skills in the course of their studies'. This, I believe, is the most insidious and dangerous element in the Luddite fallacy. It is difficult to attack because of the danger of overgeneralization. There are some good practices in some sectors of under-

---

[6] See below, Ch. 12.

graduate legal education. It is difficult to attack head-on because at its root lie the complacency, inertia, vested interest, and apathy that one associates with conservative professions like that of law teaching. It is also difficult to attack because, as in most other aspects of legal education, there is a lack of hard evidence. So apart from invoking my own impressions over nearly thirty years of teaching and the impression of some of the main consumers of our products, teachers on professional courses, let me put my case in the form of some questions:

QUESTIONS
(i) In your institution how many students exhibit *excellence* by the time they leave you in respect of one or more skills that you think are worthwhile?
(ii) Whatever your personal views of the worthwhileness of the 'Reading Skills' illustrated in the *Reading Law Cookbook*,[7] how many of these are in fact learned effectively and efficiently on your degree and other courses?
(iii) How many of your students, by the time they leave, have the ability:
1. To write clear, succinct, and simple English?
2. To construct a valid and cogent argument on a question of law?
3. To construct and criticize an argument on a disputed question of fact?
4. To analyse and elucidate an abstract concept?
5. To spot elementary (a) logical (b) statistical fallacies?
6. To articulate the underlying assumptions of standard examples of legal discourse and to criticize them in terms of their internal coherence?
7. To make intelligent use of (a) a law library; (b) a general library; (c) information retrieval systems, such as Lexis?

(g) 'Sustained skills teaching is not feasible under present conditions'

Let us interpret this to mean that a major shift in emphasis along the lines indicated above is not feasible at present because of lack of (a) resources and (b) time.

Resources

It has become part of current orthodoxy to claim that direct teaching of skills is 'labour-intensive' and that, in the present economic climate, it is therefore impossible to develop it on a large scale. This is one of the reasons given for the disappointingly slow development of clinical legal education in polytechnics and universities and the failure to implement a full-blooded version of Ormrod in the professional courses. This is yet another area in need of research and development. My impression is that while certain kinds of simulation and clinical exercises do involve considerable preparation and/or supervision, the argument is often greatly overstated. There are certain counter-examples. It is now generally accepted that one reason for the survival of the Langdellian case method was that this was seen by university administrators as one of the *cheapest*

---

[7] Op. cit., n. 6.

forms of graduate education. Law schools subsidized other graduate schools. Yet the Langdellian system involved active participation by large classes in a skills-oriented enterprise, sustained in part by a combination of competition and terror. In my experience, when students are required to *do* major participatory exercises—in research or Wigmorean analysis or mooting—provided that one is efficient in the preparatory and early stages, such enterprises do not necessarily take up much more of the teacher's time than ordinary classroom teaching, even if some individual supervision is involved. The same is true of certain kinds of group projects in which the role of the teacher is supervisory and managerial. After all, it is the students who should be doing most of the work. In some instances, machines and good materials may wholly or partly replace live teachers. This is not to suggest that skills teaching is never more expensive than other forms of teaching. That is clearly to overstate the case, for example in relation to certain kinds of clinical work. Rather it is to suggest that a lot of it can be made surprisingly cost-effective by careful thought and good management.

Time

Learning a skill typically involves heightened awareness, mastering some instructions, first steps, and then increased competence through repeated practice. Insofar as we want, within formal education, to proceed beyond consciousness-raising and laying a foundation for the future development of relatively high levels of competence, the students need to be allowed time in which to exercise each skill. A number of factors mitigate against this at degree level. These include a reluctance to emulate the drill-sergeant model of instruction (one cannot master the goose-step by only doing it once), both in respect of the authoritarian and the repetitive nature of drilling, and, above all, the compulsion to cover a lot of ground. When I tell colleagues that I sometimes spend up to six weeks on a single case and set students exercises in analysis of evidence that take several months, they wonder how I get away with it. The simple answer is to slaughter the dragon, 'coverage'. In my experience this is the hardest thing to change in legal education because the attitudes 'one can't leave out' (the hearsay rule, or Kelsen, or defamation or the rule against perpetuities) are so deeply rooted in our academic legal culture.

(3) Which skills?

In the course of this paper, and on other occasions, I have dropped hints or explicitly argued for skills which seems to me to be worthwhile and suitable for development in a law degree. These include rule-handling, fact analysis, the kinds of skills of questioning, reading, and interpretation that are illustrated in the *Cookbook*.[8] More recently, the analysis and construction of plausible stories,

---

[8] Id.

and some of the skills and techniques of conceptual analysis, of articulating implicit assumptions of propositions and questions, of criticizing and re-posing questions, and, of course, of constructing and criticizing arguments. There is a pattern about these: they are all rather abstract, notionally transferable 'intellectual' skills involving reasoning, analysis, and synthesis which fall largely within the cognitive, as contrasted with the affective, domain of learning. If asked to justify emphasizing these—in the sense of giving them a high, but not necessarily an overriding priority—I would say quite simply that reasoning and analysis are central to the discipline of law and that our discipline and the rich literature associated with it, are excellent materials for developing such skills.

By way of dotting the 'Is' and crossing the 'Ts' it is worth stressing two further points. First, it is worth re-emphasising that I do not believe and am not arguing for the proposition that development of skills constitutes the only worthwhile learning objective in legal education. Secondly, the skills that I associate with the discipline of law are not coextensive with the skills of the *law student*, who may or may not be an intending lawyer. The phrase 'thinking like a lawyer' has quite deservedly taken a battering in recent years. If we were to substitute 'thinking like a law student', that is equally susceptible to caricature and derision unless we have a rather clear conception of our model law graduate. The important thing, in the present context, is surely this: in our system the role of the academic stage, and of law degrees of all kinds, is to provide a good general education in the discipline of law. This is valued by enlightened practitioners, professional trainers, and general employers as much as by academics. It involves at its core certain kinds of mental training that are of undoubted practical utility—for what is more useful than the ability to think clearly? But that is not the point. The kind of skills that I favour in the present context are those that are central to understanding law, which is the main objective of our academic enterprise.

10

Karl Llewellyn and the
Modern Skills Movement*

Skills and competency are currently high on the agenda of debates about legal education in the common law world. From British Columbia to New Zealand, from Zimbabwe to Hong Kong, from Melbourne to London (England and Ontario) the merits of direct versus pick-it-up learning, of holistic versus abstracted approaches, of clinical versus simulated training, of the balance between know how and know-what are being vigorously debated in a plethora of experimental programmes.[1] In the United States the history of the skills movement is variously told; some, with short memories, start with The Council on Legal Education for Professional Responsibility (CLEPR) or the competency debates of the 1970s;[2] some go back to a historic meeting in Asheville, Tennessee in 1965;[3] some treat the Lasswell-McDougal plan of 1943,[4] or the report of the Association of American Law Schools (AALS) Committee on Curriculum, chaired by Llewellyn in 1944,[5] or a job analysis by Wigmore in 1922,[6] as marking the start of the modern skills movement; some trace the story back to the first law school clinics or to Langdell's switch from an emphasis on knowledge to rigorous, single-minded

---

* This chapter is an extract from 'The Idea of Juristic Method: A Tribute to Karl Llewellyn', 48 *U Miami L Rev.* 119, 142–7 (1993). This was one of three versions of lectures or papers given in Chicago, Leipzig, and Miami on the occasion of the centennial of Llewellyn's birth.

[1] A useful, international bibliography of the literature in English (mainly about particular skills) up to 1988 is Jeanine Watt, *The Legal Skills Sourcebook* (College of Law, St Leonards, New South Wales, 1989).

[2] On CLEPR see William Pincus, *Clinical Legal Education for Law Students* (Council on Legal Education for Professional Responsibility, New York, 1980). On the competency debates, see e.g., Warren E. Burger, 'The Special Skills of Advocacy: Are Specialized Training and Certification of Advocates Essential to Our System of Justice?' 42 *Fordham L Rev.* 227 (1973); ABA, *Report and recommendations of the Task force on Lawyer competency: The Role of the Law Schools* (the Cramton Report, 1979); and works cited in the extensive bibliography in ABA, *Legal Education and Professional Development—An Educational Continuum* (MacCrate Report, 1992).

[3] H. Sacks (ed.), *Proceedings of the Asheville Conference of Law School Deans on Education for Professional Responsibility* (Chicago, Council on Education for Professional Responsibility, 1965).

[4] H. Lasswell and M. McDougal, 'Legal Education and Public Policy: Professional Training in the Public Interest', 52 *Yale Law Journal* 203 (1943).

[5] *Report* of the AALS Committee on Curriculum (Chair, K. N. Llewellyn), reprinted as 'The Place of Skills in Legal Education', 45 *Colum. L Rev.* 345 (1945). Interestingly, the Committee gave credit to Wigmore for pioneering the idea of making a job analysis of lawyers' operations a basis for skills training, but considered his version too elaborate to be practical: J. H. Wigmore, 'The Job-Analysis Method of Teaching the Use of Law Sources', 16 *Illinois Law Review* 499 (1922); 4 *American Law School Review* 787 (1922); cf. 30 *Harvard Law Review* 812 (1917).

[6] Id.

focus on a single set of intellectual skills;[7] some of us would even trace the story back through the long history of rhetoric to Quintillian, Cicero, and Aristotle.[8]

The recent rapid increase in interest in the common law world outside North America is sometimes known as 'the Gold Rush' in tribute to the influence of Professor Neil Gold, first in developing ideas (largely derived from American models) in British Columbia and Ontario and then disseminating them to a number of jurisdictions in Africa, Australasia, and South East Asia and most recently, and rather belatedly to England.[9] There in 1989 the Inns of Court School of Law, in a remarkably radical move, substituted a year-long skills-based course for the traditional knowledge-based one that had fallen into disrepute.[10] In 1993 Law Society of England and Wales introduced a new Legal Practice Course, which aimed to move in a similar direction while maintaining a balance between knowledge and skill.[11]

Some academic lawyers fear that the profession will seek to offload some of the substantive law topics that have been discarded at the vocational stage onto the undergraduate degree. To counter this 'knowledge backlash', they are vigorously claiming that, as liberal educators, 'we are in the skills business too', at least in respect of intellectual skills.[12]

For the past five years a very active Legal Skills Research Group has been stimulating and co-ordinating empirical research in this general area.[13] Interestingly, the recent ABA Task Force on Legal Education and Professional Development (the MacCrate Committee) acknowledged that 'the Commonwealth programs are perceived to be far more effective than our existing bridge-the-gap programs'.[14] If this is true, which is debatable, it is largely because more time

---

[7] This theme is developed by Llewellyn in 'The Study of Law as a Liberal Art' (1960), reprinted in *Jurisprudence*, Ch. 17 (Chicago, 1962).

[8] The tension between skills training (know how) and study about (know-what and know-why) runs through contemporary treatments of narrative, rhetoric, and reasoning in legal contexts. Given doubts about the validity and acceptability of 'non-rational means of persuasion', few law teachers openly claim to be directly teaching rhetorical and narrative skills. Practitioners' handbooks are only a little less inhibited. On the inevitability and potential abuses of storytelling in advocacy, see *RE* Ch. 7.

[9] For accounts of some of these developments see *LLS* and *The Journal of Professional Legal Education*. Although the quip about the 'Gold Rush' points, *inter alia*, to the delusion that one can get-wise-quick through short doses of skills training, Neil Gold should be exempted from any responsibility for this. He has regularly warned against expecting too much of direct teaching of skills and has pioneered important basic research into what constitutes excellence in advocacy and how it might be developed.

[10] A good description and evaluation of the first year of this course is Valerie Johnston and Joanna Shapland, *Developing Legal Training for the Bar* (Sheffield, 1990).

[11] The Law Society of England and Wales, *Training Tomorrow's Solicitors* (London, 1990), *Legal Practice Course—Written Standards* (London, 1991), *Training Tomorrow's Solicitors— Second Report* (London, 1992).

[12] See Ch. 9 above and 'Intellectual Skills at the Academic Stage: Twelve Theses', in P. Birks (ed.), *Examining the Law Syllabus: Beyond the Core* (Oxford, 1993) 93.

[13] Institute of Advanced Legal Studies, London, *Legal Skills Working Papers* (1992 continuing).

[14] MacCrate Report, op. cit., n. 2, at 405.

is available in the Commonwealth courses: most of them involve six to nine months full-time study after the completion of the first law degree.

The modern skills movement is diverse and controversial. However, a predominant orthodoxy can be discerned. This is exemplified by the MacCrate Report in 1992, the much skimpier Marre Committee Report in England in 1988, and the writings of Professor Neil Gold.[15] The basic tenets of this orthodoxy can perhaps be restated as follows: one of the primary objectives of legal education and training is to enable students to achieve minimum standards of competency in basic skills before being let loose on the public; what constitute such basic skills depends on a job analysis of what different kinds of lawyers in fact do. Lawyer-jobs can be analysed into transactions or operations, which can be further broken down into tasks or sub-operations; a skill or skill-cluster denotes the ability to carry out a task to an acceptable, specified standard. Minimum acceptable competence is to be distinguished from excellence, and it is the main function of law schools and bridge-the-gap programmes to ensure that all entrants to the profession satisfy minimum competence in a range of skills, measured by actual performances which satisfy articulated criteria under specified conditions. Problem-solving is, in this view, seen either as one of the most important basic skills or, as some would have it, the master skill under which all lawyering tasks can be subsumed.[16] Finally, there is an ethical dimension: not only does the standard list of skills include ability to recognize and to resolve ethical dilemmas,[17] but issues of ethics, values, and professional responsiblity must be involved in the learning of each skill. This supports the idea of a pervasive approach to professional responsibility.

At first sight this looks like a restatement of Llewellyn's views. In 1941 he wrote: '[S]ound sociology of law is the precondition to sound legal technique';[18] the 1943 Lasswell-McDougal plan and the 1944 AALS Report, which was mainly drafted by Llewellyn, are widely recognized as pioneering attempts systematically to relate legal education to what lawyers in fact do and to move from one rather narrow set of intellectual skills to a broader and more systematic prepa-

[15] Id.; Lady Marre, *A Time For Change: Report of the Committee on the Future of the Legal Profession* (London, 1988). For additional information see the numerous articles and reports by Neil Gold on New Zealand (1986, 1989), Zimbabwe (1986), England and Wales (Bar) (1987), Hong Kong (1989–92); also *LIS*, Ch. 11; J. Kilcoyne and N. Gold, 'Instructional Technology: The Systematic Design of Legal Education', in R. Matas and D. J. McAwley (edd.), *Legal Education in Canada* (1987); and the research project on exemplary performance of advocates for the Advocates Society Institute (Ontario), reports by A. G. Tobin and D. Rusnell, Advocacy Training Project (1987).

[16] e.g., S. Nathanson, 'The role of problem-solving in professional legal education', 2 *Journal of Legal Education* 167 (1989); P. Jones, 'Skills Teaching in Legal Education—the Legal Practice Course and Beyond', in P. Birks (ed.), op. cit., n. 12, at 102–4; cf. Lasswell and MacDougal, op. cit., n. 4; C. Kelso, 'In Quest of a Theory of Lawyering: Some Hypotheses and a Tribute to Dean Soia Mentschikoff', 29 *U of Miami L Rev.* 159 (1975); A. Amsterdam, 'Clinical legal Education—A 21st Century Perspective', 34 *Journal of Legal Education* 612 (1984).

[17] e.g., MacCrate Report, op. cit., n. 2, at 203 (*et passim*).

[18] Llewellyn, *My Philosophy of Law* (Boston, 1941), at 197.

ration for all important aspects of legal practice. Llewellyn helped to set the fashion of drawing up lists of skills, although his modest list of six looks rather meagre compared to MacCrate's list of ten skills groups (each with subdivisions) and Lady Marre's twenty-four. 'Problem-based learning' is now in fashion, and significantly Llewellyn's *Law in Our Society* had a substantial section devoted to 'Theory of Problem-solution in General'.[19] His courses on Elements and Appellate Advocacy at Chicago were clear attempts to develop direct teaching of specific skills;[20] and he summed up the importance of the ethical dimension in the much-quoted aphorism: 'Technique without ideals may be a menace, but ideals without technique are a mess.'[21]

Undoubtedly many of the developments in skills-based legal education since 1944 in North America and beyond could be interpreted as attempts to implement, refine, and develop Llewellyn's own programme. Contemporaries, such as Frank Strong and David Cavers, and former students, such as Irvin Rutter, Charles Kelso, and Terence Anderson explicitly acknowledged his direct influence, which could also be seen in particular programmes at Cincinnati, Ohio, Antioch, and Miami.[22] Soia Mentschikoff and Irwin Stotzky edited and expanded the Elements materials which are still used as the main book for the first-year foundation course at the University of Miami School of Law and a few other schools.[23] In my own work on interpretation and fact-analysis and more generally in legal education I am happy to acknowledge Llewellyn as a seminal influence.[24]

Thus Llewellyn clearly has a place as an important pioneer in this area, and his influence lives on. Yet one wonders whether the powerful modern orthodoxy is entirely in tune with his vision and ideas. If Karl Llewellyn were to return today and read the MacCrate and Marre reports, one suspects that he would react with a mixture of enthusiasm and dismay. On the one hand, he would probably welcome the broadening of the focus of legal education and training, the concern to be more realistic about what lawyers do, the increased educational

[19] Llewellyn, *Law in our Society* (unpublished teaching materials) at 93–104 (Lecture 13). Llewellyn emphasizes the interplay between conscious and unconscious aspects of problem-solving.
[20] Extensive teaching materials for both courses survive and are contained in the Llewellyn Papers at the University of Chicago Law School (Elements is in File M and Legal Argument in File N). The Elements materials provided the basis for Soia Mentschikoff and Irwin P. Stotszky, *The Theory and Craft of American Law—Elements* (New York, 1981).
[21] With slight variations in wording: e.g., Llewellyn, op. cit., n. 5, at 162; 'The Adventures of Rollo', (1952) *U of Chicago Law School Record*, vol. 3, no. 1, at 23.
[22] Examples include, F. Strong, 'The Pedagogic Training of a Law Faculty', 25 *Journal of Legal Education* 226 (1973); D. Cavers, 'Skills and Understanding', 1 *Journal of Legal Education* 396 (1949); I. Rutter, 'A Jurisprudence of Lawyers' Operations', 13 *Journal of Legal Education* 301 (1961); C. Kelso, *A Programmed Introduction to the Study of Law* (Indianapolis, 1965); T. Anderson and R. Catz, 'Towards a Comprehensive Approach to Clinical Education: A Response to the New Reality', 59 *Washington University Law Quarterly* 727 (1981); H. Russell Cort and Jack L. Sammons, 'The Search for "Good Lawyering": A Concept and Model of Lawyering Competencies', 29 *Cleveland State Law Review* 397 (1980).
[23] Mentschikoff and Stotzky, op. cit., n. 20. [24] e.g., *HDTWR; ANALYSIS.*

professionalism, the emphasis on professional responsibility and problem-solving, and attempts to develop an empirical base for skills training.[25] However, let me on his behalf, express some concerns.

First, consider the precept that 'sound sociology of law is the precondition to sound legal technique'.[26] It is very doubtful whether compiling lists of discrete skills which practitioners say they think are important goes very far in the direction of a sound sociology of law. This is not to denigrate the work of Zemans, Rosenblum, and Garth in Chicago[27] nor that of Joanna Shapland in England.[28] But the outcome to date seems to be longer and longer check-lists, with little analysis of interconnections, and only rather primitive efforts at setting priorities. As the lists get longer, the time available for study stays the same or even decreases. The almost inevitable result is the sacrifice of detail, depth, and transferability to the dragon of 'coverage'—in this case coverage of longer and longer lists in the name of a mechanistic form of bureaucratic rationalism that is threatening to engulf formal legal education.

In England, perhaps even more than in the United States, the legal profession has been obsessed by coverage, that is the idea that there are certain fields of law that every student should have covered, however superficially, before being admitted to practice. This has been most obviously exhibited in the old style bar and solicitors' examinations—not very different from state bar examinations, which traditionally tested short-term memory of masses of technical detail. The shift to skills has not reduced the obsession. Once competence has been defined in terms of a list of skills, the gatekeepers may even feel that they have to adopt the position that someone who has failed on even one item on the list has to be treated as incompetent. As the list grows, so detail, depth, repetition, and skilfulness are sacrificed. At one institution, after I persuaded the powers that be that 'fact-management' was an important skill-set, I learned that within two years it had been squeezed into three hours of classroom instruction. One symptom of this tendency is found in disclaimers for the new-style skills courses. For example, the Inns of Court School of Law claims that its one-year full-time course is no more than a preparation for pupillage, in other words apprenticeship.[29] Similarly 'bridge the gap' increasingly means the gap betwen law school and apprenticeship or starting practice under supervision. What is at risk in this primary school model is the idea of formal legal education as a long-term or

---

[25] Johnstone and Shapland, op. cit., n. 10; *LLS*.   [26] Llewellyn, op. cit., n. 18, 197.

[27] e.g., F. Zemans and V. Rosenblum, *The Making of a Public Profession* (Chicago, 1981); B. Garth, D. Landon, and J. Martin, ABF Surveys (preliminary findings summarized in the MacCrate report, App. B, 379–84).   [28] Op. cit., n. 10.

[29] Statements about the course indicate that it aims to prepare students to perform adequately in work they might do in their second six months of pupillage and for this reason 'the course aims to be extremely general, aiming at more or less the lowest common denominator for the practising bar', (Council of Legal Education, *The New Vocational Course, Introductory Paper* (London, 1988)); Johnstone and Shapland, op. cit., n. 10, at 2.

lifelong investment.[30] In his passionate plea for 'The Study of Law as a Liberal Art', Llewellyn commented on Langdell's contribution, which involved a historic switch from emphasis on substantive knowledge to emphasis on one set of case-law skills as follows: 'The resulting skills, though sharp and well-instilled, were narrow, and remained so. The wherewithal for vision was not given.'[31] There is a danger that a future historian of the modern skills movement might write: 'The resulting technical skills were broad, but they were neither sharp nor well-instilled. And there was a total neglect of the vision thing.'

[30] This theme is developed in W. Twining, 'Developments in Legal Education in the Commonwealth: Beyond the Primary School Model', 2 *Legal Education Review* 35 (1990).

[31] Llewellyn, *Jurisprudence*, op. cit., at 377.

11

*Reading Law**

I. CANNIBALISM, LOVE LETTERS, AND YESTERDAY'S NEWS: SOME NEGLECTED MATERIALS OF LAW STUDY

The phrase 'reading law' can be variously interpreted. It can mean studying law, as in the phrase: 'He read law at Cambridge'. It could mean interpreting law, according to one or another theory of interpretation. It could, perhaps, refer to the kind of law they do or study at the University of Reading, as in the phrase 'LA Law'. But I shall be concerned with a more mundane and general usage of 'reading law' as the intellectual activity of studying and using various kinds of texts.

My thesis can be summarized in four propositions. First, the range of materials available for the study of law is much wider and more varied than orthodox Anglo-American practice suggests. Second, attempts to broaden the range of materials used in law study have often failed to establish themselves because of a lack of clarity about objectives and methods. Third, the tools for providing such clarity are readily available. They are called questions. The central theme of these lectures is putting texts to the question. Fourthly, broadening the range of materials of law study in this way is not only illuminating; it can also be enjoyable.

I shall deliver on my promise to talk about love letters and cannibalism. As a bonus I shall also say something about the law reports. But these examples will merely serve to illustrate a general thesis: that in reading any text it pays to ask: Why? What? How? In the second part, I shall go into more detail about the How? with particular reference to newspapers and juristic texts.

The term 'materials of law study' was first popularized by Professor Brainerd Currie in a seminal article on academic law in America.[1] It is rather ungainly, but it accurately delineates my subject. 'Law study' is broader than legal education as conventionally conceived. For it also encompasses legal research and individual study for a variety of purposes, including self-education about law. 'Materials' is rather more homely than the more forbidding and fashionable term

* This is a revised text of the sixth Seegers Lectures delivered at Valparaiso School of Law on 12–13 Apr. 1989. Parts of the lectures have been adapted from the F. H. Lawson Lecture, delivered at the University of Lancaster on 30 Apr. 1987. Some of the themes are further developed in *BT*, Ch. 5.
[1] Currie, 'The Materials of Law Study', 8 *J Legal Educ*. 3 (1955); Currie, 'The Materials of Law Study', 3 *J Legal Educ*. (1951).

'text'; the latter carries associations of swarms of semioticians, phenomenologists, hermeneuticists, discourse analysts, structuralists, narratologists, literary theorists, and even jurists declaiming abstrusely and abstractly about 'discourse' and 'texts'. I am not entirely sceptical about the value of these recent fashions. But here I want to be more pragmatic and down-to-earth. 'Materials' suggests something to be used for specific purposes.

The first step in my argument is quite familiar. Despite many attempts, Anglo-American legal scholars and teachers have never managed to break the stranglehold of the law reports on the study of law. Compare today's legal literature with that of twenty or thirty years ago and there is no question that it is broader and more varied than it used to be: cases and materials now coexist with casebooks; contextual studies compete with black-letter texts; and most law students are exposed to Reports of Committees and other policy documents, empirical studies, and other kinds of materials. There is even reputed to be a Law and Literature Movement with at least thirty-eight American law schools claiming to offer courses in Law and Literature.[2] Legal scholarship is also more varied than it was in respect of perspectives, methods, and sources. But the one thing that we do well in a sustained way is to read and use the law reports. I wish neither to overstate nor to labour the point, so let two examples suffice. First, legislation. We pay lip-service to the idea that legislation is at least as important as case-law in our political, social, and legal life. Courses on legislation were pioneered in the United States at the start of the century, if not before.[3] Yet in England in 1968, Patrick Fitzgerald could entitle an article 'Are Statutes Fit for Academic Treatment?';[4] in England in 1989, legislation does not appear to be the subject of much more sustained attention than it was twenty years ago. There are a few courses[5] and the *Statute Law Review*,[6] but generally speaking our handling of cases is much more assured and systematic than our handling of statutes. I am not aware that the situation is very different in the United States, where the case method has survived repeated attacks to a truly remarkable

[2] Gemmette, 'Law and Literature: An Unnecessarily Suspect Class in the Liberal Arts Component of Law School Curriculum', 23 *Val. UL Rev.* 267, 268 (1989).
[3] In the Anglo-American tradition pleas for the systematic study of legislation go back at least as far as Bentham: J. Bentham, 'Proposal for a School of Legislation' (c. 1794) (unpublished manuscript available at University College, London, CVII 31–6). One of the pioneers of teaching legislation in the US was Ernst Freund of the University of Chicago, who clashed with Joseph Beale and James Barr Ames on this issue. See K. Llewellyn, *Jurisprudence: Realism in Theory and Practice*, (Chicago, 1962), at 379; see generally F. Ellsworth, *Law on the Midway* (Chicago, 1977); E. Freund, *Standards of American Legislation* (Chicago, 1917), at 310–14. Freund introduced courses on statutes at Chicago but, from a longer view, it was a Pyrrhic victory over Langdellism.
[4] Fitzgerald, 'Are Statutes Fit for Academic Treatment?', 11 *J Soc'y Pub. Tchrs. of Law* 142 (1971).
[5] The longest established is probably that in the University of Edinburgh. See Henderson & Bates, 'Teaching Legislation in Edinburgh: An Outline' (1980) *Statute L Rev.* 151; Miers & Page, 'Teaching Legislation in Law Schools' (1980) *Statute L Rev.* 23.
[6] The *Statute Law Review* was established in 1980 as an offshoot of the Statute Law Society, an organization devoted to the improvement of the form, organization, and accessibility of legislation.

degree. Even leading members of the Critical Legal Studies Movement are primarily case-law scholars.

My second example is so-called 'contextual studies'. For over twenty years I have been associated with the 'Law in Context' series, which sought to break the mould of orthodox 'black-letter' textbooks and casebooks in the United Kingdom. I remain a committed contextualist, but I would be the first to acknowledge that contextual works in England and elsewhere in the common law world are not based on a coherent theory of law either as a phenomenon or as a discipline.[7] The case-law tradition is a tough tradition in a way that its challengers seem not to be. I shall suggest some reasons for this; but here I am concerned less with the Why? and the Whether? than with the How?

The following are examples of potential materials of law study that are used only spasmodically, if at all, by law teachers and scholars: trial records; contracts and legal documents; manuals of advocacy; historical studies; newspapers; stories, plays, and other works of the imagination; and films. Insofar as we use other kinds of materials that I have mentioned, such as legislation, policy documents, or empirical studies, we tend to use them irregularly and uneasily.[8]

Before proceeding to the second stage of the argument, let me anticipate two possible objections. Some students may wonder what all of this has to do with them. 'Here is this fellow telling us what we are missing in our legal education. If he's right, there's not much that we can do about it, as we don't control what we have to study—and we are given too much to read anyway.' I do not have too many illusions about law students, but it may not be totally unrealistic to think that at least some students, out of interest or necessity, may have occasion to do some law-related reading after they graduate (or even sooner). The gist of my message is that should they ever have occasion to read a statute or a newspaper or a legal biography or a novel or a love letter, they should pause before starting and ask: Why? What? How?

A second objection needs to be considered. It might be asked: What has he got against law reports? The answer is: not much. There is, of course, a familiar list of their limitations: they are unrepresentative of the law in action—in legal practice and society; they emphasize the pathological rather than the routine and the prophylactic; the problems they treat tend to be narrowly focused; they are at best slices of legal life abstracted from the total process of litigation; and so on. Far from denigrating the law reports as source material, I believe that they are a vast anthology of concrete, real life problems, solutions, and arguments, selected, organized, and presented in ways that are convenient, accessible, and open to a variety of uses.[9] I shall argue that, in a sense, they represent neglected materials of law study because they tend to be used for a narrower range of purposes than they need be. There is little wrong with the law reports except our

---

[7] *RE*, Ch. 11; see also, TAR.   [8] This theme is developed in Ch. 12, below.
[9] See also Twining, 'Cannibalism and Legal Literature', 6 *Oxford J Leg. Stud.* 423 (1986).

tendency to be obsessed by them. Rather it is more useful to treat orthodox use of the law reports as a paradigm of the approach that I wish to advocate.

One reason why reading cases is a successful practice in our tradition is that, generally speaking, we have relatively clear ideas about the Why? the What? and the How? of our readings. In orthodox study we read a case or a series of cases with one or more objectives in mind: for example, to discover how a particular doubt about the law has been resolved; or to garner raw material for constructing an argument; or to find a concrete illustration of some general rule, principle, or problem; or to study an episode in the development of a particular doctrine or a general, authoritative disquisition on a legal topic. We also have a rather clear idea about the nature of the material: how it is constructed and organized, who is responsible, why it has been published, and what is its official status as an authoritative text. Our tradition also does reasonably well in respect of ways of reading, although I think that these could be improved by a more self-conscious and direct concern with method.[10] Most students learn to adjust their methods to their purposes—they learn how and when to do a simple précis or a closer or more critical reading and how to case, skim, browse, précis, delve, analyse, compare, synthesize, criticize, or deconstruct.

It has been estimated that American law students on average read more than 2,000 appellate cases during three years of law school.[11] English undergraduate law students probably read less than half that number. The frequency with which practising lawyers read the law reports varies considerably. But how many law students have read the whole of one trial record? Five? Ten? How many have read one or more secondary analyses of a *cause célèbre* for a serious purpose, i.e., not just for entertainment? For example, how many have studied a serious account of the Sacco-Vanzetti case or Dreyfus or Jack the Ripper or Alger Hiss or the Kennedy assassination, or a volume in one of the Notable Trials Series? If you have read such material, ask yourselves what, precisely, was your purpose? What was the nature of the material? What equipment did you have for reading it? Why? What? How? If you have not asked such questions, ask why not?

The question remains: What justification is there for neglecting this kind of material in our legal cultures? There are some prima facie reasons. Let me quickly dispose of two. First, 'these materials are not as accessible as the law reports'. Insofar as this is true, this is a self-confirming argument. Published records and detailed scholarly accounts of trials are less extensive than the law reports partly because there is little demand for them, other than as entertainment. But, largely because there has been a popular market for such works, there is an extensive literature. The market fluctuates and what gets published is open

---

[10] On the advantages of the direct as opposed to the 'pick-it-up' approach to learning legal skills, see *HDTWR*, Preface.

[11] Andersen & Catz, 'Towards a Comprehensive Approach to Clinical Education: A Response to the New Reality', 59 *Wash. ULQ* 727, 733 (1981).

to the charge of being even more unrepresentative than the law reports. Sensational murders and spy stories dominate the genre. Nevertheless, there is a mass of material that is relatively accessible; there could be more, if there were a demand.

A second reason for neglect relates to the nature of the materials (What?). Trial records, it is said, tend to be longer, more diffuse, and less well-organized than the law reports. They are unmanageable, even if one knew what one was managing them for. In my opinion, these criticisms are only partly correct. Trials are highly structured events and most trial records are almost as uniformly organized as law reports, though less well-provided with indexes and other furniture. They do tend to be less succinct than the law reports, and it takes time and experience to read them in a disciplined way. But this reasoning can be turned on its head: insofar as records are difficult to use because of unfamiliarity, this reflects a general tendency to neglect procedure and trials at first instance in academic law.[12] The use of this kind of material may help to remedy that neglect. Similarly, it is bizarre that the subject of evidence is still largely studied through appellate cases. Insofar as trial records are inherently difficult to manage, this is an additional reason for using them as educational material. For surely an important intellectual skill in legal practice, administration, or academic life is the skill of organizing and managing a complex body of amorphous data. As we shall see, that is one of the main objectives for which I use materials relating to famous trials in my own teaching. The law reports are too neatly packaged for the purpose.

The judicious use of trial records and similar materials can serve other aims. For example, Professor Landsman of Cleveland-Marshall Law School uses them for the purpose of analysing the conditions and dynamics of alleged miscarriages of justice. When do they occur? What goes wrong? How far can the risks be lessened by improved institutional design? He tells me that his teaching and research in this area floundered and lacked focus until he found and adopted a suitable theoretical framework for undertaking this kind of analysis.[13] A seat-of-the-pants approach did not work.

During the past fifteen years or so, I have used and adapted John Henry Wigmore's method of analysing mixed masses of evidence, using trial records as the main raw material.[14] The primary learning objectives are fairly clear: students who have undertaken such exercises should have begun to develop techniques of macroscopic analysis (structuring complex arguments from extensive, seemingly amorphous data) and microscopic analysis (very detailed and

---

[12] Much more emphasis is placed on the study of procedure in the curriculum of American law degrees than in the UK. But trial records are neglected in both systems, and more theoretical and 'scientific' attention is generally paid to procedure in the continental European tradition than in the English-speaking world.

[13] Personal communication to the author. See also Landsman, 'When Justice Fails', 84 *Mich. L Rev.* 824 (1986).   [14] See generally *ANALYSIS*, Ch. 3, App.

precise construction and criticism of arguments based on single items of evidence). After some preliminaries, the whole class reads some sixty pages from the trial of Frederick Bywaters and Edith Thompson.[15] As some of you may know, Edith Thompson was hanged for inciting or conspiring with Freddy Bywaters, her lover, to murder her husband. The main, but not the only evidence, against her was a collection of her love letters to Freddy. We spend approximately four weeks in class reading Edith's love letters. I chose the case deliberately for its complexity and because, on one view, if one can analyse Edith's prose, one can analyse anything. Thereafter each student selects a case that interests him or her and subjects it to intensive analysis. It is great fun and rewarding to teach; it is a great sweat, but rewarding to learn. We try not to lose sight of the primary objective, which is to master a fairly simple, but demanding, intellectual procedure. The educational rewards tend to go far beyond the development of a single analytical skill.

What, precisely, are these other rewards? I am unable to give a confident answer, partly because the rewards vary from student to student and are unplanned. It is also because it is often the case that what we learn or teach goes beyond our capacity to articulate clear learning objectives or precise criteria of success. For example, I recommend to my students that they should read the novel based on the case by F. Tennyson Jesse, *A Pin To See The Peepshow*.[16] This excellent book produces very positive reactions from those who read it, but who is to say what, if anything they have learned from the experience? What, precisely, did you learn from the last novel that really gripped you?

This poses some difficult questions in educational theory: to what extent must our answer to the Why? be formulated as learning objectives that can be specified in behavioural terms?[17] To what extent should teachers or learners embark on educational enterprises in an open-ended way with no clear objectives? My bias is to try to articulate learning objectives in a disciplined way, but not to allow the theories of Bloom and Mager to force me to distrust my intuition that some text is really worthwhile in some open-ended way.

In the history of legal education there have been some brave attempts to teach law through literature.[18] After all, *Bleak House*, the *Antigone*, *A Man for All*

---

[15] Id., Ch. 4. The case is analysed in detail in *RE*, Ch. 8.

[16] F. Tennyson Jesse, *A Pin to See the Peepshow* (London, 1934) (reissued in the UK by Virago as a feminist novel, 1979).

[17] See R. Mager, *Preparing Instructional Objectives* (2nd edn., Belmont, 1975); B. Bloom, *A Taxonomy of Educational Objectives Handbook I* (New York, 1956); D. Krathwohl, B. Bloom, & B. Masia, *A Taxonomy of Educational Objectives Handbook II* (New York, 1964). On the application of the approach to legal education, see Pirie, 'Objectives in Legal Education', 37 *J Leg. Educ.* 576 (1987).

[18] These have been usefully surveyed by Gemmette, op. cit., n. 2. A striking feature of this survey is that almost none of the statements of objectives of the courses covered conforms to the Bloom-Mager model for the formulation of educational objectives. The most succinct statement is by Barbara A. Burnett: 'Fun.' Gemmette comments that this is not only the most honest statement, but also 'one of the best reasons for teaching the course'. Gemmette, op. cit., n. 2, at 311.

Seasons, Kafka's *The Trial*, *One Flew Over the Cuckoo's Nest*, and many court-room dramas seem to beg to be used in enlightened courses that seriously try to live up to the claims that the study of law can be a vehicle for genuinely liberal education. Law journals contain occasional descriptions of attempts to use litera-ture in law teaching. I myself have tried to base a class about interrogation and confessions on the marvellous passages in Dostoyevsky's *Crime and Punish-ment* in which Porfiri Petrovich plays cat-and-mouse with Raskolnikov.[19]

On the last occasion that I tried to use it, the dialogue proceeded along the following lines:

SELF.   How do you find the readings this week?
CLASS.   [*in chorus*] Great!
SELF.   What did you think of the account of the second meeting between Porfiri and Raskolnikov?
STUDENT. It said it all, man.
SELF.   That's it, then.

This experience did not undermine my belief in the text, but the class was a failure. The fault lay with the teacher rather than the material—I just did not know *how* to use it.

What is striking about most such experiments is that they have failed to become institutionalized, even at the margins.[20] The major exception to this generalization is James Boyd White's *The Legal Imagination*.[21] This is an American coursebook-anthology that draws very largely from literary sources and includes a significant amount of poetry. It explores in great detail and depth analogies between literary and legal interpretation, and the operation of lan-guage and values in legal and literary imagination. Not only has White taught successful courses in Chicago and Michigan based on these materials, but his book has been reissued in paperback.[22] I happen to disagree with White's theory of legal interpretation[23] and I am frankly sceptical of any suggestion that Jane Austen's *Emma* is a book about law,[24] but the success of the enterprise is both significant and welcome. Perhaps the key lies in the fact that James Boyd White is a Professor of both Law and Literature and that he has borrowed techniques from literary education in presenting his materials to law students.

---

[19] F. Dostoyevsky, *Crime and Punishment* (trans., D. Magarshack, Harmondsworth, 1951), esp. III. 5, IV. 5, V. 2.

[20] Gemmette's survey suggests that this statement may no longer be true in the US. She found that, out of 135 law schools that responded to her survey, 38 offered a course on Law and Literature in 1987. Whether these will become regular offerings remains to be seen. Gemmette, op. cit., n. 2, at 267–8.

[21] J. B. White, *The Legal Imagination* (Boston, 1973, abr. edn. 1986). On the surprisingly modest sales figures and adoptions, see Gemmette, op. cit., n. 2, at 269, n. 6.

[22] J. B. White, op. cit., n. 21. See also J. B. White, *When Words Lose Their Meaning* (Chicago, 1984); J. B. White, *Heracles' Bow* (Madison, 1985).

[23] See *RE*, Ch. 7.   [24] *When Words Lose Their Meaning*, op. cit., at 163–91.

On this note of caution, let us turn to cannibalism. In recent years there has been published a number of contextual studies of leading cases, such as M'NAGHTEN, CARLILL V. CARBOLIC, RYLANDS V. FLETCHER, PALSGRAF V. LONG ISLAND, AMERICAN BANANA V. UNITED FRUIT, HADLEY V. BAXENDALE, AND REGINA V. DUDLEY AND STEPHENS.[25] In each instance, a leading case familiar to most law students has been studied in detail in its particular historical context. Very often such treatment significantly changes one's perceptions or understanding of the original case. One enthusiastic advocate of this approach, Professor (now Judge) John Noonan has said: '[It] is my own belief that about half of law school should be devoted to studying cases in this historical way. A curriculum based almost totally on appellate opinions, while excellent for stimulating analysis, distorts what actually happened.'[26]

Although I have both enjoyed and benefited from these studies, I think that this is overselling contextualism. Some of the reasons for this are illustrated by Brian Simpson's book *Cannibalism and the Common Law*.[27] This is a learned, ghoulish, and highly entertaining study of REGINA V. DUDLEY AND STEPHENS, the leading case on the defence of necessity at common law. The defendants were convicted of murder for killing and eating the cabin boy of the shipwrecked vessel *Mignonette* in order to save their own lives. The book is well-written, scholarly, enjoyable, and illuminating. But what, precisely, does it illuminate? From it you can learn about the immediate background to the case; about the custom of the sea in respect of emergencies; about cannibalism on land and sea, its culinary and gastronomic aspects, and the songs it provoked. You can also read about the growth of the Merchant Shipping Acts; about Sawney Bean and Liver-eating Johnson and the devious Baron Huddleston; about how a leading case was fixed; and about the golden age of yachting.[28] One even gains quite a lot of insight into the dilemmas and hypocrisies of necessity as a justification and excuse. And like other such studies, it shows that the law reports often conceal as much as they reveal about the cases that they report.

---

[25] On M'NAGHTEN'S CASE, 8 Eng. Rep. 718 (HL 1843), see 1 N. Walker, *Crime and Insanity in England* (Edinburgh, 1968), Ch. 5.

On HADLEY V. BAXENDALE [1854] 9 *Ex.* 341, 156 Eng. Rep. 145, see Danzig, 'HADLEY V. BAXENDALE: A study in the Industrialization of the Law' 4 *J Legal Stud.* 249 (1975).

On RYLANDS V. FLETCHER (1868) LR 3 HL 330, see Simpson, 'Legal Liability for Bursting Reservoirs: The Historical Context of RYLANDS V. FLETCHER', 13 *J Legal Stud.* 209 (1984).

On AMERICAN BANANA CO. V. UNITED FRUIT CO., 213 US 347 (1909) and PALSGRAF V. LONG ISLAND RR, 248 NY 339, 162 NE 99 (1928), see J. Noonan, *Persons and Masks of the Law* (New York, 1976), 65–151.

On CARLILL V. CARBOLIC SMOKE BALL CO. [1893] I QB 256, see Simpson, 'Quackery and Contract Law: The Case of the Carbolic Smoke Ball', 14 *J Legal Stud.* 345 (1985).

On REGINA V. DUDLEY AND STEPHENS [1884] 14 QBD 273, see Simpson, op. cit., n. 27 and accompanying text. [See now Brian Simpson, *Leading Cases in the Common Law*, (Oxford, 1995).] This general theme is explored further in Ch. 12, below.

[26] Noonan, 'Review of Cannibalism and the Common Law', 63 *Tex. L Rev.* 749, 752 (1984).

[27] A. W. B. Simpson, *Cannibalism and the Common Law* (Chicago, 1984).

[28] Id. See also the amusing index, especially the entry under 'Cannibalism.'

'The fox knows many things; but the hedgehog knows one big thing.'[29] *Cannibalism and the Common Law* is definitely a foxy book. Both as a work of scholarship and as potential educational material, it is a splendid failure. The best scholarship and the best education focus on specific questions and have at least some fairly clear touchstones of relevance. *Cannibalism and the Common Law* lacks focus. It is in essence a product of serious scholarship that has been presented to the world as a work of entertainment. Some of the colourful characters and stories that add to our enjoyment divert attention from any central theme or theories that there might have been. Yet, sadly, I fear that Professor Simpson may have made the right choice. For if he had presented us with a more focused case-study of necessity or strategic litigation or official hypocrisy, it would have attracted far less attention with no corresponding benefit. Presented as material for law study it would probably have been neglected. Simpson was faced with a dilemma familiar to legal scholars. If you present unconventional material in unusual form, it probably will not be used; if you present it in palatable form, it may be consumed, but for no apparent purpose. The paradox of contextual studies of leading cases is that a case becomes leading because it raised and perhaps resolved an issue of law of general significance; this issue becomes abstracted from the original context of the particular historical event. It is largely a matter of serendipity whether or not leading cases provide good material for detailed case-studies. The significance of a historical case-study is normally determined by criteria other than doctrinal importance. Thus, works like Simpson's can play a useful role in reminding us of the connections between law and ordinary or not-so-ordinary life, but I do not think that they can provide a staple diet for even a truly humanistic study of law.

To restate the argument to date: in our practice of the discipline law we tend to neglect a wide range of potentially valuable texts. But if such texts are to become a regular part of the materials used for studying law in our legal culture, we need to develop clear ideas about why we are reading them, their nature and limitations as raw material, and what methods of reading a given kind of material are suitable for different purposes. We should recognize that our capacity to learn and to understand often outruns our capacity to articulate clear learning objectives, but this should not be an excuse for abandoning a relatively purposeful approach.

The next step is to propose a reasonably disciplined method for exploiting this rich heritage of neglected materials. The germ of such a method is found in the general precept that I have already given: in approaching any text, ask Why? What? How? (Why am I reading this text? What is the nature of this text? What method is suited for reading this text for this purpose?) To a large extent the Why? should determine the What? and the How? By and large, purpose should determine the selection of material and should indicate (or at least provide a test

---

[29] Archilocus (Diehl, Frag. 103).

of) what method is appropriate. Of course, life is not in practice so simple, but this general approach is a straightforward way of maintaining a sense of direction. One implication of the proposition that the Why? tends to dominate the What? and the How? is that a systematic methodology for exploiting potential materials of law study presupposes a coherent theory of the nature and objectives of such study. This opens up the Pandora's box of the competing aims and objectives of legal education and legal research.[30] My central thesis, however, will fit a wide range of different educational and scholarly priorities.

Suppose we decide that we want to explore our notions of what constitutes excellent or deviant behaviour by an appellate judge. An obvious, but not yet hackneyed, approach would be to select a sample of judgments that are conventionally viewed as models of excellence, or the reverse, and to consider what reasons might be given for admiring or criticizing them. An exercise I sometimes do with first-year students is to take some well-known judgments of Lord Denning at his best (e.g., CANDLER V. CRANE CHRISTMAS[31]) and at his worst (e.g., WARD V. BRADFORD[32]) and then to move on to a case that tends to produce more ambivalent reactions, MILLER V. JACKSON.[33] The following is from the opening paragraph of Lord Denning's judgment in *Miller*:

In summer time village cricket is the delight of everyone. [The Millers, one asks?] Nearly every village has its own cricket field where the young men play and the old men watch. In the village of Lintz in County Durham they have their own ground, where they have played for these last 70 years. They tend it well. The wicket area is well rolled and mown. The outfield is kept short. It has a good club-house for the players and seats for the onlookers. The village team play there on Saturdays and Sundays. They belong to a league, competing with the neighbouring villages. On other evenings after work they practice while the light lasts. Yet now after these 70 years a judge of the High Court has ordered that they must not play there any more. He has issued an injunction to stop them. He has done it at the instance of a newcomer who is no lover of cricket. This newcomer has built or has had built for him, a house on the edge of the cricket ground which four years ago was a field where cattle grazed. The animals did not mind the cricket. [How was this proved?] But now this adjoining field has been turned into a housing estate. The newcomer bought one of the houses on the edge of the cricket ground. No doubt the open space was a selling point. Now he complains that, when a batsman hits a six, the ball has been known to land in his garden or on or near his house. His wife has got so upset about it that they always go out at weekends. They do not go into the garden when cricket is being played. They say that this is intolerable. So they asked the judge to stop the cricket being played. And the judge, much against his will, has felt that he must order the cricket to be stopped; with the consequences, I suppose, that the Lintz Cricket Club will disappear. The cricket ground will be turned to some other use. I expect for more houses or a factory. The young men will turn to other things instead of cricket. The whole village

---

[30] My own biases as a scholar and teacher are clear: I tend to favour broad understanding of legal phenomena closely linked to sharply honed intellectual skills, such as skills of analysis and reasoning. See, e.g., Ch. 9, above.   [31] CANDLER V. CRANE CHRISTMAS [1951] 2 KB 164.
[32] WARD V. BRADFORD [1972] 70 LGR 27.   [33] MILLER V. JACKSON [1977] QB 966.

will be much the poorer. And all this because of a newcomer who has just bought a house there next to the cricket ground.[34]

In the course of three pages Denning uses the word 'newcomer' five times and '70 years' six times. What is he up to? Is this judge-like behaviour?

Tempting as it is, I do not intend to analyse this passage here.[35] The judgment as a whole has received a mixed reaction: cricket lovers and environmentalists love it; property owners and precedent lovers tend to dislike it; many are ambivalent—some like the outcome, but sense that 'the rhetoric' (note the term) is 'over the top'. 'Lord Denning departed from the high standards of the judge and adopted the mantle of the advocate', wrote one critic.[36] Yet the same commentator considered it an excellent example of the art of persuasion.[37] It is fairly obvious that one can have great fun analysing Lord Denning's intentions, who he thought his audience was, how persuasive his argument is, and in what respects he is deviating from conventional norms of judicial excellence and propriety. Whether one adopts a common sense approach or borrows more sophisticated techniques from a neighbouring discipline, such as literature or rhetoric or semiotics, it is obvious that the Why? of this reading requires a different How? from the conventional ones. It is only slightly less obvious that all judgments can be viewed as exercises in rhetoric and can be subjected to scrutiny as such.[38] The differences between sophisticated and common sense techniques is that the former tend to subject the text to sharper questions. Both seem to me to be valid and neglected ways of reading the law reports for this purpose. Why? To clarify notions of excellence in writing judgments. What? Examples of judgments considered to be excellent or deviant or about which there is some ambivalence. How? Asking questions of the text designed to elicit what are considered to be acceptable criteria of propriety, validity, and cogency in judicial reasoning.

A very different kind of analysis involves trying to diagnose in depth what factor or factors in a reported case occasioned difficulty or doubt either in the minds of the judge(s) in the case itself or in subsequent cases. This involves the systematic diagnosis of what can be called 'the conditions of doubt' in a given context of interpretation. I have elaborated this method elsewhere.[39] It can take one far beyond intuition in identifying the factors that made or make the case problematic and in providing a basis for constructing arguments. The technique is quite simple: it involves little more than running through a check-list of

[34] Id., 340–1.
[35] See *RE*, at 235–8; cf. B. Jackson, *Law, Fact and Narrative Coherence* (Merseyside, 1988), at 94–7.
[36] Atiyah, 'Contract and Tort' in *Lord Denning: The Judge and the Law* (edd., J. L. Jowell & J. P. W. B. McAuslan, London, 1984), at 73.   [37] Id.
[38] There is now an extensive literature about different kinds of reading of the law reports, which is by no means confined to different fashions in 'deconstruction'. Recent English examples include P. Goodrich, *Reading the Law* (Oxford, 1986) and Davies, 'Reading Cases' 50 *Mod. L Rev.* 409 (1987).   [39] See *HDTWR*, Ch. 6.

possible factors that tend to give rise to difficulties in interpretation. These fall into four broad categories:[40] events before the creation of the rule; factors relating to the nature and form of the rule itself, such as bad drafting or a poor fit between instrument and purpose; factors coming into existence after the rule, such as changes in values or other legal rules or technology or the social or political context; and finally, peculiar features of the particular case, such as particular conditions of sympathy or fairness (what Karl Llewellyn called 'fireside equities'[41]) or the likely undesirable consequences of a particular outcome of the case, such as creating a diplomatic incident. What is striking about this kind of analysis is that it involves a different kind of reading from normal case analysis. It involves systematically asking a series of more sharply focused questions about why a given rule or text is difficult or puzzling or controversial, before moving on to conventional analysis. More often than not one finds that several factors combine, some of which may be overlooked or underplayed by more intuitive reading.

So far, I have suggested that there is a wide range of materials of law study that are under-exploited largely because we have not developed conscious and systematic techniques for reading and using them. The potential of even the law reports is not realized in our practices largely because we are unselfconscious about our methods of reading. I have also hinted that the key lies in knowing what questions to ask and developing habits of asking such questions in a systematic way. In the next section I shall try to develop this theme in relation to some specific kinds of reading of some particular kinds of text. Some of what I am suggesting may sound at once simple-minded and radical. But perhaps we can agree on one point: the art of questioning should be one of the main skills of any law-trained person. Knowing what questions to ask is the first step to wisdom, as Kipling clearly recognized:[42]

> I keep six honest serving-men;
> (They taught me all I knew)
> Their names are What and Why and When
> And How and Where and Who.
> I send them over land and sea,
> I send them east and west;
> But after they have worked for me,
> *I* give them all a rest.

> *I* let them rest from nine till five,
> For I am busy then,
> As well as breakfast, lunch and tea,
> For they are hungry men.
> But different folk have different views.

[40] Id., at 220–6.
[41] K. Llewellyn, *The Common Law Tradition* (Boston, 1960), at 121, and Index.
[42] R. Kipling, 'The Elephant's Child' in *Just So Stories* (London, 1902).

I know a person small—
She keeps ten million serving-men,
Who get no rest at all!

She sends 'em abroad on her own affairs,
From the second she opens her eyes—
One million Hows, two million Wheres,
And seven million Whys!

II. READING LAW II: SOME APPLICATIONS AND IMPLICATIONS

In this section, I propose to illustrate some of the potential of a systematic approach to texts by considering two specific examples in more depth. The central theme remains the idea of putting texts to the question. In order to do this I shall focus on two texts that I use in my own teaching. I shall concentrate on some specific educational objectives, but for present purposes education and scholarship in this context have shared aims: they are part of the general enterprise of understanding law. First, we shall look at one specific exercise involving newspapers. Next, we can have a second helping of cannibalism, by examining Lon Fuller's *The Case of the Speluncean Explorers* as a vehicle for exploring the nature of legal theory.[43] Finally, I shall try to link my thesis about materials of law study to a broad conception of legal theory within the discipline of law.

The Newspaper Exercise

In recent years I have persuaded my colleagues to join in a collaborative effort that we call 'The Newspaper Exercise'. This is the very first assignment we give to entering law students; indeed, we ask them to prepare for it before they arrive in our law school. We ask each of them to read every word of a non-tabloid (i.e., up-market) newspaper published in the week before they embark on their legal education. One version of the precise instructions is as follows:

The Newspaper Exercise: The Pervasiveness of Law in Society
Buy a copy of the *Guardian* or *The Times* or the *Telegraph*, preferably for the last week of September of this year. Read through *all* of it marking with a coloured pencil or pen all the passages which have some clear 'law-related' content. Calculate the number of column inches which, in your view, are devoted to legal or law-related matters. Then answer the questions below.

Before starting on this exercise:
  (i) stipulate your working definition of 'legal' and 'law-related';
  (ii) work out a method for calculating the amount of space devoted to 'law-related' content; and
  (iii) devise a rough scheme for categorizing the type of material.

43 Fuller, 'The Case of the Speluncean Explorers', 62 *Harv. L Rev.* 616 (1949).

Questions

1. What branches of the law would you expect regularly to feature in or be relevant to understanding items in:
   (i) the sports pages;
   (ii) the Arts section;
   (iii) the Business section; and
   (iv) advertisements.
2. Identify the national legal systems and other bodies of law (e.g., Public International Law) that would be directly relevant to the items reported on *one* of the foreign/international pages in the particular newspaper you have read.
3. Which features more prominently in your newspaper: legislation? case-law? 'non-legal' rules?
4. Identify *two* passages in your newspaper that you would expect would be more easily understood by a person with a law degree.
5. What lessons have you learned from doing this exercise?

Bring your marked copy with you to the first tutorial. To do this exercise should take you not less than four and not more than six hours.

This exercise can be interpreted and used in various ways. The constraints of time, team-teaching, and the particular context dictate that we treat this quite lightly and informally. We devote only one hour of classroom time to discussing it, and later I make some informal comments in part of a lecture. In short, we do not try to exploit its full potential. Despite, or perhaps because of, this relatively light treatment, the exercise is generally well-received, but one wonders whether it makes a lasting impact. In the first tutorial my colleagues ask different questions and emphasize different points. Students, when asked, claim to have learned, or to have been reminded of, a remarkable range of lessons: that contract is everywhere; that administrative law is almost as important as contract in interpreting the sports pages; that it helps to know something about Islamic law in order to understand reports in the business section as well as foreign news; that the *Financial Times* contains rather good drama criticism. Perhaps the highest compliment about his undergraduate legal education that I have heard paid by a former student was that he left equipped to read every page of the *Financial Times* with a discerning and critical eye.

The Newspaper Exercise is designed to convey one central set of messages to beginning law students: law is interesting, pervasive, dynamic, and relevant to most aspects of private and public life; it features on the sports pages, the arts pages, in the business section, and the foreign section, as well as in the more obvious places; all school-leavers know quite a lot of law already and they have had practical experience of it as criminals, tortfeasors, licensees, contractors, tenants, debtors, violators of copyright, and slanderers. What is encompassed by the notion of 'law' is highly elusive, but the most important message of all is that law is capable of being fascinating as a subject of study.

One way of evaluating the potential of this and other kinds of readings of newspapers as a means of understanding law is to seek to formalize this exercise in terms of learning objectives. To put the matter briefly, one could rationalize the pedagogical objectives of the exercise in some such terms as these. The exercise has both affective and cognitive objectives, as well as some that fall in the grey area of 'consciousness-raising'. The affective aspects are probably achieved, at least temporarily, for most students merely by spending a few hours on a single newspaper. At least the idea is shown that it is *possible* for law study to be fascinating, dynamic, and concerned with issues that are truly important for ordinary people as well as in political and economic life. This, in turn, may start the process of undermining a different image of law as fustian, esoteric, drily technical, and tedious. Such an image may represent the expectations of English students more than their older American counterparts, and it may be less prevalent in England today than it was twenty years ago.

There are also some cognitive lessons built into the exercise. One learns that it is difficult to identify what is 'legal' or 'legally relevant', that the first step in legal diagnosis is classifying legal issues in terms of fields of law, and that real life situations do not come neatly parcelled in legal categories—torts do not walk typically into your office ready labelled, and that this is one reason why law reports and legal textbooks tend to be artificially decontextualized and abstracted from 'real life'. More fundamentally, reading a newspaper through legal lenses can provide one starting-point for developing two related themes about the broader significance of legal perspectives. First, consider how much the discourse of newspapers is expressed in terms of concepts that take their meaning from law. 'Murder', 'marriage', 'alien', 'income tax', 'tenant', and 'heir', are obvious examples of terms in everyday use that are both constituted and given precision by law. Turn to the business section and the phenomenon is even more striking: 'corporation', 'bankruptcy', 'debentures', 'mergers', 'take-overs', 'insider dealing', 'charities'. Indeed, one might ask, which important concepts of the business news do not derive their precise meanings from law?

Perhaps less obvious is how many institutions and dignitaries can only be defined and explicated by reference to law: What is the Federal Trade Commission or the FBI? What are the powers, authority, and status of the Director-General of Fair Trading, a Commissioner for Baseball, an Archbishop or an Ayatollah? These are all legal questions. And the legal perspective as a lens for interpreting the news goes beyond concepts. For example, only legally-informed people can give answers to some questions that are central to in-depth interpretation of the Salman Rushdie affair. What is the meaning of the alleged death sentence? Who has authority to pronounce it in what circumstances? With what specific offences against Islam is Rushdie charged? Are these 'offences' against religion or law, or is there no such distinction? What, if any, crimes have been committed in England by those who have supported or repeated the Ayatollah's sentence? Is there anything in the book itself that is criminal or actionable or otherwise illegal in any of the countries in which it has been distributed? Is a given government's decision to take no action against the book based on law or policy or a combination of the two? What are the limits of freedom of speech for authors and Ayatollahs in different countries? Take any public event and one cannot go far before in-depth understanding and interpretation involve addressing lawyers' questions.

Reading a newspaper in this way illustrates the point that legal lenses are essential to understanding society as much as non-legal lenses are necessary to understanding law. But having created or reinforced awareness of the general point, can we use newspapers to carry it further? The short answer is 'yes', but as with other under-exploited materials of law study, one cannot go very far without disciplined answers to the What? the Why? and the How? The uses and limitations of newspapers (and other types of public media) for purposes of understanding aspects of the interrelations between law and society depend on a sophisticated understanding of the What? Who owns them? How are they structured, constructed, and produced? What is the influence of economic, ideological, and other factors on the selection, presentation, and interpretation of news? And so on. My impression is that to date, in England and the United States, there are some interesting particular examples, such as studies of law-related 'moral panics' and the image of law and lawyers in the media[44] but little sustained research or literature. There are some well-developed tools within media studies, such as content analysis, and from a different quarter, deconstruction, but so far I know of no sustained attempt to address the What? the Why? and the How? of using newspapers and other public media as materials for studying law.

Cannibalism Again: *The Case of the Speluncean Explorers*

For my next example, I want to turn to a classic of Jurisprudence in order to carry one stage further the notion of putting texts to the question. The text is Lon Fuller's *The Case of the Speluncean Explorers*. The fact that I intend to subject it to quite stringent criticism should be taken as a compliment: normally, only classics deserve such attention.

Before describing and criticizing the text from a particular perspective, let me briefly state my own view of legal theory.[45] Jurisprudence is the theoretical part of law as a discipline. A theoretical question is a question posed at a relatively high level of generality; a philosophical question is one posed at a very high level of abstraction. 'What constitutes valid reasoning?' is a philosophical question. 'What constitutes valid reasoning about questions of law?' is a question of

---

[44] e.g., S. Chibnall, *Law and Order News* (London, 1977); S. Cohen, *Folk Devils and Moral Panics* (London, 1972); Chase, 'Lawyers and Popular Culture: A Review of Mass Media Portrayals of American Attorneys', 1986 *Am. B Found. Res. J* 281; Chase, 'Toward a Legal Theory of Popular Culture' (1986) *Wis. L Rev.* 527; 'Symposium: Popular Legal Culture', 98 *Yale LJ* 1545 (1989); Rosen, 'Ethical Soap: LA Law and the Privileging of Character' 43 *U Miami L Rev.* 1229 (1989).

[45] See *LTCL*, Chs. 4, 13; *RE*, Ch. 11.

legal philosophy. 'What constitutes valid reasoning in American state appellate courts?' or 'in the English Court of Appeal?' are still sufficiently general to be regarded as questions belonging to legal theory, but they are not purely philosophical questions, because answering them also requires some familiarity with particular institutional contexts.[46] Jurisprudence is thus equivalent to legal theory, but is wider than legal philosophy. Since generality is a relative matter, theory cannot be sharply separated from particular fields of study. Theory knows no boundaries. Since there is no necessary correlation between generality and utility or uselessness, the idea that all theory is useful or useless is a fallacy, just as contrasting theory and practice involves a false dichotomy.

Teachers of Jurisprudence generally fall into one of two categories—those who teach *about* Jurisprudence and those who ask their students to *do* it. In most countries Jurisprudence is seen as a vast heritage of classic or near-classic texts, from which a very few are selected for study; so one reads bits of the work of Hart or Fuller or Aristotle or Aquinas or Dworkin; one learns about their ideas; and one interprets and criticizes them. In the other approach, theorizing is seen as an *activity* involving posing, refining, answering, and arguing about important general questions relating to law, ideally to stimulate students to work out their own positions in a coherent and relatively informed way.[47] The range of significant questions is not as vast as the heritage of attempted answers, but nevertheless selection is still necessary in almost any Jurisprudence course. So even in the activity courses, attention tends to be focused on a few questions from one sphere of legal theory, such as ethical or epistemological questions or questions about reasoning about disputed issues of law. I am a late convert to the idea of treating theorizing as an activity rather than a subject. I still use selected texts as the main means of raising questions and getting students to develop their own answers through dialogue with the text. The difference is one of emphasis, but it is significant: we study questions raised by Bentham or Dworkin and their attempted answers as a means to clarifying our own views on the significance of the questions and the validity of our own answers. We are not studying Bentham or Dworkin as such.[48]

My conception of legal theory and legal theorizing is relevant here because I start my courses on Jurisprudence with *The Case of the Speluncean Explorers*. I use it, first, to present and discuss different conceptions of Jurisprudence, and, second, to suggest a particular method of reading juristic texts as a vehicle for stimulating students to clarify their own ideas.

Given that the objective of reading juristic texts is to enter into intelligent

---

[46] e.g., philosophers who contribute to discussions of 'legal reasoning' tend to assume that the distinction between the questions of fact and questions of law can be treated as unproblematic in judicial contexts and that 'legal reasoning' is the only or the main or the most distinctive kind of reasoning engaged in by lawyers, judges, and other participants in legal processes. See *RE passim* and Ch. 17, below.   [47] *LTCL*, Ch. 13.

[48] The problems of anachronistic reading of juristic texts are explored further in RB.

dialogue with them, and given that the texts are selected because they raise important questions and suggest answers, reasons, and perspectives bearing on those questions, what might be a reasonably systematic way of reading such texts for this purpose? Over the years I have developed a quite simple and flexible method. I ask students to approach any juristic text at three levels: the historical, the analytical, and the applied.

The extent to which the historical context of a work is important in interpreting and evaluating it has been a matter of central concern to theologians, intellectual historians, literary theorists, and jurists, among others. Here one can bypass some of those controversies,[49] because our reading is for a specific ahistorical purpose: the text is being used as a means to clarify one's own views on significant questions *today*. Why, then, bother about history at all? A brief answer is that at the very least setting the text in its historical context can help one to identify the central concerns of the author and hence enter into an intelligent dialogue with the text in a way that avoids some of the cruder caricatures that contaminate much secondary writing about Jurisprudence. It also can have other uses, as I shall illustrate with reference to 'the Speluncean Explorers'. Usually it is quite sufficient for this particular purpose to learn enough about the background of the text and its author to establish the general nature of his enterprise and its underlying concerns. In short: What was biting him? (Most classical jurists are, alas, still male.)

Translating concerns into questions marks the transition from the historical to the analytical mode of reading. And as Professor Hart has shown, some articulated questions are very poor expressions of their underlying concerns.[50] If one is puzzled about the meaning of a familiar abstract word, such as 'law' or 'right' or 'justice', a question expressed in the form of a request for a dictionary definition is unlikely to be helpful. If one interprets Holmes's *The Path of the Law*[51] as an expression of concern about legal education at Harvard becoming out of touch with the realities of everyday legal practice, then it is strange to read it as a text centrally concerned with the question What is law? and intended to launch a general theory of law.[52] Identifying, clarifying, and, if necessary, reposing questions involves interpretation and is often not a straightforward matter.

The most basic kind of analytical reading can be designated as 'reading for plot'. What questions does this text address? What answers does it propose? What are the alleged justifications for the answers? Elementary reading for plot provides the basis for the next step in dialectical reading: Do I agree with the questions? Do I agree with the answers? Do I agree with the reasons? This process of dialogue can be extended in many directions almost indefinitely, again depending on one's purposes and the value of reading this text for those

[49] Id.   [50] Hart, 'Definition and Theory in Jurisprudence', 70 *LQ Rev.* 37 (1953).
[51] Holmes, 'The Path of the Law', 10 *Harv. L Rev.* 457 (1897).
[52] Twining, 'The Bad Man Revisited', 58 *Cornell L Rev.* 275 (1973).

purposes. In my experience, Holmes's *The Path of the Law*, like *Hamlet*, yields fresh interpretations, insights, and puzzles at each reading—perhaps the highest compliment one can pay to any text. Of the analysis of texts there is no end, but in this context, the suggested method provides an economical and disciplined basis for entering into worthwhile dialogues without getting bogged down unnecessarily.

The third level, rather uncomfortably designated as 'the applied', involves exploring particular implications and applications of the questions, answers, and reasons attributed to the text and alternatives developed in the course of the dialogue. Theorizing involves considering particulars in relation to general ideas. To put the matter briefly and crudely: in studying Bentham's classic exposition of the principle of utility in *An Introduction to the Principles of Morals and Legislation*,[53] we begin by clarifying Bentham's concerns. What seems to be a plausible interpretation of this version of his utilitarianism developed in that text? Is this the least vulnerable interpretation of utilitarianism in the view of the reader (this may involve looking at other texts)? The purpose is to stimulate each student to develop an answer to the question: Am I a utilitarian? Moving to the applied level is a means of testing out a position provisionally adopted at the general level: Does utilitarianism necessarily commit you both to vegetarianism and to justifying torture and punishment of the innocent in extreme circumstances? If so, are you sure you are a utilitarian? And so on.

This, in outline form, is a simple recommended intellectual procedure for a systematic approach to the reading of juristic texts for a given purpose. Let us apply it briefly to *The Case of the Speluncean Explorers* by way of illustration.

Historical[54]

The Case of the Speluncean Explorers was written in about 1948. It was the first of a series of hypothetical examples in a course on Jurisprudence at Harvard Law School. At the time Fuller was in his mid-forties. Ten years later he was to come into prominence as the first and one of the most important critics of the positivism of H. L. A. Hart and as a leading exponent of the idea that no sharp distinction can be made between legal and moral reasoning in debating questions of law. Fuller wrote 'the Speluncean Explorers' before the appearance of Hart, Dworkin, Nozick, and Rawls. Marxism, Critical Legal Studies, and Economic Analysis of Law had not yet made themselves felt in American law schools. So it is hardly surprising that none of these feature in what can reasonably be interpreted as an attempt to provide a conspectus of rival approaches to legal argument (and, more broadly, competing visions of law). So perhaps we

---

[53] J. Bentham, *An Introduction to the Principles of Morals and Legislation* (edd., J. H. Burns & H. L. A. Hart, London, 1970).

[54] For background, see R. Summers, *Lon L. Fuller* (London and Stanford, 1984); L. Fuller, *The Problems of Jurisprudence* (temp. edn., 1949).

can impute the following objective to Fuller: to introduce Harvard students to
the subject in the late 1940s by raising a range of central and perennial questions
in Legal Philosophy and by presenting a conspectus of different approaches and
positions on those questions.[55]

Analysis I. Plot

The Case of the Speluncean Explorers is based on two leading cases involving
cannibalism and the defence of necessity in criminal law—the English cases
of REGINA V. DUDLEY AND STEPHENS[56] and the earlier American case of US V.
HOLMES.[57] Simpson's recent book reveals that Fuller had intelligently researched
the background. Fuller's version takes the form of five opinions of the Supreme
Court of Newgarth in the year 4300 (a time roughly equidistant from 1950 as
1950 was from the Age of Pericles).[58] Four members of the Speluncean Society
had been trapped in an underground cave. Stupendous efforts were made to
rescue them, at the cost of ten lives and a great deal of money. By the twentieth
day the unfortunate explorers decided that they could only avoid death by star-
vation before they could be rescued if they killed and ate one of their number.
One of them, Whetmore, suggested that they should decide who should be the
victim by casting dice. The others agreed only after much hesitation, whereupon
Whetmore declared that he withdrew from the arrangement. The others decided
to go ahead and one of them cast the dice on Whetmore's behalf. The throw
went against Whetmore and he was killed and eaten. In due course the survivors
were rescued and charged with murder. The report contains five individual judgments, each of which adopts a seemingly different approach.

Fuller's standpoint in this context was that of a Socratic teacher, and this was
not intended as a coherent statement of his own views. However, his views can
to some extent be inferred from the opinion of Foster, J, and, indirectly, from
the element of caricature in his treatment of some of the other judges. His
perennial concern with problems of value is revealed by the single question he
appended to the case in his collection of materials entitled *The Problems of
Jurisprudence*:

---

[55] Op. cit., n. 43, at 645. Fuller's general views on the teaching of jurisprudence are outlined in
Fuller, 'The Place and Uses of Jurisprudence in the Law School Curriculum', 1 *J Legal Educ*. 495
(1949) (roughly contemporaneous with the first publication of *The Case of the Speluncean Explorers*); see also Summers, op. cit., n. 54, at 8.

There have been several attempts to adopt Fuller's device of the imaginary case for similar
purposes. See, e.g., Seidman, 'The Inarticulate Premiss', 3. *J Mod. Afr. Stud*. 567 (1965) (the case
of Kwame s/o Nighili); A. Hutchinson, *Dwelling on the Threshold* (Toronto, 1988), Ch. 6 (the case
of DEREK AND CHARLES V. ANNE AND MARTIN); A. D'Amato, *Jurisprudence: A Descriptive and
Normative Analysis of Law* (1984), Ch. 12 (further proceedings in the case of the Speluncean
Explorers).

[56] *Dudley and Stephens* [1884] 14 QBD 273, aff'd. [1885] 14 QBD 560.

[57] US V. HOLMES, (1842) 26 *Fed. Cas*. 360.   [58] Op. cit., n. 43, at 645.

It is fairly clear that the root difficulty in the case of the Speluncean Explorers lies in the fact that values ordinarily protected by law have come into irreconcilable conflict, so that one must be sacrificed if the other is to be preserved. In the case as it is put the values in conflict are human lives. Would it be possible to construct a similar case in which one property value was pitted irreconcilably against another? If it is more difficult to construct such a case, why is this so?[59]

The standard way of reading the case is to identify the issues and the competing positions taken on each of them. It is widely regarded as an excellent way of starting a Jurisprudence course. However, in the present context, let us look at it in terms of Fuller's conception of Jurisprudence: What did he consider to be central questions and what did he consider to be the most important competing approaches or theories?

We can restate the main issues in the case in non-Fullerian language as follows:

1. Is it ever morally
    (*a*) justifiable
    (*b*) excusable
    to kill and eat a fellow human being?
2. Whether or not it is morally justifiable or excusable, is it legally justifiable to kill and eat a fellow human being in order to save one's own life. Alternatively, is necessity a defence to a charge of murder?
3. What is the connection, if any, between questions 1 and 2?
4. What is the proper role of an appellate judge in deciding a hard case on a question of law? How does this differ from other officials?
5. What kinds of reasons are admissible, valid, and cogent in
    (*a*) reaching
    (*b*) justifying
    a judicial decision in a hard case? What is the relationship between (*a*) and (*b*)? In particular, should public opinion be taken into account in reaching and justifying such decisions?
6. Do (a) citizens (b) judges owe an indefeasible duty of fidelity to law?

The five judges take a variety of positions on each of these issues. Three of them think that the killing was excusable to some degree, allowing for mitigation. Keen, J, implies that it may be completely justifiable, and Tatting, J, seems unsure of the morality of the action. Truepenny and Keen consider that the accused were nonetheless guilty of murder; Handy and Foster, JJ, would quash the conviction; Tatting, J, considers the case too hard and withdraws, with the result that, the court being equally divided, the conviction is affirmed. In justifying their decisions, Truepenny and Keen concentrate on the wording of the statute, which they consider to be clear; Tatting relies on precedent and analogy; Foster appeals to purpose, which he considers to be in conflict with and to

[59] See Fuller, op. cit., n. 53, at 645.

override the wording; and Handy decides on 'common sense' backed by articulated public opinion. Each of the judges expresses his views on the role of judges in hard cases and their relationship to other officials (in this case the prosecutor, the Chief Executive, and the Legislature).

Analysis II. Critique

The Case of the Speluncean Explorers raises a rich range of issues and arguments. It is splendid pedagogical material; it is readable, profound, and calculated to engage the interest and concern of all but the most closed-minded students. It forces students to clarify their own positions on a number of questions and to see how those views relate to different intellectual traditions. Subliminally, it communicates two important messages: Jurisprudence can be enjoyable and 'relevant'. When, like many teachers, I use it in class, we address the substantive issues it raises, and I ask students to note with which judge they have instinctively identified to start with and to review this at the end of the course. It is not a bad touchstone of self-definition.

Here, I want to consider the text as an indication of Fuller's picture of the world of Jurisprudence. In a Postscript Fuller claims that 'the case was constructed for the sole purpose of bringing into common focus certain divergent philosophies of law and government . . . [which] presented men with live questions of choice in the days of Plato and Aristotle and which are among the permanent problems of the human race'.[60]

How far is the last claim sustained from the perspective of 1989? *Speluncean Explorers* brings together a number of standard issues in legal theory and illustrates their interconnectedness: positive law and the law of nature; the relationship between law and morals; different modes of interpreting statutes and reasoning about questions of law; the proper role of judges and its relationship to the roles of the legislator and various executive roles; the relationship between law and public opinion; the ultimate basis of government and the nature of fidelity to law.

Single cases or case-studies are useful as dramatizing and concretizing devices, but they have limitations as vehicles for presenting comprehensive or systematic overviews. In 1948 one might then have been able to suggest a number of improvements; for example, instead of presenting a near-consensus on the morality of the action, one judge could have been a moral absolutist maintaining an indefeasible right to life, another a moral nihilist or sceptic, maintaining that moral judgements are nonsensical or purely subjective expressions of opinion, a third a utilitarian, and so on. Similarly, more than one different kind of purposive interpretation could have been illustrated (for example, principled, consequentialist, or the Golden Rule) and a wider range of philosophies

---

[60] Op. cit., n. 43, at 645.

of government. One could also suggest that standard kinds of Legal Positivism (as represented by Austin and Kelsen) could have been presented more starkly and that Handy, J, is a rather unsympathetic caricature of a Realist.

These are by no means fatal flaws. Indeed, a good discussion can bring out most of the points. Similarly, it is not difficult to update Fuller's version. It is quite possible, as an example of working at the applied level, to set an exercise of writing a judgment in the case from some point of view not canvassed by Fuller, especially approaches that have come into prominence since his day. This works well with approaches, such as that of Ronald Dworkin or Economic Analysis of Law or some versions of Critical Legal Studies, that share Fuller's concern with the nature of appellate judging. It also works quite well with actual judges, such as Lord Denning, Lord Simmonds, or Judge Posner. It does not work so well with approaches that are less court-centered or are concerned with other issues, such as Marxism, Anarchism, Feminism, or macro-sociological theories. The central questions addressed by such theories tend to be rather different. Thus, one student purporting to write a feminist judgment in the case concluded that it raised no difficult issues at all since the person eaten was a man. Whether or not one finds that amusing, it trivializes the concerns of feminism precisely because those concerns are not central to the text. Similarly, while it is possible to subject the case to a Marxist analysis, this does not work, firstly, because the situation does not bear intimately on central Marxist concerns about power, class, etc. and, secondly, because both the author and the reader are invited to adopt the standpoint of appellate judges *within* a legal system, some of the ideological and institutional aspects of which are taken for granted in ways that Marxists are concerned to attack or at least to question.

For me, it is highly significant that *The Case of the Speluncean Explorers* works quite well in regard to some of our stock of theories of and about law, but does not work so well for others. It indicates a key point of difference between Fuller's conception of Jurisprudence, as expressed in this text,[61] and my own. To put it bluntly, for the sake of succinctness, Fuller's case-study, and theories that fit it well, exhibit the classic symptoms of what Jerome Frank called 'appellate court-itis', in this case treating a hard case on a question of law as paradigmatic of legal theorizing. It is revealing that some central ideas of Fuller, Dworkin, and critical scholars (and their critics) who debate about legal interpretation and even some brands of Economic Analysis of Law fit the case quite easily. These have at least some shared concerns and issue is joined.

Given time I would argue that the positivisms of Hart and Kelsen and even Holmes sit less easily precisely because the root concerns of positivism are not

---

[61] I am here criticizing the text read on its own for a particular purpose. A defence of Fuller could be mounted along the lines that he himself acknowledged that 'The Speluncean Explorers' did not present a comprehensive view of jurisprudence and, indeed, he included some other hypothetical cases in *The Problems of Jurisprudence*. My concern here is not to be fair to Fuller, but to consider the uses and limitations of the text, read on its own, as an introduction to jurisprudence.

about how appellate judges and their satellite functionaries should reason or choose.[62] I would also argue that American Legal Realism is caricatured by Fuller for similar reasons. In my view, it is a common fallacy to interpret the Realists as being solely or even primarily concerned with appellate court judging.[63] One move away is to broaden our concerns to include disputed questions of fact, as Frank suggested, or to extend this to all important decisions in litigation, as has been done by those who view litigation as a complex total process in which contested trials and appellate decisions are in practice exceptional events. But if one's view of law extends beyond appellate courts to trial courts, and beyond trial courts to pretrial and post-trial events, and beyond litigation to dispute prevention and resolution, and beyond these to the kind of pervasive transnational phenomenon that is illustrated by the newspaper exercise, then a conspectus of legal theories that uses a case-study set in the particular institutional context of a common law appellate court will not do. It is too narrowly focused, too unrepresentative, and too culture-bound to provide a basis for capturing a balanced overview of the range of general questions that need to be asked and tackled as part of a general understanding of the subject-matter of the discipline of law.

It is just because *The Case of the Speluncean Explorers* illustrates a view of Jurisprudence that I am concerned to attack that I continue to use it in teaching the subject. The fact that it also suggests that studying the subject can be fun is a bonus. In this context, my purpose has been twofold. First, I have tried to illustrate how the development of quite simple intellectual procedures for questioning texts in a disciplined way can yield results in terms of economy, purposiveness, and I hope, insight. Secondly, the case for developing ways of broadening the range of standard materials of law study is really part of a plea for a broader, richer, and more systematic vision of our discipline. My view of what constitute worthwhile materials of law study stems from my view of legal theory as embracing a vast range of important issues at a number of levels of generality. On this foundation, I rest my case.

---

[62] See further, Ch. 8, above at 171–7.   [63] This theme is developed in TAR.

12

*The Reading Law Cookbook**

A PRIMER OF SELF-EDUCATION ABOUT LAW

Abbreviations

BT	W. Twining	*Blackstone's Tower* (1994)
CLT	K. Llewellyn	*The Common Law Tradition: Deciding Appeals* (1960)
FD	J. Farrar & A. Dugdale	*Introduction to Legal Method* (3rd edn., 1990)
HDTWR	W. Twining & D. Miers	*How To Do Things With Rules* (3rd edn., 1991)
KLRM	W. Twining	*Karl Llewellyn and The Realist Movement* (1973)
LLR	J. Holland and J. Webb	*Learning Legal Rules* (1991)
MP	D. Miers and A. Page	*Legislation* (2nd edn., 1990)
TCAL	S. Mentschikoff & I. Stotzky	*The Theory* and *Craft of American Law* (1981)

For other citations and abbreviations, see any standard work on how to use a Law Library.

1. Clarification of standpoint

Who am I?
At what stage in what process am I?
What am I trying to do?
Ref: *HDTWR*, 64 ff., 120 ff., 190 ff.

2. Reading any text: What? Why? How?

What are the salient characteristics of this kind of text?
For what purpose(s) am I reading this text?
What technique(s) of reading are appropriate for my purpose(s) in reading *this* text?

---

* This is a revised version of a text used in teaching Legal Method since the mid-1980s. An earlier version was published as an app. to *HDTWR*; parts of the original version were appended to Ch. 11.

3. Legal literature in general

(a) Two useful distinctions

(i) within legal discourse: law talk and talk about law. For example: any proposition of law (for instance the rule in HADLEY v. BAXENDALE (1854) 9 Exch. 341) is law talk; any historical, sociological or critical statement about legal rules or phenomena falls under 'talk about law'. Legal discourse is often a mixture of law talk and talk about law, with the latter predominating.

(ii) within legal literature a corresponding distinction between law books and books about law.[1] 'Law books' include primary sources (for instance law reports, legislation, and secondary accounts of legal doctrine such as treatises, restatements, reference works); 'books about law' is a much wider and more varied category, including historical, philosophical, and critical works by legal scholars and many kinds of writings by non-lawyers. These distinctions are, of course, not clear-cut and often break down.

(b) A total picture of legal literature

Walk around the law library identifying the main types of books, distinguishing between law books and books about law. Then explore the rest of the library and ask: how many law books are there here? How many sections do *not* contain a significant number of books about law? What kinds of legal literature are not in this law library? (*BT*, Ch. 5).

4. Newspapers

(A) Introductory: the Newspaper Exercise

See above, Ch. 11, at 210–13.

HOW? (a) Reading a *whole* newspaper per instructions.

(b) Systematic content analysis.

(B) Media treatment of law (and order)

WHY? (a) To explore various aspects of the relationship between law and public opinion and opinion-formation—for instance 'moral panics'.

(b) To analyse or deconstruct media treatment of legal issues and events.

---

[1] R. L. Abel, 'Law Books and Books about Law', 26 *Stanford L Rev.* (1973), 175.

WHAT? News as socially constructed forms of 'knowledge'.
HOW? (a) Case studies of media treatments of particular issues or events.
(b) Deconstruction (see below).

References
Steve Chibnall, *Law and Order News* (1977)
S. Cohen, *Folk Devils and Moral Panics* (1972)
Jane Gaines, *Contested Culture: The Image, the Voice and the Law* (1992)
Steve Redhead, *Unpopular Cultures* (1995)
A. Chase, 'Lawyers and Popular Culture', *ABF Res. Jo.* (1986), 281
Symposium, 98 *Yale Law Jo.* (1989), 1545

(C) Routine up-date

WHY? Keeping up to date (a) generally, (b) on specific issues.
WHAT? This week's or today's news (newspaper, Law-Tel, Lexis, *New Law Journal*, specialized services).
HOW? Skim, mark, digest, file.

5. Policy documents

WHAT? Reports of official committee, private organizations, etc. and other documents dealing with issues of public policy or law reform or perceived 'problems' to which law might contribute. For example Royal Commissions; Reports and Working Papers of Law Commissions and Law Reform bodies; JUSTICE Reports; First Report of Select Committee on Violence in Marriage (*HDTWR*, 76–84, 128–9); cf. Women in Prison Committee (Florida): *Battered Women in Prison: Casualties of Domestic Violence* (Tallahassee, Fl., 1993).
WHY? For example diagnosis and analysis of a problem to the solution of which it is thought that law might contribute. (Cf. 'There oughta be a law.') Part of legislative history of a particular statute.
HOW? (i) *Quick*
Why? When? Who? To do what? How? What conclusions and recommendations? Then what? So what?
(ii) *Slow*
Why? The historical context of the enquiry leading to the report. Why *then*? Motives for giving the task to this committee (whitewash; delay; public demand; to stimulate or dampen public debate; to remove an issue from party politics; social engineering).
When? Main dates in sequence of events from initial triggering event to 'end' of story (for example enactment, implementation, shelving or rejection of recommendations).

Who? Membership of committee. Who chose them how? (Spread of interests; orthodox 'great and good'; loaded; significant absentees.)
To do what? Precise terms of reference. How were these interpreted by the committee?
How? Procedures followed. Oral 'evidence'? Specially sponsored research? Public meetings? Discussion documents ('Green papers') etc.
What? Conclusions and recommendations. Perception and diagnosis of the problem. History, context, date. What were perceived to be the main controversial issues? What options considered, rejected? Overt/covert disagreements within the committee.
Then what? Post-report events.
So what? Historical, analytical, theoretical significance of the report and its story for this reader.

Some variants

1. Other kinds of report (for example 'fact-finding' enquiries); other kinds of policy document.
2. Some official reports provide exceptionally useful syntheses and statements of existing law, historical background, public debates, and social data. They are accordingly useful as materials of law study for a variety of purposes.

Note: Reports of Royal Commissions, official committees, and the like have probably been more *politically* significant in UK than in USA. Nevertheless it is fair to say that they number among neglected materials of law study in both countries.

References

HDTWR, Ch. 2; symposium, 48 *MLR* (1980), 558; MP Ch. 2.
M. Komarovsky, *Sociology and Public Policy: The Case of Presidential Commissions* (1975).
R. A. Chapman, *The Role of Commissions in Policy-Making* (1973).
A. M. Platt (ed.), *The Politics of Riot Commissions* (1971).
S. Cretney, 'The Politics of Law Reform', 48 *MLR* (1985), 505.
R. T. Oerton, *A Lament for the Law Commission* (1987).

6. Legislation

(i) Quick

WHY? e.g.   (a) To learn about the structure and content of the instrument as a
            whole.

        (b) To find and interpret the exact words in the text applicable to a particular point of law.

        (c) To use as raw material for a legal argument.

        (d) Other.

HOW?   For (a), chart the design of the statute (*HDTWR*, App. I, section 8; FD, 302–5); thereafter depends on exact purpose. For (b) and (c), clarify standpoint; identify relevant statutory materials; where appropriate, locate exact words in text giving rise to doubt; consider immediate textual context; adjoining words; this section; statute as a whole; collect relevant non-statutory materials; state competing interpretations; specify the conditions of doubt; construct argument.

References

HDTWR, Chs. 9 and 10; *LLR* Chs. 7 and 8; FD, Chs. 9–11; MP, Chs. 11 and 12; *KLRM*, 239–45

G. Engle and J. Bell, *Cross on Statutory Interpretation* (3rd edn., 1995)

F. Bennion, *Statutory Interpretation* (1992)

G. Calabresi, *A Common Law for the Age of Statutes* (1982)

D. N. MacCormick and R. Summers (edd.), *Interpreting Statutes: A Comparative Study* (1991).

(ii) Slow

No cookbook can make you skilful at handling statutes.

7. Law Reports I: Orthodox reading

(A) The single case

(1) Précis ('briefing a case')

(i) Quick

WHY?   A necessary foundation for most purposes for which cases are read.

WHAT?   A kind of document. 'A case is the *written memorandum* of a *dispute or controversy* between *persons*, telling with varying degrees of completeness and of accuracy, *what happened, what each of the parties did about it*, what some supposedly impartial *judge or other tribunal* did in the way of bringing the dispute or controversy to an *end*, and the avowed *reasons* of the judge or tribunal for doing what was done.' (Adapted from N. Dowling, E. Patterson, and R. Powell, *Materials for Legal Method* (2nd edn., 1952), 34–5. See *HDTWR*, 280 ff.)

HOW?   A standard form of précis covering:

        (a) Title; citation; court; topic(s); outcome (who won?); order.

(b) Facts; question(s) of law; competing answers to questions; holding (court's answer to question); reasons for decision; comment. For example case note of REGINA V. ALLEN, *HDTWR* Ch. 8, at 288.

Alternative method: *TCAL*, xxviii ff.

(ii) Slow

Additional details, for example on procedure; arguments of counsel; treatment of prior authorities; reasoning of individual judges; historical background to this case (see below, 8B).

(2) Attacking an adverse precedent

WHY?   To weaken authority and persuasive force of a precedent.
WHAT?   A potentially adverse precedent.
HOW?   Precedent techniques—i.e., cumulation of *reasons* for not following or applying prior case to the case at hand.

For example treatment of *Fanning* in *Allen* (*HDTWR*, 268). This was an *Irish* case; four judges dissented; *Fanning* based on misinterpretation of prior cases; *Fanning* inconsistent with prior cases.

NB: Cockburn CJ could have distinguished *Fanning*, but chose not to do so. Why not?

Ref. *HDTWR*, 301 ff.; *CLT* 77–92 (extracted in *TCAL*, 437–47).

(3) Boosting the precedent value of a favourable precedent

For example this case is indistinguishable from the present case; it is a judgment of *Scrutton* (or some other respected judge); the reasoning was impeccably based on principle and authority; it has been followed in subsequent cases; it makes sense (*TCAL*, 427–36).

(B) Groups of cases

(1) Synthesizing *all relevant precedents on a single question of law.*

WHY?   For example to resolve a doubt about the law; constructing a legal argument; exposition of a legal topic.
WHAT?   A collection of authoritative decisions and arguments about the issue in question.
HOW?   Grand style synthesis of potentially conflicting precedents.

(2) Studying a sequence *of cases on a topic.*

WHY?   *TCAL*, 297–8.
WHAT?   A temporal sequence of precedents in a single jurisdiction.
HOW?   See FD, Ch. 8; *TCAL*, 297–8.

Example: E. Levi, *Introduction to Legal Reasoning* (1949) on Negligence/
            Product Liability and the Mann Act.
            C. Manchester et al., *Exploring the Law* (1996) Part 3.

8. Law Reports II: Less orthodox readings

The law reports tend to be over-emphasized in legal education in respect of
orthodox reading, at the expense of other materials of law study. On the other
hand, they are also an under-exploited resource in terms of other purposes and
methods of analysis. The following is a sample of alternative modes of reading
and using law reports.

(A) *Reconstructing* the arguments in a single case. For example charting the
structure of the arguments in *Allen, HDTWR*, 248–54.
(B) *Analysing the conditions of doubt* giving rise to disagreement or doubt
about the law.
   Objective: to diagnose in depth *why* there was a doubt or dispute about the
law in a past case.

WHAT?   The reported opinion(s) (and, if available, summary of arguments of
          counsel and/or the briefs).

WHY?   (i) as a preliminary to reconstructing the arguments in the case; or
          (ii) to analyze the case in depth as raw material for constructing an
             argument on a point of law; or
          (iii) for some other purpose.

HOW?   (i) *Quick*
          What conditions give rise to the doubt(s) in this case?
          Which of these conditions relate to
          (a) events preceding the creation of the rule or doctrine relevant to
             the case?
          (b) incompleteness, indeterminacy or imperfection of applicable doc-
             trine at the time;
          (c) events after the original creation of the rule or doctrine;
          (d) special features of *this* case?
          (ii) *Slow*
          (a) Which of the check-list of 35 conditions of doubt (*HDTWR*, Ch.
             6) apply to this case?
          (b) Are there any others?
          (c) Which of these conditions formed the basis, on its own or in
             combination, for a colourable argument for one side?
          (d) Was this an appellate case worth appealing or was it foredoomed?
             (*CLT*, 25 n, 27; *KLRM*, 248–9.)
          (e) Was this a 'hard case' in Dworkin's sense? Did any of the issues
             relate to matters that are 'essentially contested'?

(C) *Analysis of styles of reasoning of judicial opinions.*

Objective: to analyse a single opinion or a collection of opinions in terms of the style employed.

WHAT?   Judicial opinions.

WHY?   (a) to determine whether an individual judge or a particular court conformed to a given style of reasoning at a given moment of time or during a given period; or

       (b) as an aid to predicting how a known judge or court is likely to respond to a particular point or line of argument; or

       (c) to compare and contrast predominant styles of individual judges, courts or legal traditions in different times or places. For example to compare the judgments of Lord Mansfield and Lord Eldon; the opinions of the US Supreme Court or speeches in the House of Lords in 1900, 1950, and 1990; appellate cases in different common law and civil law jurisdictions; the styles of the European Court of Justice and the European Court of Human Rights.

HOW?   (i) *Quick*   To what extent does the material fit into Llewellyn's ideal types of Grand Style and Formal Style reasoning?

     (ii) *Slow*   See *TCAL*, 316–22; Gillis Wetter, *The Styles of Appellate Judicial Opinions* (1960), discussed *CLT*, 465 ff. and *KLRM*, 265–6, 455; *LLR*, Ch. 10.

(D) *Critical analysis of the corpus of opinions of a single judge.*

For example:

J. Jowell and J. P. W. B. McAuslan, *Lord Denning: The Judge and the Law* (1984); B. H. Levy, *Cardozo and the Frontiers of Legal Thinking* (1938); Felix Frankfurter, *Mr. Justice Holmes and the Supreme Court* (1938); Samuel Konefsky, *The Legacy of Holmes and Brandeis: A Study in the Influence of Ideas* (1956)

(E) *Critical analysis of alleged political biases of one or more courts*, by considering treatment of cases involving women, ethnic minorities, students, labour unions, etc.

For example:

J. A. G. Griffith, *The Politics of the Judiciary* (4th edn., 1994);

Richard H. Sayler, Barry B. Boyer, and Robert E. Gooding, Jr. (edd.), *The Warren Court: A Critical Analysis* (1969);

Herman Schwartz (ed.), *The Burger Years: Rights and Wrongs in the Supreme Court* (1987)

(F) *Deconstruction of judicial opinions and other critical readings.*

For example:

Murphy and Rawlings, 'After the Ancient Regime', 44 *MLR* (1981), 617

C. Husson, 'Expanding the Legal Vocabulary: The Challenge Posed by the Deconstruction and Defense of Law', 95 *Yale Law Jo.* (1986), 969

D. Balkin, 'Deconstructive Practice and Legal Theory', 96 *Yale Law Jo.* (1987), 743

M. D. A. Freeman, Lloyd's *Introduction to Jurisprudence* (6th edn., 1994) Ch. 12 (critical legal studies) and Ch. 13 (feminist jurisprudence).

(G) *Quantitative analysis of judicial opinions*

For example:

Glendon Schubert, *Judicial Behavior* (1964);

(H) *Economic analysis of legal doctrine*

R. Posner, *Economic Analysis of Law* (1986)

(I) *Narrative*

W. Twining, 'Lawyers' Stories', *Rethinking Evidence* (1990), Ch. 7

B. Jackson, *Law, Fact and Narrative Coherence* (1988)

W. Wagenaar, P. van Koppen, and H. Crombag, *Anchored Narratives* (1993)

(J) *Participant perspectives*

The experience and consequences of being involved in litigation from the standpoint of the parties or other participants (for example witnesses; legal worms). C. Knapp: 'no study of law is adequate if it loses sight of the fact that law operates first and last *for, upon* and *through* individual human beings.'

For example:

John T. Noonan, *Persons and Masks of the Law* (1976); Charles Dickens, *Bleak House*.

(See further below, 10. Contextual studies.)

9. Trial records

One of the most neglected kinds of materials of law study.

(A) Analysis of evidence in cases involving disputed questions of fact

WHY? (a) Organizing a mixed mass of evidence in order to structure an argument about a disputed question of fact.

(b) Microscopic analysis, construction, and evaluation of arguments from evidence.

WHAT? For example trial records and secondary accounts of trials involving disputed questions of fact. National trial competition problems.

HOW? Wigmore's Chart Method and complementary techniques of analaysis.

References

J. H. Wigmore, 'The Problem of Proof', 8 *Ill. L Rev.* (1913), 77

T. Anderson and W. Twining, *Analysis of Evidence* (1991) (for a short version, see *LLS*, Ch. 8; for a critique, see *TEBW*, Ch. 3 and appendix).

(B) Miscarriages of Justice

WHY? Analyse what factors contributed to acknowledged or alleged failures in the criminal justice system.

WHAT? Trial records or secondary accounts of *causes célèbres* (for example Sacco-Vanzetti; Alger Hiss; Bywaters and Thompson; Luke Dougherty in the Devlin Report).

HOW? Various methods. See for example Landsman, 84 *Michigan Law Rev. No. 2* (1986); Twining, *Rethinking Evidence* (1990), Ch. 8; R. Weis, *Criminal Justice: the True Story of Edith Thompson* (1988); Ludovic Kennedy, *The Airman and the Carpenter* (Hauptman, 1985); Paul Foot, *Who Killed Hanratty?* (1971); Bob Woffinden, *Miscarriages of Justice* (1987); J. Kadane and D. Schum, *The Sacco-Vanzetti Case: A Probabilistic Analysis* (1996).

(C) Models

For example famous cross-examinations. F. Wellman, *The Art of Cross Examination* (various editions).

10. Contextual studies of leading cases

WHY? In-depth study of a leading case in its historical context.
WHAT? Contextual studies of particular cases.
HOW? Problematic. See W. Twining, 'Cannibalism and Legal Literature', 6 *Oxford Jo. Legal Studies* (1986), 423.

Examples

HADLEY V. BAXENDALE, R. Danzig, 4 *J Leg. Studies*, 249 (1975)

BROWN V. BOARD OF EDUCATION, R. Kluger, *Simple Justice* (1975)

PALSGRAF V. LONG ISLAND, John T. Noonan, Jr., *Persons and Masks of the Law* (1976), 111–51

CARLILL V. CARBOLIC SMOKE BALL, A. W. B. Simpson, 14 *J Leg. Studies* 345 (1985)

RYLANDS V. FLETCHER, A. W. B. Simpson, 13 *J Leg. Studies* 209 (1984), (see now A. W. B. Simpson, *Leading Cases in the Common Law* (1995))

R V. DUDLEY AND STEPHENS, A. W. B. Simpson, *Cannibalism and the Common Law* (1984; Penguin, 1986)

LIVERSIDGE V. ANDERSON, A. W. B. Simpson, *In the Highest Degree Odious* (Oxford, 1992)

11. Reading a juristic or other secondary text: the historical, the analytical, and the applied

Assuming the purpose is to enter into a dialogue with the text on issues on which it is potentially significant:

Historical

  (i) *Quick*   What were the author's central concerns in writing this text? What
                was biting her?

 (ii) *Slow*   *Who* was the author?
                When was the text written, published?
                What was the immediate (practical, intellectual, personal, cultural)
                context of its creation?
                Where does it fit in the author's total opus/intellectual development?
                Whence? Sources, 'influences' etc.
                What were the author's main concerns?

Analytical

(a) Exposition

  (i) *Quick*   What questions does the text address?
                What answers does it give to those questions?
                What are the reasons (evidence, premises, arguments) advanced in
                support of the answers?

 (ii) *Slow*   Detailed textual analysis and interpretation.

(b) Dialogue

  (i) *Quick*   Do I agree with the questions?
                Do I agree with the answers?
                Do I agree with the reasons?

 (ii) *Slow*   Critical analysis of multiple interpretations.
                Which is the least vulnerable interpretation of the question(s),
                answer(s), reason(s) etc.?

Applied

Implications and Applications:

  (i) *Quick*   So what?
                What are the logical implications of the answers?
                What is the historical significance of the text?
                What is the contemporary significance of the text?

 (ii) *Slow*   Detailed study of implications, consequences, and other
                'significance'.

Examples:

Quentin Skinner, *Machiavelli*

On *Bramble Bush*, *KLRM*, 140–52

On 'The Path of the Law', (*TCAL*, 524), see 58 *Cornell Law Rev.* (1983), 275

'Reading Bentham', LXXV *Procs. of the British Academy*, 97 (1989)

12. Casebooks

See: B. Currie, 'The Materials of Law Study', 3 *Jo. Leg. Ed.* 331 (1951), and 8 *Jo. Leg. Ed.* 1 (1955), 1 *KLRM*, 128–40.
A feminist perspective: Frug, 34 *Am. UL Rev.* (1985), 1065.

13. Textbooks

Twining, 'Is your Textbook Really Necessary?', 11 *JSPTL (NS)* 81 (1970); cf. 12 *JSPTL (NS)* 267 (1973).
D. Sugarman, 'Legal Theory, The Common Law Mind and the Making of the Textbook Tradition', in *LTCL*, Ch. 3.

14. Law Reviews

Symposium, 36 *Jo. Leg. Ed.* (1985), 1
F. Rodell, 'Goodbye to Law Reviews', 23 *VL Rev.* (1956), 38

15. Cookbooks (nutshells, swots, outlines, etc.)

standpoint:	law student why?	law teacher why not?
	To save effort.	It saves effort.
	It provides structure.	It reveals the ball.
	It succinctly summarizes information.	It substitutes for skill and understanding.
	It is useful for professional exams.	This is not a cram course.
what?	Well-organized, concise summary.	Superficial nutshell of facts.
how?	Memorize.	Don't!

Comment: Some Cookbooks teach skills, for example, . . .

16. Not dealt with

Reference works, treatises, restatements, treaty series, legal history, constitutions, contracts, wills, conveyances, articles of association, etc., etc. (*BT* 111–18).

17. Reading about law

See: Main library.
Why? What? How?—That is another story.

Ref. J. J. Marke (ed.), *Deans' List of Recommended Reading for PreLaw and Law Students* (1984).

E. Gemmette, 'Law and Literature: An unnecessarily suspect class in the Liberal Arts Component of Law School Curriculum', 23 *Valparaiso L Rev.* (1989), 267.

Alexander Welsh, *Strong Representations: Narrative and Circumstantial Evidence in English Law* (1992).

Richard Posner, *Law and Literature: A Misunderstood Relation* (1988).

Appendix

Horizontal Reading[2]

Can you really be said to have had a general education in law, if you have never read (or seen) *Crime and Punishment* or *Antigone* or *Bleak House* or *A Man for All Seasons* or *To Kill a Mocking-Bird*? Can anyone claim to be 'well-read' in law, if they are not familiar with the writings of Bacon or Maine or Maitland or Holmes or other classic legal writers? And can a practising lawyer be said to be a worthy member of a learned profession if she knows nothing of Plato or Aquinas or Bacon or Blackstone or Bentham or Rawls? These are all questions inviting the answer 'No'; yet hardly any of these works or authors will feature on reading-lists for courses that you take in the LL B. One can construct a strong case for 'reading around the subject' for such reasons. This note, however, is based on a different premise: Law is *interesting* and there is a vast mass of literature which tends to fall outside the official curriculum, but which can add to the enjoyment of your legal education as well as to its quality.

There is no need for me to produce my own list of Great Books or Legal Classics, but I shall include some personal favourites at the end. There are many such lists. Among the most accessible are A. W. B. Simpson, *Invitation to Law*, Ch. 9; Glanville Williams, *Learning the Law*; and William Twining, *Blackstone's Tower: The English Law School*, chapter 1. More systematic, but somewhat heavier, are the American work, Julius Marke and Edward Bander, *Dean's List of Recommended Reading for PreLaw and Law Students* (various editions) and Appendix III of *How To Do Things With Rules*. Much lighter, but somewhat dated, is Robert Megarry, *Miscellany at Law*.

My advice is: follow your interests. If you like literature, there is a host of novels and plays that might appeal to you. Many are mentioned in the works listed in the last paragraph; there is now a Law and Literature Movement in law schools and a readable, though sceptical guide, is Richard Posner's *Law and Literature: A Misunderstood Relation*. More high-minded and serious are James

---

[2] This is a handout given to entering law students at University College, London as part of their 'Introduction to Law'.

Boyd White's *When Words Lose Their Meaning* (*Emma* a law book?) and *Heracles' Bow*—mainly for *aficionados*. For the middlebrow reader, Julian Symons and Frances Fyfield are up-market crime novelists who know what they are writing about; so too do most of the new breed of American lawyer-novelists (John Grisham, Scott Turow, Richard North Patterson) who are also more 'popular' in style. For legal humour, A. P. Herbert, Henry Cecil, and John Mortimer are standard, nostalgic favourites. Accounts of libel cases are often amusing. Tom Wolfe's *Bonfire of the Vanities* belongs to a more satirical genre. Legal biographies and autobiographies tend to be very uneven in quality, but there are good, readable books on, for example, Francis Bacon, Thomas More, Marshall Hall, Henry Maine, Albert Venn Dicey, O. W. Holmes Jr., various Lord Chancellors, and Lord Denning.

If you wish to read about law schools, John Osborn's *The Paperchase* (*Love Story* with a contracts teacher instead of leukaemia as the villain) and Scott Turow's *One L* are both about Harvard. English law schools do not feature in our campus novels, so you will have to do with *Blackstone's Tower* (above). There is a mass of literature relevant to law in legal anthropology, sociology, ethics, politics, psychology, ecology, and, indeed, most of the social sciences and the humanities, but here it is generally sensible to seek guidance from specialists in particular areas (legal or otherwise). Do not hesitate to consult one or more of our resident experts if you have some special line of interest that you would like to pursue. Legal history also has a rich storehouse of literature and at some stage a legally educated person ought to have read at least something by Maitland, Maine, E. P. Thompson, and Willard Hurst. Here again, it may be advisable to consult one of our legal historians about where to begin.

For some the easiest starting-point for general background reading may be famous cases. The literature is massive and very varied: campaigning journalism about alleged miscarriages of justice, transcripts or potted accounts of famous trials, scholarly monographs, sensational treatments of gruesome crimes, and a mass of faction and fiction. The American *cause célèbre*, the Sacco-Vanzetti case, stimulated so many novels, plays, and poems that it was even referred to as 'the only major literary event in the United States between two wars'. In France, the Calas, Dreyfus, and Dominici cases (the last involved the murder of a UCL professor and his family) occupy a similar position. Perhaps our nearest equivalent is the trial of Edith Thompson (the case even featured in Joyce's *Finnegans Wake*; and see further below). 'The Birmingham Six', O. J. Simpson, and even 'Death on the Rock' may, in time, attain a similar status. Here, as with some of the other categories mentioned, you are as likely to find many of these books in a good public library as in a law library.

Follow you interests and consult me or any of my colleagues about where to look. Let me end with my personal list of winners. If you do not find *any* of these interesting, then maybe you should not be reading law. Start with one of these: Brian Simpson, *Cannibalism and the Common Law* (Penguin) and/or

Sibyl Bedford, *The Faces of Justice*, and/or Patrick (Lord) Devlin, *Easing the Passing* (the Bodkin Adams case), and/or F. Tennyson Jesse, *A Pin to See the Peepshow* (an early feminist novel about Edith Thompson, reissued by Virago). If you enjoyed Simpson's book, move on to his *In the Highest Degree Odious*; if you liked either or both of the next two, try Bedford's, *The Best We Can Do* (also about Adams). If you liked *Peepshow*, follow up with *Criminal Justice: the True Story of Edith Thompson* (Penguin) by Rene Weis (English Dept., UCL). Closer to your first year studies are books by and about Lord Denning (start with his *The Discipline of Law*). And, as you are at UCL, you ought to find out about Jeremy Bentham. A good short introduction is John Dinwiddy, *Bentham* (Past Masters). As the Americans say: 'Enjoy'.

13

*Access to Legal Education and the Legal Profession: A Commonwealth Perspective**

INTRODUCTION

Once upon a time the Law Faculty of the University of Xanadu, tired of perpetu-ally debating curriculum, decided to turn their attention to Admissions.[1] They started by analysing who their students were; this did not take long as they already knew that they were much of a muchness. So they resolved to take on the broader question of who were not their students.

We seem to have a problem of Access, said the Dean, over 90 per cent of our student body are drawn from only 5 per cent of the population.

Educational institutions should not try to solve society's problems, said the Sub-Dean.

There is no problem, said the Vice-Dean, we have never had any complaints.

There is no problem, said the Admissions Tutor, we are prohibited by law from discriminating on grounds of gender, colour or religion and we select solely on the basis of the school-leaving examination.

Last year's survey showed no correlation whatsoever between school-leaving results and degree performance.

There used to be a problem about women, but now they represent 45 per cent of our intake: the problem is solved.

---

* This is a revised version of the annual Access of Justice Lecture, delivered at the University of Windsor on 2 Apr. 1986 and published in 7 Windsor Yearbook of Access to Justice 157–208 (1987) and reprinted in R. Dhavan, N. Kibble and W. Twining (edd.), *Access to Legal Education and the Legal Profession* (London, 1989) (*ALELP*). I am grateful to many people for help with this paper. Most of them are acknowledged in the first published version. A select bibliography on access to legal education and the legal profession is included in *ALELP*.

[1] The discussion is set in the mythical jurisdiction of Xanadu with a view to making the presenta-tion more concrete and more provocative. Xanadu is a composite with many familiar features. Far from being presented as typical it is designed to bring out some of the great variety of circumstances and problems relating to access in different jurisdictions of the Commonwealth. Constructing a mythical country frees one from both the incubus of data and expatriate inhibition. But the main purpose is to invite my audience to engage actively in the comparative method: by comparing and contrasting the position in your own jurisdiction with each circumstance in Xanadu, the nature of problems of access and prospects for effective action in your own country may be clarified in the context of a quite simple framework of analysis and comparison. For prior reports from Xanadu see 'Keeping Up to Date in Xanadu', *Proceedings* Seventh Commonwealth Law Conference, Hong Kong and Chs. 3 and 8 above.

The problem is not solved: it is merely postponed to a later stage in the process. Women still suffer discrimination in apprenticeship, employment, and promotion. Anyway 80 per cent of the women applicants are from the Northern middle class.

We get very few Southerners; but that is not our fault: they just do not apply.

Of course we have a problem: our student body should be broadly representative of the population at large.

That is not the problem: our student body should represent the best potential practitioners.

That is élitist: everyone should have an equal opportunity to enter law school.

We have a near monopoly over entry to the legal profession: at present we prefer academic high-flyers many of whom probably won't practise to sound men who would be the backbone of the profession. We should only admit those who intend to practise.

We are not a trade school.

We should try to get the best and the brightest.

Ask not who is the best; rather ask who is most likely to learn the most.

Ask not who will take the most, but rather who will contribute the most to our intellectual community.

It is in our interest to favour the children of the rich.

Admission by auction would maximize revenue.

Admission by lottery is the most efficient and objective method of selection.

There is a problem, but it is insoluble.

There are plenty of solutions: for example mature student entry.

I am against reverse discrimination.

That is not discrimination: our mature students do as well as 18-year olds and they both learn and teach more.

If the South continues to feel that it does not get its fair share of places in the education system we shall have a civil war.

We should have quotas: 50 per cent women; 30 per cent Northerners; 85 per cent rural; 90 per cent working class and so on.

No. What we need is variety: let us have two policemen; two convicted felons; two divorcees; two single parents; two married men; a trade unionist; a managing Director; and a foreign diplomat.

If you want variety, why not admit mainly foreign students?

At least we should look to the experience of other countries for models or success stories.

No country in the world has solved the problem of access: there are no success stories.

Eventually the Oldest Member spoke up: 'None of us know what we are talking about: let us consult an expert.' 'There are no experts', howled his colleagues. 'Then let us make one by appointing him', he replied. That is how, without any prior expertise, I came to write the report from which the following extracts are taken.

WHOSE PROBLEM?

Under what circumstances is it true to say that a problem of access exists? Obviously this depends largely on the standpoint and values that are adopted. For example, from the standpoint of an individual who wishes to study law or become a lawyer any obstacle between him/her and these goals represents part of their problem of access. And she may feel aggrieved if it seems that the barriers are artificially high or irrelevant or unnecessary or unfair in some way. For example an applicant may resent any of the following:

1. a strict limit on numbers at one or more stages of legal education or training or qualification;
2. negative discrimination, direct or indirect, against him/her as an individual or against members of a class or group to which he/she belongs;
3. positive discrimination in favour of some other class or group;
4. arbitrary or biased selection, treatment or certification at any stage;
5. a longer minimum period of education, training, apprenticeship or limited practice than seems justifiable according to agreed criteria of minimum 'competence', if such exist;
6. an arbitrary academic standard for professional qualification;[2]
7. restrictions on upward or lateral mobility that seem unnecessary or unfair or unduly rigid;
8. barriers that result from structural features of the economic, social or educational system rather than specifically from the organization of legal education or the legal profession;
9. absence of a 'second chance' to remedy a failure or poor result at a particular stage; and so on.

To what extent such grievances in fact exist and to what extent they are remediable depends very largely on circumstances. To what extent others will sympathize with such grievances or feel that they are justified is, of course, a matter of evaluation in the given context.

From the standpoint of those who control different stages or routes—the various gatekeepers—some of these matters will be of direct concern; but others will be felt to be outside their control or jurisdiction. For example, in formulating an admissions policy for a particular law school, criteria of admission and selection, and efforts at recruitment, must take account of the pool of actual and

---

[2] e.g., the requirement of second class honours in one's first degree as a condition of admission to the Bar, introduced in England by the Senate of the Inns of Court in 1981, taking effect in 1983.

potential applicants from whom their students can be realistically recruited and selected. They cannot take on full responsibility for all prior and subsequent stages in the process.[3] And at times different gatekeepers may be at odds with each other.

I propose to look at problems of access from a different standpoint, that is from the perspective of the system as a whole where the concern is to devise workable general strategies for improving access to legal education and the legal profession in a given jurisdiction. My concern is to suggest a way of diagnosing the problem from this point of view in different contexts and of considering the range of possible strategies and devices that might be employed at different points in the system.[4] Where power over the total process is dispersed, an important factor is likely to be the willingness or otherwise of each of the gatekeepers to co-operate with others in tackling the problem.

From this perspective, the extent and nature of actual grievances, the existence of particular barriers to access, and the attitudes, interests, and circumstances of particular gatekeepers are all relevant. But insofar as we are concerned with describing, analysing, and improving existing systems in respect of access, we need to adopt a broader perspective and a longer time frame than those of individual applicants or particular gatekeepers. We may also need to take into account additional factors that may be marginal or irrelevant to these particular participants.

In diagnosing the problem, we need first to look at the following, in the broad context of the particular society under consideration: politico-economic factors,

[3] For a powerful plea that higher education should acknowledge a share of the responsibility for low participation rates of some groups, see Neil Kibble, 'Race, Class Access to Legal Education', 8th Commonwealth Law Conference (1986). See also *ALELP*, Ch. 7. Accidents of birth are often the biggest single factor affecting equality of opportunity. In Sri Lanka, e.g., up to 1970 it was estimated that approximately 94% of the population were effectively excluded from university legal education and hence entry to the legal profession by virtue of competitive entry based on academic standards, in particular a stringent English language requirement. (Cooray, 1985, discussed below.) In most countries one's chances of reaching university are to a large extent predetermined at birth (or before) given that gender, colour, class, geographical location, and family background are all likely to be significant factors in determining one's life chances, especially in the educational system. For certain purposes, e.g., in devising practical ways of improving access, it may be sensible for the gatekeepers in the system, such as law school admissions tutors and those who control entry to the practising profession, to take a later baseline for analysis. For example, in Xanadu it may be sensible to concentrate on increasing recruitment from those who left school after 16 and to recognize that it may not be practicable for an access policy to do much for those who have been eliminated at an early stage. But if one is to take the notion of opportunity seriously it is important to recognize that for the vast majority of the population in most countries the opportunity to study law or to qualify as a lawyer has effectively been lost at an earlier stage.

[4] My terms of reference prescribe that I have to advise the Law Faculty (and no one else) about the problem. This at least helps to clarify my role: what I shall try to do in this report is to suggest a general approach to analysing problems of access to legal education and the legal profession in any common law country; I shall suggest questions to be asked and factors to be considered in devising a general strategy for improving such access; and I shall draw attention to some relevant experience and literature, but it is beyond my brief to make specific recommendations. My job is to intellectualize the problem: it is for locals to contextualize it, and to try to reach agreement on a common strategy. This, given the diffusion of power within legal education, is a highly political matter.

such as the state of economic development; existing power structures and domin-ant ideologies; sectarianism, racism, sexism, and other forms of prejudice; the demography of the country; the education system and, in particular, the organ-ization, scale, and financing of tertiary education; national policies concerning such matters as language, educational opportunity, and the delivery of legal services; the nature of the legal profession in both private and public sectors; and the social functions—both manifest and latent—of law schools. Above all, in diagnosing the problem and considering possible strategies and particular measures, the whole discussion needs to be set firmly in the particular historical context. Our concern is with feasible policy, not with Utopia.

Since 'Xanadu' is an explicitly heuristic device, it would be artificial to present a very detailed historical scenario, but it may be useful at this point to present some elementary 'facts': the country of Xanadu is an artificial construct from a series of recognizable types: independent ex-colony; politically stable (a mildly socialist democratic government); a fragile mixed economy; per capita income of say £300 (US $500) per annum; ethnically varied, multicultural and multi-lingual, its population of eight to ten million is divided unequally between the South (mainly Muslim and local religion) and the much smaller, predominantly Christian, North; its legal system is also plural (national constitution and legis-lation; customary law, Islamic law, and received common law) with the lan-guage and traditions of the common law presently being the dominant influence on the legal profession. This is distributed almost equally between public sector lawyers (including a career judiciary) and private practitioners (advocates) who are members of a fused profession. The education system is largely government-run, with a few private and mission schools. There is a single national university with a Law Faculty that was established in 1962; five years ago a private law college was set up in response to market demand and, after a struggle, its degree has been recognized as fulfilling the academic stage of qualification for practise. Foreign exchange difficulties have made study abroad increasingly difficult especially for lawyers. Perhaps the single most important feature is that there is a single stream method of qualifying as a lawyer whether in the private or public sector. Almost without exception the route is national school-leaving certificate, local three-year law degree (at 18 plus), one year's professional training suc-ceeded by a bar examination, two years' apprenticeship (with an advocate or in the public service) followed by two years' restricted practice, before an advocate can practise on his or her own—a total of six to eight years post-18.

DIAGNOSIS

One quite simple way of diagnosing the problem in a given jurisdiction is to set up a model of the different stages through which a potential law student or lawyer must pass and to ask four sets of questions of each point in the process:

1. What are the barriers to progress beyond this stage? Do the barriers operate against members of disadvantaged groups?
2. Who controls entry and exit at this stage?
3. From the point of view of the individual: by what means might each barrier be surmounted or circumnavigated?
4. From the point of view of the gatekeepers and of those concerned with general strategy: what are acceptable and feasible means of eliminating or mitigating or circumnavigating the barriers or easing the passage of individual members of disadvantaged groups in the interests of improved access?

In order to simplify the presentation I propose to make some working distinctions not all of which are of general application. First, taking birth as the baseline it is useful to distinguish between stages and barriers that a potential recruit must pass through to come within range of being eligible for admission, and stages and barriers that confront actual applicants, students, and aspirants in the process leading towards professional status. In Xanadu the line can be drawn at about the seventeenth birthday. For the sake of simplicity I shall treat all the factors that serve to eliminate potential recruits before that stage as falling outside the purview of this report, whether these be accidents of birth, filtering out of the school system, premature specialization or career choice, linguistic deprivation or whatever.[5] Again, in order to simplify matters, I shall confine my analysis to the point in the process when the recruit to the legal profession becomes fully qualified to practise on his/her own—while recognizing that some barriers to access or progress may be as great or greater at later stages in his/her career. This study is limited to initial qualification.

In analysing a given situation it is useful to make a number of working distinctions, most of which are familiar.[6] We need to distinguish:

1. between *selection* among applicants and active recruitment of applicants;
2. between *minimum standards* of entry or eligibility and *criteria of selection* in situations of competition;

[5] Legal education and training in Xanadu broadly approximates to jurisdictions that have adopted the 'Gower' model of legal education and training. This was pioneered in Nigeria in the early 1960s, consolidated in England after the Ormrod Report on Legal Education in 1971, and adopted, with several variants, in many Commonwealth jurisdictions. Perhaps the most significant divergencies from the Xanadu pattern of legal education and training are as follows: (a) a requirement of a first degree or a minimum period of undergraduate study before entry to law school (e.g., Canada, Australia, the US); (b) no formal provision for apprenticeship (e.g., Nigeria, most Australian states); (c) multiple routes of entry to the profession (e.g., non-graduate, non-law degree entry), as in England and Wales: (d) provisions for qualification through external degrees and other forms of distance learning. On variations between systems see International Legal Center, *Legal Education in a Changing World* (New York, 1975), Ch. II (hereafter ILC (1975)).

[6] Several of those distinctions are elaborated in Oliver Fulton, 'Overview of Access and Recruitment to the Professions', in S. L. Goodlad, *Education for the Professions* (London, 1984), Ch. 7. On 'discrimination' and 'preferential treatment', see below, 258 and 265.

3. between competition for *any* place and competition for more *desirable places* (for example in an élite law school or a prestigious law firm);
4. between *selection* on entry to higher education and *certification* at the end of the educational process;
5. between *certification* for practice (has the candidate satisfied certain academic tests and training requirements?) and *evaluation* of professional competence;
6. between *direct* (or intentional) and *indirect discrimination* (both in a negative sense) and between '*reverse discrimination*' and other kinds of '*positive action*';
7. between criteria of selection which involve *preferential* treatment and those that are *different* without being discriminatory.

In respect of admissions to an educational programme, we need to distinguish between such questions as: is the candidate likely to *complete* the course; to *excel*; to *benefit*; and to *contribute* to this institution or the community at large? One can, for example, benefit from a course that one fails to complete and excel in a course from which one has learned little or nothing, perhaps because one is overqualified for it; and one can excel in a course to which one has contributed nothing.

Two distinctions are particularly important for our purposes. First, we need to differentiate between selective and mass systems of higher education, including legal education.[7] At one extreme, applicants compete for a strictly limited number of places in a single institution which aspires to provide intensive, high quality education for the chosen few. At the other pole, there is no *numerus clausus* (or quota) and anyone who satisfies some minimal criteria, for example passing a national school-leaving examination, is entitled to a place. Large-scale systems are often characterized by very large classes, poor facilities, high failure rates, and very formalized instruction. In such contexts the legal education system sometimes serves as a dumping ground for surplus demand for higher education, along with other subjects that are perceived by politicians and administrators to involve low costs.[8]

A second distinction is between single and multiple routes of entry. In England, for example, it was for a long time possible to qualify as a solicitor either solely through a combination of apprenticeship plus professional examinations, or after obtaining a law degree that exempted holders from the first part of the professional examinations, or after obtaining a degree in a subject other than law. Although in recent years there has been a strong trend towards all-graduate

---

[7] See ILC (1975), paras. 68–71.

[8] Prima facie the absence of quotas remains one of the main barriers to access. However, as the authors of ILC (1975) have argued, mass systems of legal education may be quite dysfunctional in respect of both the legal system and more basic manpower objectives. Furthermore, because of high failure rates and graduate unemployment, they offer only the illusion of increased economic opportunity for most of the students.

entry, there is still provision for qualification by graduates with degrees in subjects other than law. This is a route followed by a significant minority of candidates. There is also a good deal of variety in the types of degree available (full-time; part-time; external; mixed degrees (for example law and language; law and sociology); and sandwich courses). All these provide a degree of flexibility, especially for late developers, mature students, and people who decide that they wish to become lawyers at a relatively late stage in their education. At the other extreme stand systems in which there is only a single route of entry, typically involving a whole series of barriers or filters, at any one of which a candidate's opportunity to become a lawyer may be irrevocably destroyed.

Partly because it is a small country, partly for reasons of historical contingency, Xanadu is very near to the ideal type of a system with a single route of entry. With almost no exceptions, anyone who wishes to qualify as a lawyer has to pass through a uniform series of stages, each of which may result in the elimination or filtering out of a potential aspirant, often with no further chance of re-entry. Thus in reverse order, before being allowed to practise as a sole practitioner, a lawyer must have been employed in legal work in government or in private practice for two years after qualification as an advocate; by no means all those who qualify as advocates obtain employment of a kind that satisfies this requirement. In order to qualify as an advocate a graduate has to complete two years of apprenticeship after passing bar examinations; the failure rate in the bar examinations is quite high and candidates are allowed to resit only once; by no means all those who pass manage to obtain places as trainee advocates (the equivalent of articles or pupillage in the English system). In order to take the bar examination one must have attended full time for one year at the professional law school, for which there is intense competition for a limited number of places. Until recently holders of certain foreign law degrees or professional qualifications were eligible for direct entry to the professional school. But pressure from local law graduates has led to a considerable narrowing of this provision and, in any event, opportunities to study law abroad have declined to almost nothing in recent years. For all practical purposes, an intending lawyer must obtain second class honours in the local law degree from one of two institutions. There is in fact a significant wastage rate, by failure in examinations and otherwise, especially in the less highly regarded private law school; this is despite the fact that only about 30 per cent of all applicants obtain a place in one of these institutions. This figure is misleading on its own, because it is well-known that only those who perform well above average in the national school-leaving examination have a chance of being accepted, and so many do not bother to apply. Also, although those who have specialized in science at school are theoretically eligible, few apply and even fewer are selected. The school system is itself a pyramid, from which students are filtered out at every stage. In theory there is universal primary education, but it is estimated that in some rural areas as many as 30 per cent of children never in fact complete primary school.

The aspiring lawyer has to pass through a series of gates or filters, each of which is controlled by a largely autonomous authority. The highly selective school system is controlled largely by, or through, the Ministry of Education; entrance to and exit from the two local law schools are controlled by the University and the private Law College respectively, each of which is largely autonomous. Formal qualification for the legal profession is controlled by a Council of Legal Education, on which the judiciary and the two law schools are represented, but which has a majority of private practitioners. Selection for places for apprentices and for limited practice is almost entirely controlled by employers; these include local law firms, the Ministry of Justice, and various other institutions in the public sector, including the larger municipal councils. Thus, as in many other countries, control over access is split among several different authorities in such a way that the diffusion of power tends to make life harder rather than easier for the aspirant: at each stage in the process he or she has to please a different gatekeeper.

Xanadu, therefore, corresponds very closely to an extreme 'ideal type' of single stream entry which has the following characteristics:

1. The education system is a monolithic pyramid with many students eliminated at every stage.
2. Progression at nearly every stage depends on success in competition for a limited number of places.
3. There are few second chances for those who failed in such competition.
4. Career choice for law (for those who have such a choice) generally has to be made in theory by the age of 18, in practice for most by 16, when the decision has to be made whether to specialize in Science or Arts. Most people never reach a point where such choices are open to them at all.[9]
5. Except for minimal provision for mature student entry to university, and the residue of recognition of foreign qualifications, there are no alternative routes of entry to the legal profession.
6. All intending lawyers, including those who are destined for the judiciary or the public service, have first to qualify as private practitioners. At first sight this looks like postponement of specialization, but it can be argued that much of the training at the professional stage is irrelevant to public sector work.[10] It does not follow from this that the best solution is to stream people earlier.

[9] School-leavers 'specializing' in Science are eligible for admission to the Xanadu Law School, but only a small number apply. Of course, one needs to distinguish between point(s) in time at which opportunity to become a lawyer is effectively eliminated and the point(s) in time at which one is effectively committed to becoming a lawyer. Even in countries where occupational mobility is restricted, the latter points tend to occur significantly later.

[10] Some students in the professional school complain that the curriculum and bar examinations are too heavily oriented towards the needs of sole practitioners and small practices. The official response is that this is the best way of trying to ensure minimum competence of all those entering practice, that specialization at this stage would be premature, and that large organizations in both

7. The gatekeepers at each stage and the criteria they use are significantly different, which does not mean to say that they do not have some shared biases.

8. There are no special programmes of remedial education and few second chances within the system of legal education and training.

Other jurisdictions deviate from the model in significant respects, though few even approximate to the ideal type which represents the polar opposite; for example, a jurisdiction which has the following features:

1. progression depends on satisfying minimum criteria of eligibility rather than selection in competition (no *numerus clausus*);
2. multiple routes of entry to higher education and to the legal profession;
3. active recruitment, encouragement, and support of members of disadvantaged groups;
4. second chances at each stage within each route;
5. specialization and career choices are deferred;
6. generous provision for occupational mobility (for example transfer from one occupation to another);
7. generous or partial recognition of foreign qualifications;
8. special programmes for remedial or accelerated education;
9. a co-ordinated strategy for dealing with problems of access.

WHY SHOULD WE BE CONCERNED? ARE LEGAL EDUCATION AND MEMBERSHIP OF THE LEGAL PROFESSION SOCIAL GOODS?

According to Jeremy Bentham the interests of lawyers are in constant opposition to the interests of the community.[11] In a single work he likened them to leeches, sharks, cuttlefish, poisoners, idolators, dog-trainers, savages, slave-dealers, swindlers, lottery-keepers, spiders, depredators, tinkers, shoemakers, and fish-wives . . . to mention only a few.[12] Without making too fine a point of it, one might infer from this that Bentham did not think that membership of the legal

private and public sectors should be able to provide further training 'in-house'. More generally it has been argued, in the context of professional education in the UK that short of massive social change 'the only hope of changing [existing patterns of differential access] in a progressive direction . . . is to attempt major changes not just in entry criteria but in the structure of higher education (for which the only irresistible lever available to governments may be finance) . . . Probably the best general recipe is simply to delay choice by delaying specialization.' (Fulton in Goodlad (1984) at 89). Part of the thinking behind this is that systems of professional qualification that require early specialization or are inflexible in similar ways tend to operate to the detriment of the underprivileged.

[11] e.g., J. Bentham 4 *Works*, Bowring ed. (Russell and Russell, New York, 1962), 495. In this passage, Bentham qualifies his generalization with the phrase 'with very inconsiderable exceptions'.

[12] J. Bentham *Rationale of Judicial Evidence*, J. S. Mill ed. (London, 1827), *passim*. Bentham's vituperations against lawyers in this work were usefully assembled by William Empson in a review of the *'Rationale'* 48 *Edinburgh Rev.* 457 (1828) 473–82.

profession is self-evidently a social good. Indeed, one might reasonably infer that utility dictates reducing rather than extending opportunity to join such a band of swindlers, cuttlefish, and spiders.

Bentham was not merely, or even mainly, echoing familiar quips about the unpopularity of lawyers. He was putting forward a serious argument, though some think that he rather spoiled his case by overindulgence in invective. Before dismissing him out of hand it is useful to consider his thesis, if only because it provides a convenient peg on which to hang some preliminary points.

First, Bentham's polemic against the legal profession was part of an impassioned plea for simplifying the law and the administration of justice by freeing it from all artificial technicality. For him justice under the law involved enforcement of rights with a minimum of vexation, expense or delay. The law needed to be simple, clear, and genuinely accessible to all. He saw nearly all complexity and technicality as obfuscations attributable to the sinister interests of judges and lawyers ('Judge and Co.').[13] Whatever we think of his argument as a whole, it serves as a reminder that increasing access to legal education and the legal profession does not necessarily increase access to justice. In some circumstances it may have the opposite tendency.

Secondly, Bentham was, of course, attacking the legal profession and the judiciary as it was organized in his day. In his ideal polity salaried judges would have a pivotal role and there would even be a limited place for professional lawyers in both private and public sectors. Legal education both for specialists and the public at large would be an important aspect of access to information about law. Rather than hanging all lawyers, let us hang three points on this peg:

1. not all lawyers are private practitioners;[14]
2. access to legal education may raise different issues from access to the legal profession;
3. any rational strategy for increasing access to the legal profession needs to address questions about what kinds of lawyers such a strategy is intended to encourage: more of the same? Law-trained people who might be expected to perform a variety of roles significantly different from those traditionally ascribed to barristers and solicitors? Possibly even people who by their membership would transform the nature of the legal profession from within? Questions about who should be lawyers are inseparable from questions about what lawyers are or might be for. Similarly questions about who are or should be law students are intimately connected with questions about what kind of legal education they want or need or are likely to get.

[13] See *TEBW*, Ch. 2.
[14] For a critique of the 'private practitioner' image on the development of legal education in anglophonic Africa in the 1960s see Twining, 'Legal Education within East Africa', in *East African Law Today* (London, 1966) and L. C. B. Gower, *Independent Africa: The Challenge of the Legal Profession* (Cambridge, Ma. 1967), at 132–4.

All of these considerations apply to Xanadu. Thus, as in many other Common-wealth countries, lawyers working in the public sector—as judges, in central and local government, in public enterprise—outnumber those in private practice. Our concern here is with access to the legal profession in this broad sense.

There is, however, a complicating factor. At present anyone who wishes to qualify as a 'lawyer' in Xanadu has to qualify as an advocate, even if he/she intends to pursue a career in the public service or the judiciary.[15] This require-ment has been a matter of public controversy, partly because of the existence of a career judiciary on the French model. It is beyond my terms of reference to consider this complex matter in detail; however it is relevant to point out that while the present position undoubtedly facilitates mobility between public and private sector legal occupations, it provides an extra, somewhat artificial barrier to becoming a lawyer in the public service. As commentators have pointed out, there is much criticism of the bar examinations as an instrument for preparing or certifying a person as a competent advocate; these examinations place a strong emphasis on knowledge rather than skill and on knowledge of private law and, in particular, on a limited range of transactions which are mainly of impor-tance to business and to middle class individuals (conveyancing, probate, com-mercial sales, matrimonial, accident compensation, and bankruptcy). Some of these matters are of marginal relevance to intending magistrates and public sector lawyers. Some of the implications of this will be considered below. Here it is worth making the general point that problems of access to the legal profes-sion in a broad sense look quite different in jurisdictions with a single generalist qualification, common to all lawyers, from jurisdictions with streamed routes of entry of one kind or another.

My terms of reference make it clear that increasing access to the legal pro-fession in this broad sense is *assumed* to be socially desirable. There is not a consensus as to the reasons for this. Some support the policy as part of a wider concern with *access to justice;* others are concerned with educational and occu-pational opportunity for disadvantaged *individuals;* yet others with increasing *representation* of disadvantaged or minority groups or classes; some maintain that the Bar should *broadly reflect the composition of society* at large.[16] Advo-cates of *increased social mobility* are interested in facilitating entry for older people, both the educationally deprived and members of other professions or occupations who wish to transfer. There are also supporters of much greater *cross-jurisdictional reciprocity* in respect of recognition of foreign or external qualifications.[17]

[15] Gower (1967) Ch. 3.

[16] Traditionally the profession has been recruited almost entirely from urban, middle-class males. Recently the proportion of women recruits has risen fast, but most them come from the same social background as their brethren. In other respects lawyers in both public and private sectors are unrep-resentative in terms of class, religion, and geography.

[17] e.g., Symposium on 'Freedom of Movement in the Commonwealth Legal Profession' (contrib-utions by Linda Spedding, Campbell McLachlan, and John Hamilton *The Commonwealth Lawyer*, vol. I, No. 2, 7–39 (1986) and *ALELP*, Ch. 14.

These reasons (access to justice, individual opportunity, group representation, balance or pluralism within the profession, and mobility between occupations and jurisdictions) are different. To some extent they reflect broader ideological views. They interact in complex ways. Of course they are not necessarily mutually exclusive, but the different concerns are often in competition with each other. In order to simplify my analysis I shall interpret my terms of reference as being based on the assumption that in Xanadu the highest priority favoured by those responsible for policy is increasing representation of various groups, especially women, Southerners, and Muslims, but that this has to be fitted within the broader policy of improving both individual educational opportunity and access to justice.

DEVELOPMENTAL RELEVANCE AND THE NUMBERS GAME

I have said that it is assumed that increasing access to the legal profession is socially desirable. This needs to be qualified: there has been a long-running debate about the 'developmental relevance' of law and lawyers.[18] In many countries, including Xanadu, legal education and training is almost entirely financed from public funds.[19] As in many countries at this stage of development there is an acute shortage of 'high level manpower'. Accordingly questions have been asked, especially by the Treasury, manpower planners, and donors of foreign aid, about the priority to be given to legal education and training in the education budget and about the desirability of having strict manpower planning in respect of lawyers.

In theory there is a close connection between the two. Historically the reality has been very different. In the immediate post-independence period an attempt was made to set rigid quotas in all subjects in tertiary education on the basis of a national manpower plan that was regularly revised. To start with the target for lawyers was set so low that it would not have been possible to justify a local law school.

The story is a quite interesting variant on a common pattern: the 1960 manpower plan set an initial target of 5 new lawyers by 1975, rising to 15 by 1985. This represented approximately 1 per cent of the anticipated intake into tertiary education. Thus the manpower planners decreed that only one lawyer should be produced every three years for the first fifteen years after independence; thereafter the rate of production would be permitted to treble to one per year. These targets could be achieved by sending students abroad to study law. What actually happened was very different: in 1962 a local law school was set up in

---

[18] e.g., International Legal Center, *Law and Development* (New York, 1974). A recent example is Keith Patchett, 'The Role of Law in the Development Process', 48 *CLEA Newsletter* 33 (1987).

[19] It is estimated that in Xanadu approximately 50% of the total income of private practitioners is derived from public funds. In some countries with more developed systems of legal aid or in which private practitioners regularly act as prosecutors the percentage is significantly higher.

response to pressure from politicians, many of whom were lawyers. The first intake was 25; when a second (private) law school was established in 1970 in response to strong market demand, this time mainly from middle class parents, the university law school intake had already risen to 60. In addition, for about a decade starting in the early 1960s, a substantial number of individuals went abroad to study law: some were privately financed, but many more were on scholarships from foreign governments of varying political and legal complexion. Most, but not all, returned home after obtaining one or more legal qualifications of even more diverse provenance. By 1985 the population of law-trained personnel had risen to 1,500, exactly 100 times the original 1960 projection. This repeated, in (only slightly) more dramatic form than elsewhere, a very widespread (possibly the predominant) pattern in former British dependencies in the post-colonial period.[20] At about the same time an independent professional school was established to provide one year's full-time postgraduate training for law graduates. The establishment of such a programme was recommended, by a team of foreign experts, on what is known as the 'Gower' model that was originally instituted in Nigeria and then was widely imitated in the Commonwealth, including in the three jurisdictions of the United Kingdom.[21] Contrary to their recommendation the Law School was entirely separate from the University and because of this was lucky to receive any financial support from government. This added to the cost of formal legal education and training, but not to the overall numbers of those qualifying. In fact it served as a brake on numbers both by having a quota of places and because it provided another financial disincentive.

What explains this phenomenon of the popularity of law? It is a complex matter and, pending further research, we cannot be sure of the answers. However, some factors are reasonably clear. First, even more than in other sectors of tertiary education, recruitment to particular disciplines was almost entirely demand-led, despite the efforts of the planners. Law was extremely popular, and remained so, with only minor fluctuations. This seems to have been an extremely widespread pattern internationally.[22] Secondly, the manpower planners underestimated the output of the secondary schools and the availability of foreign aid for education in the first decade after independence. They also made some elementary errors about law, in particular equating law graduates with practising lawyers and practising lawyers with private practitioners.[23] In fact, here as elsewhere, the law degree served as a multifunctional feeder to a variety of occupations and more lawyers (i.e., advocates) found employment in the public sector than in private practice.

---

[20] e.g., Twining, op. cit. (1966); ILC (1975) paras. 135–9; J. S. Bainbridge, *The Study and Teaching of Law in Africa* (South Hackensack, NJ, 1972), Ch. 1; J. C. N. Paul and W. L. Twining, *Legal Education and Training at UBLS* (Inter-University Council, London, 1971) (Botswana, Lesotho, and Swaziland).   [21] Above, n. 5.

[22] This phenomenon has received surprisingly little attention and deserves further study.

[23] Above, n. 14.

There was also a political dimension: an uneasy alliance of law teachers, leaders of the Bar, senior judges, and middle class parents exploited the planners' errors from a mixture of motives: the law teachers needed students; the Bar wished to develop 'critical mass'; many of the older generation of legally qualified people remembered that the colonial regime had restricted access to legal education for fear that it would be a breeding ground for politics, as indeed it was; students from diverse backgrounds and middle class parents saw the Law as financially attractive; and an international 'Law-and-Development' lobby articulated the case for the developmental relevance of law with great fervour and mixed success.

About 1970 the Law Society reversed gear and started complaining of 'overcrowding', but with conspicuous ambivalence and no success at all. They were too late. The lawyer factories were in full production sustained by their own momentum, by self-interest, and by continuing public demand. Today the rate of production is considerably higher than the national birth rate. If current trends continue it will take until AD 3050 until there are more lawyers than people in Xanadu. According to a recent projection, the United Sates is due to reach that happy state of affairs considerably earlier despite the recent fall in law school applications.[24]

Of course, manpower planners and governments concerned with public expenditure are not the only parties who have been interested in control of numbers. Legal educators have regularly seen size of classes as a major factor in determining the nature and quality of legal education: large law schools may provide more opportunities for offering a variety of options but, more significantly, large classes and mass legal education are nearly always seen to be in conflict with high standards. Again, 'overcrowding' of the Bar has been a recurrent concern of practitioners and their professional associations at different times in various countries. This is a surprisingly neglected topic in the comparative study of legal professions. It is too large and complex to consider in detail here, but it may be illuminating to highlight a few examples in the literature: for example, there is a quite extensive literature on debates about 'overcrowding' in the United States in the 1930s.[25] At the height of the controversy leading academics, such as Karl Llewellyn and Lloyd Garrison, pointed out that complaints about overcrowding coexisted with significant unmet needs for legal services.[26]

---

[24] Unwarranted extrapolation from figures in Frank T. Read, *Demand for Legal Education into the Twenty-First Century*, paper presented to the ABA section on Legal Education (London, July 1985).

[25] For a useful review, see J. Willard Hurst, *The Growth of American Law: The Law Makers* (Boston, 1950), 255, 314–17, see generally R. Abel and P. Lewis, *Lawyers in Society* vols. I & II (Los Angeles, 1988).

[26] L. Garrison et al., 'The Economics of the Legal Profession', ABA, Chicago, 1938. K. Llewellyn, 'The Bar Specialises—With what Results?', 167 *Annals* 177 (1933); and 'The Bar's Troubles and Poultices—and Cures?', 5 *Law and Contemp. Problems* 104 (1938); reprinted *Jurisprudence* (Chicago, 1962), 343.

The problem was that there was strong competition for one sector of the market for the delivery of services to élite groups, but neglect of the needs of much of the rest of the population. Such arguments have been echoed in recent years in various parts of the Commonwealth.

Two of the more sustained attempts to analyse the problem of numbers are worth mentioning: one in New South Wales in 1979 (Bowen Report), the other in Ontario in 1981–2.[27] Both reached no firm conclusions on the control of numbers in the context of quite sharp disagreements. The NSW Enquiry vaguely recommended that the Law Society 'should give serious attention to the need to reduce the number of people embarking on legal education with regard to the capacity of the community to utilise their training', but significantly failed to specify any particular measures.[28] More candidly, the Ontario Report concluded, after much controversy, that 'if in fact there was overproduction, there was little that could or should be done about it'.[29] Calls for quotas or other overt limits on numbers have been rejected in Canada, the United Kingdom, several European countries, and many American jurisdictions.[30] Perhaps this is because the idea is seen to be incompatible with a free market ideology or with the notion of a liberal profession or because of a genuine concern not to limit access or because other brakes on numbers (for example excluding non-citizens, shortage of places in educational institutions or for apprentices or allowing the market to take its toll after admission) are seen to be as effective and more acceptable.

As we have seen, in Xanadu the production of law graduates has greatly exceeded the projections of planners or the expectations of anyone. It would be comforting to suggest that, given this boom in the production of law-trained persons, there is no serious problem of access to legal education and the profession. I would not have been invited to undertake this exercise if there had been no perceived problem and my impression is that there probably is one. This is a bit puzzling, for prima facie the single best way of improving access is to increase student numbers and reduce competition for places. It is difficult to fathom the extent and nature of the problem because here, as elsewhere, reliable information is strikingly patchy; experience elsewhere suggests that the compilation and interpretation of adequate statistics, especially statistics based on race, is both difficult and controversial. We have a fair idea of the social demography of the Bar, but not of lawyers in the public sector and even less information about law graduates not engaged in legal work. We know fairly accurately the composition of the present law student body in the Law Faculty and the private Law College. We can guess that nearly all of the diminishing numbers of those

---

[27] *Legal Education in New South Wales* (Bowen Report) (NSW: Government Printer, 1979): Law Society of Upper Canada, 'The Report of the Special Committee on Numbers of Lawyers' (1983) 17 *LSUC Gazette* 222. See further, T. C. Colchester, 'Views on the Numbers Game from the Sidelines: The New South Wales and Ontario Enquiries', 37 *CLEA Newsletter* (1984). See further *ALELP*, Chs. 5 and 6.

[28] Colchester (1984), 2.   [29] Ibid., 3.   [30] Information supplied by Richard Abel.

who are studying abroad (or have studied law abroad in recent years) have been privately financed (mainly by affluent parents), for one of the minor victories of the manpower planners has been that it is against government policy to award scholarships for law at either undergraduate or postgraduate level.[31] We can also make a rough estimate of the breakdown of applicants to the Xanadu Law Faculty: 45 per cent women; 80 per cent class I and II; 90 per cent Northerners; a clear majority urban; only a handful of overseas students. On the whole, these figures are reflected in the composition of the student body, except that the percentage of Southerners and mature students is higher, suggesting a slight element of indirect positive discrimination in selection.

Some of these figures may be useful as a basis for looking in detail at particular barriers to access, for example in university admissions, but much more is needed if a serious attempt is to be made to analyse such matters as the recruitment of mature students (how large is the pool?) or broader issues such as alleged overcrowding. Compilation of such statistics has sometimes been resisted on the ground that they would serve to perpetuate existing divisions or provide data that may help discrimination. However, it is my impression that there is a significant international trend in opinion favouring compilation of statistics about particular categories of people—by race, gender, class etc.—for the benefit of the disadvantaged.[32]

BARRIERS AND OBSTACLES

A systematic analysis of the problem of access in a given jurisdiction would need to consider each of the points of entry and exit in a total process which may involve several different routes. Some barriers—such as finance, language, inadequate schooling may pervade the whole process; others such as overt discriminatory hiring practices or unfair admissions criteria or shortage of apprenticeship places may operate at some points only. For example, the fact that nearly 50 per cent of Xanadu law students today are now women does not mean that there are no gender-related problems regarding access in Xanadu: very few southern women reach law school; women encounter both direct and indirect discrimination and other barriers at later stages of the process—and, indeed, many of them move out of the system in anticipation of such barriers.

In the space available, I can only look briefly at four examples of barriers that

---

[31] Cf. Patchett (1986) op. cit.

[32] On controversies about collecting such data in India see M. Galanter *Competing Equalities* (Delhi and Oxford,1984) *passim* (index under census). The American Bar Association, Section on Legal Education and Admissions to the Bar compiles and publishes statistics on women and minorities and individual law schools. On the UK, see e.g., *Education for All* (Report of the Committee of Inquiry into the Education of Children from Ethnic Minority Groups) (The Swann Report) (Cmnd. 9453, 1985), 173–6, 600–61 *et passim*. On some ways of presenting such statistics see *ALELP* App. at 312 ff.

are particularly important, but seem to operate in different ways in different contexts: language; the length of period of qualification; negative discrimination;
and opposition to positive action.[33]

Obstacles to access

(a) *Language*

In almost all societies language is a major factor influencing opportunity; in
multilingual societies the problems can be both acute and complex. A recent
study on Sri Lanka by Mark Cooray provides a graphic illustration of some of
the problems in relation to law.[34] In Sri Lanka the mother tongue (*swabasha*) for
the bulk of the population was either Sinhala or Tamil, but the language of
administration between 1858 and 1970 was English. Until 1970:

> the legal profession was closed to the vast majority of the people of the country who did
> not possess a western education. Legal education was in English and therefore it was
> open to that class which had been educated in English. The degree of knowledge of
> English which was required of a person who wished to proceed to higher education and
> legal studies could only be obtained by attending one of the good English schools, and
> almost all such schools were situated in the principal towns. Thus in effect the legal
> profession was open only to those living in urban areas whose parents could afford to
> send them to English schools. The English schools prior to 1945 were fee-levying. Social
> class was not necessarily a barrier to an English education, but economic circumstances
> and residence in non-urban areas [were].[35]

Even after the introduction of free education, those who came from affluent
backgrounds, went to fee-paying schools, and spoke English at home, had an
overwhelming advantage.

After 1945 political pressure for a national language switchover began to
mount. The pressure came particularly from the Sinhalese majority who had
three main objectives: (1) equality of opportunity in education for all classes; (2)
equality of opportunity in obtaining employment; (3) gradual resurgence of Sinhala
culture and development of the language.[36]

A language switchover began to be implemented in 1945, but it was not until
1970 that teaching of law in *swabasha* was introduced in the University of
Ceylon. Cooray documents in fascinating detail the politics, law, and logistical
difficulties of this change. Not surprisingly, a rearguard action to preserve the
use of English was fought by some law teachers and members of the legal

---

[33] Other barriers and obstacles are considered in *ALELP* Chs. 3 (Mosston), 4 (Cannon), 7 (Kibble),
and 15 (Dhavan).
[34] M. Cooray, *Changing the Language of the Law: The Sri Lankan Experience* (Quebec, 1985).
See also the same author in W. Twining and J. Uglow (edd.), *Legal Literature and Legal Information* (Ontario and London, 1982), Ch. 12.   [35] M. Cooray (1985), 147–8.
[36] Ibid., 49. On the position of the Tamil minority, see especially 41–3.

profession. They argued that English was the language of law in the courts and the legislature and, with greater force, that there were almost no books and materials on law in *swabasha*.[37] These arguments were in part valid, for as Cooray points out, in the circumstances a switch to *swabasha* in legal education inevitably meant a lowering of standards, 'at least temporarily if not permanently', especially because of the problem of literature.[38] But they also used delaying tactics and their resistance resulted in almost complete unpreparedness when the inevitable switch came. The battle depicted by Cooray involved what was perceived as a tension between what he calls 'the educational ethic' and 'the socialist ethic'.[39] One side argued for the maintenance of standards at all costs; the other side pointed out that legal education in English effectively excluded 94 per cent of those who qualified for admission to the Arts stream in the university; since this was essentially the only route of entry to the legal profession, it excluded the vast bulk of the population from the chance of becoming lawyers. A political choice had to be made and in Sri Lanka 'the socialist ethic' prevailed.

In other countries similar choices have to be made but, of course, it is not only socialists who support national language policies and increased opportunity. In 1975 the ILC *Report on Legal Education in a Changing World* noted the importance and complexity of language as a factor in legal education and observed:

The greater challenge to legal educators comes through the adoption of a local language as the medium of instruction. This has been happening in a number of countries recently. Some Indian law schools now teach in Hindi; in Sri Lanka there are now three streams, Sinhala, Tamil and English; in the Sudan much of the teaching is in Arabic, and it is intended that instruction in Ethiopia and Tanzania will eventually be in the Amharic and Swahili languages, respectively. In Indonesia the law schools have for a number of years now taught in Bahasa Indonesia. The switch in the language of instruction is generally part of a wider national policy to change the language of the legal system and of education.

There can be various reasons for such policy—the local language may be intended to be used as a vehicle for national unity (Tanzania, Indonesia); it may be a manifestation of nationalism (Sudan); it may be used in effect to reallocate resources or to undermine the dominant position of one ethnic group (especially in plural societies). But in each case there is a further important consideration—a legal system which operates in a language which is not understood by the majority of the citizens may fail to inspire confidence in its fairness. The parties to a litigation may fail to understand the proceedings (even more so than in other countries). Countries which are striving towards models of popular participation in the machinery of justice find the use of the local language to be an essential preliminary.[40]

The ILC Report noted how very little attention had been devoted to the relationship between law, education, and national language. This is still true today.

---

[37] Ibid., 122–5.   [38] Ibid., 124.   [39] Ibid., 124.
[40] ILC (1975), para. 247. This passage is in certain respects outdated on some points of detail, but the general argument still holds. E.g., on India see Cottrell (1986).

Mark Cooray's work is a shining exception that could serve as a model for further studies. In the present context Sri Lanka is a particularly interesting case study because the national language switch-over was largely motivated by concern for educational and occupational opportunity.

However, the particular, situation of Xanadu is rather different from that in Sri Lanka and, sadly, there is almost no reliable information about the relationship between language and access to legal education and the legal profession—a critical gap in our knowledge. Xanadu is a multilingual society; there are said to be over fifty indigenous languages, but there is no indigenous lingua franca. There are several official languages, but English in practice dominates. English is still the main language of secondary and tertiary education, but it is being rapidly displaced in the schools by instruction in the main vernaculars. The time will come when this inevitably will affect legal education. The situation in Xanadu is different from Sri Lanka in important aspects—for example, customary law is probably much more important in Xanadu—but at least three general lessons can be extracted from Cooray's study: first, research on the relationship between law and language in multilingual societies is feasible and deserves a high priority; secondly, legal educators need to prepare the ground carefully and well in advance for a switch in the medium of instruction. This raises particularly acute problems in respect of legal literature.[41] Where, as in Xanadu, the language of education in schools is changing, this inevitably will have important implications for legal education. Thirdly, in this respect as in others, there is perceived to be a tension between concern for high standards and concern for access.[42] Difficult choices have to be made and such choices are inevitably political.

(b) Length of period of full qualification

Another point at which there is regular tension between access and standards is the length of the period of legal education and training in law. In order to make approximate transnational comparisons it is convenient to take the standard baseline as 18 and to include in the total process all formal requirements for education, training, apprenticeship, internship, and restrictions on solo practice, since all of these have a direct bearing on access. There is, of course, a great divergence in the standard routes of entry. Canada follows a pattern rather similar to the United States. In England the law degree is a first degree, but only represents the first (or academic) stage of a three-stage system of training. An intending solicitor, for example, has to take a full-time twelve-month course in a professional law school, pass a stiff final examination, and then do two years of articles, followed by five years of continuing legal education. On the other hand, one does not need a law degree at all in order to qualify and a significant

---

[41] See generally Twining and Uglow (edd.) (1982).   [42] See further below, 274–7.

number of Arts and Science graduates become barristers or solicitors by a different route. In India the traditional pattern has been a three-year BA, followed by a three-year LL B, with no Bar exams or apprenticeship. But it is now proposed to collapse this into a five-year LL B.[43]

Despite great divergences, it is possible to venture a few general observations. First, in the past fifteen to twenty years there has been a near-universal international trend towards graduate entry to the legal profession, with law degrees being the normal and in most countries a necessary academic qualification.

Secondly, variations in the length of the total minimum period for qualification for full practice are not as great as is sometimes supposed. Thus it is almost unknown for someone to be allowed to 'hang out a shingle' as a sole practitioner below the age of 23; yet in very few countries does the minimum period extend beyond 27. The greatest differences in formal requirements relate to the differences between jurisdictions in the emphasis placed on general education, formal legal education, and formal apprenticeship or internship. Of course, the actual pre-qualification careers of intending lawyers are much more varied than the minimum requirements suggest. For example, many American students spend four years over their undergraduate degree, a significant number 'intermit' or do postgraduate work or have a period of judicial clerkship or decide to qualify as lawyers when they are much older than 18—and the point at which making such a decision becomes crucial varies considerably between and even within systems.

Thirdly, almost nothing is known about the relationship between access and different patterns of qualification. However, on the basis of particular studies of access, backed by common sense impressions, it is possible to formulate a general hypothesis: in almost all countries, the longer the period required (in practice) for qualification, the more access is reduced for less privileged members of society. This hypothesis needs to be tested and refined in different contexts. But there are good reasons (some backed by research) for believing that it is generally true.[44] For example, even in systems in which there is relatively generous financial support for legal education and training, these provisions very rarely remove all the economic barriers to qualification for the less well off. This point extends far beyond problems of fees, accommodation, books, vacation living, etc. to the economic expectations and needs of the families and dependents of students from poor backgrounds. Besides direct economic barriers, there may be significant cultural, social, and other disincentives inherent in a prolonged period of education and training—and one would expect these to vary quite considerably from place to place.

---

[43] Jill Cottrell, '10 + 2 + 5: A Change in the Structure of Indian Legal Education', 36 *Jo. Legal Educ.* 331 (1986). See Sathe, *ALELP* Ch. 8.

[44] See generally O. Fulton (ed.), 1983. Jill Cottrell points out that India may provide a counter-example: 'In some states it has been remarkably easy to enter the legal profession, although it takes a long time. The new (10 + 2 + 5) scheme, which is shorter, is part of a strategy designed to restrict access.' (Cottrell, private communication.)

The length of the period of qualification is another area in which there seems
to be a regular tension between concern for high standards (what Cooray calls
the educational ethic) and concern about access. I have to acknowledge that in
several jurisdictions in which Law has been a first degree I have regularly
supported moves to extend (or maintain) the length of first degrees in law from
three to four years (and, in one instance, to five years). In the process of thinking
about access, I have become much more aware of the close connections between
the length of education and barriers to access. Yet my enthusiasm for four-year
undergraduate degrees in law (and, for mixed multi-disciplinary degrees) has
been tempered, but by no means extinguished. How can this be justified? A
simple answer is as follows: first, in the circumstances of the United Kingdom
there are overwhelming educational arguments in favour of four-year degrees in
law. The strength of the purely *educational* case is not diminished by the argument concerning access. Indeed, in respect of some categories of disadvantaged
students (for example those with a poor command of the language of instruction), the case may be stronger. It is quite misleading to suggest that a concern
for educational excellence is intrinsically élitist. As a teacher of law I believe in
aspiring towards excellence. This does not involve indifference to problems of
educational opportunity, but it does create a dilemma. Secondly, in all the contexts in which I have supported four-year degrees, there have been multiple
routes of entry to the legal profession. Thirdly, support for the opportunity to
spend four years over a law degree is not incompatible with support for one-year
conversion courses or two-, three- or even five-year programmes in certain
circumstances. I would not favour many four-year law degrees in the USA, for
example.

(c) Discrimination

The Constitution and laws of Xanadu forbid discrimination in employment,
education, and most sectors of public life on grounds of religion, sex, race,
ethnic origin or, in certain particular cases, age. Anti-discrimination legislation
relating to race and sex has recently been extended to cover 'indirect' as well
as 'direct' (or intentional) discrimination, along the lines of modern British
legislation.[45] Preferential treatment, generally in favour of under-represented
groups, is permitted in certain limited spheres (including admission to educational institutions), but is normally not required.[46] The exact scope of these latter
provisions is a matter of uncertainty. It is clearly narrower than the kind of
mandatory scheme that exists in India.[47]

The framework of anti-discrimination laws cannot be written off as merely
'paper rules'. Since Independence successive governments have proclaimed an

[45] L. Lustgarten, *Legal Control of Racial Discrimination* (London, 1980); D. Pannick, *Sex Discrimination Law* (Oxford, 1985).
[46] On 'preferential treatment' see below, 263–70.   [47] Below, 272.

egalitarian ideology and have made genuine efforts to try to enforce anti-discrimination legislation, especially in respect of race and sex, and to promote anti-discrimination policies and practices, especially in public sector employment and institutions. There have been some modest programmes of positive action, but almost none so far that relate directly to legal education and the legal profession.

Despite genuine attempts over a long period to tackle problems of under-representation and discrimination, it is openly acknowledged that the reality falls far short of the aspiration. The situation in legal education and the legal profession broadly reflects general patterns in society at large. The great bulk of the existing legal profession originally came from urban, middle class backgrounds. Southerners, women, Muslims, rural communities, the urban working class, and some religious and ethnic minorities are hardly represented at all. This pattern is largely repeated in legal education, except that the number of women law students has increased rapidly (to about 45 per cent); but, as we have seen, nearly all of these are drawn from the urban middle class.

There is widespread acknowledgement that there is a serious 'problem' and that it is directly rooted in fundamental problems of poverty, underdevelopment, cultural diversity, and political conflict. Not surprisingly, there are sharp disagreements about the precise nature of the problem, its causes and what, if anything, should be done to tackle it. These disagreements reflect profound differences in ideology, expectations, and material interests. In Xanadu some of the most passionate public debates have recently centred around the related topics of discrimination, reverse discrimination, and affirmative action. This is a minefield where both angels and outside 'experts' fear to tread. All that I shall attempt here is to try to clarify some key concepts and to comment briefly on some of the more accessible literature from elsewhere, notably the United States and India. These concepts, it is hoped, may be helpful in eliminating some unnecessary disagreements; the admittedly selective comments on the American and Indian experiences are intended to serve as a reminder that one needs to be discriminating in looking to foreign experience and 'solutions' for guidance.

I suggested earlier that it is useful to distinguish between direct (or intentional) and indirect discrimination (both in a negative sense) and different kinds of positive or preferential treatment; and between reverse discrimination and other forms of 'positive action'.[48] These concepts need to be elucidated and related to other standard terms in common use, such as 'institutional discrimination' and various 'isms' that carry a strong condemnatory charge, such as 'sexism', 'racism', 'sectarianism', and 'tribalism'. The present purpose is to produce a reasonably clear and workable vocabulary rather than to explore in depth some of the complexities and refinements that are inevitably associated with them.

---

[48] Above, 243. 'Changing Notions of Discrimination', in S. Guest and A. Milne (edd.), *Equality and Discrimination* (Wiesbaden, 1985).

It is probably fair to say that lawyers have contributed a good deal to the development of a more precise and less emotionally laden vocabulary in this area.[49] However, what is needed here is a usable vocabulary for analysis of problems of principles and policy in different national contexts, shorn of the technical refinements associated with specific legal doctrines in particular jurisdictions. In this regard, some of the Anglo-American legal vocabulary is suggestive, but is not entirely appropriate for present purposes. What follows is an attempt to sketch the outline for a simple and admittedly crude lexicon of concepts for diagnosis and prescription of access problems in widely differing contexts.

As a start, it is useful to distinguish between two spheres of morality:[50] individual morality is concerned with the rightness, or more broadly, the goodness of individual actions. Moral principles, in this sense, are concerned with guiding and evaluating the conduct of individual actors. *Social or political* morality, on the other hand, is concerned with guiding and evaluating choices, decisions, and actions made by or on behalf of groups, institutions, or a whole community. This reflects Bentham's classic distinction between the principles of morals (how ought I to behave?) and of legislation (on what principles(s) ought the legislator to decide?).[51] In the present context, we are concerned directly with political morality and only indirectly with individual morality, for we are concerned with devising and evaluating strategies for dealing with a perceived problem on behalf of the community as a whole.

The concept of 'morality' in this usage is directly related to concepts of choice, responsibility, and action. It focuses on the choices and actions of responsible actors or agents and falls within the sphere of 'the philosophy of action'. However, in considering a perceived problem of maldistribution and inequality we may need to go beyond the sphere of the philosophy of action to include evaluation of states of affairs, which may or may not be blamed on any human agency. This involves switching attention from the choices and responsibilities of actors to the interests, needs, and concerns of victims.[52] From the

---

[49] On the uses of 'persuasive definition' in the Anglo-American context see J. C. McCrudden (1985). Implicit in the thesis presented here is the assumption that a fairly sharp distinction needs to be drawn between diagnosis of 'the problem' and prescription of feasible strategies for action. Strongly emotive terms and 'persuasive definitions' may have a role to play in promoting particular policies, but tend to be unhelpful in diagnosis.

[50] See further W. Twining, 'Torture and Philosophy', *Procs Aristotelian Soc.*, Suppl. Vol. LII, 1978, 143, 144–7; and 'Academic Law and Legal Philosophy: the Significance of Herbert Hart', 95 *LQR* 557, 571–3 (1979). See further, J. L. Mackie, *Ethics: Inventing Right and Wrong* (London, 1977).

[51] J. Bentham, *An Introduction to the Principles of Morals and Legislation*, J. H. Burns and H. L. A. Hart edd. (London, 1970). The significance of this distinction between morals and legislation within utilitarian theory is explored by A. J. Ayer in 'The Principle of Utility', *Philosophical Essays* (MacMillan, London, 1963), 254 *et seq.*

[52] The arguments for and against three different rationales for affirmative action (compensatory justice; distributive justice; and social utility) are usefully explored in Myrl L. Duncan, 'The Future of Affirmative Action', 17 *Harvard Civil Rights and Liberties L Rev.* 503 (1982). However, the

point of view of victims of disastrous events or situations it may be of secondary importance, or even of indifference, whether their plight is attributable to human agency or to other factors, such as chance or historical contingency or Acts of God. The primary concern of a starving person is to obtain food, not to find a scapegoat for his/her situation. Similarly, radical inequalities of distribution of goods in society represent a bad state of affairs independently of the extent to which it is possible to attribute blame for the situation on individual or collective human agencies.[53]

It follows from this that it is important to distinguish between past-directed and future-directed 'responsibility': a human agency may be held 'responsible' (R1) for the occurrence of an event or situation that has occurred for any one of a number of reasons—for example, in lawyers' terminology, because of intention, recklessness, negligence, omission or on some notion of strict liability. Or a human agency may be 'responsible' (R2) for taking future action to try to remedy or compensate for an undesirable state of affairs independently of how this is thought to have come about. For example, many governments, groups, and individuals feel that they have a duty to succour victims of natural as well as man-made disasters.[54]

In countries such as the United States and the United Kingdom, discussions of problems of access have been to a striking extent agent-oriented. Public debate and even legislation has tended to be conducted largely in terms of words like 'discrimination', 'prejudice', 'racism', 'sexism', which focus attention more on the attitudes and behaviour of powerful individuals, groups, and institutions rather than on the interests, needs, and aspirations of those who have suffered. As discussion has become more sophisticated, some of these terms have been extended to cover behaviour and situations for which agents are held responsible (R1) even though their attitudes and conduct are not necessarily morally reprehensible. Thus, for example, the concept of 'discrimination' was originally restricted to intentional acts of unjustified unfavourable treatment of others. Over time it became accepted that this was too narrow, not only because intention was difficult to prove, but also because many examples of unfavourable treatment were recognized to result from structures and practices which were not attributable

analysis is rather too rooted in the agent-oriented vocabulary of 'discrimination', 'affirmative action', 'treatment', etc. What is suggested here is that the rationales of distributive justice and social utility are more clearly articulated in victim-oriented terms that treat the past behaviour of agents as merely contingent factors that may have contributed to a greater or lesser extent to the existence of the 'problem' in different contexts.

[53] Some of the conceptual difficulties about the scope of 'morality' are explored in debates about 'moral luck'; e.g., Bernard Williams and Thomas Nagel in *Procs. Aristotelian Soc.*, Supp. Vol. L (1976).

[54] Compare the analogous shifts in recent writings from fault based notions of liability in tort to a broader notion of compensation for accidents caused by human agents to a yet broader concern with all kinds of misfortune, including disease. *Atiyah's Accidents, Compensation and the Law*, Peter Cane 4th edn. (London, 1987); Jane Stapleton, *Disease and the Compensation Debate* (Oxford, 1986).

to deliberate intent to discriminate. Accordingly, following American models, the British Sex Discrimination Act 1975 and the Race Relations Act 1976 were extended to cover 'indirect discrimination' which required those subject to the legislation, such as employers, to adopt criteria and procedures which took into account prior existing disadvantages and the effects of such practices on the opportunities and interests of racial minorities and women. While this represented a significant enlargement of the scope of the legislation, the focus remained on 'how the distribution was arrived at rather than the outcome'.[55] Such agent-oriented perspectives may be appropriate in legislation establishing tortious or criminal liability, especially in countries in which past and present prejudice are major factors in the situation. However, a victim-oriented perspective and language may be more appropriate to a country like Xanadu in which racial (though not sexual) prejudice is almost certainly only a minor contributing factor to what is widely recognized to be a situation involving radical maldistribution of opportunity in the particular spheres of access with which we are concerned. If one were looking for scapegoats the facts of geography, natural disaster, centuries of conflict, and the policies of former colonial rulers would no doubt be prime candidates. But our task is to try to ameliorate a bad situation, whatever its causes, rather than merely to allocate blame. We are concerned with devising positive and realistic measures, including allocating responsibility (R2), for the future and only incidentally in attributing blame for the past. For this purpose, the language of distributive justice, utility, and positive action is more useful than that of moral culpability.

There are, however, two contexts in which notions such as discrimination are important. First, although Xanadu is a remarkably tolerant and friendly society, it would be foolish to assert that prejudice and unfair discrimination are unknown. So far as racial prejudice is concerned, it is fair to say that the legislation and the machinery that exists for its implementation are the most that can be hoped for in the circumstances. The problems of sexual equality in a multicultural society, with a large Muslim population, are too complex and delicate to be dealt with in this paper. Suffice to say that successive governments have consistently proclaimed their commitment to principles of sexual equality and such proclamations are broadly reflected in the Constitution and laws of the country.[56] To sum up: direct and indirect discrimination has probably contributed less to the existence of a problem of access in Xanadu than in some other countries and a fairly standard range of anti-discrimination measures has already been implemented.

---

[55] McCrudden op. cit. (1985), 84.

[56] Some non-legislative anti-discrimination measures, such as explicit non-discriminatory admissions criteria and voluntary codes of practice in respect of selection, promotion, etc., in employment have yet to be implemented.

(d) Opposition to positive action

A second context in which an agent-oriented vocabulary is clearly relevant and in need of clarification is in the area commonly referred to as 'affirmative action'. Here again the Anglo-American debates may obscure as much as they illuminate. Such terms as 'affirmative action', 'preferential treatment', 'positive action', and 'reverse discrimination' have been used in a variety of different senses. In the context of local debates some have become associated with specific measures that have aroused strong opposition. As a preliminary to considering the acceptability of different measures, it is useful to construct a working vocabulary.

It is helpful to have a broad general term that refers to all measures specifically designed to address the kinds of problems with which we are here concerned. Because the term 'affirmative action' has over time acquired some rather specific associations, let us substitute the less familiar 'positive action'. This is both broad and vague and so we need to distinguish between different species within the genus.

Adapting a useful set of working distinctions recently suggested by Christopher McCrudden in the context of employment,[57] let us differentiate five species of positive action as follows:

1. *Direct preferential treatment*, such as quotas or goals in admissions, which explicitly discriminate in favour of particular groups as such at the expense of identifiable groups and individuals in situations of competition or scarcity. This is nearest to the standard case of 'reverse discrimination'.[58]

2. *Indirect preferential treatment*, for example criteria for selection which in practice have the effect of benefiting members of disadvantaged groups[59] at the expense of others, but without using criteria which explicitly refer to those groups. For example, reserving a quota of places for 'the unemployed in Handsworth', where it can be shown that the vast majority of those eligible will be blacks. This is the converse of 'indirect discrimination' as used, for example, in British anti-discrimination law.

---

[57] I am grateful to Christopher McCrudden for help with this section. See especially, McCrudden, op. cit. (1985) and 'Rethinking Positive Action', 15 *Industrial Law Jo.* 219 (1986). The vocabulary adopted is slightly different from that suggested by McCrudden, who was writing with specific reference to discrimination in employment. The distinctions are almost identical and the main thesis that many objections to 'reverse discrimination' do not apply to other forms of positive action is the same.

[58] Direct preferential treatment includes situations where factors such as race, gender, locality are used as a sole criterion, or as one of several relevant factors, or to 'break ties'. If the more emotive term 'reverse discrimination' is applied to all of these, it is important to recognize that arguments for and against such measures need to take account of these different species.

[59] This is slightly wider than McCrudden's 'facially neutral but purposively inclusionary policies', op. cit. (1987), 57, in that it includes all measures that have such effects whether or not this is their primary purpose.

3. *Anti-discrimination measures*, directed at specific practices and acts of direct and indirect discrimination; for example, prohibitions on unfavourable treatment in such areas as employment and education in modern legislation in many Commonwealth jurisdictions.[60]

4. *Functional preferential treatment*, that is measures which explicitly resort to criteria normally associated with disadvantage, such as race or sex, because these criteria are claimed to be functionally relevant to the situation concerned.[61] For example, prescribing that women will be preferred to men, or blacks to whites, as performers for parts portraying women (or blacks). Or, having a quota or goal for members of minority groups in admission to law school on the grounds that the educational programme will benefit by the presence of members of these groups. Such provisions are only clear examples of 'positive action' when they are introduced for the primary purpose of furthering positive action.

5. *Non-preferential positive action*. This is a residual category covering all forms of positive action not falling under 1.–4.[62] Typically these will arise in situations where there is no direct competition in respect of a finite 'cake' of resources. For example, access courses, remedial teaching or encouraging members of disadvantaged groups to apply. Here more resources may be allocated to the disadvantaged than to others on the basis of need, but within a framework in which formal criteria of eligibility, selection or certification remain standard.

These are only 'ideal types' and rather vague ones at that. However, they are useful as a way of making broad differentiations between types of positive action that may meet opposition in particular contexts. For example, in England 'direct preferential treatment' is a matter of continuing controversy; 'indirect preferential treatment' has not attracted much opposition, perhaps because it has not been a focus of attention; anti-discrimination measures have, over time, become a broadly accepted aspect of the order of things; whereas it is probably fair to say that categories 4. and 5. have been relatively uncontroversial. In the Xanadu Law School the term 'reverse discrimination' has been applied indiscriminately to admissions quotas, and mature student entry and, even on one occasion, to the allocation of funds to visits to schools in a part of the country from which no law students had previously been recruited. Such examples differ both in respect of the kinds of arguments that are relevant to justifying (or opposing) particular measures and in relation to their general acceptability in practice in a given context. In Xanadu, for example, public controversy has been most acute in respect of quotas for admission to University. This is a clear example of direct preferential treatment, which is, not surprisingly, the area in

---

[60] Cf. McCrudden, op. cit. (1986), on 'Eradicating discrimination', 223.

[61] This is approximately equivalent to McCrudden's redefining 'merit', ibid., 225.

[62] This includes, but is wider than, McCrudden's 'outreach programmes', ibid., 223–4.

which opposition to positive action tends to be most virulent and to be supported by the most plausible arguments. Accordingly it is worth looking more clearly at opposition to direct preferential treatment, as the most problematic kind of positive action.

DIRECT PREFERENTIAL TREATMENT

In the English-speaking world debates about such policies in respect of admission to professional schools have been both stimulated and dominated by the controversy surrounding the American cases of *DeFunis, Bakke*, et al.[63] It is, of course, an enormous advantage to be able to draw on the rich and sophisticated literature that has developed around this controversy. However, one needs to sound a note of caution in the present context.

The most obvious point is that the terms of the debate were established in the context of American culture at a particular point in history.[64] For example, the ideological frame of reference did not accommodate the kinds of state socialism that would form the context of such a debate in say India or Sri Lanka or Tanzania. Secondly, the central issues in the American cases concerned the legality and legitimacy of certain kinds of provision for direct preferential treatment (notably racial quotas and differential criteria of selection). In some countries there is no doubt at all that such provisions are permitted by law and this not only in countries that have few or no anti-discrimination laws; in some, as in India, such provisions have been legally *mandated*.[65] In such contexts the main focus of controversy is as likely to be on the general costs and benefits and effectiveness of such provisions and policies as on problems of detailed implementation. Again, most of the leading American cases concerned competition for places in a limited number of relatively prestigious institutions in an educational context characterized by an extraordinary hierarchy of institutional prestige, on the one hand, and varied educational opportunity on the other. I am told that at no time since 1945 has there been an absolute shortage of law school places in the United States (medical schools may be different) and that, if one includes unaccredited schools, by and large the number of places in all law schools exceeds the demand from applicants who satisfy some minimal criteria

---

[63] DEFUNIS V. ODEGAARD 82 Wash. 2nd 11, 507 P 2nd 1169 (1973), treated as moot 416 US 312 (1974). REGENTS OF THE UNIVERSITY OF CALIFORNIA V. BAKKE 438 US 265 (1978).

[64] On some alleged parallels between the Indian and American experience see A. Blumrosen, 'Some Thoughts on Affirmative Action There and in India: Galanter's *Competing Equalities*', (*ABF Res J* 1986), 653.

[65] Galanter op. cit., (1984) categorizes the Indian approach as 'compensatory discrimination', because 'it does not blink at the fact that some are left out, that we are dealing with something more than a benign process of inclusion. At least where scarce resources are distributed, it employs a principle of selection that is akin to the old discrimination' (2–3). However, he acknowledges that there are also 'non-discrimination and general welfare themes' in the Indian policies (ibid., 3).

of entry.[66] Bakke and DeFunis, for example, were not fighting for an opportunity to qualify at all, but for the right to compete for a place in relatively prestigious institutions on the basis of 'merit' alone.[67] The focal point of the American legal debates has been an opportunity to enter élite institutions and to have access to the higher echelons of a stratified profession. Whatever the imperfections of the American system of education, by and large the disadvantaged seem to have more chances of obtaining some legal education than in most other countries (but, again, India may be an exception).

In many countries there is intense competition to have any opportunity to study law or become a lawyer. For example, in Xanadu, someone who fails to obtain a place in one of the two local law schools is with minor exceptions denied any chance of obtaining a law degree or of qualifying for practice. On the other hand in some countries large-scale legal education has been one of the dumping grounds for surplus demand for higher education.[68] Anyone with minimal educational qualifications can study law but very few are destined to reap much economic or social advantage by doing so.

Furthermore in interpreting the American situation it is difficult for the outsider to discern what was the likely impact of the *Bakke* line of decisions (insofar as it permitted certain kinds of affirmative action) and how far this has anything to do with figures concerning participation rates in legal education by women and members of certain minorities. For example, the extensive figures published by the ABA Section on Legal Education in 1984 suggest that between 1971 and 1984 minority enrolments in ABA approved schools doubled and the number of women increased by a factor of five.[69] It seems rather unlikely that programmes involving direct preferential treatment of the kind that were at issue in *Bakke* directly account for more than a small proportion of these increases. Other, less controversial measures, such as anti-discrimination rules and policies and non-preferential positive action programmes, together with much broader social trends and changes in the climate of opinion are probably more important.[70] Moreover these figures only relate to ABA approved schools; yet in some American States it is possible to obtain a law degree and to qualify to practise as a lawyer in non-approved schools.

A second caveat about American literature relates to the level of abstraction of the debate. American constitutional litigation is known for its tendency to

---

[66] e.g., Clyde Summers in *University of Toledo L Rev. Symposium* (1970) 383. Confirmed by R. Stevens (Private Communication). Periodically, American law schools become concerned about a fall in law school applications.

[67] On different interpretations of the precise nature of such claims, see R. Dworkin *Taking Rights Seriously*, London (1985) 298–9. As Dworkin points out, '[t]here is no combination of abilities and skills and traits that constitutes "merit" in the abstract' (299).

[68] ILC (1975) paras. 68–71.   [69] ABA (1985) 66–8.

[70] However, Stevens (1983) 245–7, suggests that CLEO and other 'headstart programmes' for minority students played a major role in the increase of minority enrolments in law schools between 1969–79.

convert fundamental philosophical questions into legal issues. One reason for the intense academic interest generated internationally by *Bakke* et al. is that the topic of 'reverse discrimination' is philosophically interesting. In the process of justifying direct preferential treatment utilitarians may be found to be committed to justifying all kinds of discrimination. Can an egalitarian justify unequal treatment to further a long-term goal of equality? Do not measures which constrain benefits in the pursuit of policy smack of coercion of individuals and curtailment of rights? As Richard Tur puts it: 'Any practice which can simultaneously embarrass the utilitarian, confound the egalitarian and challenge political individualism is worthy of study in its own right.'[71]

The philosophical issues raised by direct preferential treatment are intellectually interesting and of some practical importance. However, they are not the only examples of positive action that have aroused opposition. Moreover, in many countries the problems are so acute that over-concern with philosophical niceties may inhibit effective action by sowing confusion. If in a particular country over 90 per cent of the population is effectively excluded from access to certain kinds of educational and occupational opportunity, it is not difficult to transcend philosophical differences to reach a broad consensus that something is badly wrong. The main issue is not whether, but how? Thus some measures such as opening up multiple routes of entry or investing more in remedial or second chance education or in scholarships, may win widespread support from people of quite different political and philosophical persuasions. So too, in extreme circumstances, exceptional measures may be widely accepted, some of which might be considered unjustified in other contexts. Philosophical clarity need not inhibit positive action: rather it can provide a basis for devising coherent strategies and, by differentiating between different kinds of positive action, it may help to reduce unnecessary controversy.

The notion of 'reverse discrimination', as an example of direct preferential treatment, implies deviation from a system purporting to apply uniform conditions of merit; it presupposes three conditions:

1. That fair competition involves all candidates competing according to a single set of criteria of selection on merit;
2. That these criteria are in fact good indicators of 'merit' in that either
   (*a*) the criteria are good predictors of relevant future performance (potential) or
   (*b*) the criteria are reliable indicators of either intelligence or past achievement or experience that deserves to be rewarded by success in this competition;[72]
3. That the competition is in practice fair to all applicants.[73]

---

[71] Richard Tur, 'The Justification of Reverse Discrimination', in M. A. Steward (ed.), *Law, Morality and Rights* (Dordrecht, 1983) 271.
[72] On 'Merit', *supra*, n. 67.   [73] Cf alleged cultural biases in law school admission tests.

A sceptic might suggest that none of these criteria is satisfied in Xanadu. There is no good reason for suggesting that a uniform test of admission is appropriate for candidates drawn from such diverse backgrounds: for example the language of the schools and the school-leaving examinations are different in the North and the South, and educators despair of making confident comparisons of these examinations as tests of academic 'excellence', given the radically different traditions of the two school systems. Mature students are selected by yet other criteria which are different, but their performance in law school examinations suggests that these criteria are at least as good predictors of this kind of performance as the school-leaving examination. It is misleading to say that this type of mature student entry is an example of 'reverse discrimination', i.e., direct preferential treatment. In this context, it merely provides alternative criteria of selection which are considered to be equally valid.

The sceptic can go on to doubt that selection of school-leavers is in fact made on 'merit': the school-leaving examinations are acknowledged to be unreliable indicators of first year performance in law school;[74] they are even less reliable in respect of final degree results;[75] being largely tests of memory (especially in the South) they may be better indicators of likely success in bar examinations, but that is mere speculation. There is no evidence at all that they have any claim to be predictors of likely success in legal practice; nor are these examinations highly regarded as tests of 'intelligence' or capacity for clear thought. They make no claim to be indicators of such qualities as honesty, compassion, and commitment to democratic ideals of law and justice, that Chief Justice Dickson of Canada has recently suggested should weigh heavily in training and selecting

[74] e.g., R. G. Lee, 'A Survey of Law Schools Admissions', 18 *The Law Teacher* 165 (1984) on 'A' Levels in England.

[75] Defenders of aptitude testing are prepared to acknowledge that little is known about the relations between test scores and long-term performance. E.g. Jennek Brittel and William B. Schroder state: 'Far too little research using broader and longer-range measures of success has been done. In part, this unsatisfactory state of affairs is attributable to the lack of agreed upon indicators of success in college or success in life, and to the fact that research in this field is costly and difficult. Admissions testing is, however, vulnerable to the criticism that too little is known about the relationship of test scores to college and career success.' 'College Admissions Testing in the United States' in International Council for Educational Development, *Access Policy and Procedures and the Law in U.S. Higher Education* (New York, 1978). The Australian experience of aptitude testing, for example in Queensland, may be at least as relevant to some Commonwealth countries as the American. In most Commonwealth countries, with the exception of Canada, almost no use is made of aptitude testing in law. One argument put forward in its favour is the converse of the US criticism: viz. that some educationally disadvantaged candidates may have a better chance through selection through aptitude testing than through their academic record, especially if the latter is based—as happens in many countries—on a uniform national examination. The core of American criticism of the LSAT seems to be that, at least in its present form, it is used as a means of eliminating large numbers of candidates who might turn out to be capable of becoming competent lawyers. The core of the objections relate to the test (which may have class, ethnic or other biases) and to its use as a condition of qualifying for law school. It seems that they are not fundamental objections to aptitude testing in general, which has great potential in increasing access, not least in providing certain kinds of short cuts. (See further n. 78, below.)

future lawyers.[76] No use is made here of legal aptitude testing (on which more later). Accordingly, as in most Commonwealth countries, it is arguable that there is no baseline of 'merit' from which a policy of 'reverse discrimination' could be said to deviate.

The sceptic could go on to point out that the standard complaint against direct preferential treatment is that meritorious candidates are denied opportunity despite their success in a fair competition. But it is generally acknowledged that to obtain the same result in the school-leaving examination there is no uniformity in the number of barriers each candidate has had to surmount (nor in the amount of assistance he or she has received). In this view the educational rat race is an obstacle course with a variable number of obstacles and aids for each candidate. It can hardly be said to be a fair competition. A variant of this argument is advanced by Katherine O'Donovan: arguments against reverse discrimination as advanced by whites, men, etc. are based on denial of equal opportunity to them. But where there have been past disadvantages, minority or women applicants typically have not had equal opportunity themselves, taking birth as the baseline.[77]

It may be objected that the sceptic has overstated her case: because existing criteria of selection fall short of perfection, it does not follow that they are completely unmeritorious as tests of 'merit'. If one accepts 'merit' as the most important, or at least an important, criterion of selection the question is not: 'are existing criteria perfect?' but: 'are they the best available?' In practice, some of the factors mentioned by the sceptic are taken into account in admission, admittedly in a rough and ready way (for example that some candidates have had to surmount more barriers than others). To suggest that school-leaving examinations (or other academic records) are useless as indicators of past academic excellence or future potential, is greatly to overstate the case.

How reliable and useful they are varies according to circumstances. The American LSAT, whatever its limitations, is a subtle and flexible instrument; it is carefully monitored and is capable of continuous refinement, adjustment, and improvement on the basis of extensive data.[78] English 'A' levels are much less reliable predictors of performance in law school, but nevertheless they serve to eliminate large numbers of clearly unsuitable or indolent candidates who would

---

[76] Chief Justice Brian Dickson (1986). In another context Chief Justice Dickson has written:'The primary goal of legal education should be to train for the legal profession people who are, first, honest; second, compassionate; third, knowledgeable about the law; and fourth, committed to the rule of law and justice in our democratic society.' Introduction to the *Canadian Law Schools Admission Handbook* (1986). In the context the author makes it clear that legal education prepares people for a variety of other careers.

[77] K. O'Donovan, 'Affirmative Action', in Guest and Milne (1985), op. cit., at 77, 79.

[78] See LSAC Research Studies (1959–83). The most common charge against the American LSAT relates to alleged racial or cultural biases (e.g., David M. White, *Towards a Diversified Legal Profession* (Berkeley, 1981). See further *ALELP* Chs. 3 and 4. My personal view is that aptitude tests can both promote and restrict access, depending on how they are designed *and used*.

not satisfy either the 'benefit' or 'success' entry standards.[79] As for fairness, it
can be pointed out that national examinations and aptitude tests at least provide
public, external criteria, known in advance by candidates, and which are more
relevant and less arbitrary than lotteries and other random mechanisms favoured
by some.[80] Without such criteria admissions processes would be susceptible to
allegations of corruption or abuse or arbitrariness.

Even if one accepts some or all of these objections as valid, they by no means
completely dispose of the sceptic's thesis. In particular, it is worth stressing
(1) that by no means all admissions criteria other than past academic record or
aptitude tests are examples of 'reverse discrimination'; (2) that standard arguments against direct positive action are weakened insofar as particular criteria of
alleged 'merit' are shown to be deficient in one way or another; (3) that the
'fairness' of a particular competition is also a relative matter; and (4) that access
can often be increased by means of other kinds of positive action in admissions
(for example remedial education; taking account of past circumstances in assessing 'merit' either as desert or predictor; pursuing the goal of a diverse educational community).

India: a case-study

A recent article by Jill Cottrell on Legal Education in India (as it was in 1983)
highlights some features of the Indian scene that contrast quite sharply with the
situation in North America and England.[81]

Indian legal education is, not surprisingly, vast and complex. As in North
America, law degrees are postgraduate, although there are moves to change this.
The three-year LL B is both a necessary and a sufficient qualification for practice. There are no Bar examinations, no formal requirements for apprenticeship,
and no longer any requirements for limited practice. India presents a striking
example of mass legal education. Nearly 350 institutions offer legal education
to nearly 150,000 law students. In some places, there is a policy of 'unlimited
admissions regardless of merit'.[82] Standards are very variable; classes tend to be
large; staff/student ratios range from 50/1 to 150/1;[83] the students tend to be very
poorly motivated and, in some places, they are both restless and powerful;
cheating is endemic in some institutions; the curriculum is largely dictated by

---

[79] Dee (1984) and Kibble (1986), op. cit., both acknowledge this.

[80] e.g., Duncan Kennedy's 'Utopian Proposal': 'There should be a test designed to establish
minimal skills for legal practice and then a lottery for admission to the school: there should be
quotas within the lottery for women, minorities and working class students. There should be a
national publicity campaign about our goal of modifying the social composition of the bar.' *Legal
Education and the Reproduction of Hierarchy: A Polemic Against the System* (Cambridge, Mass.,
1983), 121–2.

[81] Cottrell (1986). Cottrell's article was based largely on material collected in 1983. This section
does not take account of developments since then.

[82] Ibid., 6. Citing a report on Uttar Pradesh.   [83] Ibid., 11.

the profession, yet over 90 per cent of law graduates do not enter practice. The overall impression given to the outsider is that neither the institutions themselves nor governments (state and central) nor the profession is able to exercise much control over numbers, standards or even orderly conduct of classes and examinations. There are some centres of excellence, and some have degrees of high standing, but Cottrell reports that much legal education is described by one law teacher as 'a refuge for the unemployed and the rejects from the science and technical courses'.[84] On the other hand it offers to many what may be a last chance of upward mobility. Thus despite the requirement of a first degree before starting the study of law, access to legal education is not as acute a problem as in many countries, at least for those who have reached the tertiary level of education. Nor is normal admission to practice. It has been estimated that only between 5 per cent and 10 per cent of law graduates enter practice, many of them because of lack of a more attractive alternative.[85]

Over the years energetic efforts have been made by the Bar Council of India, by many institutions, and by individual law teachers to exert stronger control over legal education and to improve its quality. Recently the main focus has been on a scheme to substitute a five-year degree in law, starting at 18 plus, for the present 3 plus 3 (Arts followed by Law) pattern. The objects of this proposal are to reduce the scale and improve the quality of legal education by increasing student motivation, controlling numbers, cutting the period of formal education post-18 by a year, encouraging a broader approach to the study of law, and greatly strengthening quality control. The proposals have received a mixed reaction and it remains to be seen to what extent they will be implemented with what results.

At first sight this looks like yet another example of the conflict between Access and Excellence. In many ways it is. But this tension can exhibit itself in complex ways: undoubtedly the reduction of numbers and the imposition of higher standards will reduce access, but it is access to a system of legal education that may not offer very much increased opportunity to the vast majority of its students. One of the main objectives of the scheme is to increase student motivation; yet the effect of making law degrees full time will be to eliminate part-time, evening courses that are said to contain more highly motivated students, many of whom are drawn from underprivileged backgrounds.[86]

The proposal is also seen as an example of the leaders of the profession abdicating responsibility by seeking to exercise control only indirectly:

There is some criticism of the role of the Bar Council itself. Some teachers have expressed resentment at what they see as the autocracy of the Council—though this is not a widespread reaction, possibly because the LL B degree has been for so long structured by the demands of the profession. There is a feeling that the Bar is expecting the universities to do its dirty work for it. The profession wants to achieve two things: a

---

[84] Ibid., 7 (quoting S. K. Agrawala).   [85] Ibid., 12.   [86] Ibid., 12.

reduction in the number of entrants to the profession and a raising of the standard of education of those who do not enter. In theory these could be achieved by the profession's raising its own gateways to practice—by requiring the passing of professional examinations set by itself, or by running its own professionally oriented post-graduate courses, or by an apprenticeship requirement—and each of these approaches has its advocates among university teachers. But the Bar Council feels it lacks the capacity to administer and enforce any such restrictive devices and is in effect saying to the universities: 'You build the gateway—to our specification.'[87]

Galanter's study

As I suggested above, in recent years perceptions of the nature of the problems of access to legal education have been strongly influenced by the extended debates surrounding the American cases of *Defunis* and *Bakke*.[88] As so often happens, American constitutional litigation has stimulated profound and searching analysis of fundamental issues. But some tough questions have to be asked about the relevance of this debate to other countries. Conversely, one may ask have not the American debates been too sharply focused on some narrow issues and have they not been unduly parochial and isolationist? For example, on one interpretation, the *Bakke* case presents an inconclusive answer to some highly specific questions about selection for élite professional schools.[89]

For non-Americans, trying to make sense of the American literature can be as perplexing as it is seductive. The issues seem universal, yet they are posed in their own unique context. One striking feature of that literature is that it almost never refers to experience outside the United States. A major step away from this isolationism has been taken by the publication of Marc Galanter's monumental work, *Competing Equalities*.[90] This is a detailed study of the vast and bold Indian system of 'compensatory discrimination', in which preferential treatment in respect of such matters as legislative representation, the public service, education, and employment has been required by law. I cannot attempt to do justice to this superb work here, nor can I explore some of the (minor) reservations that I have about it.[91] But, it is worth pointing out that it raises a host of questions that are worth asking, and which may have been relatively neglected in the familiar American debates, at least by lawyers. Galanter shifts the focus of attention from questions about the legitimacy of positive discrimination to questions about implementation, especially legal implementation. For example,

---

[87] Ibid., 22–3. By 1989 several instititions, including the newly established National Law School of India at Bangalore, had introduced five-year degrees.

[88] e.g., the discussions in Guest and Milne (1985), McCrudden (1986), and reviews of Galanter (1984) cited below at n. 91.

[89] R. Dworkin, *A Matter of Principle* (Cambridge, Ma., 1985), Ch. 15.

[90] Galanter (1984).

[91] See reviews by J. Cottrell (1985) 34 *ICLQ* 658; J. D. M. Derrett (1985) *Jo. Commonwealth and Comparative Politics* 272: R. Dhavan (1985) *Law and Policy*; Lance Liebman (1985) 98 *Harv. L Rev.* 1679; R. Meister (1985) *Wisc. L Rev.* 937.

given such a policy, who exactly should be the beneficiaries? What sorts of benefits should be included with what priorities? Can individuals leave or enter a beneficial class through marriage, conversion, or economic success or failure? On the basis of what criteria should quotas be set? What are the economic constraints and consequences of such provisions? What rights, if any, should be recognized for those excluded from beneficial treatment? What are the political implications of the very real sense of grievance that such programmes tend to generate? What are the broader political implications of such programmes? What are the global costs and benefits of such a strategy? Can any coherent rationale be articulated for compensatory discrimination? What differences does it really make to the overall position of the disadvantaged groups? And so on.[92]

Because the Indian Constitution and legal system have been directly influenced by the common law and by some American ideas and because it is by an American scholar, Galanter's study will no doubt have more direct resonance for many American readers than some other accounts of Commonwealth experience. The context of the problem may be exotic, but the response and Galanter's interpretation have echoes in American experience. Conversely, to an Englishman, some aspects of the Indian approach to the problems and Galanter's treatment of it seem remarkably American, not least in the way in which some problems of access have been transformed into legal issues and have been the subject of litigation. In my own country, and I suspect in the great majority of other Commonwealth jurisdictions, it seems strange to perceive law and the courts as having such a significant role to play in addressing problems of access. This, too, raises a host of fascinating questions that cannot be pursued here.

Thus it is extremely difficult to judge how much direct relevance the American debates and Galanter's work have to diagnosing the problem of formulating access strategies in the very different circumstances of my own country and of Xanadu. In Xanadu preferential treatment is neither required nor prohibited. Following Ronald Dworkin, who is at his most persuasive on this issue, positive discrimination is justified if it is directed towards increasing the participation of minorities in certain professions.[93] Applicants to professional schools do not have a right to a place nor a right to be considered on the basis of a single set of criteria based on academic 'merit'. It is one thing to treat people as equals, it is another to treat them equally.[94] Such positive discrimination does not violate rights, but it can involve costs, including costs for those who are meant to benefit. In India, for example, Galanter characterizes the overall story as 'A costly success'.[95] These costs include:

1. a sense of grievance on the part of disappointed applicants and others who consider themselves to have been harmed by the practice;

---

[92] See Cottrell, op. cit. [93] R. Dworkin (1977), Ch. 9; (1985), Chs. 14–16.
[94] R. Dworkin (1977), 1, 227. [95] Galanter, 563.

2. a loss of respect, and possibly of self-respect, for beneficiaries who are perceived not to have won a place on 'merit';
3. disputes, possibly litigation, about the legitimacy of a particular programme or some specific aspect of it;
4. uncertainty about application of criteria;
5. rigidity leading to absurd results and invidious decisions when rigid criteria or fixed quotas are instituted; accusations of corruption or favouritism where more flexible arrangements are prescribed;
6. if formal criteria of positive discrimination are based on race or caste, it is claimed that this may have the effect of perpetuating the very divisions and categories that are under attack;
7. by no means all programmes of positive discrimination have been successful in practice in significantly increasing opportunities for disadvantaged groups.

Given the social and economic costs of programmes of positive discrimination it is always worth considering whether the same goals may be furthered as well by other means. Yet the symbolic significance of such measures also needs to be taken into account. Galanter is careful to emphasize that 'no single big lesson' can be drawn from the Indian experiences;[96] he points to many ironies, vagaries, and inconsistencies in the system; but he concludes that the benefits of this bold experiment outweigh the costs and that the system he describes is 'more congenial in practice than in theory'.[97] As a recent article in the Harvard Law Review suggests, this fascinating study has considerable potential relevance and resonance for those concerned with the subject of access in very different contexts.[98]

ACCESS VERSUS EXCELLENCE?

A recurrent theme of the literature that I have cited and of some parts of this paper is that there seems to be a regular tension between Access and Excellence.[99] Cooray presents the debate in Sri Lanka as a conflict between the Socialist and the Educationist ethic.[100] In that debate both sides acknowledged that a rapid switch-over from English to *swabasha* in legal education would almost inevitably result in a lowering of standards, at least for a period. It was a price that the socialists were prepared to pay. Conversely it is acknowledged in India that most measures currently being advocated for improving the quality of legal education will involve some restrictions on access.[101] Those of us who have advocated four-year degrees for most undergraduate law students in England

---

[96] Ibid., 563.   [97] Ibid., 567.   [98] Liebman, op. cit., n. 91.
[99] The *locus classicus* is J. W. Gardner, *Excellence: Can We be Equal and Excellent Too?* (New York, 1961).
[100] Op. cit., 122–5.   [101] Cottrell (1986).

recognize that an extra year means an additional financial and psychological barrier for most students. In the United States some historians of the legal profession have attributed an alleged decline in the American Bar to its democratization during the Jacksonian period.[102] Again the debates about accreditation and homogenization of American law schools in the 1920s and 1930s were often depicted as a direct conflict between standards and opportunity. I hope that I have made it clear that I think that all such interpretations are too simple. Modern historians doubt whether the Jacksonians made much impact on the quality or role of the American Bar generally.[103] They probably hastened the demise of apprenticeship; yet ironically this method of qualifying has probably offered better prospects of upward mobility in some jurisdictions, at least to some groups, than institutionalized legal education. And as for India: what real opportunities are in fact offered to their students by many of the non-élite programmes that are under attack?

However, the theme is too persistent for one to be able to ignore the question: are Access and Excellence inherently incompatible? I personally find this question worrying because I both believe in increasing access and as a teacher and educator I am committed to the idea of excellence. I do believe that they are compatible in principle and practice, though I readily acknowledge that in particular contexts they can give rise to acute dilemmas and conflicts. So let me conclude by justifying this belief.

To begin with let us ask: excellence in respect of what? To me excellence in legal education relates to the quality of learning and excellence in legal practice, to the scope and quality of services offered to clients, and to the community. The best educational experience is the one in which one learns most about something that is worth learning. The best educational institution is one in which students best learn worthwhile things. An excellent legal profession is one which delivers needed services well to the whole community.[104]

It is easy to lose sight of these simple ideas. For example, there are many well-documented instances in history where the rhetoric of excellence of 'standards' has cloaked other interests and motives.[105] When a legal profession fights to raise entry standards the primary concern may be to enhance the prestige and status of the group as part of the process of 'professionalization' or to reduce competition by restricting numbers or to improve its public image or as part of

---

[102] e.g., Charles Warren, *A History of the American Bar* (Boston, 1911); A. H. Chroust, *The Rise of the Legal Profession in America* (Norman, Oklahoma, 1965).

[103] e.g., Robert Stevens, *Law School* (Durham NC, 1983), Ch. 1.

[104] To assert that the primary function of law schools is to provide opportunities for learning does not involve a denial of the point that they also play a role (which varies from place to place) in selecting and certifying individuals for legal practice. All too often, in practice, the educational function is subordinated to these other, secondary, functions.

[105] See generally, Stevens (1983). On the tendency to confuse academic standards and quality in university education, see Eric Ashby, *Universities: British, Indian, African* (London, 1966), 237–8, 259–60.

a power struggle with government or the law schools. These motives may be mixed in with a genuine concern for the quality of the services offered by the profession to its clientele. Even so, in this context it is always worth asking: the quality of which services *to whom?* For sometimes the standards are being raised in the interests of one sector of the potential clientele at the expense of the rest.

Academics are at least as vulnerable to such charges of hypocrisy or self-deception. Take, for example, the claim that a law school selects students on the basis of 'merit'. Such claims are not universally false, but we have seen that there are several strategies of scepticism in respect of such claims.

1. A particular test of 'merit' may be:
   (*a*) unreliable as an indicator of past academic performance;
   (*b*) a poor predictor of academic performance in law school;
   (*c*) a poor predictor of or largely irrelevant to professional competence;
   (*d*) discriminatory or otherwise unfair to some types of candidate.
2. Many competitive tests are not governed by rules that make the competition fair.
3. Where a test of merit is both reliable and relevant to future performance, it could be used as a pre-test to exempt people who already have the skills or knowledge that the course in question is designed to develop. Yet such tests are sometimes used in practice to select people for an education that they do not need.[106]
4. In practice methods of testing and selection for admission to law school and to practice are governed, perhaps inevitably, as much by administrative convenience as by genuine concern for 'merit'.

Merit claims cannot be dismissed entirely, but they always deserve scrutiny. Similarly with talk about 'excellence'. When my colleagues boast that our institution attracts 'good students', they may mean students who have performed better than others in one or more tests of 'merit' or who are good examinees or people who are already well-educated or professionally or economically ambitious or well-connected or stimulating or interesting to have around. Whatever the attractions or otherwise of some of these qualities they are conceptually different from the notion of excellence in education that is used here.

In many countries law schools perform functions of selection, elimination, certification, career guidance, placement, and control of numbers. They often offer security, prestige, fun, and freedom to the faculty. These are not necessarily

---

[106] Cf. Military training, in which pre-testing of skill in rifle-shooting may exempt (or even disqualify) individuals from particular aspects of training. Insofar as many 'legal skills' represent applications in a particular context of more general intellectual or human skill, many of those who enter legal education need little or no training in such skills, whereas this may be a prime need for others. In view of the fact that much skills training tends to be labour-intensive and expensive, this is a matter of considerable potential significance for professional legal training.

bad or wrong, but they are incidental to the enterprise of education. At its heart education is not about status or prestige or winning competitions or certification or selection or placement or entertainment; it should be about learning (whether for its own sake or for some other end). Above all one should not confuse excellence resulting from opportunity to learn or to perform a useful social role with prestige by association. If one keeps this clearly in mind the tensions between access and excellence can, at least to some extent, be dissolved.

There is a fundamental and obvious reason for rejecting the idea that conflicts between access and excellence are inevitable. If extending access means broadening the pool of talent from which law students and lawyers are recruited, it would be paradoxical to maintain that this must lead to a general lowering of standards. Whatever the ideological fine-tuning of particular access strategies, surely part of the motive force is the idea that potential talent is being wasted. Whether one emphasizes individual opportunity or social equality or group representation or the general welfare, increasing access is generally favoured because of a basic faith in some potential for excellence and the rejection of the idea that the disadvantaged are inferior. To assert this as an article of faith need not blind one to the formidable constraints, the complexities, and the acute dilemmas that have to be confronted in particular contexts.

Most practical measures will involve costs, including sometimes short-term sacrifices of excellence or standards. But it is surely a denial of faith in human nature shared by people of many different religious and political persuasions to suggest that increasing opportunity for the development of talent will necessarily be inimical to excellence in legal education and legal practice.

CONCLUSION

The primary purpose of this essay has been to raise some questions and suggest some concepts that may be pertinent to analysing practical problems of access in different contexts. It precedes rather than reports on some detailed investigations. However, it may be useful to suggest a few tentative hypotheses and conclusions arising from this preliminary inquiry.

1. Access to legal education and the legal profession is part of a much broader problem of access to education and to élite occupations. There are some factors which are effectively beyond the control of those who are in a position to do something about the legal sector: for example, accidents of birth; what happens in the school system; many aspects of economic, social, and linguistic disadvantage. Nevertheless, those responsible for that sector have a duty to try to mitigate the effects of such barriers.
2. What specific measures have much hope of making a significant impact depends very largely on context. However, it is worth offering a few tentative hypotheses:

(a) A general policy of flexibility in respect of routes of entry and occupational mobility is likely to provide the most effective way of surmounting or circumnavigating barriers to access. For example:

    (i) multiple routes of entry;

    (ii) avoidance of premature specialization;

    (iii) generous provision for mature entry, external qualifications, and lateral mobility;

    (iv) the provision of second chances at every stage.

(b) Systematic diagnosis and monitoring of the barriers to access in a given jurisdiction depend on adequate information, including regular statistics concerning potentially disadvantaged classes.

(c) Intensive remedial education targeted directly at the needs of particular groups that have suffered educational disadvantage offers one of the most promising avenues of improving access. Remedial education can be general or specialized; this can be offered either pre-law or within legal education. The costs tend to be high, the numbers affected small, but there is ground for thinking that measures, such as the American CLEO programme and the specialized access courses that are beginning to develop in England, can be remarkably cost-effective.[107]

(d) Law school admission policies that include:

    (i) multiple, alternative criteria of admission and selection;

    (ii) positive recruitment programmes aimed both at attracting applicants from particular groups (for example mature students from particular localities) and overcoming psychological barriers to applying;

    (iii) communication of full information about admissions policies and selection criteria to all potential applicants.

(e) Financial assistance that takes account of the total economic situation of those in need of help.

(f) In multilingual societies, sensitivity to the importance of language in respect of admission, instruction, and examination and of available literature must be a high priority, often requiring long-range planning and considerable adjustments in teaching.

(g) Aptitude testing validated in respect of disadvantaged groups can be an efficient and more objective method of selection than many other methods which are more likely to be biased in favour of more privileged groups (for example interviews, certain kinds of examination). However, the very advantages of such tests may lead to their overuse; for example, when uniform tests are used to eliminate

---

[107] On Law Access courses in England see Kibble (1986). On CLEO, see *Unversity of Toledo L Rev. Symposium* (1970); Stevens (1983), 245; and *ALELP*, Chs. 3 and 6.

law school applicants who might have the potential to be competent lawyers.[108]

3. My personal view is that there is nothing wrong in principle in employing positive action, or even direct preferential treatment, in selection for education or training to further an important social purpose. As the Indian experience shows, such provisions can give rise to extremely complex, often intractable, problems of implementation; they almost invariably give rise to deeply felt grievances and other social costs. Whether the benefits outweigh the costs in a given context will often involve difficult and contentious issues of political judgement.

4. Attempts artificially to control numbers at the point of entry to the profession rarely succeed in the long term and tend to operate to the detriment of the disadvantaged.

5. There is often a perceived tension between access and standards of excellence at least in the short term. However, it is a fallacy to assert that increasing the pool of talent from which law students and lawyers are recruited necessarily involves a 'lowering of standards'. In the long term improved access is the ally, not the enemy, of excellence.

6. Problems of access are complex and intractable. They tend to be context specific. Nevertheless there is much to be gained from looking at these problems from an international perspective and pooling experience of problems and attempted responses. Commonwealth countries can learn a great deal from the American experience as well as from each other; it may be that looking at the experience of other Commonwealth countries may suggest some new perspectives on your own situation.

[108] On the dangers of some kinds of aptitude tests and their possible misuse see *ALELP*, Ch. 5.

14

*Preparing Lawyers for the Twenty-first Century**

We are already preparing lawyers for the twenty-first century. Whether we are doing so as efficiently, as imaginatively or as professionally as we might is another matter. Higher education of any kind tends to be an expensive enterprise which, even from a purely utilitarian point of view, can only be justified as a long-term investment. Those who are currently undergraduates or who are undergoing professional training or apprenticeship, or who are learning by experience as fledgling practitioners will only be able properly to evaluate their basic education and training after the year 2000. Accordingly this topic is concerned with the here and now.

In the first part of this paper I shall draw attention to a number of recent trends and developments in legal education in the Commonwealth that give some grounds for optimism. In the second part I shall argue for a concerted effort to foster realistic and enlightened expectations about their legal education among law students and young lawyers.

One hopes that a significant proportion of the current generation of law students and young lawyers will look back to the 1990s as a period of relative enlightenment in which some of the truisms of educators in the late twentieth century were transformed in a sustained way from pious aspirations into practical working principles. These truisms include the following: that education is a life-long enterprise; that most higher education should be self-education; that the main role of undergraduate education is learning how to learn; that standard distinctions between academic and practical, theory and practice, liberal and vocational are false dichotomies that are mischievous as well as misleading; and that any body of lawyers worth preserving must take seriously its claims to be a learned profession.

These truisms are part of the standard aspirational discourse of Law Day addresses, after-dinner speeches, public lectures, and Commonwealth Law Conferences. But those who control recruitment, vocational training, professional examinations, and related matters, by their practice and example as well as their

---

* This paper was prepared for the Ninth Commonwealth Law Conference, held in Auckland in 1990. It builds on and develops some themes in an earlier paper, 'Developments in Legal Education in the Commonwealth: Beyond the Primary School Model'. This was presented at a conference to commemorate the twentieth anniversary of the Faculty of Law of the University of Hong Kong and was published in R Wacks (ed.), *The Future of Legal Education and the Legal Profession in Hong Kong* (1989).

talk often send quite different messages to law students and intending lawyers. These contradictory messages include the following: that studying law is mainly a matter of acquiring knowledge; that coverage is more important than depth; that what legal subjects one covers in primary legal education is more important than whether they are good vehicles for intellectual training; and that one is finished with academic study, critical analysis, and even reading as soon as one graduates—that 'theory' is something one grows out of about the age of twenty-one. Such ideas are almost the exact opposite of the noble aspirations enumerated above. Just because they are more often assumed in practices and attitudes than in public statements they can have a more direct and subversive influence on the expectations and attitudes of law students and intending lawyers than pious sermons. One purpose of this paper is to make a plea to those responsible for vocational training, professional examinations, and above all recruitment, to take seriously the content of the messages they communicate to the young and, where appropriate, to consider changing their tune.

I. TRENDS AND DEVELOPMENTS

First, the good news. During the past thirty years the discipline of law in the Commonwealth has been undergoing an unprecedented period of expansion, experimentation, and development. It has been transformed from a small-scale, cheap, low prestige subject into an unrecognizably more sophisticated, pluralist, and ambitious enterprise. A report prepared in 1984 by the Heads of University Law Schools in England (HULSC) and endorsed by the Heads of Polytechnic Law Schools and Heads of Scottish Law Schools provides a convenient starting-point for considering these changes.[1] From the vantage point of 1984 we identified a number of key trends and developments in our discipline in the period beginning in the early 1960s and extending to the early 1990s: a great increase in the scale of legal education at all levels, backed by steadily buoyant demand for opportunities to study law; a new pluralism in academic law, signalled by such phrases as socio-legal studies, law in context, law and development, and clinical education; a diversification of types of undergraduate study through mixed degrees, sandwich courses, and degrees with a large foreign component, (but only relatively modest provision for part-time study outside the London external system). There was a substantial increase in the number of courses seen as standard or as part of the core of legal studies: for example, administrative law, company law, consumer law, welfare law, labour law, intellectual property, domestic civil liberties, international protection of human rights, and, in the

---

[1] Heads of University Law Schools, *Law as an Academic Discipline* (London, 1984). An abbreviated version was published in the Society of Public Teachers of Law, *Newsletter*, Summer, 1984. The author was chairman of the working party that prepared the Report. The account in the text adds a few Commonwealth glosses to the Report, which was confined to England and Wales.

United Kingdom, the laws of the European Community. The computer age in law got off to a slow start and at first was perceived as being mainly relevant to information retrieval. In a few places clinical work found a modest place in undergraduate studies. Perhaps more important in the present context, beginning in Ghana and Nigeria in the 1960s, there developed what has sometimes been referred to as 'the Gower model',[2] that is a rather rigid structuring of professional legal education and training into three or four discrete stages: academic, vocational, apprenticeship, and continuing—although in most countries continuing legal education was still at a rudimentary level.

By 1984 further developments were predicted: greater emphasis on commercial subjects, including some interesting newcomers with a strong international flavour: transfer of technology, financial regulation, credit transfer, and specialized aspects of international trade. Computer applications and implications were perceived to go beyond information retrieval to include expert systems and many aspects of office management. In the same year the Commonwealth Law Ministers included on their agenda the important subject of education about law for non-lawyers, which may prove to be one of the biggest growth areas of the 1990s.

Since 1984 a new series of buzz words and phrases signals the pace of change: critical legal studies, in-house trainers, distance learning, access to legal education and the legal profession, skills research, multi-disciplinary practice, multi-national practice, international mobility of lawyers, law teaching clinics, training the trainers, judicial studies, law and medicine, records management, and, of course, autopoiesis.[3]

Looking forward into the 1990s we can expect to hear a lot more about

---

[2] Professor Gower tells me that the decision to provide the vocational stage outside university law faculties in Ghana and Nigeria was taken before he became involved in developing local legal education in those countries. A similar structure was adopted in other jurisdictions where he served as a consultant, including Hong Kong, Uganda, and, later, England and Wales (on which see *Report of the Committee on Legal Education* (Ormrod Report) 1971 Cmnd. 4594 HMSO, London). Part of my argument in this paper and its predecessor (op. cit., n. *) is that this kind of rigid structure tends to marginalize the contributions of professional law teachers after the primary stages and to entrench unhealthily sharp distinctions between 'theory' and 'practice'. This argument is not intended as a criticism of decisions in Ghana and Nigeria thirty years ago, still less of Jim Gower's many contributions to legal education and training in the Commonwealth.

[3] Many of these developments are described in the Commonwealth Legal Education Association (CLEA) *Newsletter*. On critical legal studies, see Mark Kelman, *A Guide to Critical Legal Studies* (Cambridge, Ma., 1987); on in-house trainers, see *Commonwealth Directory of In-House Training Professionals*, Commonwealth Institute of Legal Education and Training (CILET), Windsor, Ontario, (1988); on distance learning, see John Goldring 'Distance Teaching in Law: A Proposal for Commonwealth Co-operation', (1989) 57/58 CLEA *Newsletter*, Annex II; on access, see *ALELP* and Ch.14, below; on skills, see *LLS* and J. Watt (ed.), *The Legal Skills Sourcebook* (Sydney, NSW, and CILET, 1989); on international mobility of lawyers, see Campbell McLachlan in *LLS*, Ch. 14; on autopoiesis, see G. Teubner (ed.), *Autopoietic Law: A New Approach to Law and Society* (Florence, 1987). A lot is likely to be heard of Records Management in the 1990s. It is significant that the Association of Commonwealth Archivists has changed its title to the Association of Commonwealth Archivists and Records Managers (ACARM). They have recently turned their attention to legal records.

specialist certification, compulsory continuing legal education, and, especially important in the Commonwealth, law in multilingual societies.[4] It is perhaps also significant that in respect of human rights the 1990s are being spoken of as the decade of implementation. Also important in the present context has been the very substantial shift from emphasis on acquisition of knowledge to development of skills at the vocational stage, illustrated by new courses pioneered in Canada and rapidly spreading to, for example, Australia, Hong Kong, Lesotho, New Zealand, and, in 1989, even to the Inns of Court in London.

Amid all these changes there have, of course, been some equally important continuities in attitudes and practices. Two are directly relevant to this paper: a revival of interest in general principles and the reassertion of some of the central values of classical liberal education.[5]

Several points are worth noting about these impressionistic lists. First, most of these trends were international. While there have, of course, been many local variants and differences in timing, most of these items should today at least be familiar as ideas to legal educators throughout the Commonwealth. We are fortunate to belong to a strong and vital international network in which news of new developments, experiments, and ideas is rapidly disseminated.

Secondly, these developments have continued during more than a decade of financial cuts, squeezes, and crises in higher education in most parts of the Commonwealth. Law has generally been better cushioned than most other disciplines. The reasons for this are complex, but the main factor has almost certainly been the extraordinarily high demand for legal studies. In most countries (India is perhaps the main exception) law is one of the most popular and prestigious subjects with the result that there is rarely a problem of unfilled places and competition ensures that it attracts a high proportion—some would say a disproportionate share—of the academically most promising (or most successful) school-leavers. There have, of course, been serious problems: the outdated views that law is naturally a cheap subject and that it is not 'developmentally relevant" still persist in some quarters,[6] leading to endemic underfunding and other brakes on progress. Cuts and squeezes have made the recruitment and retention of law teachers increasingly difficult. In poorer countries many law faculties struggle to keep going in situations of appalling economic difficulties. Yet even in such countries, law faculties often benefit from attracting an academic élite of highly motivated, relatively well-educated students. In an important sense legal education is demand-led and as a result the attitudes and

---

[4] Problems of law in multilingual societies were a recurrent theme of the Hong Kong conference, mentioned in n. *. The best study to date of the implications of such problems for legal education is Mark Cooray, *Changing the Language of the Law: the Sri Lankan Experience* (Quebec, 1985).

[5] See especially op. cit., n. 1.

[6] 'The case for law' is well argued by Keith Patchett in 'The Role of Law in the Development Process', (1987) 48 CLEA *Newsletter* 33. From the late 1980s law became a priority area for the World Bank and Western aid agencies under the rubric of 'democracy, human rights and good governance'.

expectations of its clients, the students, fundamentally affect the practice of the enterprise.

The main object of the English HULSC Report to which I have referred was to challenge outdated ideas about the financial needs of our discipline. Law has been traditionally treated as one of the cheapest subjects with poor staff-student ratios, library-bound (with no need for equipment other than books), and, in most countries, standard academic salaries. The Report argued that many recent developments inevitably increase unit costs: access courses, clinical education, and skills training are all labour-intensive; book prices have generally increased at a faster rate than inflation in a period when student spending power has often decreased; new developments have expanded needs for international travel, field research, sabbatical leave, modern technology, four- or even five-year degrees, etc., all of which are relatively expensive. As we mentioned above, in many countries there is a serious problem of staffing where academic salaries have fallen behind other comparable occupations and the gap between the earnings of practitioners and academics has widened. The main conclusion of the HULSC Report was that law remains one of the most cost-effective disciplines, but perceptions of its financial needs have to be adjusted to take account of the changing nature of legal education, training, and research. The same point applies to changing conceptions of continuing legal education.

Fourthly, many recent developments mandate a broader vision of legal education as an enterprise. At the conference to celebrate the twentieth anniversary of the Hong Kong University Law Faculty, I argued that the contemporary agenda of issues in legal education is expanding our perceptions of the scope of the enterprise and requires a rethinking of the role of law schools.[7] Until recently most reports and discussions of the subject have focused on law degrees and initial qualification of private practitioners (the primary school model). Academic lawyers have generally played only a marginal role in post-degree education. The new agenda includes not only continuing legal education and judicial training, but also law in schools, paraprofessional training, and increasing legal awareness in society as a whole. That this is not merely a peripheral extra for 'outreach programmes', 'service teaching', and token exercises in public relations is illustrated by recent trends in dissemination and education about human rights, where priority is being given to such matters as classes for women's groups, community education, and the training of social workers and police and prison officers. My argument in that paper was that law schools, as the core institutions of any national system of legal education, need to move beyond the 'primary school model' to be redesigned as multifunctional resource centres for providing and assisting legal education at all levels in society. This will require significant shifts in the ways in which they are organized, staffed and funded.[8]

---

[7] Op. cit., n. *; see further below, Ch. 15.

[8] Ibid. The idea was first developed in *Legal Education in a Changing World* (International Legal Center, New York, 1975).

On the way back from Hong Kong I had the privilege of visiting the new National Law School in Bangalore, which has been established by the Bar Council of India as a model law school, designed to help to upgrade the whole system of legal education in India. It approximates very closely to the multi-functional model for which I argued in my paper. To be sure, it gives pride of place to an intensive, imaginatively conceived five-year first degree that integrates a multidisciplinary approach to legal study with clinical experience, placements, and skills training. But that is only one part of its activities: already it has organized intensive refresher courses for law teachers, judicial training seminars, legal literacy courses for women, and legal awareness programmes for community workers and others. It is producing a law journal and a legal information service about current law, advanced continuing legal education workshops, and is developing plans for distance education using modern techniques and technology. The National Law School promises to become a model not only for India, but for many other countries in the Commonwealth, not least because it is relatively modestly financed.[9]

One final point on recent trends. 'The knowledge explosion' in law is not confined to standard and core subjects. Options have proliferated at undergraduate and postgraduate level. Thirty years ago the standard three-year LL B curriculum rarely listed more than twelve to fifteen subjects; today some extend to over fifty. In 1965 about thirty subjects were offered in the London LL M; today it lists over one hundred and also makes provision for taking cognate subjects in other disciplines that are not listed. This proliferation of subjects has coincided with the shift from emphasis on knowledge to skills and with other demands on curriculum while the standard time allowed for primary legal education has generally remained unchanged. The result is that the pressures to overload the curriculum have become immense. The situation is exacerbated where a switch to skills teaching at the vocational stage is accompanied by increased demands on coverage at the academic stage either through a formal extension of the number of 'core subjects' or by informal pressures on students to select 'practical' options. In some countries the danger of a knowledge backlash is very real. This is one area in which clearly contradictory messages are being sent down from above to our students. For while undergraduates are encouraged to cover more and more areas of substantive law, teachers in some vocational courses often say that they prefer non-law graduates with uncluttered minds to law graduates who lack basic intellectual and research skills such as the capacity to express themselves clearly, to construct an argument or to use a law library. The vocational teachers and the profession cannot have it both ways. The arguments against coverage have been well summarized by Peter Wesley-Smith:

---

[9] [This account is broadly confirmed by the *Report* of The Expert Review Panel on NLSIU in 1996, of which I was a member.]

[M]ere acquisition of legal knowledge in law school is of little value to a practitioner because that knowledge (a) can only be a tiny portion of the whole, (b) can be understood only superficially, (c) is easily forgotten or only partially or inaccurately remembered, (d) is rarely needed in practice in the form in which it is learned, (e) is likely to be quickly outmoded and thus dangerous to rely on, and (f) is of little use when new problems arise to be solved.[10]

There are encouraging signs that university and polytechnic law teachers are responding by insisting that 'we are in the skills business too' and that the main function of the academic stage is to develop intellectual skills.[11] This amounts to a reassertion of some of the basic values of classical liberal education, but if the law teachers are to be believed by their students these values need to be reinforced rather than undermined by the practising profession.

II. MAKING THE TRUISMS COME TRUE

Many recent developments in legal education concern the structure, functions, and financing of legal education systems as a whole and the legal educational needs of non-lawyers. Most of these recent trends and the arguments for a broadened conception of legal education in society are directly relevant to the narrower topic of the professional formation and development of practising lawyers in the private and public sectors. For they reflect a growing realization that the general educational truisms enumerated at the start need to be taken seriously not only at the level of primary legal education but also in respect of such matters as continuing legal education, specialization, retraining, recertification, and multi-disciplinary and international practice. Each of these topics raises difficult practical issues of policy and implementation that are beginning to receive detailed attention. Fundamental to all of them are the attitudes and expectations of the recipients and purveyors of legal education. These attitudes and expectations are most likely to be formed at the early stages of the process —in systems on the Gower model at the academic and vocational stages.

In the limited space available I can only sketch some of the implications of these truisms as they bear on the who, the when, and the how of professional education.

A. Legal Education For Whom

The most obvious implication of the idea that education is a lifelong process is that it concerns not only undergraduates and intending practitioners, but also the

---

[10] Peter Wesley-Smith, 'Neither a Trade nor a Solemn Jugglery: Law as Liberal Education', in Wacks (ed.) op. cit., n. *, at 62.

[11] J. McFarlane, M. Jeeves, and A. Boone, 'Education for Life or Work?', *New Law Journal*, 4 Sept. 1987, 835–6; and Ch. 9, above.

recently qualified, leaders of the bar, and senior judges. It applies to lawyers in the public sector and in industry as well as to private practitioners. How far the later stages can and should be left to self-education and learning by experience rather than formal continuing education will be touched on briefly below. One reason for welcoming the belated development of institutionalized continuing legal education is that it offers by far the best hope of relieving pressures on the overcrowded curriculum at the primary level. It should be a further truism that the basic formation of a professional lawyer is at least a ten-year process which does not stop at the point of admission and that law students should be encouraged not to try to cross bridges before they come to them. When I tell this to my first year students, I sense that they do not really believe me.

Less obvious perhaps is the question of access: who does and who does not have the opportunity to become lawyers? One of the more important conclusions of a recent Commonwealth symposium on the subject[12] is that in systems where there is strong competition for places in law school, the criteria for admission have very little to do with suitability for legal practice. Another lesson of that exercise was that systems with multiple routes of entry (via degrees other than law, external degrees, apprenticeship, conversion courses, overseas qualifications, etc.) tend to present fewer barriers to access than do those which require a full-time law degree as a necessary qualification for practice. I admit that I used to be opposed to non-law graduate entry and looked down on external degrees, but as a result of this exercise I am converted to 'open study'[13] and multiple routes to qualification as providing opportunities for many suitable and highly motivated people who have contributed much to legal practice. Another lesson of the access study is that changes in law school admissions policies by themselves are unlikely to make a significant contribution to problems of access unless backed by other measures such as access courses, adjustments to curriculum, and general flexibility in educational provision.

B. Continuing Legal Education and Specialization

Our truisms suggest that continuing legal education (CLE) should be a lifelong matter, but that most of it should take the form of self-education. Some of the main issues in this area relate to how far it should be required or controlled,

---

[12] *ALELP*; see also Ch. 14, below.

[13] From its early days, almost 150 years ago, the London External System was based on the twin principles of 'open entry' (no *numerus clausus*, i.e., all who satisfied General Entrance Requirements were eligible to register) and 'open learning' (i.e., no prescribed courses or methods of study). The first principle seems to have served the purpose of extending educational opportunity admirably; the second has been more controversial. Until recently the University of London served only as an examining and accrediting body and offered no instruction and little guidance to candidates. In recent years the policy has been modified to allow some direct instruction, but the principle of 'open learning' still operates.

what is the optimal mix of learning by experience and formal study, and how much time it needs or deserves.

A Sellar and Yeatman history of CLE might read as follows: stage one was characterized by occasional lectures on recent developments in legislation and case-law designed to help practitioners to keep up to date with legal doctrine in a relatively painless way. Stage two involved rather more substantial half-day or even one-day 'courses', especially for the recently qualified, often designed to fill in gaps in their basic training in, for example, office management, communication skills, trial advocacy or substantive law subjects they had not 'covered' in their formal studies. This mode sometimes runs over into rather more high-powered and expensive workshops or conferences involving star speakers, glossy handouts, and heavy lunches—at the top end of the market extending to whole weekends in Oxbridge colleges or other congenial settings. In North America the CLE industry now includes use of distance-learning devices, such as audio cassettes, home videos, and specially prepared materials of varying degrees of sophistication. Such devices are beginning to catch on in richer jurisdictions within the Commonwealth. At their best each of these modes can meet real needs in a quick, efficient, and congenial way. They often adequately serve the functions of updating, keeping in touch, and refreshment within existing frameworks. It is less clear that the quick fix, canned wisdom or heavy lunches are suitable for more ambitious objectives of breaking bad habits, introducing new skills, building specialisms or moving beyond competence to excellence.

The main limitation of all of these methods is that they make heavy concessions to pressures of time. They generally proceed on the assumption that busy professionals are too busy to devote more than a few hours a year to CLE, including reading, listening or viewing on one's own. From an educational point of view it is difficult to see how it is possible for even the most sophisticated, intelligent, and interested learners to deal in depth or even adequately with new ideas or approaches and their implications and applications without time for reading, critical reflection, and exercise. The same considerations apply with even greater force to specialization.[14] If certification of specialists is to develop within legal professions it would be very strange if this were to be left entirely to learning by experience or if it were to be tested mainly or solely by outmoded forms of examination. This would be to revive in a mischievous way the false dichotomies between academic and practical or theory and practice. And it is doubtful whether any profession can stay learned solely on a diet of canned

[14] In the *White Paper on Legal Services* (Cm. 740, London, 1989), the Lord Chancellor recommended that the proposed Advisory Committee should include among its functions: 'To offer advice on whether schemes for areas of accredited specialization put forward by the professional bodies or other organizations are likely to serve the efficient delivery of legal services to the public; and to consider on its own initiative whether any new areas of accredited specialization are necessary; and to advise the relevant organizations accordingly.' (7.6 (iv)). See now, the Courts and Legal Services Act, 1990.

learning. In short, to echo Holmes, we have too little theory within CLE rather than too much.[15]

I am well aware that any suggestion that jurisprudence should have a place in CLE is likely to be greeted by scepticism, if not derision, by most practitioners. As a legal theorist I am also vulnerable to charges of special pleading. So let me make it clear that I am not arguing for refresher courses on Austin and Bentham or updates on the latest fashions in legal semiotics or autopoiesis. Nor do I think that most existing postgraduate courses are necessarily well-suited to providing the academic component of specialist training. High-grade CLE will require changes in academic practice as well as the attitudes of practitioners.

Let me illustrate what I have in mind by some practical examples drawn from recent developments in legal theory. One of the central concerns of the most prominent of contemporary jurists, Ronald Dworkin, is with what constitutes a valid and cogent argument on a question of law in a hard case.[16] Dworkin's own concerns are philosophical, but his ideal judge, Hercules, provides a model for argument which any judge or advocate who accepts his premises might seek to emulate. Dworkin's chief critics include Judge Bork and Judge Posner, who offer rival models of legal argumentation. At present many undergraduates learn *about* Hercules in courses on jurisprudence, but so far as I am aware few practical courses are directed to teaching *how* to construct Herculean arguments (or alternative kinds). One reason for this is that nearly all formal skills teaching is at an introductory level, concerned with competence rather than excellence,[17] and most courses on advocacy concentrate more on presentation rather than on construction and criticism of arguments.[18]

A second example relates to evidence, proof, and fact-handling. The last ten years has seen a remarkable revival of theoretical interest in this area. Two aspects of this 'new evidence scholarship' are directly relevant here.[19] First there has been a series of debates about probabilities and proof and the application of Bayes theorem and other theories of probability to arguments about disputed questions of fact. While some of the debates are indeed rather recondite, the use

---

[15] O. W. Holmes Jr., 'The Path of the Law', 10 *Harv L Rev.* 457 (1897).

[16] R. Dworkin, 'Hard Cases' in *Taking Rights Seriously* (London, 1977) and *Law's Empire* (London, 1986).

[17] At present nearly all skills teaching involves a very limited number of introductory exercises. It is significant that the Council of Legal Education in London makes no higher claim for its new vocational course for intending barristers than that it is a preparation for pupillage. Success in the course does not *per se* certify minimum competence: at present in most jurisdictions the development of excellence in respect of skills is still left almost entirely to 'learning by experience'.

[18] The Ontario Advocates' Institute has recently conducted an interesting enquiry into what is thought to constitute excellence in advocacy. While highly regarded advocates were found to be rather inarticulate about their skills, the study concluded that preparation is the main key to effective advocacy. This might seem to underline the obvious, but most courses on advocacy have concentrated more on presentation than preparation. See *LLS* at 323–4.

[19] The phrase was coined by Richard Lempert (66 *Boston U L Rev.* 439 (1986)). For a critical discussion, see *RE*, Ch. 11.

of statistical arguments in court and other related matters is developing fast in the United States[20] and is likely to spread to many other parts of the common law world well before the year 2000. A century ago Holmes agreed that the lawyer of the future would need to have a mastery of economics and statistics,[21] but in my experience most lawyers are innumerate and most law students are terrified of figures. It is likely that Holmes' dictum will be incorporated in standard conceptions of competence by the year 2000. It is extremely unlikely that competence in these areas can be developed by quick fixes of CLE.

'The new evidence scholarship' is also concerned with a number of other topics that are relevant to the daily work of practising lawyers and judges, such as methods of ordering large masses of data and complex arguments, story telling, and the use of computers in fact investigation.[22] Some of these deserve to be at the core of primary legal education, but it will be difficult in practice to make space for them; all involve an admixture of theory and practice.

One pattern that emerges from many of these new developments is that there is a growing convergence between new trends in professional training and traditional values of liberal education, especially in relation to such questions as: what constitutes excellence in respect of legal skills?; how is it best fostered? This convergence is one reason why those old educational truisms need to be taken seriously by all who are involved in the process. The starting-point for this is a vision of the total enterprise of legal education that embodies these ideas and is reinforced by messages from those who are in a position to influence attitudes and expectations such as those responsible for professional examinations, recruitment, and post-qualification training. The kind of message I have in mind is embodied in a mundane document produced by one of the newer institutions of legal education in the Commonwealth, the Practising Law Institute of Xanadu. This is what they write to those to whom they have offered places on their vocational course:

At the Xanadu Practising Law Institute we accept graduates from a variety of educational backgrounds. They come to us with quite different stocks of specialized knowledge of varying degrees of freshness. What we expect of all of our entrants is a command of basic intellectual skills and a capacity to work on their own. In particular we expect all entrants to be able to express themselves clearly and precisely, both orally and in writing; to distinguish the relevant from the irrelevant; to construct and criticize an argument on a question of fact or law; to make intelligent use of a law library and to get up or refresh their memory on a specific legal topic quickly and efficiently on their own.

---

[20] Lempert, op. cit., cites figures that indicate that about 4% of reported District Court opinions in the US between 1960 and 1979 involved some use of statistical evidence and that this was on a steadily rising curve. See generally, Sir Richard Eggleston, *Evidence. Proof and Probability* (2nd edn., London, 1982) and David W. Barnes, *Statistics as Proof* (Boston, 1983).

[21] Holmes (1897), op. cit.

[22] See generally op. cit., n. 22 and David Schum and Peter Tillers. *Marshalling Evidence Throughout the Process of Fact-investigation: A Simulation* (Arlington, Va., 1989): cf. D. Binder and P. Bergman, *Fact Investigation: From Hypothesis to Proof* (St. Paul, Minn., 1984).

From the first day of term we shall take for granted an up-to-date grasp of the basic concepts and general principles concerning the topics listed in Note 1, including a working familiarity with the statutes listed in Note 2. If you are unfamiliar with any of these or if your memories about them are a bit rusty, you are asked to fill in the gaps and refresh your memory before the start of term. You are also asked to bring with you draft answers to any two of the problems set out in Note 3.

(Note 1 contains a quite short list of selected topics (falling mainly but not exclusively within the area of the local 'core' subjects) that will be the basis of preliminary exercises in the first weeks of the course. Note 2 contains a list of not more than ten important statutes that will be relevant to the early exercises. It includes at least two statutes that have come into force or been amended in the last year. Note 3 contains three or four problem situations raising issues that will test basic library skills. They are also directly relevant to practical exercises scheduled in the first weeks of the course.)

I have suggested that there is a strong convergence between recent developments in skills training and some central values of liberal education in that they both give a high priority to transferable intellectual skills rather than particular techniques or specific knowledge, especially in the primary stages. If this is correct, the model of an intellectually mature, liberally educated law graduate assumed in the letter might win widespread support within all sectors of legal education and training. Insofar as it embodies an acceptable set of expectations not only for future practitioners but also for recipients of continuing legal education, it is worth asking of any jurisdiction: to what extent do our law graduates fit this model? To the extent that they do not, why is this so? Are there any current practices (in bar examinations, criteria for recognition of law degrees, questions asked at interview, CLE practices, etc.) which undermine these aspirations? And what might be done positively to foster them? Let us hope that by the year 2000 academics and practitioners will be singing in unison and that our students will have got the message.

15

*What are Law Schools for?**

INTRODUCTION

Once upon a time when I was postgraduate tutor at Rutland,[1] a newly-married couple came to consult me in October about their choice of options for a taught Master's degree. They were holding hands. They had chosen to attend two courses together and two each that they would take separately. All six were essentially bread-and-butter courses within the general area of commercial law. I suggested that this was a rather unadventurous menu; and that their postgraduate year should be transformative and not just more of the same. My advice was: 'Each of you should choose one unexpected option that intrigues you in the hope that it might blow your mind.' At the end of the academic year they courteously came to say goodbye. They were still holding hands. One of them said: 'Thank you for your excellent advice. We followed it and our mind is blown.'

This parable is open to several interpretations: it could be read either as a story of success or of failure; it could be the start of a satire on obsession with performance indicators, behavioural learning objectives, and other bureaucratic academic 'newspeak'; it might be taken as relating postgraduate legal education to family values; or it could just be the statutory joke at the start of a serious talk.

My choice of title is similarly ambiguous. To ask: 'What are law schools for?' is rather like asking: 'What are flowers for?' Depending on one's standpoint it could be a question about the stated aspirations of institutions themselves; the uses to which they are put by different constituencies (central and local government, funding agencies, the legal profession, educational administrators, parents, teachers, and above all the students themselves);[2] the question could also be about manifest and latent functions of institutions or even their ideological commitments. In some countries governments use law schools as a cheap dumping ground for excess demand for higher education; in some the legal profession

---

* This is a revised and expanded version of an essay published in a symposium commemorating the 150th anniversary of the founding of Queen's College, Belfast (46 *NILQ* 291 (1995)). It originated as a keynote address given at the Conference of the Association of Law Teachers in Cambridge (England) in Mar. 1994. Although it mainly relates to the situation in England, much of the analysis applies to aspects of the situation in many other common law jurisdictions. This paper can be read as a development of the argument in *BT* (Ch. 3 and Epilogue), which incorporates part of the original text.

[1] Rutland is a mythical middling law school in middle England, not to be confused with Xanadu. See further, *BT* Ch. 4 and 'Postgraduate Legal Studies' in P. Birks (ed.) *Reviewing Legal Education* (Oxford, 1994), Ch. 10.

[2] On the wide dispersal of power over legal education in England, see *BT* 44, n. 18.

uses them as convenient filters, as finishing schools that select, certify, and socialize intending entrants to the profession; in some they are used by students for a whole variety of purposes and motives, often before they have made a final career choice; sometimes they are used by parents as safe and potentially useful emporia for increasing the marketability of their offspring.

I intend to be more straightforward than these preliminaries might suggest. I shall argue that legal educators need to rethink in a quite fundamental way the nature, objectives, and actual and potential role of law schools as institutions. My purpose is to suggest that too much tends to be taken for granted about such matters when issues of legal education policy are debated. In particular, there is a need to draw a clear distinction between the *process* of professional formation of lawyers, only part of which takes place in law schools in any country, and the nature and roles of law schools as *institutions*. Most official committees have been concerned with the process of professional formation and have often been precluded by their terms of reference from looking at law schools as institutions in the round.[3] When this distinction is blurred, important aspects of institutional life tend to be downplayed or overlooked and the range of possible strategies open to the institutions themselves is unnecessarily narrowed. Even the most sophisticated American discussions tend to equate 'legal education' with what takes place in law schools and to assume that law schools are essentially pre-paratory schools for the private profession.[4] This tendency has the dual effect of reinforcing inflated expectations about the potential contribution of law schools to the total process of professional formation and, by concentrating on the needs of intending private practitioners, of marginalizing or totally ignoring other poten-tial beneficiaries of law school services both within and outside legal practice.

My standpoint will be that of a university teacher and educator arguing for developments that I think are desirable in common law countries; I wish to make the case for persuading the relevant constituencies that it is generally in their interest that university law schools should adopt a broader and more ambitious role than they have in the past—in crude terms that they should grow out of being rather constricted primary schools in the direction of being multifunctional institutions that regularly serve a wide variety of constituencies at a variety of levels—from legal literacy to judicial training; from different kinds of law for non-lawyers to advanced specialist studies for a variety of consumers; from primary academic and vocational studies to continuing education that ranges across the whole spectrum from get-skilled-quick to get-wise-slow. In short that we should adopt a different picture of the actual and potential role of law

---

[3] There are some notable exceptions, mainly by committees sponsored by organizations respons-ible for higher education, see below n. 16.

[4] Two recent books which display this tendency in varying degrees are Anthony Kronman, *The Lost Lawyer* (Cambridge, Ma., 1993) and Mary Ann Glendon, *A Nation Under Lawyers* (New York, 1994), which are discussed in Ch. 16 below. The tendency to focus on process rather than institu-tions extends to comparative law: e.g., M. A. Glendon, M. W. Gordon, and C. Osakwe, *Comparative Legal Traditions* (2nd ed., St Paul, 1994), Ch. 12 and the works cited there.

schools from the one that is currently assumed in most discussions of legal education.

SOME ASSUMPTIONS

For reasons of space, let me make explicit a number of assumptions by way of assertion rather than argument, although they are potentially controversial. I have explored most of these topics at length elsewhere.[5]

1. The primary mission of a university is the advancement, stimulation, and dissemination of learning. Learning in this context encompasses know how, know-why, and know-what. It is broad enough to encompass both theoretical studies and such aspects of practical professional training that can appropriately be carried out in institutions with this kind of mission. There is plenty of room for differences about priorities, objectives, methods, and values within this conception and about the relationship between teaching and research. But this idea of the university as a House of Intellect is unequivocal in its rejection of strong analogies with factories or emporia or evangelical churches or ideological seminaries.

2. Everyone in society needs some legal education from cradle to grave. Not all of this education is formal. And law schools do not, could not, and should not have a monopoly of formal legal education.[6] As Lawrence Friedman has said, Western society is 'one, vast diffuse school of law'.[7] But law schools, as institutions specialized to the study of law in all its aspects, can play a key role in the advancement and dissemination of knowledge and understanding about law at many levels and in many constituencies.

3. Law schools come in many shapes and sizes, including independent professional schools, Continental European institutions of mass legal education, Islamic law colleges, commercial law tutors, and specialized institutions, such as judicial training colleges. This essay is concerned with the actual and potential roles of one kind of law school: university faculties and departments of law in common law countries.

4. In most common law jurisdictions the modern university law school is largely a post-World War II phenomenon. In this respect, as in some others, American law schools are exceptional.[8] In England, the scale of our national system of legal education has been estimated to be more than

---

[5] Points 1–6 are discussed in *BT*. On 7, see Ch. 14 above.

[6] e.g., it is one thing for law schools to train teachers for legal awareness programmes or law in schools; it is quite another for them to try to be the main agencies for delivering such programmes. Again, the case for having legally qualified people 'in-house' in business schools or engineering departments may be as strong in some contexts as the case for including 'non-lawyers' on the staff of law schools and for developing genuinely multi-disciplinary arrangements; in each case one can identify a long litany of costs and benefits.

[7] Lawrence Friedman, 'Law, Lawyers and Popular Culture', 98 *Yale Law Jo.* 1579, 1598 (1989). See further *BT*, Ch. 1 and Glendon, op. cit., Ch. 12.   [8] *BT* 23.

twenty times what it was in 1945 and about four times what it was at the time of Ormrod Report in 1971.[9] This has at least two implications: first, expansion has facilitated diversification in respect of role and pluralism in respect of ideas. Second, the modern law school as a relatively young institution has not made up its mind what it wants to be or do. It is in process of coming of age—witness the number of 21st and 25th birthdays that have been celebrated recently.[10] In this context, there is still scope for rethinking institutional roles.

5. In most parts of the common law world law schools have traditionally played a quite limited role compared to their potential. In recent years some have extended the range of their activities, but this has usually been constrained by a highly restricted self-image, viz. that they are mainly providers of first degrees in law or other introductory courses; in short they are primary schools almost always concentrating largely or entirely on first steps. This applies as much to contributions to law for 'non-lawyers', to the vocational stage, and even to continuing education as it does to under-graduate degrees. Advanced or specialized study, where it exists at all, is almost invariably treated as marginal.

Rutland is one rather clear case of this tendency: when people talk about the students or the curriculum, nearly always they are referring to under-graduates. Only in 1986 did postgraduate teaching count in the official teaching loads of full-time staff; to this day no agreement has been reached on the amount of credit to be given for supervision of research students; there is student representation on a number of faculty and university com-mittees, but all of the law students involved have been undergraduates—despite the fact that postgraduates (full-time and part-time) now exceed 20 per cent of the 'student load' in the Law School; similarly, postgraduates are eligible to join The Rutland Student Law Society, but few do and none has ever been elected to any office; recently some rather half-hearted attempts have been made to create a postgraduate community in the uni-versity, but by and large postgraduates in law are treated at best as mar-ginal, sometimes as invisible.[11] When members of faculty teach other people, for example in continuing education or extramural or access courses, it is normally referred to, and remunerated, as 'outside work'.

6. The discourse of legal education tends to focus on issues and trends that are internal to law. It tends to downplay or ignore the context of higher education as a whole, which may be at least as important. For example, in England, almost all important changes in primary legal education since World War II have reflected changes in higher and further education more than conscious decisions by the legal community: student numbers, admis-sions standards and criteria, unit costs, staff-student ratios, the grant sys-tem, the terms of service and career development of law teachers, gender

---

[9] *BT*. Ch. 2.   [10] See below, Ch. 16.   [11] *BT*, Ch. 4.

ratios, resourcing, and quality assurance were not determined with specific reference to law, which has been almost invisible in modern discussions of higher education. So far as the economics, scale, and infrastructure of legal education as an enterprise are concerned, most debates and reports, which have focused mainly on process, curriculum, and method, have been largely irrelevant.[12]

7. Almost all attempts at artificially limiting the supply of lawyers and law graduates in the common law world, through manpower planning, quotas, and other devices have failed, at least in the medium term.[13] From Botswana to Ontario, from the United States to Northern Ireland, almost invariably the scale of the enterprise has been demand-led. I once helped to quadruple the estimates for lawyers in Botswana's manpower plan in a single morning: this was in 1971; the manpower planners had provided for the production of only two new lawyers by 1980; by talking to various senior civil servants we upped the estimate to eight. I am told that by 1980 over 100 more local people had graduated in law.[14]

PROCESSES AND INSTITUTIONS: A MATTER OF EMPHASIS

The difference between focusing on process and on institutions is illustrated by two recent reports. The Lord Chancellor's Advisory Committee on Legal

[12] In England, the one major exception is the post-Ormrod settlement: the four-stage structure of professional formation—academic, vocational, apprenticeship, continuing—had the dual effect of excluding university and polytechnic law schools from systematic contribution to the last three stages and, because the three legal constituencies could not reach accord, of freeing government from having to finance the vocational stage. See further *BT*, Ch. 2.

[13] The Lord Chancellor's Advisory Committee on Legal Education and Conduct (ACLEC) has recently given strong support to this view: 'The Committee has not found evidence of successful models of planning and control of entry into professions in this country or internationally. The current decline in the number of applications for the LPC and BVC indicates that, over time, the market can be relied upon to respond to imbalances in the supply and demand for new entrants. Restrictions on numbers would require bureaucratic machinery. We are not satisfied that workable arrangements are possible. Not only is it wrong in principle for professional bodies which have a monopoly over entry to impose restrictions on the right to train and to work, but any such restrictions are likely to have an adverse and unjustifiably discriminatory effect on entry, particularly by those from disadvantaged educational and social backgrounds.' The Lord Chancellor's Advisory Committee on Legal Education and Conduct, *First Report on Legal Education and Training* (1996) para. 3.10 (cf. 3.12). See further above, Ch. 13.

[14] In the US the annual output of law graduates increased from about 17,000 in 1960–1 to about 35–40,000 in the 1980s (ACLEC, *Annual Report*, 1991–2). The numbers stabilized in the 1980s, but a period of recession contributed to what was widely perceived to be a severe crisis in the legal profession in the late 1980s, Glendon, op. cit. There the scale of the law school enterprise seems to be almost as strongly demand-led as in other countries, despite the expense; the lack of a formal apprenticeship system, legal inhibitions on restraint of trade, and the place of law in American culture combine to impose fewer brakes than elsewhere on the continuous expansion of the legal profession. Nevertheless by the mid-1990s a decline in applications led some law schools to talk seriously of 'downsizing', which significantly is normally equated with reducing undergraduate numbers (see below).

Education and Conduct (ACLEC) published its *First Report on Legal Education and Training* in April 1996.[15] This is one outcome of the first major official review of legal education and training in England and Wales since the Ormrod Report of 1971.[16] The report can be read as an expression of 'humane professionalism': it is liberal in spirit and contextual in approach;[17] it recognizes that law is a good vehicle for a general education leading to a variety of careers; it welcomes the diversification that has taken place in academic law in the wake of the expansion of higher education; it favours multiple approaches to the study of law and multiple routes to professional certification; and it is sharply critical of over-prescription by professional bodies, especially in respect of undergraduate degrees.[18] Yet ACLEC is required by its terms of reference to focus on the education and training of providers of legal services and this requirement constrains its whole approach.[19] The main focus is on the process of professional formation and development and the needs of one constituency, potential, intending, and certified providers of legal services. This colours its treatment of such matters as institutional funding, quality assurance, and student finance; legal research is viewed largely in terms of its utility for the practising profession and legal development; and libraries are judged by their adequacy for the needs of this constituency and of their clients. More subtly, this perspective underlies the committee's conception of liberal or general education. The Committee makes a plea for university autonomy and strongly recommends that 'the degree course should stand as an independent liberal education in the discipline of law, not tied to any specific vocation'.[20] However, in criticizing sharp distinctions between education and training, academic and vocational, and theory and practice, the

---

[15] ACLEC, *First Report*, op. cit.

[16] There have, of course, been numerous reports since Ormrod that dealt with aspects of the subject, (for references see above, 194n., and the ACLEC report, App. C), but this justifiably claims to be the first 'full-scale review' since 1971 (para. 2). None of these reports focuses on law schools as institutions. This contrasts with Canada and Australia where the two main reports were sponsored by bodies concerned with higher education and research respectively: the Pearce Report (D. Pearce, E. Campbell, and D. Harding, *Australian Law Schools* (Canberra, 1987) was sponsored by the Commonwealth Tertiary Education Commission; *Law and Learning* (the Arthurs Report, Ottawa, 1983)) was sponsored by the Social Sciences Research Council of Canada; both considered the functions and infrastructure of law schools in the round. See also, *Law as an Academic Discipline* (Head of University Law Schools, London, 1983).

[17] The report sets professional legal education and training in the context of its history, patterns in other countries and other professions, changes in higher education and in legal practice. The idea of 'humane professionalism' owes much to the Arthurs Report, op. cit.

[18] Id., 4.7–4.13.

[19] Under the Courts and Legal Services Act, 1990 (schedule 2. para 1 (1), the Committee is required to:

'(a) keep under review the education and training of those who offer to provide legal services;
(b) consider the need for continuing education and training for such persons and the form it should take; and
(c) consider the steps which professional and other bodies should take to ensure that their members benefit from such continuing education and training.'

[20] Id., 4.6.

Committee is drawn back into a professional perspective. The guiding principle of the report is that the process of professional formation should be seen as a continuum and that, as far as is feasible, artificial divisions between stages of professional formation should be broken down.[21] 'Practice' tends to get equated with lawyers' action rather than with the much broader idea of 'the law in action';[22] and the later stages of the professional continuum inevitably cast a shadow on how the earlier stages are conceived.

I am in sympathy with the general thrust of the ACLEC report and its recommendations.[23] I would also agree that law degrees that are guided by this kind of enlightened vocationalism can be appropriate vehicles for one kind of general education in law.[24] However, ACLEC, like most other committees on legal education, was precluded by its terms of reference from taking a comprehensive view of legal education or of law as a discipline or of law schools as institutions.

A recent report on *Legal Education in Xanadu* had no such inhibitions. It provides a striking contrast. It is unusual in three main respects: first, it looks at the national system of legal education as a whole, including formal and informal legal education, and all its recipients. It takes a quite narrow view of law (confining itself to state law, including officially recognized 'customary law'), but a broad view of education, which includes learning about the what, why, and how of legal phenomena, however that learning is acquired. Secondly, it focuses on institutions as well as processes and includes in those institutions some that are not specialized to law, such as business schools, secondary schools, police training colleges, and institutes of public administration. Thirdly, it articulated some general hypotheses that might apply to any national system of legal education. Here, it is worth quoting the summary of the main hypotheses underpinning this 'total picture' of legal education.

---

[21] Id., 2.20, 2.25. The idea of legal education as a continuum involving lifelong learning is borrowed from the American MacCrate Report, which is less ambivalently focused on mainstream private practice (Report of the American Bar Association Task Force on Law Schools and the Profession, *Legal Education and Professional Development* (Chicago, 1992).

[22] *BT* 16–21.

[23] I should acknowledge a partial responsibility for both reports discussed here. The Xanadu report is an extension of the trajectory of two reports that I helped to prepare: Financial and Legal Management Upgrade Project (FILMUP, Tanzania), *Legal Education Report* (1994) and *Review of the National Law School of India University: Report by a Panel Experts* (1996). I was also involved in the deliberations and discussions preceding the ACLEC Report. Indeed, it has been a source of modest satisfaction to have been a member of a consultative panel to an advisory committee which accepted that the logic of pluralism precluded making detailed prescriprions about most issues (id., Introd. 5).

[24] In *The Quiet Revolution* (North Ryde, NSW, 1994), Marlene Le Brun and Richard Johnstone argue that 'many of the skills that are vocationally focused in fact provide an appropriate framework within which broader educational goals can best be achieved. By placing learning in a meaningful context, learning becomes relevant and thus, more meaningful.' (At 13 *et passim*.) Clearly to study law from the point of view of important participants is *one* very important route to understanding. Within any given programme difficult choices have to be made as to which participant perspectives should be emphasized and what balance to strike between internal and external points of view. In this context the weasel word 'relevant' begs questions about to whom and for what purposes.

In (almost) all societies

1. almost everyone receives some legal education;
2. that process lasts from cradle to grave;
3. the amount of informal legal education (i.e. outside educational programmes) greatly exceeds the amount of formal legal education, even for career lawyers;[25]
4. actual and potential demand for formal legal education almost invariably exceeds the supply;
5. most formal legal education is delivered in institutions other than law schools;[26]
6. within most countries, specialized institutions called law schools can be quite varied.[27] For example, they vary within and between countries in respect of wealth; size; manifest and latent functions; prestige and influence; the age, class, and gender of students, faculty, and other staff; academic standards; conceptions of scholarship; and even architecture.[28]
7. the culture of law schools is to some extent international within legal traditions or families, but it is also much influenced by local historical, economic, ideological, and other factors, including the structure and financing of higher education, distributions of power and authority, and the nature of the legal system and the legal profession.

Official reports are typically produced in response to particular local concerns. The ACLEC and Xanadu reports are no exception. Both purported to be 'full scale' or comprehensive, but each had quite specific aims. ACLEC's central concern has been about the contribution of formal legal education and training to ensuring the quality of legal services in England and Wales in a period marked by expansion, rapid change, diversification, and financial uncertainty in higher education, private legal practice, and publicly funded legal aid. The Xanadu report was directed to establishing needs and priorities for upgrading a national system of legal education in a poor country. Despite enormous differences in the local contexts, both reports are examples of responses to perceived problems in common law countries in the post-socialist era. There is a shared background in

---

[25] 'Informal' in this context includes matters learned from firsthand experience (e.g., getting married, being arrested, negotiating a loan, entering into a contract), from newspapers, television, novels, and other popular media, firsthand observation, bar-room conversation, and gossip. A fascinating chapter on 'Legal miseducation' deals at length with the influence of inaccurate, misleading or sensationalized information and of the portrayal of foreign practices that have no local relevance (such as depictions of atypical American courtroom scenes either live, as in the O. J. Simpson case, or in fictional form). Institutionalized apprenticeship, however casual, organized work experience placements or 'stages', public lectures, law in schools, moot competitions, and even bibulous weekends or lunches that are part of continuing professional development are treated in the report as 'formal'.

[26] e.g., in Xanadu: the Police College; the Civil Service College; the Institute of Public Administration; business schools and social science departments; the multi-disciplinary Centre for Environmental Studies; and secondary schools, both as equivalent of 'A' level law and as part of civics or general studies.

[27] In 1994 Xanadu had one local campus university law school, a law department in the Open University, two law departments on branch campuses of foreign universities, a professional law college, a Judicial Training Institute, and several firms of commercial law tutors, some of which are branches of foreign-based businesses. [28] See further *BT* 51–52.

common themes of globalization, privatization, expansion, and change. Both take 'the public interest' as their benchmark. Despite differences in concern and approach, both concentrate more on structure, infrastructure, and economics than on traditional concerns about curriculum content, teaching methods, and different perspectives on law.[29] And some basic assumptions about legal education are shared: both emphasize context and 'liberal' educational values; transferable skills; a balance between knowledge, skills, and basic theory; ethical values and professional reponsibility.

Institutions and processes are, of course, not mutually exclusive as focuses of attention. The difference is one of emphasis, but it can be significant. The Xanadu report deals with a system that is heavily dependent upon public funding in a relatively poor country so that difficult questions of priorities have to be tackled. This is the main reason for the concentration on different clienteles and the role of law schools and academic lawyers. Within this framework the Xanadu report ranges much more widely than conventional documents in this genre; it deals with informal as well as formal legal education, including the role of law in general culture and intellectual life. It includes within its remit judicial training, the education and certification of specialists, and what is sometimes patronizingly referred to as 'law for non-lawyers' (including legal awareness, law in schools, access courses, police training, law and medicine, and intellectual property for engineers). It contains an interesting discussion of the actual and potential contribution of the discipline of law to other disciplines and to intellectual life. Naturally, 'mainstream' or 'traditional' legal education and training is given due attention, but it is considered within the context of a total picture of needs and demands for learning about law by a more varied clientele and at a number of levels. Similarly, a great deal of attention is paid to specialized law schools, but as part of a broader picture of other legal education provision.

Here we are concerned with the role of university law schools, which are the main specialist institutions, but by no means the only providers of legal education. The report set out to undermine a number of entrenched ideas about such law schools inherited from the traditional culture of the common law. These include the following widespread assumptions:

1. that all university law schools have the same mission and should be judged by identical criteria. Like football clubs, they compete with each other in a single hierarchy of prestige (the football league model);
2. that the core of that mission is primary legal education and that the term 'law student' refers only to someone taking a first degree in law (the primary school image);

[29] The ACLEC Report deals with the general aims of legal education and training (2.3), 'the prescribed common element' (formerly known as 'the core') for qualifying law degrees (4.11–4.19), and teaching methods and assessment (4.4.21), but only in respect of first degrees, conversion courses, and the one year vocational stage.

3. that the main priority need for legal education is basic education and training for intending and newly qualified private practitioners of law, even in contexts where the absorptive capacity of the legal profession exceeds the supply of new lawyers and most law graduates start their careers in the public service (the private practitioner image);[30]
4. that the supply of entrants to the legal profession can be artificially controlled by manpower planning, the pass rate in the bar examination, apprenticeship requiremernts or other restrictive practices (the numbers game);[31]
5. that providing legal educational services for other clients is beneath the dignity of university law schools and that this is reflected in treating such teaching as 'outside work' and in the derogatory use of such terms as 'service teaching', 'law for non-lawyers', and (mainly in the United States) 'legal studies' and 'pre-law courses' (the professional snob syndrome);
6. that law is by its nature one of the cheapest subjects in higher education.[32]

WHAT ARE LAW SCHOOLS FOR? TWO MODELS
AND SOME VARIANTS[33]

Despite the prevalence of such orthodox asumptions, law schools are in fact quite varied, both internationally and within particular countries. Accordingly, in analysing a particular national legal education system it is useful to locate institutions within a framework of 'ideal types'.

In modern industrial societies, despite the complexities, two main conceptions of the role of the law school have competed for dominance: the first is the law school as a service institution for the profession (the professional school model); the second is the law school as an academic institution devoted to the advancement of learning about law (the academic model).[34] Each 'ideal type' has significant variants; most actual law schools are hybrids combining elements of both models.

There have been several variants of the professional school model.

First, and most prestigious, is an institution which purports to be the practising legal profession's House of Intellect, providing not only basic education and

---

[30] See William Twining, 'Legal Education Within East Africa', in *East African Law Today* (London, 1966) at 139–44.   [31] See above, n. 13.

[32] The case against this assumption was made, with only limited success, in *Law as an Academic Discipline* (1983), op. cit.   [33] This section was adopted almost verbatim in *BT*, Ch. 3.

[34] In England, the national system of legal education and training involves a rather greater variety of institutions than in most countries: independent professional schools, a bewildering number of kinds of higher and further educational institutions, and even commercial law tutors. I shall focus here on university law schools, but much of what I have to say really relates to our national system of legal education seen as a whole: no single institution can hope to take on the whole range of potential functions that a law school could perform.

training, but also specialist training, continuing education, basic and applied research, and high level consultancy and information services. The nearest analogy is the medical school attached to a teaching hospital, which, *inter alia*, gives a high priority to clinical experience with live patients as part of an integrated process of professional formation and development. In no modern Western country has this model been realized in law.[35]

An intermediate form is the graduate professional school. Typically it is within a university, but stands somewhat apart. Its main function is to provide basic vocational education for intending practitioners, who have obtained at least a first degree in some other subject. The graduate business school is the prototype. The classical American law school approximates to this model. British academics tend to cast envious eyes at the better American law schools—with good reason in respect of resources, pay, status, willingness to experiment, and a generally more 'grown-up' atmosphere. Yet the structure in the United States has created an acute and persistent tension between the vocational and academic functions, not least in respect of scholarship. In its higher forms this ideal type includes being institutionally involved at all levels and in effect performing the role as the legal profession's House of Intellect. The nearest approximation is the élite American law school, but it rarely contributes to teaching non-lawyers and, with some notable exceptions, is only peripherally involved in substantial forms of continuing legal education and advanced studies. When it expands its research and teaching beyond what the profession and the judiciary considers relevant to them, it comes under attack, as has happened recently in the *Michigan Law Review*, where Judge Harry Edwards strongly criticized law schools for neglecting their traditional role as producers of 'practical doctrinal scholarship'.[36]

A third variant, which is more developed in some civil law jurisdictions, is the staff college, which provides in-service and advanced training, typically for a specialized cadre such as prosecutors, the judiciary, or senior law enforcement officials. Leading examples are the École Nationale de la Magistrature (ENM) in Bordeaux and the Legal Training Research Institute in Japan, both of which

---

[35] Harvard Law School may claim to be the institution that has come closest to this model: it has an extensive postgraduate programme; it runs many advanced courses and workshops; all JD students have an opportunity to gain clinical experience, and many in fact do so; and a substantial portion of the faculty is engaged in high level consultancy and litigation. But in respect of structure and priorities it is significantly different from a medical school (especially in relation to specialist training and the idea of a teaching hospital) and, of course, Harvard is not representative of even the better American law schools. Those who complain that law schools have departed from their traditional mission, interpret that to be preparing people for practice and systematizing doctrine (see below, n. 36). When Antioch Law School tried to develop as an essentially clinical institution, built around a law office, it ran into difficulties in respect of accreditation. This was only one of the factors that led to its demise in 1988. Non-vocational 'legal studies' have relatively low prestige. One reason why the ordinary first degree in law is not widely perceived as a suitable vehicle for general education is its expense from the students' point of view.

[36] Harry T. Edwards, 'The growing disjunction between legal education and the legal profession', 91 *Michigan L Rev.* 34 (1992); similar concerns are expressed by Kronman and Glendon, op. cit.

provide extended initial training for those who have been admitted to the judicial cadre after very stiff competition.[37]

A fourth variant is the independent professional school run for—and typically by—the practising profession. Examples of this include the Law Society's College of Law and the Inns of Court School of Law in England, some professional schools in the Commonwealth, and the National Institute for Trial Advocacy (NITA). These institutions have often performed a useful role under difficult conditions. But only very occasionally in history have they flourished in the long term—one exception being the Inns of Court in their heyday. There are two reasons for this fragility: they find it difficult to attract public funding and they lack prestige within both the legal profession and the university system. However, as continuing legal education has become established, commercial institutions, such as NITA, may find a stable niche market for their services.

The professional school model can be contrasted with the academic model. Again there are variants, mainly in respect of ambition and prestige. The most ambitious version of this is set out in a report by the International Legal Center (ILC) on *Legal Education in a Changing World*, which states:

Law schools, perceived as multipurpose centres, can develop human resources and idealism needed to strengthen legal systems; they can develop research and intellectual direction; they can address problems in fields ranging from land reform to criminal justice; they can foster the development of indigenous languages as vehicles for the administration of law; they can assist institutions involved in training paraprofessionals; they can help to provide materials and encouragement for civic education about law in schools and more intelligent treatment of law in the media; they can organise, or help organise, advanced specialized legal education for professionals who must acquire particular kinds of skills and expertise.[38]

This is a rather idealized statement of what might be termed the idea of the law school as the Legal System's (or less parochially, Law's) House of Intellect, dealing with all aspects of the advancement and dissemination of knowledge about law in the modern world and serving many constituencies, including the legal profession in both public and private sectors.[39] I shall refer to this as the

---

[37] For brief accounts of training institutions in several countries, see Alan N. Katz, *Legal Traditions and Systems: An International Handbook* (New York, 1986). High level Staff Colleges should not be confused with bodies which mainly run much shorter in-service training for judges, such as the National Judicial College (US), the Judicial Studies Board (England), and the Richter Academie (Germany). Of course, over time some of these may evolve in the direction of the more ambitious staff college model.

[38] International Legal Center, *Legal Education in a Changing World* (New York, 1975) at 39.

[39] The only law school that I know that uses this model as an aspiration is the National Law School of India in Bangalore, which is involved in judicial studies, continuing legal education, refresher courses for law teachers, paraprofessional training, legal awareness (again especially teacher training), clinical work, postgraduate studies, in addition to a five-year integrated undergraduate degree. It works under severe financial constraints, but the key point is that *all* of these activities are considered to be part of the normal role of the institution. See above, n. 23.

ILC model. It overlaps with the professional model in that it includes practical training and other services to the legal profession as part of its remit. But it differs in three key respects: it is independent of the legal profession, it has a much wider clientele, and its mission is more in tune with the academic ethic. In countries with only one or two law schools this puts heavy demands on the institution, often involving difficult choices about priorities.[40]

A second version of the academic model is the Law Faculty as a full part of the university, pursuing original research and offering a general education in law at undergraduate level and a range of postgraduate courses, including research training, advanced academic studies, multi-disciplinary work, and some kinds of specialist education and training. This has been the aspiration of many Continental European Law Faculties, with many variations in time and place.

A third variant of the academic model is the law school which is essentially an undergraduate teaching institution. This may or may not have a commitment to research and, typically, it sees other teaching activities as secondary.[41] The danger of this kind of self-image is that an institution may get the worst of both worlds, if it treats undergraduate teaching as its main function and the undergraduate degree is perceived and used mainly as the first stage of professional formation. For what is such an institution except a primary or even a nursery school for the profession?

USER PERSPECTIVES

It might be objected that all of these 'models' are essentially 'top-down', design models reflecting the stated objectives of those with power over general policy rather than the interests and viewpoints of those whom the institutions are meant to serve, the customers or consumers. Such a perspective might be criticized on three main grounds: first, it leaves out the interests and goals of students, and behind them, their main reference groups, such as parents, partners or employers. Second, it is unrealistic in that it focuses on official aspirations and it glosses over the latent functions of educational institutions as gatekeepers, filters, and

---

[40] A partial analysis of the actual and potential role of the Law Faculty of the University of Dar-es-Salaam in a country in which it is the only university law school is to be found in the FILMUP task force report on *Legal Education* in Tanzania in 1994 (op. cit.). One of the main issues was to what extent general legal education, primary training for advocates, training for the judiciary (from court clerks to senior judges), specialist training for government lawyers, and legal awareness programmes should be distributed among a variety of relatively specialized institutions or whether most should be concentrated in two or three, such as the Law Faculty, a National Legal Centre, the Institute of Public Administration, and possibly a Judicial Training College. Final decisions have yet to be taken, but there was common ground that the Law Faculty should serve a variety of constituencies and that proliferation of institutions was generally undesirable.

[41] In the UK there is a well-grounded fear that many universities will soon be relegated to the staus of 'teaching only' institutions. It is particularly important for them to look beyond undergraduate teaching for outlets for their services.

socializing agencies. For example, it is sometimes suggested that the main functions of leading American law schools are to select and socialize talented recruits for a limited range of élite occupations, such as corporate law practice or law teaching. From this point of view, admissions criteria, the grading system, and placement are more important than curriculum, teaching methods, or educational philosophy. The fact that you were at Harvard Law School is more important than what you learned there. Third, it ignores how institutions are in fact used by its clients and consumers. For example, law students have more or less clear personal agendas which may diverge significantly from the mission of the institution or the aspirations of their teachers. The desire of many law students to get through the professional examinations and qualify as quickly and painlessly as possible often conflicts with the more high-minded learning objectives that their teachers may try to prescribe, recommend, or impose. In short, law students and potential employers may use law schools for quite different purposes from those to be found in mission statements and other official formulations of objectives.

These points are important and I have dealt with them at length elsewhere.[42] One of the central themes of these essays is that some of these tensions can be reconciled within a conception of enlightened vocationalism, but there are other dilemmas that are endemic because of the plurality of interests and values within law school culture and the best that one can hope for is some kind of balance or compromise.

None of these points subverts the present argument, which relates to such questions as who should be treated as clients or customers and which of the many competing demands for legal educational services university law schools might be best suited to serve. The nub of the matter is that if everyone in society needs some formal legal education then, in most societies, universities can only meet a small part of the need and that, in some contexts at least, this provides law schools themselves with some leeways of choice and that it is in most people's interests that they should concentrate on those sectors that they are best equipped to serve. Tensions become particularly acute when the main customers are demanding things which an institution is either unwilling or unable to provide.

On this analysis, élite American law schools experience an acute tension between the intellectual aspirations and interests of a substantial part of the

---

[42] e.g., in *BT* I argued that power has been widely distributed through a variety of constituencies in the English system of legal education, but that the single most influential constituency has been students (and their families), who have usually voted with their feet. To a large extent legal education has been demand-led: the scale of the system has been strongly influenced by the popularity of law as a subject; students choose their law schools, and to a lesser extent options, and they exercise influence in other ways; the expectations of employers (including professional organizations) have been largely filtered through students' interpretations of such expectations. Some of the most persistent tensions in law school culture occur because educators consider such expectations to be unrealistic, or short-sighted, or incompatible with the academic ethic. Sometimes the tensions arise because of familiar conflicts between teaching and scholarship.

faculty and the demands and expectations of their main clientele, who are assumed to be intending practitioners. Much of the discourse of American legal education just assumes that this is the significant group of clients and does not seriously consider the possibility of substantial diversification of their clientele (for example, by making major regular contributions to interdisciplinary or mixed degrees at undergraduate and postgraduate level). They appear to be locked into a rather rigid version of the professional primary school model. American colleagues may rationalize this in terms of tradition or finance or prestige or quality, or they may point to some of the other obstacles to breaking out of the mould. To an outsider a more plausible interpretation is that the assumption is so deeply embedded in settled ways of thought as well as vested interests that other possibilities have not often been given sustained consideration.[43]

From the perspective I am adopting, it seems likely that the potential demand for formal legal education will nearly always exceed the supply. From the point of view of the academic legal profession the good news is that any individual institution, if it plays its cards right, can over time choose between a variety of potential clients, consumers or markets. But what it has to offer needs to adjust to demand and to the situation of consumers. One cannot just lay on a full-time LL M and expect practitioners to apply in large numbers; jurisprudence for judges needs to be packaged differently from jurisprudence for undergraduates; courses for school teachers on human rights education or advanced courses for engineers or doctors or businessmen need to be carefully designed and often require interdisciplinary co-operation.

The application and suitability of these various models depend to a large extent on context. The American law school model is no more likely to be easily transplanted to the United Kingdom or Latin America than the Dutch or German model is likely to be introduced in the United States. But within a given context there may be some leeway for choosing between various strategies, especially in respect of clientele, and I propose to illustrate this by applying this perspective to the current situation in England and Wales.

THE SITUATION IN ENGLAND: A CASE-STUDY

Legal education systems around the world vary considerably. Once the mould has been set, it is often very difficult to break. For example, to an outsider American law schools seem to be locked into a remarkably rigid structure, that

---

[43] That there are some notable exceptions is not denied: e.g., the joint degree programmes at Yale and Berkeley. What I am questioning here are the standard ways of thinking and debating about legal education and law school policy, exemplified in some of the assumptions identified in the Xanadu report, especially the football league model (1.); the primary school image (2.); the private practitioner image (3.); and the professional snob syndrome (5.).

is a paradigmatic example of 'the football league model'.[44] They play the same game in different divisions of a single league. In England, the centralization of higher education and the introduction of various kinds of external quality assurance mechanisms are pushing universities in a similar direction.[45]

When, in 1993, the Lord Chancellor's Advisory Committee began the first comprehensive review of legal education since 1971, it fairly quickly dismissed a number of possibilities as impracticable, without exploring their desirability in any detail. At the top end of the scale, the clinical medical school model (or, as a variant, Jerome Frank's clinical lawyer school), the postgraduate law school (as in the United States), and the five-year undergraduate school were not considered to be feasible options in a system heavily dependent on public funding. At the other end, there was no suggestion that serious consideration should be given to moving towards the mass open entry model, as in some Continental European and Latin American countries; nor are we are likely to adopt the populist Jacksonian model or to abolish all law schools as happened in China during the Cultural Revolution. None of these seem to be serious options in the foreseeable future.

Once established, a given structure is often difficult to break. However, there is more room for manoeuvre than many discussions of policy allow. The First Report by ACLEC emphasized the need to break down artificial barriers between different stages of professional formation and it gave strong support to continued pluralism in respect of types of programme and different pathways to professional qualification.[46] However, the Committee's terms of reference restrict it to concentrating on the provision of legal services and professional formation. Law schools have a wider and more flexible remit. Despite the constraints, financial and otherwise, three main strategic possibilities seem to be open for law schools in England and Wales in the coming years.

1. They can continue to conform largely to the academic version of the primary school model, concentrating on introductory legal education at undergraduate and other levels. They can serve undergraduates, and possibly a variety of other constituencies, but mainly at primary level—with

---

[44] e.g., the controversial annual ratings of law schools by *US NEWS AND WORLD REPORT* attract a lot of publicity and a lot of criticism, perhaps because they are taken seriously by applicants and others. On the fate of the Antioch Law School which tried to break out of the mould, see above n. 35.

[45] One mitigating feature of the system of 'quality assurance' introduced under the Further and Higher Education Act, 1992 is that students' learning experiences are evaluated within the framework of a programme's stated aims and the overall mission of each institution. This allows for a degree of pluralism, but can still inhibit innovation. On the application of this to law see, HEFCE, Subject Overview Report QO 1/94, *Quality Assessment for Law* 1993–94 (discussed in the ACLEC *First Report*, op. cit., Ch. 7).

[46] The *First Report* argues for 'our preferred model of integrated education and training, with multiple entry and exit points for those who will provide different types of legal services'. (Introd. 14 and Ch. 2.)

programmes such as postgraduate studies, advanced multi-disciplinary work, specialist education and training, judicial studies, and training trainers, treated as occasional, extramural or marginal.

2. They could move in the direction of becoming service institutions for the profession, as in the United States, but be more involved in post-degree vocational training at all stages, including continuing, advanced, and specialist training; or

3. they can move clearly in the direction of the ILC model, diversifying outwards as well as upwards, extending both their clientele and the levels of study, with some division of function between institutions.

In *Blackstone's Tower* I argued that it is in the interests not only of law schools, but also of the legal profession and society at large that something like the third option should be embraced as the model for our system as a whole.[47] In the English context, where law schools are agreeably small by international standards, few law schools could take on such a wide range of functions on their own, but there is no reason why collectively university law schools could not be at the hub of a healthy and diverse national system of legal studies. I argued that in recent years we have moved haltingly in this direction, but our practice outstrips our self-image and there is a danger that an opportunity may be missed unless there is a conscious effort to move quite boldly in this direction.

On recent visits to the United States I have been forcibly reminded of the power of entrenched assumptions about the functions and clientele of law schools. Because they focus very largely on single-subject first degree courses in law, American law schools are just as much primary schools as any other institutions in the common law world. To an extraordinary extent, postgraduate studies, specialization, advanced research, and even continuing legal education are marginalized or ignored. Even when such programmes exist, they are not perceived, from within or without, to be part of the core of the institution. In respect of statistics, prestige, and policy-making the primary school image dominates: typically, 'students' refers to JD candidates and 'legal education' to JD (i.e. first degree) programmes only. The much-debated league table ratings of *US News and World Report* are based on Law School Admission Test (LSAT) scores, 'student selectivity rank', and placement success only in relation to first degree programmes. When undergraduate applications fall, talk of 'downsizing' similarly refers to numbers of first degree students. In my experience little or no serious consideration is given to alternative markets for law school educational services. American law schools are the envy of the world, especially as to what money can buy in respect of libraries, staff, and support services. Yet the entrenched self-image of being a primary school for the legal profession and not much else creates intellectual inhibitions which are all the more powerful for being buried. The prototypical American law school compares unfavourably

[47] *BT*, at 197–8.

with their medical schools and science faculties in respect of specialist training, postgraduate research, clinical teaching, and certain kinds of pure and applied research at the frontiers of knowledge. Tensions between the scholarly aspirations of the faculty and the demands of practice-oriented first degree students are endemic. Ironically, it is likely to be much easier for some poor relations to move briskly in the direction of the ILC model than our richer American cousins.

The case for embracing this model in the English context can be restated as follows:[48]

1. It is in the interests of students and individual law teachers that law schools should broaden their range. In many respects English university law schools have outgrown the three-year undergraduate law degree at 18 plus. From the point of view of undergraduates, breaking free from the vocational culture of the old 'academic stage' has two great advantages: first, it opens the way for greater choice both within and between law degrees which are less constrained by outdated notions of a core curriculum; and, secondly, it allows the great majority of law students to postpone important career decisions until they àre more mature and better informed—a theme given great emphasis in the ACLEC Report. The ILC model also opens up access to legal education to a much wider range of clients.

   From the point of view of academic lawyers, to focus mainly on primary legal education within a narrowly-oriented vocational culture constrains their professional activities in respect of both reach and depth. The undergraduate curriculum is overloaded, undergraduate options have increasingly been squeezed, and vast tracts of law are conspicuously under-researched. Law teachers need more varied outlets in order to flourish.

2. At a mundane level, law schools need to diversify in order to ensure a stable economic base in a context in which opportunities to enter private practice, or even to qualify, appear to have contracted, while other needs for legal education have begun to surface. Given the wide range of possibilities, individual law schools can increase their control over their own destiny by diversification. They can to some extent choose where to concentrate their efforts, but they will have to be realistic about demand.

3. It is in the interests of the legal profession that law schools should diversify in this way. At the lowest level it will relieve the so-called problem of 'oversupply' of law graduates: if undergraduate law degrees are and are perceived to be genuinely liberal and academic in the best sense, this would maintain a broad pool of talent from which to select, would lessen pressures to make premature career choices, and it would help to reduce the expectation that a law degree is an automatic passport to practice. In the context of the United Kingdom, university law schools can best maintain demand for undergraduate places, if undergraduate legal education is

---

[48] This is an abbreviated version of the argument advanced in the Epilogue of *BT* at 196–9.

designed, delivered, and sold as being genuinely multifunctional and as vocationally relevant for many other occupations as most degrees in the Arts and Humanities. This will only happen if law school culture changes and if undergraduate legal education is both organized and presented as being as interesting and as good a vehicle for general education as philosophy, history, sociology, politics or English. 'The case for law' has to be made persuasively to the relevant constituencies, schools, parents, and employers as well as potential applicants.[49] To get the message across and to make it credible requires the co-operation of the legal profession and other employers and it is in their long-term interest to co-operate in this way.[50]

There are further good reasons why it is in the interests of the practising profession that law schools and law teachers should be professionally involved in teaching and writing about much more than the core subjects, a few undergraduate options, and elementary skills. It is in the interests of the profession that academics should have the opportunity to explore and develop new fields, and to take a longer-term, more detached, and more critical view of trends and developments than front-line practice normally allows. It is also in the long-term interest of the legal profession that law schools should maintain a balance between fundamental and applied research.

4. Finally, it is in the social interest that our law schools should be involved in the systematic advancement and dissemination of learning about all aspects of law from a variety of perspectives, not just in those aspects that relate to the knowledge and skills of private practitioners of law. It should be a truism that law and law-in-action are much broader than lawyers' law and lawyers' action.[51] Law schools on their own cannot hope to meet all of society's needs for legal education and legal understandings—but they can and should be a focal point of such activities. It is almost certainly in the public interest that the law school enterprise should be quite large and diverse rather than being confined to a small élite that focuses mainly on the upper reaches of the legal system and primary training for private practice. Academic lawyers are much more likely to make useful contributions to legal practice and legal development, as well as to more general understandings, if their routine professional activities are not confined to primary education and deal with all aspects of law from a variety of perspectives. In an increasingly complex and interdependent world, the

---

[49] *BT* 58–61.

[50] See above, Ch. 14. One inhibiting factor has been a fear on the part of practitioners, especially the Bar, that in order to recruit 'the best and the brightest' it is necessary to catch them young. This places a remarkable faith in the predictive value of academic tests at 18 and 21 and an even more remarkable discounting of the value of maturity and informed career choices. I have long suspected that the costs of cradle-snatching by the legal profession greatly outweigh the benefits, except in respect of short-term recruitment of academically bright helots.

[51] This theme is developed in *BT*, Ch. 1.

problems of interpreting the objects of one's studies tend to increase. They should aspire to create a culture that facilitates the blowing of minds. Law is a grown-up subject and law schools need to be given the space to develop into broad-ranging mature institutions concentrating on what they are meant to be good at—the intellectual advancement, stimulation, and dissemination of learning about law.

16

*Pericles Regained?**

In 1981 Professor Anthony Kronman, who was later to become Dean of the Yale Law School, addressed the student editors of the *Yale Law Journal* about the difference between scholarship and advocacy. Scholarship aims at the truth, he said, but advocacy is only interested in persuasion. Accordingly, 'scholarship is a better and higher calling than the advocate's [which] . . . corrupts the soul by encouraging a studied indifference to truth'.[1] Afterwards, two colleagues asked Kronman how he could continue training students for a practice which he despised. Did not legal practice require 'a practical wisdom as honorable as the scholar's love of truth but very different from it'?[2]

Disturbed by the question, Kronman has returned to it repeatedly in his published writings, culminating in a substantial book entitled *The Lost Lawyer*. There he explores in depth the idea of practical wisdom as the central quality of the ideal of 'the lawyer-statesman'. He concludes that judges, private practitioners, and law teachers in their capacity as trainers of lawyers can and should all aspire to this ideal. Hence it is possible to 'live greatly in the law'.[3] However, between 1960 and 1990 three main factors have combined to undermine the ideal and make its realization very unlikely. These are the growth and commercialization of corporate legal practice, modern trends in legal thought, and the bureaucratization of the courts in response to their increased case-load. All are antithetical to the lawyer-statesman ideal. As a result, there is a crisis of identity for all those who have chosen a life in the law. Kronman's analysis is optimistic and idealistic in respect of the possibility of living honourably in the law, but pessimistic about its feasibility under present conditions in the United States.

Nearly thirty years ago, in 'Pericles and the Plumber' I argued that most discussions of 'lawyer education' were based on two contrasting images of the end-product of the process of professional formation: the image of Pericles (the enlightened policy-maker, the lawgiver, the wise judge) and the image of a

---

* This essay, which has not been published before, was stimulated by a reading seminar at Boston College in the Spring of 1995 during which several works dealing with the state of the legal professions and law schools in the US and the UK were discussed. I learned a great deal from the colleagues who participated in these discussions in Newton, but the perspective and views expressed here are my own.

[1] A. Kronman, *The Lost Lawyer* (Cambridge, Ma., 1993) (hereafter *LL*), Preface at 7; the central thesis of the book is anticipated in the article 'Living in the Law', 54 *U of Chicago L Rev.* 835 (1987) (hereafter, *Chi.*), which still repays study. [2] *LL*, Preface.

[3] O. W. Holmes Jr., 'The Profession of the Law' (1886), *Occasional Speeches*, (Cambridge, Ma., 1962) at 29.

plumber, a no-nonsense, competent technician concerned with socially useful, but essentially mundane tasks.[4] The gist of my argument was that neither image was appropriate as a model for lawyer education, largely because they were both too simple: the image of the lawyer as Pericles was too elevated and the image of the plumber was too mundane. Furthermore legal practice is too complex and too varied to be reducible to a single model for intending lawyers. That lecture has sometimes been misinterpreted as suggesting that these are competing images between which any programme of preparation for practice must choose; or, more subtly, that every lawyer should seek to combine the technical competence of a plumber with the breadth of vision and high ideals of a Pericles. While the second interpretation was nearer to the mark, it ignores the point that I was questioning reductionist models of 'the lawyer'.

Since 'Pericles and the Plumber' was first published two trends have reinforced the thesis: first, sociological studies of the legal profession have documented how far legal professions in the modern world are so stratified, hierarchical, and fragmented that concepts like 'the lawyer' or 'the legal profession' are little more than fictions.[5] Secondly, legal practice has further diversified in increasingly complex ways so that scepticism of generalizations or of the search for a core of 'lawyering' is more than ever justified. Accordingly it is interesting to examine the recent resurgence of attempts to set up models of 'the good lawyer' and 'fundamental lawyering skills' by people who are well aware of these diversifications.

The Lost Lawyer is only one among many such attempts. These are generally more sophisticated and complex than the old question-begging formulations of the objectives of university legal education in terms of 'knowing the law' or 'thinking like a lawyer'. For example, in the United States the ABA's MacCrate Report, while acknowledging the pluralism of practice, asserts at the outset that the legal profession 'is more organized and unified as a profession than at any time in its history' and that 'the law has remained a single profession identified with a perceived common body of learning, skills and values'.[6] The report is built around a statement of 'fundamental lawyering skills and values', which places 'problem-solving' at the head of its list of skills, although it does not go as far as subsuming all skills under that head. In England, the Lord Chancellor's Advisory Committee on Legal Education and Conduct (ACLEC), in formulating general aims for a common system of basic legal education and training for barristers and solicitors, rather more tentatively formulated five general 'outcomes' that legal education and training should aim to achieve: intellectual integrity and independence of mind; core knowledge; contextual knowledge;

---

[4] Above Ch. 3.

[5] The literature is usefully surveyed in Roger Cotterrell, *Sociology of Law: An Introduction* (London, 2nd edn., 1992) Ch. 6.

[6] *Legal Education and Professional Development*, Report of the ABA Task Force on Law Schools and the Profession (Chicago, 1992) (The MacCrate Report) at 11.

legal values; and professional skills.[7] ACLEC was struggling with the problem of retaining some shared objectives in a context in which there was criticism of the idea of 'core subjects' at the academic stage and resistance to common training from those who opposed fusion of the 'two branches' of the legal profession. They were themselves supporting a policy of promoting diversity of background in recruitment of intending lawyers. While the MacCrate Report flirted with the idea of lawyers as problem solvers, ACLEC seems to have been more influenced by the idea of 'humane professionalism' that explicitly underpinned the approach of the Canadian report on *Law and Learning* in 1983.[8] Another model that has become influential in legal educational circles is Donald Schon's 'reflective practitioner', who is equipped to move from 'the high ground' of technical competence into 'the swamp' of non-routine, important problems which arise in situations of uncertainty.[9] Schon's ideas are the starting-point for the first text which introduces issues of 'professional responsibility' to English undergraduates.[10] They also influenced the most substantial manual for law teachers yet published, *The Quiet (R)evolution*, which developed out of law teaching clinics in Australia.[11]

In a similar vein, Mary Ann Glendon of Harvard sets out a model of 'the art of lawyering' that emphasizes dispute prevention and dispute settlement as well as litigation.[12] She lists nine qualities of the lawyer as 'peacemaker' that can provide a basis for professional pride: '*The Eye for the Issue . . . The Feel for the Common Ground . . . The Eye to the Future . . . Mastery of the Apparatus . . . Legal Architecture* (constructing institutional structures and frameworks) . . . *Procedure*.[13] . . . *Problem Solving . . . Strong Tolerance* (a combination of empathy and detachment) and *Incremental Change*'.[14] Glendon is careful not to make strong claims for the uniqueness of this interesting list. She does not suggest that every lawyer has or should have all of these characteristics, but rather that the legal profession comprises a pool of talent in which these qualities abound:

---

[7] ACLEC, *First Report on Legal Education and Training*, (London, 1996) para. 2.4.

[8] *Law and Learning*: Report to the Social Sciences and Humanities Research Council of Canada (The Arthurs Report, Ottawa, 1983).

[9] Schon rather overstates the case when he says: 'The practitioner must choose. Shall he remain on the high ground where he can solve relatively unimportant problems according to prevailing standards of rigor, or shall he descend to the swamp of important problems and non-rigorous inquiry?' Donald Schon, *Educating the Reflective Practitioner*, (San Fransisco, 1987) 4.

[10] C. Maugham and J. Webb, *Lawyering Skills and the Legal Process* (London, 1995).

[11] M. Le Brun and R. Johnstone, *The Quiet (R)evolution: Improving Student Learning in Law* (North Ryde, NSW, 1994).

[12] Mary Ann Glendon, *A Nation Under Lawyers: How the Crisis in the Legal Professon Is Transforming American Society* (New York, 1994) (hereafter *NUL*) at 102. This book is a wide-ranging polemic by a leading Catholic member of the new communitarian movement. It is less closely argued and focused than *LL*. I am here only concerned with those aspects of the book that bear on Kronman's thesis. For a cautionary review, see Sanford Levinson, 45 *Jo. Legal Education* 143 (1995) at 102.

[13] 'Procedure pervades the lawyer's world. Love of procedure makes the diverse members of the legal profession cousins, if not siblings, under the skin.' (*NUL* 105.)   [14] Id., 102–8.

Yet competent accomplishment of the everyday task of lawyers deserves to be celebrated in our complex, pluralistic nation oriented to the rule of law, representative government, and fundamental freedoms. Lawyers cannot claim to have a monopoly on any of [these] qualities, but no other occupational group in American society displays the ensemble in the same degree.[15]

Thus recent literature presents us with several new aspirational models of 'the lawyer' as problem solver, reflective practitioner, humane professional, peace-maker, and statesman. Although they involve differences of detail and emphasis they clearly share some important family resemblances. All, for example, stress adaptability, problem-solving skills, integrity or trustworthiness, and technical competence. Though generally 'thicker' in conception, they are clearly closely related to earlier images, such as Lasswell and McDougal's 'supreme policy maker'[16] and Karl Llewellyn's 'craftsman'.[17] Indeed, Kronman and Glendon explicitly claim to build on and develop Llewellyn's ideas. Yet are these not just more sophisticated forms of reductionism and élitism designed to serve as a legitimating ideology for the independence, monopoly, and privileges of what is no longer a single profession?

I shall argue first, that legitimating professional privilege is only one of a number of different, though related, concerns underlying this proliferation of models; second, that the central ideas in these images fit some concerns better than others; and, third, that the search for a 'core' that differentiates legal prac-tice or the discipline of law from other professions and fields of study is a chimera. Rather, I shall suggest, the most worthwhile ideas in these images or models emphasize the continuities rather than differences between lawyers and other professionals and between the study of law and other disciplines. How-ever, it is first necessary to look in more detail at the main ideas underlying these images of 'the lawyer'. I shall focus on Kronman's 'lawyer-statesman' because it looks remarkably like a resurrection of the image of 'the lawyer' as Pericles and because it is at once the most philosophically sophisticated example of recent reactions to an alleged crisis of identity in the legal profession and yet, at first sight, it seems vulnerable to several formidable lines of criticism. How-ever, I shall suggest that the concept of 'practical wisdom' as elaborated in *The Lost Lawyer* is worth rescuing and can be reframed in a way that avoids the pitfalls of reductionism.

THE CONTEXT

From Plato's *Gorgias* through Jack Cade and Jeremy Bentham to contemporary lawyer jokes there runs a nearly universal theme: legal practice is often considered to be ignoble; at best it is morally ambiguous. The reasons for condemnation are

---

[15] Id., 102.   [16] See above, Ch. 4, at 77.   [17] See above, Ch. 10.

various, but they point to a single conclusion, summed up in a strong form in Jeremy Bentham's dictum: 'The interests of the legal profession are in all respects opposed to those of the community'.[18]

The tradition of introspection and self-castigation is not new;[19] nor is it confined to the United States. But it seems to be more sustained, more open, and more seriously discussed in a society in which the legal profession has been traditionally perceived as being the American counterpart of an aristocracy.[20] There is a continuous tradition of linking these themes.[21] An outside observer may be equally struck by the persistence of the concerns, the sophistication of the debates, and the difficulty of disentangling genuine ethical questions from worries about public image and a search for a legitimating ideology.

The Lost Lawyer shares some of the characteristics of this genre: it laments the commercialization of legal practice; it harks back nostalgically to earlier times when the ideal of the lawyer-statesman was accepted at least as an aspiration, a claim that is disputed by some historians;[22] it blames jurisprudential movements, especially critical legal studies and law and economics, for undermining the ideal; and it makes some standard, and in my view, dubious assumptions about the nature and length of the process of professional formation and the role of law schools within that process. It is, however, distinctive in three important respects: first, it advances an elaborate philosophical interpretation of 'practical wisdom' as a civic virtue; secondly, it links the ethos of judges, practitioners, and academic lawyers to this single ideal; and, thirdly, it focuses on the question of the individual who is contemplating a life in the law: can I live honourably in the law? This is to do with professional pride, job satisfaction, and personal fulfilment. Kronman's topic is individual morality.

Kronman's arguments in support of his thesis are wide-ranging and intricate. I am generally more attracted by his conclusions than his premises. If this was a book review,[23] I would be inclined to challenge the plausibility of his history,[24]

---

[18] J. Bentham, iv *Works* 95. In this passage Bentham qualifies the statement with the phrase 'with very inconsiderable exceptions'. See further, *TEBW*, 75 ff.

[19] e.g., the commercialization of the American bar has been a recurrent theme of public comment for over a century. Typically the corporate law firm is singled out for attack and nostalgic contrasts are made with some earlier Golden Age with indeterminate or movable dates.

[20] The *locus classicus* is Alexis de Tocqueville, *Democracy in America* (G. Lawrence trs., New York, 1969) at 268.   [21] See above Ch. 10.

[22] Kronman borrowed the term 'the lawyer-statesman' from an address by Chief Justice Rehnquist in which he sketched pen portraits of outstanding wise and public-spirited lawyers of the past who had served as role models for their contemporaries. William H. Rehnquist, 'The Lawyer-Statesman in American History', 9 *Harvard Jo. of Law and Public Policy* 537 (1986); *LL* 11–13.

[23] I have drawn on the following from among the many reviews: James M. Altman, 'Modern Litigators and Lawyer-statesmen', 103 *Yale L Jo.* 1031 (1994); Mark Aaronson, 'Dark Night of the Soul', 45 *Hastings L Jo.* 1379 (1994); Neil Duxbury,'History as Hyperbole', 15 *Oxford Jo. Leg. Stud.* 477 (1995); Marshall B. Kapp, (1994) *Jo. of Psychiatry and Law* 287; J. H. Schlegel, review in *Law and History* (forthcoming, 1995); David B. Wilkins, 108 *Harv. L Rev.* 458 (1994).

[24] Several commentators, including Altman, Duxbury, and Schlegel, (op. cit.) have questioned Kronman's interpretation of American legal history.

some details of his philosophy,[25] and his claim to be doing sociology.[26] We also have quite different views about the desirability of pluralism and diversity in legal theory and legal education. Here, however, I wish to concentrate on the concept of 'the lawyer-statesman' and to make the case for taking its central ideas seriously.

THE LAWYER-STATESMAN AS AN IDEAL

Kronman's concept of the lawyer-statesman is prescriptive rather than descriptive. He is careful to distinguish between what he considers to be desirable in general (optimistic) and his assessment of its feasibility in American legal practice, especially corporate practice, in the 1990s (pessimistic). The ideal is explicitly old-fashioned and high-minded.[27]

'[T]he outstanding lawyer—the one who serves as a model for the rest—is not simply an accomplished technician, but a person of prudence or practical wisdom as well.'[28] In addition, he is 'a devoted citizen'. 'He cares about the public good and is prepared to sacrifice his own well-being for it, unlike those who use the law merely to advance their private ends.'[29]

There are accordingly three conditions that must be satisfied to qualify as a lawyer-statesman: technical competence, civic mindedness, and practical wisdom.

Kronman has relatively little to say about technical competence and what he says is controversial. It is a necessary but not a sufficient condition for being a good professional; on its own it is merely instrumental and so does not provide a basis for a concept of professionalism based on character. The expertise of the competent lawyer does not lie so much in knowledge of legal rules or of a mixture of techniques from other fields, but rather in the art of handling cases:[30]

---

[25] Kronman's interpretation of Aristotle is controversial (see Altman (1994) op. cit., 1038–40). I deal briefly below with the problematic link between process and outcome in the idea of 'good judgment' and question Kronman's insistence that 'practical wisdom' is necessarily linked to a conception of the public interest. However, it is not possible here to do justice to these and many other issues at the level of philosophy.

[26] Although Kronman, who is an expert on Max Weber, claims that the the second half of the book is more 'sociological' (*LL*, 6), he ignores almost all of the modern sociological literature on the legal profession and on legal professions generally, except a few studies of corporate law firms. E.g., he assumes the unity of the legal profession, yet a central theme of sociological studies is that legal professions, especially in the US, tend to be highly stratified, hierarchical, and fragmented; they serve a very wide range of clients and interests in a variety of roles with strikingly different levels of reward; and, of course, access to legal services is unequally distributed. Kronman focuses almost entirely on the upper reaches of the legal system: large law firms, the senior judiciary, and élite law schools. His justification is that they are the main standard-bearers (273) and incubators of the lawyer-statesman ideal. On the significance of Kronman's élitist tendencies see below at 323–5; on his use of Max Weber, see below n. 81.

[27] *LL*, 3–4.   [28] Id., 2.   [29] Id., 14.   [30] Id., 359–62.

What lawyers are particularly trained to do and can generally do better than philosophers and economists is think about cases—imaginary future cases . . . but real past ones too. The ability to fashion hypothetical cases and emphatically to explore both real and invented ones is the lawyer's professional forte.[31]

This extraordinarily reductionist interpretation of technical competence provides the basis for a passionate defence of an idealized version of the Langdellian case method of instruction. This has, not surprisingly, attracted some sharp and, in my view, well-merited criticism.[32] Fortunately, Kronman's conception of technical competence is severable from the proposition that such competence is a necessary but not a sufficient condition of being a good lawyer. One can substitute a much richer conception of what that involves without undermining the basic argument.

Kronman interprets civic mindedness or public-spiritedness as an attitude which involves commitment to the general interest rather than to sectional interests; to the public good and to public service, rather than private gain. He follows modern thinkers, such as Alasdair MacIntyre and Stuart Hampshire, rather than Aristotle, in adopting a pluralist view that political ends are unavoidably varied and incommensurable.[33]

Kronman stresses three points: first, civic mindedness is a necessary condition of being a good professional and that 'any lawyer who lacks it altogether is to that extent a professional failure';[34] second, zealous commitment to public interest law is not the only ethically defensible conception of legal practice;[35] and third, public-spiritedness on its own does not provide an adequate basis for making legal practice intrinsically satisfying.[36]

The position of the judge is the clearest example of a legal role in which the incumbent is meant to act consistently in the service of the public good. But the roles of the practising lawyer—as counsellor, as representative, and even as advocate—and of the law teacher as mentor of intending practitioners, are satellites to those of the judge. This is not merely because it is often necessary to predict how a judge will react or decide, but also because they too are required to be judicious.[37] The co-operative negotiator, the wise counsellor, and the persuasive advocate all have to internalize as well as to anticipate a judge's sense of what is prudent and for the public good. This is a point to which I shall return.

Kronman devotes most attention to the elusive concept of 'practical wisdom'. The core of the book is an elaboration of an ideal based on an interpretation of Aristotle's notion of 'phronesis', glossed by neo-Kantian ideas and a touch of

---

[31] Id., 362.

[32] e.g., Wilkins (1994) and Aaronson (1994), op. cit. Ironically, Kronman's hero, Karl Llewellyn, was a leading proponent of the idea that case-law skills were only one part of technical competence.

[33] 'This attitude, of course, is compatible with great diversity of opinion regarding the nature of the public good itself, and to subscribe to it one need not subscribe to any particular political orthodoxy . . .' (*Chi.*, 842, cf. 838, A. MacIntyre *After Virtue: A Study in Moral Theory* (Notre Dame, 1981); Stuart Hampshire, *Morality and Conflict* (Cambridge, Ma., 1983)).

[34] Id., 842.   [35] *LL*, 154–62.   [36] Id., 365–6.   [37] Id., 150–1.

Freudian psychology.[38] The components of practical wisdom are 'traits of character, permanent dispositional attitudes rooted in the realm of feeling and desire'.[39] Such traits can only be developed by a combination of formal education and practical experience. Life in the law can provide an opportunity to develop such dispositional attitudes as well as an outlet for exercising them.

At the core of practical wisdom is the notion of good judgment. 'By judgment I mean the process of deliberating about and deciding personal, moral, and political problems.'[40] To say that a person has 'good judgment' refers to the deliberative procedures they employ (process) and the decisions or choices that they make (outcomes). Judgment involves more than intuition or deduction; it is a process of deliberation that combines empathy and detachment in a harmonious balance; it includes an ability to imagine a range of unknown possibilities and to reflect on them coolly and calmly. This process involves feeling as well as cognition.[41] It is most clearly exhibited in situations in which difficult choices have to be made between incommensurable values.[42] It cannot be subjected to formal rules or algorithmic formulae.

Good judgment involves deliberating well. Kronman treats the link between process and outcome to be like connoisseurship: the judgments of connoisseurs 'are assumed to be more reliable and on the whole to reflect a better and more informed view of the aims of the enterprise in question'.[43] He seems, however, to acknowledge that this connection is largely a matter of faith: 'I also believe ... that the choices of a person who deliberates well—with sympathy and detachment—are themselves likely to be sound or practically wise'.[44] This may be analogous to the academic's faith in reason; for example, the belief that it is worth teaching law students how to construct logical arguments, because cogency in argumentation is not solely a matter of employing irrational means of persuasion.[45]

Although it is elusive, Kronman's idea of practical wisdom is a significant improvement on previous attempts to express the model of 'the good lawyer'

---

[38] Kronman follows Hannah Arendt quite closely in his interpretation of Kant. Interestingly, he finds a close affinity between Llewellyn and Aristotle: 'Llewellyn's notions of craft, habit and experience mark an important similarity between his view of law and Aristotle's account of the nature and aims of political education generally.' (id., 217.)

[39] Chi., 841.   [40] Chi., 846.   [41] *LL*, 74–5.   [42] MacIntyre (1981), op. cit.

[43] *LL*, 139.   [44] Chi., 854, *LL*, 66–76.

[45] e.g., *ANALYSIS* at 117–31. Despite his elaborate and illuminating treatment, Kronman's concept of good judgment remains elusive. This particularly applies to the connection between process and outcome. There are many contexts in which one assesses 'good judgment' solely or mainly in terms of results: a sportsman who has 'a good eye' for a ball or a person who is recognized as a good judge of character (or racing form or the stock market) are assessed mainly by the regularity with which they prove in retrospect to have made correct predictions. (E.g., W. Galway, *The Inner Game of Tennis* (London, 1975).) The process by which they arrived at their conclusions may be attributable to intuition or innate talent or inside knowledge or informed experience or a combination of these. Conversely, there is no necessary or established connection between lengthy deliberative processes, which may approximate to Kronman's ideal, and decisions that in retrospect turn out to have been good or wise.

in terms of policy-making, craftsmanship or problem-solving. Lasswell and McDougal's 'policy making', Llewellyn's theory of crafts, and current notions of problem-solving can all be said to represent an advance on more formalistic images of 'the lawyer' whose expertise resides mainly in knowledge of legal rules or ability to interpret, apply or manipulate them. But none seems adequate as an account of why 'lawyerlike' characteristics are to be admired or emulated or why an individual can take pride in being 'a good lawyer'.

Kronman in his criticism of Lasswell and McDougal and of Llewellyn and in his own construction of practical wisdom provides one possible answer. He suggests that the Lasswell-McDougal Policy Science is too scientistic and cerebral. By advocating a science of values and facts which owes nothing to tradition and experience, they focus solely on rather abstract intellectual skills and leave out key elements of the idea of good judgment, especially as that is embodied in the common law tradition. Similar objections can be made to rationalistic conceptions of problem-solving, which are intellectual, instrumental, and often presented as being reducible to protocols, algorithms or other intellectual procedures capable of being codified and applied almost mechanically by humans or even by machines.[46]

Kronman acknowledges that Llewellyn caught some of the missing elements in his analysis of the common law tradition and craftsmanship. It accommodates tradition, learning by experience, and unconscious or semi-conscious ways of knowing. Llewellyn's 'horse sense' is informed intuition, based on experience, analysis, and discriminating judgment.[47] However, Llewellyn's model of the craftsman falls short of the lawyer-statesman ideal in two ways: first, he failed to give his 'sympathies a solid philosophical defense'.[48] And, second, it is incomplete because it fails to address 'the important but obscure connection between character and judgment'.[49] In Kronman's view judgment is not only a matter of intellectual skill; it involves a capacity to combine sympathy and detachment routinely as a matter of habits nurtured by both education and experience. More controversially, he links this capacity to a concern for and even 'a superior ability to discern the public good'.[50] Because practical wisdom is a trait of character, that is a habit of feeling as well as thinking, it is intimately linked with a person's sense of self and their idea of what is a meaningful and honourable way of life.[51]

---

[46] Not all treatments of problem-solving in legal contexts are overly rationalistic: compare, e.g., the relative emphasis on analytical and 'holistic' approaches in Margot Costanzo, *Problem Solving* (London, 1995), C. Maugham and J. Webb, *Lawyering and the Legal Process* (London, 1995), and John R. Hayes, *The Complete Problem-Solver* (Hillsdale, NJ, 1989). For a recent psychological interpretation, see Herbert Simon, 'Problem Solving and Education' (1980), reprinted in Simon *Models of Thought* Vol. II (New Haven, 1989).

[47] Kronman elegantly reformulates the notion of 'horse sense' as 'the ability of those who have mastered an activity to pursue it with subtlety and grace, employing powers of discernment irreducible to rules'. (*LL*, 349). Cf. Llewellyn's formulation in *The Common Law Tradition* (1960) at 298 and *Law in our Society* (reproduced in *KLRM* at 502–4).

[48] Id., 49.   [49] Id., 24.   [50] Id., 35, discussed below.   [51] Id., 74–6.

Mary Ann Glendon, a pupil and even more enthusiastic disciple of Llewellyn, also senses that something is missing from his idea of the craftsman. She approvęs a modified version of Karl Llewellyn's ideas of craft, practical wisdom, and love of the common law tradition as a worthy ideal for practising lawyers and judges and for those who train them. She endorses Kronman's notion of practical wisdom as a virtue of character as well as of intellect. However, she would gloss it with a more philosophically sophisticated account of practical reasoning.[52] This is attractive not least because it suggests a bridge between two intellectual traditions: analytically rigorous, but rather abstract accounts of reasoning about questions of law[53] and more 'realistic', but looser, treatments of practical skills. What Kronman and Glendon add in different ways is the idea that a coherent conception of 'good lawyering' needs to have solid philosophical underpinnings. In short, skills trainers, clinicians, and teachers of professional responsibility need to take philosophy seriously.

SOME CHALLENGES TO KRONMAN'S 'LAWYER-STATESMAN': PARTISANSHIP, PATERNALISM, AND ÉLITISM

Kronman presents technical competence, civic mindedness, and practical wisdom as three necessary ingredients of the lawyer-statesman ideal. But what exactly is the connection between them? For example, is technical competence separable from practical wisdom or is the former a necessary, but not a sufficient, condition of the latter? One can think of examples, in real life and in fiction, of a general practitioner of medicine or law who is consulted because of their reputation for sagacity or good sense, even though their technical knowledge is a little 'rusty'. Similar considerations may apply to some senior partners in law firms. But a client would normally be unwise to rely on such persons as *professionals* unless they have competent technical backup, for example, in the form of junior associates or specialists to whom referrals can be made, as in medicine. It seems that a good professional as an individual needs either to be technically competent or at least be able to recognize when expertise is needed and to have access to it.

More important, can 'practical wisdom' be applied to the furtherance of sectional or even wicked ends? For instance, is Don Corleone's loyal lawyer and counsellor, Thomas Hagen, in Mario Puzo's *The Godfather*, an exemplar of practical wisdom in the service of the Mafia?[54] His employer could rely on his

---

[52] Glendon (1994) 235–9. Glendon attributes the insight that practical reasoning is central to the common law tradition to Edgar Bodenheimer. This is somewhat eccentric, because the idea can be traced back through Blackstone and Coke and, in counterpoint to English positivism, to the idea of right reason or practicable reasonableness in the natural law tradition.

[53] And recently about other 'lawyers' reasonings' about questions of fact, negotiation, and problem-solving, see below Ch. 17.

[54] Mario Puzo, *The Godfather* (New York and London, 1969).

loyalty, his technical competence, and his sagacity in helping to solve his practical problems and further his interests. This suggests that 'practical wisdom' and 'civic mindedness' are conceptually separate.

For Kronman, practical wisdom and public-spiritedness are linked in that the lawyer-statesman uses his practical wisdom to discern where the public good lies and to offer advice and guidance to clients about their goals as well as the means of achieving them.[55] As we have seen, the office of the judge is presented as the clearest example of a situation in which practical wisdom and public-spiritedness are expected to be combined, but the roles of practitioners and law teachers are to be viewed as satellites to those of the judge. This is not merely because it is often necessary to predict how a judge will react or decide, but also because they too are required to be 'judicious'.[56]

This is prima facie unconvincing. In politics a leader who rises above sectional interests to produce a new vision or way forward that transcends past divisions is recognized as a 'statesman'. And there are occasions when lawyers in their role as professionals are called on to be statesmanlike in this way. But the standard view of the role of the private practitioner, especially in the Anglo-American system, is to represent the interests of particular clients in a partisan fashion solely within the constraints of legality and canons of professional ethics.[57] Good judgment may be needed to understand and to further those interests even if they are in conflict with other interests or others' conceptions of the public good. The standard justification of the partisan approach to advocacy is that the ideology of the adversary system postulates that it is in the public interest that all legal persons should be properly represented.[58]

Kronman directly confronts the notion of the advocate, and more generally the lawyer, as 'hired gun' and argues that a lawyer's role is to further the interests of clients only within the parameters of the public interest, because lawyers and judges are involved in a common practice. This idea of the lawyer as 'statesman' whose role is to harmonize the interests of clients with the public good challenges the standard view, accepted by most practising lawyers. This is so, even in respect of the narrow range of situations where the client requires advice on ends as well as means or where the lawyer is seeking to anticipate how a court will react in the context of litigation.[59] He argues strongly that commitment to the public good is an essential ingredient of professional integrity and self-esteem. This is, of course, one of the most contested areas of professional ethics, especially in law, but Kronman's emphatic subordination of partisanship to the public interest is severable from his central thesis. For here again it is possible to separate his particular conception of 'civic mindedness' from the general idea that notions of individual ethics and of the public interest

---

[55] *LL*, 14–5.   [56] Id. 150–1.   [57] e.g., Altman (1994) at 1031 ff.

[58] Stephan Landsman, *The Adversary System: A Description and Defense* (Washington, 1984).

[59] For a cogent criticism of Kronman's judge-centredness and his simplistic conception of litigation see Altman (1994) op. cit.

are central to the ideal of 'professionalism'. One can agree that standard conceptions of 'professionalism' include notions of integrity, honesty, and 'service',
yet hold different views of professional duty when there is a potential conflict
between clients' interests and a more general public interest.

Even if we accept that lawyers often have the opportunity to shape their
clients' definition of ends as well as means, good judgment rests in reconciling
the clients' choice of *their* objectives with a judicious assessment of where their
best interests lie. The ends and means are the clients' not the lawyer's and how
far the clients' interests should be harmonized with the public good is in the
clients' control. In advocacy and in representing and advising corporate or other
clients, the paternalistic role of lawyers is often quite limited in practice. The
orthodox ideology prescribes that it is the client who has the final decision on
objectives—with or without advice—and it is wrong for the lawyer to substitute
his or her own judgment about objectives for those of the client.[60] Where the
client's interests or objectives are clearly pitted against the public interest, as in
the example of a Mafia counsellor, good judgment and practical wisdom may
still be expected of the lawyer in furthering the interests of the client.

On this view, Kronman's idea of civic mindedness looks like old-fashioned
paternalism. A striking example of this criticism is provided by a mental health
specialist, who is sympathetic to the idea of 'horse sense', but who states:

> Thus proponents of modern mental health advocacy would probably reject the élitist,
> anti-egalitarian, almost self-righteous tone of Kronman's extended sermon. For those
> who have shaped and are perpetuating the presently dominant autonomy/advocacy-based
> model of mental health law, a call for independent deliberation and prudential wisdom
> on the part of civic-minded attorneys smacks dangerously of re-emerging paternalism,
> overreaching and even conflict of interest—factors overcome only lately.[61]

Kronman's interpretation of civic mindedness is controversial, but it represents
one recognizable position on a spectrum of views about professional ethics. *The
Lost Lawyer* at first sight also seems vulnerable to charges of élitism. Kronman
writes in a high-minded way from the vantage point of the Yale Law School;
he focuses almost entirely on corporate practice, appellate courts, reported decisions on questions of law, and élite law schools. He calls practical wisdom 'an
embarrassed virtue', because in Aristotle's version it is doubly non-egalitarian:
first, for Aristotle human beings by nature are not equally fit for participation in

---

[60] Cf. 'the client-centred model' adopted by Le Brun and Johnstone: 'The model of lawyer which
we advocate places the client at the centre of a process in which the client and lawyer actively
participate in finding a solution which is acceptable to the client.' (op. cit., 41.) They contrast this
with 'the more traditional model in which the lawyer assumes responsibility and exercises predominant control and direction over the client's problems while the client remains a "passive" recipient
of the lawyer's service' (ibid.). Although Le Brun and Johnstone emphasize affective as well as
cognitive faculties and cite Kronman with approval, it seems that they fall within 'the narrow'
partisan view that Kronman attacks at length (see, however, 42–3, which suggests some ambivalence
about the tension between loyalty to clients and other commitments).

[61] Review by Kapp (1994) op. cit., at 290.

public life and, second, individuals have a differential talent for practical wisdom. Kronman would reject the inegalitarian premise in respect of eligibility, but would hold on to the idea that practical wisdom is a virtue of character that is not equally distributed. By associating the idea of practical wisdom with 'statesmanship' he invites scepticism about its relevance or applicability to those in the middle or lower reaches of a system whether they be sole practitioners, public defenders, prosecutors, middle level associates, trial judges or law teachers in middle or lower ranking law schools.

Some of the élitism is not necessary. For example, the term 'lawyer-statesman' gives an unnecessarily elevated impression as a label for the idea of practical wisdom. A similar semantic inflation was one factor in the resistance to Lasswell and McDougal's 'Law, Science and Policy'. They proclaimed that 'the lawyer is today, even when not himself a "maker of policy", the one indispensable adviser of every responsible policy-maker of our society'.[62] This conjured up images of Presidential Advisers, high level Washington lawyers, Supreme Court Justices, and other influential public figures such as Henry Stimson, Dean Acheson, John McCloy or, later, Archibald Cox.[63] But the LSP concept of policy-making was much more mundane and far-reaching: it explicitly referred to any transaction or decision involving important choices about the distribution of values, including the purchase of a house, a routine divorce or administering a trust or estate.[64] Kronman, too, uses quite homely examples: 'Should I divorce? Should my spouse and I have a child? Should I sacrifice my professional career to stay home with the children?'[65] It is unnecessarily inflationary to use words like 'statesman' in talking of such problems.

Karl Llewellyn avoided such aggrandizement by using the less pretentious, but quaintly old-fashioned, idea of 'the craftsman'. He repeatedly stressed that he was concerned not just with the upper reaches of the legal system, but with 'the plain and ordinary citizen of the craft'.[66] He emphasized minimum competence and decency for all, and excellence as an aspiration even for the many.[67]

---

[62] See Ch. 4 above at 77.

[63] *LL*, 11. Commentators have pointed out that most of Kronman's heroes or role models made their reputations in public affairs rather than in their capacity as lawyers; furthermore, some of them, such as John McCloy, are perceived by many as villains rather than as heroes. One may ask whether controversial leaders such as Dulles, McNamara, and Kissinger had 'practical wisdom' in Kronman's sense?

[64] Lasswell and McDougal (1943) op. cit. at 209. In this passage the authors include trade unionists, secretaries of trade or business associations, 'or even the humble entrepreneur or professional man' as policy-makers (id., 208–9).   [65] *LL*, 65.

[66] *The Common Law Tradition*, op. cit., 214, cited by Kronman at *LL*, 214, but not emphasized by him.

[67] Kronman misses two important points in his interpretation of Llewellyn and Lasswell and McDougal: first, in 1943 and 1944 they developed the idea that professional formation should be consciously based on a job analysis of lawyers' operations, what lawyers in fact do. This subsequently became the foundation of the modern skills movement, see above Ch. 10. Secondly, Llewellyn's 'theory of crafts' was developed as a part of his general sociology of law. Kronman conflates the idea of 'law jobs' (the tasks that have to be done in any group somehow, and certainly

Recently another less pretentious term has become fashionable—'problem-solving'. Within the skills movement this has sometimes been elevated to the status of the most important skill for lawyers or the master-skill under which all others can be subsumed.[68] The term is sufficiently broad to escape charges of élitism, but surely many problems require 'practical wisdom' for their solution.

THE EDUCATIONAL CONTINUUM AND THE ROLE
OF LAW SCHOOLS

Kronman places the main responsibility for the decline of the lawyer-statesman ideal on the law schools. He follows American convention in assuming 'the professional school model' and in placing a great faith in the power of formal education. Yet there seems to be a distinct tension between the concept of 'practical wisdom' which requires maturation through experience over a long period of time and the idea that fostering 'the lawyer-statesman ideal' is mainly the responsibility of formal education. It is one thing to assume that the main objective of a law degree is preparation for the private practice of law; it is quite another to imply that the three years in law school are the main or only part of professional formation. Kronman deplores the increasing influence of law clerks just because of their immaturity and lack of judgment.[69] It is difficult to see how law schools, especially on the primary model, can be given the main responsibility for developing the central qualities of practical wisdom that are at the core of Kronman's ideal; just as it is difficult to see how full-time career scholar-teachers of law in such institutions can be expected to be the main mentors and role models for developing practical wisdom over a ten-year time frame.[70]

It seems to me that there are three important elements missing from the kind of orthodox analysis that Kronman adopts which may have skewed his conclusions: first, the distinction between formal legal education and training leading up to some point of initial certification, such as admission to the Bar, and the longer process of professional formation resulting in a lawyer who is considered to be 'fully fledged'; second, the distinction between making a career in corporate legal practice in one or more large firms and spending a few years there at the start of one's career; and, third, the distinction between the process of professional formation and the role of law schools as institutions.[71]

When does legal education begin? I tell my first year students in London that their legal education began at birth and that they all know more about law and have had more firsthand practical experience of it than they may realize.[72] In

not only by lawyers) and 'lawyer jobs' (*LL* at 121). This paves the way for his over-simple account of the legal profession and legal practice.

[68] Stephen Nathanson, 'Problem Solving in Professional Legal Education', 7 *Jo. Professional Legal Educ.* 121 (1979); cf. *BT*, 168–71.
[69] *LL*, 347.   [70] See Le Brun and Johnstone, op. cit., 110–118.
[71] See Ch. 15, above.   [72] *BT*, Ch. 1.

England, as in most of the rest of Europe, students begin their formal legal education at 18 plus; *a fortiori*, entrants to American law schools should have had a broader general education and more legal and life experience by 22 plus, quite apart from exposure to pre-law programmes, the LSAT, and law firms or other legal institutions. Yet Kronman repeats the dubious proposition that '[a] lawyer's professional life begins the day that he or she starts law school'.[73]

Similarly, it is a truism that the process of professional formation extends far beyond law school and initial certification as a licensed practitioner. In England the structure of formal legal education and training is highly differentiated: for example, for solicitors the normal route is three years academic study; one year full-time vocational training; two years as a trainee under contract (formerly articles) before qualification; followed by a period of restricted practice and some compulsory continuing legal education, which is steadily developing into a substantial requirement. Thus the total period of formal training pre-qualification/certification is six years, but few would claim to be 'fully fledged' the moment they qualify. In Continental Europe the normal pattern is a longer undergraduate degree at 18 plus, followed by a further period of pre-qualification training for the judiciary, government lawyers, and various kinds of private practitioners. Thus in Europe the process of professional formation is generally conceived to be at least seven to ten years after 18.

It would be an extreme kind of formalism to suggest that the process of professional formation in the United States is normally shorter than in the European Union. The purely formal requirements—a first degree, three years at law school, bar examinations—ensure that Americans cannot and do not qualify at an earlier age than lawyers in Europe; indeed, the normal age for formal admission is probably later than in most other countries. More important, however, is what happens in the years after initial certification. The various American jurisdictions have almost no formal requirements for apprenticeship or other restrictions on setting up on one's own ('hanging out a shingle'). This may have removed a significant brake on expansion of the legal profession,[74] but the number of lawyers who start off on their own is small and few would hold them out as role models for others.[75] In fact there is in the United States an extensive and varied *de facto* system of apprenticeship and supervised experience which is as significant as the more institutionalized forms of *stages*, training contracts, and apprenticeship that exists in most Western countries.[76] Parts of this may be facilitated,

---

[73] *LL*, 109.   [74] See Ch. 13, above.

[75] J. Carlin, *Lawyers on Their Own* (New Brunswick, 1962); *Lawyers' Ethics* (New York, 1966).

[76] The extensive system of summer internships in the US has been referred to as 'the new apprenticeship'. This may somewhat undermine the image of law schools as total institutions that pervades some of the more grunging literature by former students (e.g., Scott Turow, *One L* (New York, 1977), Richard D. Kahlenburg, *Broken Contract* (New York, 1992)). But the term may obscure the extent and importance of the range of clerkships, mentoring of associates, and supervision of young lawyers throughout the legal system.

but almost none of it is controlled by law schools. In large law firms young associates are supervised, monitored, and 'developed' in a strongly hierarchical context in their early years—some of the literature even talks of the whole period of being an associate as 'apprenticeship'.

The informality of American provision in this respect may result in some gaps or loopholes. It may also contribute to a tendency to inflate the importance of the role of law schools in the total process of professional formation. Running through much of the extensive American literature on élite law schools is an assumption, usually unstated, that the three-year law degree is *the* key element in the whole process. 'Legal education' is often equated with what happens in law schools; they are even treated in some of the literature as if they are total institutions. Clearly they do play a key role in selection, socialization, and cer-tification as well as in education—and some would say that selection is the most important of these. The MacCrate Report sees law schools as the main instru-ment for preserving the unity of a fragmented profession[77]—a sort of 'boot camp' for a motley army—and yet it is the same report which has most strongly reinforced the view that legal education and training is a continuum that involves lifelong learning. If law schools are only responsible for three years (less vacations) of what is at least a seven to ten year process, why is so much attention focused on them? Maybe it serves to absolve the organized bar of responsibility for policing competency while inflating the importance of law teachers. Or maybe it is just a failure to acknowledge the extent to which the primary school model marginalizes formal legal education in the total process of professional formation.[78]

KRONMAN'S PESSIMISM—PERICLES LOST?

The Lost Lawyer ends on a deeply pessimistic note:

The collapse of the lawyer-statesman ideal has created a problem of identity in the legal profession. It has raised doubts about whether the practice of law can continue to be an intrinsically satisfying pursuit that offers deep personal meaning to those in it.[79]

Kronman sees the prospects for the restoration of the ideal as 'nearly hopeless'.[80] The commercialization of legal practice, the bureaucratization of the judiciary, and the divorce of academic law from legal practice, are all symptomatic of a general tendency that had been foreseen by Max Weber:

---

[77] See below 331–3.
[78] See above, Ch. 15. Both Kronman and Glendon generally assume the primary professional school model of law schools.
[79] *LL*, 368.   [80] Ibid.

The fate of our time is characterised by rationalization and bureaucratization and, above all, by the disenchantment of the world. Precisely the ultimate and most sublime values have retreated from public life . . .[81]

In the final section of the book, mislabelled 'Hope', Kronman offers cold comfort and feeble advice.[82] How should the lawyer who accepts the lawyer-statesman ideal confront his or her predicament? Practitioners should steer clear of corporate law firms and try to find solace in general practice in small cities or towns or else in their private lives; judges should delegate less to their clerks; law teachers should return to the traditional case method and emphasize the importance of particular cases. Kronman seems to doubt whether many will in fact take his advice. Indeed, his conclusion is so pessimistic and despondent that one wonders why he chose to stay on at Yale and become its Dean. He clearly has not given a convincing answer to the original question posed by his colleagues: if you believe this, how can you go on training students for mainly corporate law practice?

Many commentators, including Glendon, find Kronman's prognosis 'too gloomy'.[83] Her diagnosis of the crisis is similar, but more complex and thicker: a disturbingly high proportion of practising lawyers in the early 1990s were dissatisfied with their way of life, but on the other hand one-third did find personal satisfaction in their work and she speculates that these include not only public interest lawyers, but those who find a role as peacemakers[84] and 'in planning, prevention and problem-solving'.[85] Although she is sharply critical of romantic, bold judges, such as Justices Brennan and Douglas, whom she accuses of arrogance and abuse of power,[86] she is quite optimistic that large numbers of ordinary judges 'could turn in honorable performances' that approximate to a congeries of traditional judicial virtues.[87] Similarly, Glendon criticizes some law teachers for failing to teach law and being too prone to 'fancy theory'.[88] But she also suggests, echoing Holmes, that some individuals still teach law 'in the grand manner';[89] that some of the defects of the 1950s and the 1960s, such as the neglect of legislation, regulation, preventive legal practice, and alternative

---

[81] Max Weber, 'Science as Vocation' (*From Max Weber: Essays in Sociology*, trs. H. Gerth and C. Wright Mills, New York, 1946) 155, cited by Kronman at 368. One commentator (Aaronson, 1994, op. cit. at 1401) has suggested that Kronman is citing from the wrong paper: this passage refers to the bureaucratization of academic life, whereas Weber's essay on 'Politics as Vocation' would be more relevant to a discussion of legal practice as a public profession. But the same pessimism pervades both essays.

[82] *LL*, 375 ff.   [83] *NUL*, 244.   [84] Id., 97.   [85] Id., 101.   [86] Id., 169.

[87] 'A fair assessment of the current state of affairs, I believe is that classical and romantic attributes are competing for ascendancy, not only throughout the judicial system but within the psyche of nearly every judge. The synthesis that will emerge, if we are hopeful, may resemble Judge Richard Posner's pragmatic, neoclassical catalogue of judicial virtues: 'self-restraint, self-discipline . . . thoroughness of legal research, power of logical analysis, a sense of justice, a knowledge of the world, a lucid writing style, common sense, openness to colleagues' views, intelligence, fairmindedness, realism, hard work, modesty, gift for compromise, commitment to reason, and candor.'' Id., 172–3, citing R. Posner, *The Federal Courts: Crisis and Reform* (Cambridge, Ma., 1985) 220.

[88] *NUL*, Ch. 10.   [89] Id. 244 ff.

dispute resolution, are being remedied; that a counter-reformation is taking place in the study of constitutional law;[90] and that the pendulum is likely to swing back to a proper emphasis on teaching the basics of law, which Glendon interprets in similar terms to Judge Edwards' 'practical doctrinal scholarship', a more sophisticated form of exposition that treats doctrine as the core, but is informed by insights from other disciplines.[91] Overall, her picture of life in the law is more diversified and her prognosis is more optimistic than Kronman's:

As 'cold-eyed' young men and women take their places where judicial Caesars, courtroom Rambos, and classroom Rimbauds have temporarily held the center of the stage, it would be a mistake to look for a new consensus. Lawyers, as Weber taught us, have never been of one mind about what is the good life for a lawyer and how to live it. The glory of Anglo-American lawyers is that they have had a dynamic tradition of rational argument, about the most important questions. Long central to that tradition were notions of even-handedness in judging, public-spiritedness in practice, and open-mindedness in the pursuit of knowledge . . . [O]ne should not underestimate the resilience of the dynamic legal traditions of craft-professionalism, constitutionalism and practical reasoning. If we are hopeful, why should we not believe that the energies of those fertile traditions can be harnessed to the needs of a modern, diverse, democratic republic?[92]

Kronman and Glendon, and in a different way Edwards, criticize American law schools for abandoning their traditional professional role in favour of 'fancy theory'. The main target of their attacks is an unlikely pair: critical legal studies and economic analysis of law. Ironically, an Australian work which advances an optimistic (in the authors' words 'perhaps Pollyanaish') view of the future,[93] bases it on a model of 'lawyering' that is about half-way between Kronman and Glendon, but which Le Brun and Johnstone explicitly attribute to critical legal studies:

In perhaps an idealised conception, this new breed of lawyer remains aware that they are human beings with strengths, weaknesses, and doubts as well as convictions. . . . The model can adopt a number of alternative demeanours:

'There is the environmental [lawyer's] vision of a country who takes her resources and her unborn citizens seriously enough to take good care of the earth. There is the feminist (lawyer's) vision of a country whose laws do not allow women to be beaten with impunity, . . . There is the critical [lawyer's] vision of a country whose laws enforce the substantive imperatives . . . of racial equality . . .'[94]

---

[90] Ibid.   [91] Glendon at 197–8, 222 ff.; Edwards discussed in *BT* at 140–1.

[92] At 290–1.   [93] Le Brun and Johnstone (1994) op. cit., 41–5.

[94] Op. cit. at 42. The quoted passage is adapted from D. Bell and E. Edmonds, 'Students as Teachers, Teachers as Learners', 91 *Michigan L Rev.* 2025 (1991) at 2051–2. Le Brun and Johnstone claim that their model shares some of the characteristics of what Roger Cramton describes as a '"tender-minded" lawyer—one who is guided by principles (as opposed to "facts") and who is intellectualistic, idealistic, and optimistic.' Cramton, 29 *Jo. Legal Educ.* 247 (1978) at 261. Cramton is not normally associated with critical legal studies and I shall resist the temptation to comment in detail on what seems like an ideological stew.

Kronman is pessimistic and conservative; Glendon is quite optimistic and conservative; Le Brun and Johnstone are optimistic and 'critical'. These examples
suggest that optimism and pessimism are here largely independent of conservative and critical stances. Not being a prophet, I do not feel the need to stake out
a position in relation to the optimists and pessimists about the future of legal
professions in the United States, or Australia, or elsewhere. When called on to
give advice on legal careers in England, my starting-point is closer to Weber and
Llewellyn: there are many types of legal career and many conceptions of what
is a good life for lawyers. If one wishes to avoid strongly bureaucratized or
commercialized forms of professional life, one has to choose carefully. Such
choices are both personal and political. If there is a common thread that runs
through the main options, it is that it is almost impossible to avoid moral dilemmas in professional life.[95]

Implicit in Kronman's initial differentiation of the difference between scholarship and advocacy one suspects that there may have been lurking some rather
dubious distinctions between the ethical status of different occupations:[96] for
example, it is tempting to distinguish between 'helping professions' (such as
medicine and social work), socially useful, but unromantic, occupations (such
as garbage collection and accountancy), intrinsically worthwhile activities (such
as the Arts and scholarship), and morally ambiguous occupations (such as business, politics, the military or the law). Some career choices may have a special
prima facie legitimacy, but acute moral dilemmas can arise in any workplace:
doctors, priests, and development workers may be especially prone to certain
temptations, such as pride, hypocrisy, and complacency. As Thomas Becket
reminds us in *Murder in the Cathedral*, '[s]in grows with doing good'.[97]

IDENTITY AND REDUCTIONISM

These modern attempts to construct a single aspirational model for 'the lawyer'
are sometimes expressed in terms of 'a crisis of identity' for individual lawyers
and for the profession as a whole.[98] Most of the passages quoted above arose in
the context of discussions of legal education, but the underlying concerns are
more complex. One needs in particular to distinguish four kinds of question:
how can the legal profession justify its monopoly of legal services and other

---

[95] Glendon, deals with this theme rather well in *NUL*, Ch. 2. Compare the emergence of 'the
lawyer' as a morally ambiguous protagonist in the new genre of 'lawyer novels', discussed *BT*,
13–14.   [96] *LL*, Preface.

[97] T. S. Eliot, *Murder in the Cathedral* (London, 1955 edn.) 44. On the ethical dilemmas and
ambiguities of development aid work, see Helen Fielding's satirical novel, *Cause Celeb* (London,
1994).

[98] e.g., *LL*, 65–6, 361–3, 368; the Preface begins: 'This book is about a crisis in the American
legal profession. Its message is that the profession now stands in danger of losing its soul' (At 1);
MacCrate, op. cit.; cf. *NUL*, Chs. 2–5 and references there.

particular restrictive practices? Is there a 'core' of fundamental skills and/or knowledge and/or personal qualities that are necessary conditions for certifying competence? What should be the aims and objectives of formal legal education and training? And, in Glendon's words, what kind of life ought a lawyer to try to live?[99] These concerns overlap and interact and are sometimes related to other matters such as expanding the market for legal services or improving the public image of the legal profession, but in first instance they should be differentiated. Each is worth considering in turn.

Maintaining unity: a common calling

The MacCrate report is more open than most in acknowledging that its central concern is the problem of maintaining unity in the face of very real fragmentation. Collective identity of a unitary profession rather than competence or public image or individual satisfaction is the central theme:

If *a single public profession* of shared learning, skills and professional values is to survive into the 21st century, the law schools together with the bar and the judiciary must all work for the perpetuation of core legal knowledge together with the fundamental lawyering skills and professional values that *identify a distinct profession of law* throughout the United States.[100]

Why should lawyers be concerned with maintaining the unity of a fragmented profession or at least an appearance of unity? One standard answer is that any profession must claim to have a unique or special core of expertise linked to an ethic of 'service' that subordinates personal profit to the interests of clients and 'the public interest' in order to legitimate its privileges of self-regulation and monopoly over provision of certain kinds of service.[101] This view has been pungently criticized by Schlegel in discussing the MacCrate Report:

for over seventy years the profession has denied the fragmentation of legal practice with the same transparently flimsy argument to the effect that no matter what kind of law a

---

[99] *NUL*, 82.

[100] At 120 (italics added). Id. at 86, 'The professional ideal of a unitary profession with its core body of knowledge, skills and values, common educational requirements and shared professional standards has, to a significant degree, survived the profession's profound transformation in the 1970s and 1980s. It has survived despite enormous pressures within the profession to capitulate completely to commercialization and to divide into a series of economic sub-markets in which separate groups of lawyers sell highly specialized services to different consumer groups with little or no interaction among the various lawyer groups.'

[101] An organized profession may, of course, be concerned with its public image and good public relations for reasons other than maintaining a monopoly. The legal profession is in competition with other groups for its share of the market and it may also, like any other business, wish to increase demand for its services by raising public awareness. And concern with public image may also be a matter of status, power, prestige or morale: e.g., projecting a counterpoint to 'lawyer jokes' in order to preserve collective self-esteem. The image of the good professional—technically competent, trustworthy, and having good judgment—is no doubt an important part of the public relations of any profession.

lawyer practices, that lawyer needs the same base of legal knowledge and skill. The only redeeming feature of these assertions is their fit with the structure for the maintenance of professional privilege and autonomy that is the professionalisation project.[102]

It has been a matter of extended debate among sociologists how far the public service ideal is more rhetoric than reality and how far it can be a genuine unifying force within a fragmented profession.[103] Here, however, one needs to distinguish between factors that differentiate one professional group from others and hence might justify a monopoly and features which may give a sense of unity and identity within a profession, even though they are not unique.

The MacCrate Report is best known for its long list of 'fundamental lawyering skills'. As we shall see, few if any of these are both distinctive and common to all lawyers. Indeed, the main means of 'maintaining the unitary concept of being a lawyer',[104] is to be found under the pregnant heading: 'Law School: The Unifying Experience'.[105] On the two key premises of the report, that there is a single profession and that to maintain its identity is of paramount importance, the report proceeds by assertion rather than argument.[106]

In England public debate about the identity of lawyers has followed a different path. First, the division between barristers and solicitors has generally led the Bar to emphasize differences *within* the profession in order to resist fusion. For example, the new Bar Vocational Course, which was introduced in 1989, involved a quite radical shift to skills training; it was probably accepted by a conservative professional group not so much on educational grounds but because, through its emphasis on litigation skills, it reinforced the dubious notion that barristers are 'specialists in advocacy'. The English Bar has maintained a strong sense of unity in a highly individualistic profession through an elaborate set of networking devices that emphasize collegiality: the Inns of Court, chambers, circuits, and more recently specialist groups. Such collegiality has been relatively easy to maintain in a small, relatively centralized élite profession in a compact country. During the 1980s and 1990s a combination of factors—notably expansion, the growth of provincial bars, and challenges to its monopoly of rights of audience—created a sense of crisis, but this is more often talked about in terms of survival than of identity. The solicitors' profession has been larger, more fragmented, and geographically dispersed. Membership of the Law Society has been voluntary, and it has experienced internal strains between the trade union and regulatory functions of a professional body. Solicitors, for a variety of reasons, have been concerned only spasmodically to establish a strong,

[102] J. H. Schlegel, 'Law and Endangered Species: Is Survival Alone Cause For Celebration?', 28 *Indiana L Rev.* (1995) 391, at 406.
[103] For a balanced survey of the literature, see Roger Cotterrell, *The Sociology of Law: An Introduction* (London, 2nd edn., 1992), Ch. 6. An excellent recent account of the process of renegotiation of the concept of professionalism in the UK is Alan Paterson, 'Professionalism and the legal services market', 3 *Int. Jo. Legal Profession* 137 (1996).
[104] Id., 29.   [105] Id., 111.   [106] See especially Id., 11.

distinctive collective identity—one major exception being when their monopoly over conveyancing was challenged.

Secondly, and more interesting in the present context, recent discussions of policy regarding legal education and training, rights of audience, and the future of legal services have taken place in the context of a determined strategy by successive Conservative governments to increase competition and restrict unjustified monopoly. Thus the remit of The Lord Chancellor's Advisory Committee on Legal Education and Conduct is to consider the provision of legal services by appropriate providers from the point of view of the interests of consumers and the public at large. Underlying this is the idea that consumers should be put in a position where they can make informed choices between different kinds of services that may assist them in solving their problems.

In its first report on legal education the emphasis throughout was on the suitability of legal education (and even vocational training) as a preparation for many careers and the Committee came down strongly in favour of moves in the direction of common training for barristers and solicitors. The thrust of the report was away from maintaining a distinctive identity, yet its analysis of skills and values is not very different from that of MacCrate. This is hardly surprising, for the central elements of ACLEC's humane professionalism, MacCrate's fundamental skills, and Kronman's 'lawyer-statesman' are not features which differentiate lawyers from other professionals and hence do not justify a monopoly. Rather they are qualities of one general model of 'professionalism'.

Practical issues concerning monopoly, restrictive practices, professional self-governance, and other privileges are too complex to pursue here. One of the difficulties is the level of generality at which such issues are best treated, as is illustrated by the protracted debate about rights of audience in England. Suffice to say here that 'the lawyer-statesman' and other general images of 'the lawyer' are at best tangential to such issues. This should not worry Kronman because his concern with 'identity' relates to personal fulfilment rather than to professional monopoly.

Education, training, and certification: the search for a 'core'

Most discussions of the 'identity' of lawyers converge on issues of legal education and training. In some contexts, such as the MacCrate and ACLEC reports, formal legal education is the main issue; in others, as with Kronman and Glendon, law schools are treated as having a key role in the forging of professional identity. In *Blackstone's Tower* I conducted a sceptical survey of some of the more persistent attempts to define a core or essence of law as a subject of study.[107] I concluded that all such efforts are doomed to fail because law is too rich, complex, and many-layered to be reducible to a single formula. For example,

---

[107] *BT*, Ch. 7.

the long and tedious controversy over 'core' subjects at the academic stage in England was seen to be more a battle over territory between academics and practitioners than a serious disagreement about whether there is an irreducible core of legal knowledge. In any case, the debate only dealt with one relatively small aspect of professional formation and identity.

I shall not repeat the general argument here. However, there are certain limited practical purposes for which artificially listing 'core subjects' or a prescribed common element may be justified. Such purposes vary and need to be differentiated: for example, certification for initial admission, or for sole practice, or as a specialist in a diverse profession; specifying building blocks or prerequisites as part of an educational programme (for example, making a course on contract a prerequisite for other commercial law subjects in a modular degree); defining what counts as a 'law degree' for purposes of professional recognition; and, as was noted above, 'the boot camp' function—forging a common identity through a shared painful experience. Modern educational theory typically requires clearly articulated learning objectives, sometimes insisting that these be formulated in terms of observable and measurable 'performances'. Such concerns underlie some models of 'good lawyering', such as Le Brun and Johnstone's 'client centred lawyer'.[108]

Scepticism of the search for a 'core' does not imply denial that it is sometimes a response to genuine problems. However, experience suggests a number of cautionary lessons: first, such problems are local and contingent, and need to be differentiated from each other. Secondly, lists of 'core subjects' or 'fundamental skills' tend to be (a) arbitrary and (b) either over-inclusive or nugatory: for example, a knowledge of conveyancing or company law or family law is not relevant to every type of practice and requiring it of students who know where they are heading raises serious problems of 'relevance'; on the other hand, one might agree that every lawyer should have been exposed to contract, and possibly one or two other legal subjects, but such a list would fall far short of a minimum requirement of 'competence'. Similar considerations apply to lists of skills. Thirdly, strong definitions of 'the core' almost invariably lead to overprescription, which inhibits innovation, reduces diversity, and overloads curricula. And, fourthly, as legal professions diversify there is a temptation to specify transferable skills, such as 'problem-solving', at so abstract a level that it is too general to be helpful and contains little or nothing that is specifically legal.

It might be objected that such criticisms of 'the core' can be overstated. The 'core subjects' debate may have shown up the artificiality of most lists of 'necessary' subjects or 'fundamental skills', but surely the idea of technical competence involves some irreducible minimum of knowledge and skills that one can expect of anyone who claims to be a lawyer. Does not every competent practitioner need at least a modicum of 'local knowledge'?

---

[108] Op. cit., 41–5.

Herbert Simon puts this well in making the case for direct teaching of problem-solving in professional education:

Another thing that research on cognitive skills has taught us in recent years is that there is no such thing as expertness without knowledge—extensive and accessible knowledge. No one, no matter how intelligent, skilled in problem solving, or talented, becomes a chess grandmaster without 10 years of intense exposure to the task environment of chess. Hence in the training of professionals, the problem of coverage cannot be avoided. We cannot produce physicists without teaching physics, or psychologists without teaching psychology.[109]

Accordingly, '[problem solving] must, of course, be taught in the context of a rich environment of problems—mostly but not entirely drawn from the professional field in question.'[110]

This is eminently sensible. Every competent professional needs to contextualize know-how and know-what, including a great deal of tacit knowledge. But law is not one locality. Different lawyers need different local knowledges and many of the ingredients of these are not unique to lawyers: corporate counsel need to know about commercial life in general and the specific context in which they are operating with non-lawyer colleagues; similar considerations apply to practitioners dealing with divorce, rent reviews, treaty negotiations, or most other areas of legal practice. Nearly all competent practitioners need to have a mastery of detail, but nearly all of the detail is local.

This is quietly recognized by the MacCrate Report. Despite their anxieties about the unity of the profession, their list of 'fundamental lawyering skills' in Chapter 4 does not place much emphasis on those that are distinctive: problem-solving, factual investigation, communication, counselling, negotiation, office management, recognizing and resolving ethical dilemmas, professional self-development, and most of the 'fundamental values of the profession' could be found in similar lists for other occupational groups; conversely, the peculiarly legal elements, such as 'legal analysis and reasoning', 'legal research', and 'litigation and Alternative Dispute Resolution Procedures' are stated at a very high level of generality and almost no emphasis is placed at all on a 'core' of specifically legal knowledge. Significantly, competence is expressed in terms of attaining and maintaining 'a Level of Competence in One's Own Field of Practice'.[111]

ACLEC reached a similar position by a different route. In its first report, which deals with professional formation of barristers and solicitors up to the point of initial certification, the Committee moved sharply away from the traditional 'knowledge-based core' for law degrees, but nevertheless recommended a rather loosely defined 'prescribed common element', which includes an

[109] Herbert Simon, 'Problem Solving and Education' (1980), reprinted in Simon *Models of Thought* Vol. II. (New Haven, 1989) 278.
[110] Id., 287.   [111] Id., 140.

admixture of knowledge, skills, and values.[112] Its main concern was to promote diversity in recruitment, pluralism in legal education, and flexibility in career choice and development, while maintaining workable schemes of training and certification of competence. It emphasized the suitability of legal education (and even of the vocational stage) as a preparation for many careers and it came down strongly in favour of moves in the direction of common training for barristers and solicitors. The thrust of the report was away from maintaining a distinctive identity, yet interestingly the content of its specific recommendations is not very different from those of MacCrate. Thus two important recent reports on legal education and training identify almost nothing that is both common to all lawyers and uniquely legal.

Individual professional identity

Against this background, Kronman's discovery of a unique core 'in the art of handling cases' looks especially unconvincing.[113] Not all lawyers have or need such skills; emphasis on cases is more part of common law than civil law culture—a point of significance as legal practice becomes increasingly transnational; and case-studies and case-work, and case skills are not unique to law.[114] Yet Kronman is surely right in maintaining that the question: 'what does it mean to be a lawyer?' is intimately related to complex questions of personal identity. The alleged crisis of identity is sometimes linked to surveys that show that increasing numbers of practising lawyers are dissatisfied with their professional life.[115] Kronman is careful to distinguish job satisfaction from personal fulfilment. There are many possible sources of job satisfaction of which 'do-gooding' is only one: success measured in terms of money or power or reputation may be quite amoral or immoral; one may obtain satisfaction from work because it is interesting or enjoyable, or because the environment and one's colleagues are congenial, or from the sense of doing something well independently of external indicia of success. When it is reported that an increasing percentage of American lawyers or of English solicitors are dissatisfied with their situation, it would be naïve, indeed priggish, to explain this solely or mainly in terms of ethical

---

[112] ACLEC, *First Report* (1996), op. cit., Ch. 4.

[113] 'If lawyers have a distinctive expertise of their own, it . . . consists in the art of handling cases. There is in fact no other candidate for the position.' (*LL*, 362).

[114] Of course there is something special about the truly excellent case-trained common lawyer. Kronman may take some comfort from Hoebel's account of his collaboration with Llewellyn, which reputedly introduced anthropologists to 'the case method': 'I had with each case carried the analysis of its import to the limits of my ability. Yet again and again, as our discussions proceeded, he would challenge or add, defend what he had added, if defending were needed, with inexhaustible brilliance, until I in awe one day queried, "Karl, how do you do it?" "Why, Ad," he replied, with more pride in his profession than in himself, "I am a case-trained lawyer—and what is more I am one of the three best in the country."' (E. Adamson Hoebel, in 18 *Rutgers L Rev.* 735 (1964) at 742–3.) However, it was Llewellyn who insisted that too much emphasis had been placed on case-law skills in the Langdellian system, see n. 67 above. [115] e.g., *NUL*, Ch. 5.

considerations, although a sense of guilt or lack of moral worth may be one important source of dissatisfaction among several. But Kronman is justified in distinguishing such external, instrumental reasons for choosing or enjoying a legal career from the intrinsic satisfactions of practice as a way of life in which one can take pride:

> This crisis is, in essence, a crisis of morale. It is the product of growing doubts about the capacity of a lawyer's life to offer fulfillment to the person who takes it up. Disguised by the material well-being of lawyers, it is a spiritual crisis that strikes at the heart of their professional pride.[116]

One reason why this is persuasive is because, for many, involvement in the law can be sufficiently demanding and gripping that it becomes a way of life that goes to one's sense of identity. Kronman provides one fruitful answer to the question: 'How can I live honorably in the law?' I think that there are others, that some details of his 'lawyer-statesman' need modification, and that he is mistaken in looking for unique characteristics that distinguish 'the lawyer' from other professionals. Kronman's model of the lawyer-statesman combines technical competence, civic mindedness, and practical wisdom. His achievement is to give a rich account of this combination of qualities. One may substitute somewhat different conceptions of what each involves, as I would for technical competence and civic mindedness, and yet agree that this is a worthy ideal for individuals to try to emulate. Our main point of divergence relates to levels of generality:[117] Kronman seems to me to overgeneralize about the distinctive qualities of lawyers and yet to give an admirable account of professionalism in general.

CONCLUSION

Since 'Pericles and the Plumber' was first written, the literature on both legal professions and legal education has grown in both extent and quality. However, I would still maintain that monolithic models of 'the lawyer' are too simple as a basis for designing lawyer education or establishing individual or collective professional identities, just as I remain sceptical of attempts to reduce the subject-matter of our discipline to a single core or essence.[118] Both law and legal

---

[116] Ibid.

[117] To sum up our other differences: I personally find his account of technical competence to be over simple and regressive; I am not persuaded that civic mindedness is a necessary condition of practical wisdom, but I agree that some idea of integrity or uprightness is part of the traditional ideal of professionalism; I follow Glendon and Llewellyn rather than Kronman in thinking that there is often an inescapable tension between the interest of clients and the public interest that makes the role of lawyers, and of most other professionals, inherently morally ambiguous. I also think that Kronman exaggerates the importance of formal legal education in developing the basic qualities of the lawyer-statesman or, as I would prefer to put it, the good professional.   [118] *BT*, Ch. 7.

practice are too varied. For certain limited practical purposes it may sometimes be necessary to negotiate or prescribe some common requirements or standards, but these almost invariably deserve to be recognized as contingent compromises.

What is striking about recent talk is how much of it emphasizes matters that link rather than differentiate law from other occupations. It is said that basic legal education should aim to develop general intellectual skills of analysis, synthesis, oral and written communication, numeracy, team work, and problem-solving which are often referred to as 'transferable' not only between legal contexts but more generally. Fashionable models of humane professionalism or 'the reflective practitioner' relate to all professions, not specifically to law. The 'lawyer-statesman' combines technical competence with civic mindedness and good judgment (phronesis). Kronman himself acknowledges that the legal profession has no monopoly on the last two qualities; yet, as we have seen, technical competence has become increasingly localized to particular contexts and specialisms. A practitioner specializing in divorce or corporate law or insolvency or patents or commercial property or human rights may have more in common with colleagues in other professions and occupations than with most other lawyers. Similar considerations apply at more general levels. It is precisely such continuities that form the basis for claiming that law is potentially one of the great humane disciplines, that legal education can be a good vehicle for general education, and that legal practice, at its best, has a place among the liberal professions.

17

A Nobel Prize for Law?*

The date of birth of a law school and its coming of age are both indeterminate. In recent years there has been a spate of birthday celebrations by law schools around the Commonwealth. Among those with close associations with Warwick, the law faculties of Dar-es-Salaam and Lagos celebrated their twenty-fifth anniversaries in 1989; in the same year the Faculty of Law of the University of Hong Kong commemorated its twentieth birthday; and in 1993 the Centre for Socio-Legal Studies in Oxford chose the less fashionable twenty-one. In 1987 The *Modern Law Review* marked its fiftieth year with a special issue. Each of these events resulted in a substantial publication.[1] For Warwick to celebrate its thirtieth anniversary with a symposium devoted to legal scholarship suggests a pleasing maturity.

Of course, the timing of these celebrations is not entirely fortuitous. The 1960s and 1970s saw a massive expansion of legal education throughout the common law world, typically as part of more general developments in higher education. During this period established law schools grew larger and many new ones were set up. Local legal education in former colonies typically started just before or after Independence as part of the process of decolonization. In England and Wales law expanded largely in step with higher education: it got off to a slow start, but over time increased its share of the total. The modern English law school, like its university home, is essentially a post-World War II creation.[2] It has been estimated that the scale of the academic legal enterprise is about twenty to twenty-five times what it was in 1945 and, almost as significant, nearly four times what it was when the Ormrod Committee reported in 1971. For legal scholarship this had several implications: the number of full-time teachers increased from about 130 in 1945, to 974 in 1974–5, to nearly 2000 in 1994.[3] Expansion made space for specialization, innovation, and above all diversification in respect of ideas, methods, and perspectives. Legal scholarship today is

---

* This essay builds on and develops themes that are dealt with at greater length in previous writings, especially *BT*; *RE*; JJM; and, 'Remembering 1972', in D.Galligan (ed.), *Socio-Legal Studies in Context* (Oxford, 1995). It was originally published in Geoffrey Wilson (ed.), *Frontiers of Legal Scholarship* (Chichester, 1995).

[1] Issa Shivji (ed.), *The Limits of Legal Radicalism* (Dar-es-Salaam, 1987); J. A. Omotola and A. A. Adeogun (edd.), *Law and Development* (Lagos, 1987); Raymond Wacks (ed.), *The Future of Legal Education and the Legal Profession in Hong Kong* (Hong Kong, 1989); D. Galligan (ed.) op. cit., n. 1; W. T. Murphy and Simon Roberts (edd.), Symposium on legal scholarship in the common law world, 50 *MLR* No. 6 (1987).

[2] *BT*, Ch. 2.   [3] Ibid.

generally more varied, more lively, more sophisticated, and more self-confident than it was at the start of the period of expansion. A new pluralism in academic law has become established.

It is not surprising to find in these anniversary volumes a mixture of nostalgia, self-congratulation, critical stocktaking, and prescriptions for the future. What are birthdays for except to give some licence to retrospection, introspection, and prospective speculation? One underlying theme is that law schools have changed out of all recognition in the past thirty years, that most of the developments have been positive, and that there are many substantial achievements to celebrate. However, there is also a strong undercurrent of dissatisfaction and self-criticism. Like many other disciplines, especially those that are unsure of their full acceptance within the academy, law is endemically plagued by self-doubt. Much of this is articulated in terms of disagreements and ambivalences about objectives, priorities, and functions within formal legal education. Such problems of identity are caught by Thomas Bergin's title of 1968 'The law teacher: a man divided against himself'.[4] The gender balance in academic law has changed in the past twenty-five years, but the theme persists. What began as an educational problem has tended to spill over into legal scholarship.[5] Here self-doubt is sometimes expressed in the idea that there is no Nobel Prize for law.[6] This has sometimes been explicitly discussed in print, but doubts about the nature, achievements, and prospects of legal scholarship are much more widespread. The actual Nobel Prize is in many respects an idiosyncratic, historically contingent, and controversial institution. But it provides a convenient symbol for its stated aspiration of recognizing extraordinary contributions that benefit mankind.[7] In this context the question becomes: what, if anything, can legal scholarship contribute to human welfare or human understanding?

It is not difficult to find some negative answers, for example:

1. 'I have heard it said by a Professor of the Harvard Law School (not himself a lawyer) that the reason why there is no Nobel Prize for lawyers is that common lawyers have no respect for original thought. The system of precedent, urged this Professor, means that in a common law court you can destroy your opponent's arguments by showing that nobody has ever

[4] 54 *Virginia Law Rev.* 637 (1968).

[5] This paper assumes a close interdependence between teaching and research in English law schools, not least because teaching still provides the main economic base for scholarship. For an excellent discussion of the relationship between teaching and research in law, see *Law and Learning* (The Arthurs Report, Ottawa, 1983), *passim*, esp. Ch. 7.

[6] e.g., the passages from Atiyah and Conard, quoted below.

[7] One may discount the peculiar history and idiosyncrasies of the actual Nobel institution; but it is worth noting that two recent Nobel Laureates in economics, Ronald Coase and Gary Becker, derived some of their inspiration from legal examples and their close association with the University of Chicago Law School. And some lawyers, e.g., Sean McBride and Nelson Mandela, have been honoured as activists for their contributions to human rights, environmental protection or World Peace.

thought of them before. This is no doubt an exaggeration, but he definitely has a point.'[8]

2. 'The predominant notion of academic lawyers is that they are not really academic . . . Their scholarly activities are thought to be unexciting and uncreative, comprising a series of intellectual puzzles scattered among "large areas of description" '.[9]

3. 'A more fundamental obstacle to awarding a Nobel Prize for law is the difference between what scientists and artists do for humanity and what lawyers do. When a scientist discovers a means of making rice fields more productive, he adds to the food supply without taking food from anyone. When a poet provides us with a new insight, he makes us wiser without making anyone more ignorant.

   Law, on the other hand, is largely concerned with taking from one person to give to another.'[10]

4. '[I]t is not easy to see that law is a discipline in the usual sense. What truths do lawyers come up with? What are the great legal discoveries of the past ten years, or fifty years, or even a hundred There do not seem to be any.'[11]

5. 'Insofar as intellectual disciplines can be identified, this is usually done in terms of distinctive methods, distinctive subject matter or theory, or distinctive scientific or scholarly objectives. None of this applies to the "discipline" of law, which possesses no methods unique to legal study, no theory which is other than an application or development of social, political or ethical theory of some kind, and no distinctive scientific or scholarly objectives. All attempts to mark law off from other knowledge fields is bound to fail.'[12]

6. 'The character of English law and the English legal system, judge led, pragmatic and undoctrinal . . . [is] neither sufficiently scholarly to be attractive to scholars nor sufficiently legal to be attractive to lawyers. If putting "legal" in front of "scholarship" was like putting plastic in front of "cup", then adding "English" is like adding "disposable". The words "English legal scholarship", though high sounding have a similar function to the words "disposable plastic cup". Each adjective strengthens the message that one can not expect much in terms of quality or long-term utility from it.'[13]

---

[8] P. S. Atiyah, *Pragmatism and Theory in English Law* (London, 1987) at 7.

[9] Tony Becher, *Academic Tribes and Territories* (Milton Keynes, 1989) 30, discussed *BT*, Ch. 6.

[10] Alfred A. Conard, 'The Nobel Prize for Law', 18 *Michigan Jo.of Law Reform* 226 (1985) at 226.   [11] A. W. B. Simpson, *Invitation to Law* (Oxford, 1988) 178.

[12] Roger Cotterell, 'A "Post-disciplinary" Perspective on Law', (unpublished outline for seminar, 1991, quoted with permission of the author). Cotterell has since developed some relevant themes in print without using the phrase 'autonomous disciplines', e.g., 'Sociological Perspectives on Legal Closure', in Alan Norrie (ed.), *Closure or Critique: New Directions in Legal Theory* (1993) Ch. 10.

[13] Geoffrey Wilson, 'English Legal Scholarship', 50 *MLR* 818 (1987) at 819. Wilson is, here it seems, talking more about the achievement of English legal scholarship than its potential. He con-

Law in Context

These six quotations are by respected contemporary scholars with whom I do not often disagree. Most of the statements can be interpreted as reporting views, which may be quite widespread, rather than endorsing them. However, I would suggest that all of them, at least if taken at face value, are fundamentally misleading, largely because they are based on indefensible assumptions about the nature of contemporary legal scholarship or scholarship in general or both.

For example, to suggest (1.) that lawyers are not interested in new ideas because they argue from precedent, deals with only one small part of the practice of law and of legal scholarship, the construction, presentation, and criticism of arguments on disputed questions of law. It also mischaracterizes the activity. Ronald Dworkin's Hercules might be a strong contender for a Nobel Prize for law. So might some actual judges in our tradition.

Similarly to suggest (2.) that legal scholarship is mainly taxonomic or descriptive implies that exposition is the only kind of legal scholarly activity. Furthermore, it misconceives the nature and functions of legal dogmatics.[14]

Thirdly, it is surely misleading to suggest (3.) that all Nobel prizewinners are involved in win-win activities, whereas law is mainly concerned with redistribution. Even if both assumptions were true, a case could be made for claiming that if someone could devise a just, efficient, and cost-effective system for distributing risks, this might deserve to count as an extraordinary contribution to human welfare—and possibly also to human understanding.

To suggest (4.) that law is not really a scholarly discipline because there have been no great legal discoveries, omits the processes of invention, interpretation, and construction of ideas that are normally considered as central to the humanities and social sciences. Do historians, novelists, literary theorists, economists or sociologists make great discoveries in ways which jurists do not? A lawyer may discover a forgotten precedent in much the same way as an archaeologist may discover a new site or a lost manuscript, but such findings do not on their own win Nobel prizes; and scientists and scholars do not *discover* theories, concepts, interpretations, insights, or more controversially, facts. Sharp distinctions between discovery, construction, interpretation, and invention in the physical sciences are now doubted by both philosophers of science and sociologists of knowledge.[15] Cannot legal practice and lawmaking as forms of problem-solving take credit for some significant inventions, such as the trust or the letter of credit or the Mareva injunction or public interest litigation, to say nothing of monumental achievements such as Justinian's *Institutes* or Blackstone's *Commentaries*

---

cludes on a slightly more optimistic, if ambivalent, note: 'One cause for optimism for the future of legal scholarship is that so little has been tried.' (id., at 851).

[14] This argument is developed at length in *BT*, Ch. 6. Differences within 'legal dogmatics' in the civilian tradition are explored in J. F. Nijboer and L. T. Wemes, *Rechtspraak, domatiek en dogmatisme* (Arnhem, 1990).

[15] e.g., G. N. Gilbert and M. Mulkay, *Opening Pandora's Box: A sociological analysis of scientists' discourse* (Cambridge, 1984).

or the United States Constitution or the Uniform Commercial Code or some of the international conventions on human rights?[16]

To suggest (5.) that law as a discipline is not autonomous because it has no unique or special subject-matter or methods or forms of knowledge (which some would doubt), is to set a standard of autonomy which would disqualify most other disciplines. Is psychology or history or statistics or literature or politics or sociology autonomous in ways that law is not? Is it not strange to imply that social, political, and ethical theory are autonomous disciplines?

Finally, even if one accepts (6.) that the pragmatic, sometimes anti-intellectual tendencies of the common law tradition makes much of our academic activity fit the disturbing image of a disposable plastic cup, this metaphor hardly fits the work of Blackstone or Maitland or Hart or Kahn-Freund or Dworkin in our tradition, to say nothing of legal scholarship in other legal cultures. If there were a Nobel Prize for law, there would be some strong candidates, even from England.

If I were concerned here to take on some of the fundamental theoretical questions about the nature of scholarship in general and legal scholarship in particular, it would not be adequate to take a few quotations out of context and dismiss them so peremptorily. But my purpose is to comment on the current scene in the United Kingdom at a less fundamental level. It is to consider some of the concerns that underlie this poor image of legal scholarship and to suggest an alternative.

As a start, it is worth dealing briefly with a possible semantic confusion about the terms 'discipline' and 'scholarship'. Debates about the autonomy of disciplines typically centre on philosophical questions about forms of knowledge. From an epistemological point of view, if any disciplines can be said to be autonomous in a strong sense (which I doubt), I agree that law is not one of them;[17] but nor are most of the subjects that are generally accepted today as being part of the humanities and social sciences. If on the other hand, one views a discipline as a form of organized or institutionalized activity ostensibly directed to the advancement and dissemination of learning, then the idea of discipline marks out the intellectual division of labour which is historically contingent

[16] The potential of a technological perspective on law—viewing legal praxis as a form of institutionalized problem-solving—is explored in JJM. A great many legal inventions are products of teams of anonymous practitioners or incremental development over time rather than the work of named individuals. If one wants to look for examples of 'creative lawyering' or 'imaginative problem-solving' one is most likely to find it in lawyers' offices and chambers, where largely anonymous individuals and teams use their ingenuity and skill to solve thousands of practical problems, not least to prevent conflict, typically under a cloak of confidentiality. Many, of course, may be serving particular interests rather than the general welfare. Insofar as legal culture may be less inclined to assign credit for its main advances to individuals, it may be less wedded to a Great Person view of science than some other disciplines. On concerns about allocation of credit in the physical sciences see Bruno Latour and Steve Woolgar, *Laboratory Life* (Beverly Hills, 1979), Ch. 5. Nobel Prizes, other than the Peace Prize, are given only to individuals.

[17] *BT*, Ch. 7. Richard Posner, in his much-cited article, op. cit. below n. 331, uses autonomy in a weak sense to refer to 'a subject properly entrusted to persons trained in law and nothing else' (at 762).

and may vary according to time and place.[18] In our system, the study of law has been largely institutionalized into separate departments, faculties or schools which have developed more or less distinctive academic cultures. English law schools today might be said to be semi-autonomous: on the one hand during the past twenty years they have been treated by governments and administrators as part of the humanities and social sciences and to a significant degree have been assimilated into and share in a common academic culture. On the other hand, for complex reasons, law schools tend to have a culture that is in some respects different from that of history or sociology or English departments—with many individual variations. This is as much to do with differences of function and tradition as with the intellectual content of the activities that take place within them. There have, of course, been recurrent attempts to develop interdisciplinary studies, 'to break down the artificial barriers between disciplines', and 'to mitigate the rigidities of the departmental system'. Such attempts have met with mixed success, partly because of cultural differences, but also because of the internal political economy of universities.[19]

Similarly, 'scholarship' is an activity that goes on mainly, but not exclusively, in universities. In contrast to the situation in Continental Europe, English legal scholarship antedated our university law schools by several centuries. In ordinary usage the term 'scholarship' is notoriously vague. For example, the *Oxford English Dictionary* defines it as:

1. a. The attainments of a scholar; learning, erudition; esp. proficiency in the Greek and Latin languages and their literature. Also the collective attainments of scholars; the sphere of polite learning . . .
b. Applied by unlearned speakers, etc., to educational attainments of a more modest character.

In the present context doubts about legal scholarship can be interpreted as raising questions about its standing and whether it measures up to the standards of other disciplines. There are clearly some legitimate reasons for concern. For example, it is well-known that research training in law is less developed than in most other disciplines and in some other countries. Data from Halsey's 1989 survey of British academics indicate that at the time only 11.5 per cent of law teachers had doctorates compared with an average of 58.4 per cent in other disciplines.[20] Secondly, academic lawyers have many opportunities to participate

---

[18] Such an ethnographic perspective deals with 'the social aspects of knowledge communities and the epistemological properties of knowledge forms and how the two influence one another'. Becher, op. cit., 1.

[19] W. Twining, 'Law and Anthropology: A Case Study of Inter-disciplinary Collaboration', 7 *Law and Society Rev.* 561 (1973). In my experience attempts to develop genuinely integrated interdisciplinary degrees have more often run into difficulties because of questions of cost than because of intellectual or cultural difficulties.

[20] This is based on a preliminary analysis of data kindly provided by Professor Halsey. See further, *BT*, 200–5. This was the most significant deviation by academic lawyers from the norm in respect of Halsey's indicators. The recent ESRC report on *Socio-Legal Studies* (1994) identifies

in extracurricular activities which are either not academic or which fall on the borderline of 'research' and 'scholarship'.[21] Thirdly, the main audiences for legal writing—practitioners, vocationally oriented law students, and law reform bodies—exercise a strong gravitational pull towards applied work, towards *recherches ponctuelles* rather than *recherche sublime*, as they say in Quebec.[22] Fourthly, law has not attracted, and academic lawyers have not sought, as much outside research funding as most other disciplines, and such funding as is available tends to favour applied rather than fundamental research.

These concerns are real, but they need to be balanced against some other considerations. A good deal of work that is recognized as scholarly is produced by practitioners, judges, law reform bodies, and others outside the universities; for, at least in the upper reaches, the law has some claims to being called a learned profession. It would indeed be churlish to disqualify the more thoughtful, well-researched, and innovative products of practising lawyers and judges as not being scholarly just because they were undertaken for practical purposes. A great deal of specialist work that is undertaken by academic lawyers in other jurisdictions is done by barristers, law publishers, and government officials in England. This may reduce the opportunities and temptations for academic lawyers to be diverted away from serious scholarship. As part of the process of assimilation of law into universities, for purposes of appointment, promotion, research assessment, and terms of employment, most academic lawyers are treated in much the same ways and are judged by comparable criteria to colleagues in the humanities and social sciences. There is a certain amount of evidence that today academic lawyers are on average no less productive than their colleagues in other disciplines.[23]

Another factor that may underlie these negative images is the point that law has traditionally been seen as one of the cheapest subjects. This is an international phenomenon. A strong case can be made that this inhibits the development of legal scholarship, especially in areas which require fieldwork, foreign travel or expensive equipment. This perception of the subject is very difficult to change, as the Heads of Law Schools found in 1984.[24] Even if the unit costs of law were increased, it is quite likely that most of the extra revenue would be invested in higher academic salaries for law teachers rather than in support for research, as has happened in the United States.[25] It could be argued that law is well-equipped to deal with economic adversity just because law school culture is less dependent on outside research funding and has not developed expensive

research training as a priority need for the development of the field. See further, William Twining, 'Postgraduate Legal Studies: Some Lessons of Experience', in Peter Birks (ed.), *Reviewing Legal Education* (Oxford, 1994) 93.

[21] Arthurs, op. cit., Ch. 5.   [22] Id., Ch. 6; see further *BT*, Ch. 6.
[23] For details, see *BT*, App.
[24] Heads of University Law Schools, *Law as an Academic Discipline* (London, 1984); the bulk of the report was published in the SPTL *Newsletter*, Summer (1984).
[25] Derek Bok, *The Cost of Talent* (New York, 1993) Ch. 8.

tastes. However, in the long term, modest expectations are likely to lead to modest performance.

Negative images may also be a symptom of disappointed expectations. Many of the new law schools in the Commonwealth began life during a period of academic euphoria, and many of the postwar generation of law teachers shared in a general mood of idealism, optimism, and political commitment. The boom period for universities did not last long. What Halsey has called the 'decline of donnish dominion' began in the late 1960s and has continued in fits and starts ever since.[26] Issa Shivji's well-chosen title, *The Limits of Legal Radicalism*,[27] wryly catches the sense of frustration and disappointed expectations of many of those who started their academic careers in the 1960s or even the 1970s. Its significance extends beyond Tanzania and academic law. Our discipline may be larger, better integrated into the university and more self-confident than it was thirty years ago, but self-doubt and a sense of promise unfulfilled persists, as is illustrated by the passages quoted above.

Let us consider some examples. In the 1960s some of us launched an attack on the dominance of 'black-letter law' or 'the expository tradition' in both legal education and legal scholarship, complaining that it was narrow, conservative, illiberal, unrealistic, and boring.[28] The orthodox student textbook was selected as the target which symbolized the tradition. This was a challenge to a near monopoly rather than an outright assault on exposition as such. More radical critics challenged the validity of the methods of expositors or dismissed their writings as bourgeois mystification. As is common with such polemics there was an element of artificiality in the battles and a tendency to caricature. In curriculum discussions traditionalists fought rearguard actions, often with bitter resentment, but rarely did they join issue intellectually. Leading expositors tended to use the time-honoured technique of Ignoring and just got on with the job.[29]

Like most such battles there were no clear victors. On the one hand, academic law has diversified and the near monopoly of exposition has been broken. Some kinds of broader approach, such as socio-legal studies and economic analysis of law, have become established, alternative kinds of legal literature have developed, and there is a much greater variety in legal theory.[30] Perhaps because of the tendency to pluralism, no clear alternative genre of legal literature has developed as a rival to traditional textbooks and treatises. The expository text has survived. Indeed the taught tradition may be tougher and more sophisticated as a result of these attacks. It may become even tougher as more expositors undergo the discipline of preparing expert systems. In 1987 Lord Goff could say: 'we live in the age of the legal textbook'.[31] In the United States Judge Harry Edwards

---

[26] A. H. Halsey, *Decline of Donnish Dominion* (Oxford, 1992).

[27] Op. cit., n. 1.   [28] *BT*, at 141 ff.

[29] A notable exception was T. B. Smith, 'Authors and Authority' (1972) 12 JSPTL (NS) 1.

[30] On the new pluralism in academic law, see *BT*, Ch. 6.

[31] Robert Goff, 'Judge, Jurist and Legislator' (Child and Co. Lecture), (1987) *Denning Law. Jo.* 79, at 92.

has sharply attacked law schools for failing to perform their traditional role of providing 'practical doctrinal scholarship' for the practising profession and the judiciary.[32] Even Richard Posner, another academic turned judge, has gone so far as to say that '[d]isinterested legal-doctrinal analysis of the traditional kind remains the indispensable core of legal thought'.[33] Exposition has survived, perhaps with its dominance and prestige reduced, but it is here to stay, not least because expositors have been assigned a useful, if modest, role as participants in the legal system.[34] Even those who consider exposition to be a form of divination or jugglery concede that there is a steady demand for its products.

Let me illustrate the theme of disappointed expectations more concretely by reference to two areas that are of special interest to me: evidence and 'legal method'. When I came to Warwick I was asked what field of law I proposed to rethink or to 'Warwickise'. After some thought, I settled on evidence. My choice was fortunate, for it has recently become a very lively area. In the nineteenth century, evidence as a subject attracted some of the best legal minds: Bentham, Stephen, Thayer, and Wigmore, for example. But in the twentieth century it suffered a period of recession as an academic subject. In the United States it was difficult for scholars to break out of the shadow of two giants, Thayer and Wigmore. In England, during the formative period of university law schools, it was eccentrically treated as 'a barrister's subject' and was hardly studied at all. When Rupert Cross made the subject academically respectable, he followed American tradition in concentrating on the technical rules of evidence and ignoring the rich heritage of theoretical writings on proof and of work in other disciplines. In the last fifteen years there has been a series of developments which have been, somewhat grandiosely, labelled 'the New Evidence Scholarship'. It is an intellectual movement involving scholars from philosophy, psychology, statistics, semiotics, and history, as well as law. It treats the law of evidence as one, relatively small, part of the subject of evidence and proof; how small is a matter of controversy. Some of us believe that the importance of the formal rules is diminishing, that their importance has been greatly exaggerated, and that over concentration on them has distracted attention from subjects which are of greater practical and theoretical significance, such as the logic of proof.[35] Although this area has been widely recognized as a significant academic development, it seems so far to have a made a very modest impact on the teaching of evidence, and on the ordinary discourse and practices of practitioners. Some attention has been paid to psychological findings in debates on law reform,

---

[32] Harry T. Edwards, 'The growing disjunction between legal education and the legal profession' (1992) 91 *Michigan L Rev.* 34; see also the responses and comments in (1993) id., no. 8.

[33] Richard Posner, 'The Decline of Law as an Autonomous Discipline: 1962–1987', 100 *Harvard L Rev.* 761 (1987) at 777.　　　　　　　　[34] *BT*, at 135–141 and Atiyah, op. cit., *passim*.

[35] *RE*, Ch. 6 There has, of course been a long, though spasmodic, tradition of studying proof in Continental Europe from a variety of perspectives, as is illustrated by the work of Mittermaier, Muensterburg, Le'vy-Bruhl, and Perelman.

although this is not often reflected in actual legislative changes.[36] From time to time one may feel frustrated by the continuing failure of colleagues to take facts seriously and to embrace these developments. But perhaps one is being too impatient. Evidence as a field of study is unrecognizably different from what it was twenty years ago; there is a very active international network of scholars pursuing a variety of lines of enquiry and there is a burgeoning literature. Some expository works have begun to take notice of these new ideas.[37] Similar developments can be reported in a number of fields, family law, regulation, administrative law, for example. Scholarship is a collective enterprise which develops incrementally and in an area like this perhaps one should expect it to take a generation for new ideas to become part of the mainstream.

Perhaps 'legal method' provides a better example. In its lowest form this term is widely interpreted to encompass not much more than the doctrine of precedent, the so-called 'rules' of statutory interpretation, and a few bits of information that beginning law students need to know. That is a crude misnomer. Even in more sophisticated books and courses with this title two ideas are regularly conflated and confused: purported (typically misleading) accounts of the methods of reasoning of judges in appellate cases and the task of developing certain elementary skills—legal method as the skills of the law student. Teaching *about* the thought processes of one kind of functionary is a very different operation from getting students to learn *how* to think. Learning about the rules of precedent is tangential to both.[38]

A slightly more sophisticated interpretation of 'legal method' is to equate it with 'thinking like a lawyer' or, more narrowly, with 'legal reasoning'. These at least have the merit of focusing on method and linking the subject of study to a relatively developed body of theory. But 'legal reasoning' is still almost universally equated with reasoning about disputed questions of law, typically in 'hard cases'. In 1964, Julius Stone coined the phrase 'lawyers' reasonings'.[39] This correctly implies that lawyers are involved in a wide range of operations which ostensibly involve different kinds of ratiocination in a variety of contexts. Negotiating, arguing about disputed questions of fact, pleas in mitigation, sentencing, criticizing particular laws, institutions or practices, recommending reforms are all examples of professional activities that involve, or purport to involve, reasoning. So do many activities of other legal actors. Unfortunately, Stone followed tradition in concentrating almost exclusively on questions of law. But to confine 'lawyers' reasonings' to one kind of argumentation is, once again, to treat one small part as if it were the whole. Clearly this fits the narrow conception of academic law that is confined to legal doctrine; part of the point of 'broadening' legal studies is to break out of such confines.

[36] See, e.g., the symposium on the Royal Commission on Criminal Justice in 21 *Journal of Law and Society*, no. 1 (1994).

[37] Andrew Ligertwood, *Australian Evidence* (North Ryde, NSW 2nd edn., 1993).

[38] On the elementary distinction between the doctrine and techniques of precedent, see *HDTWR* at 299 ff. [39] Julius Stone, *Legal System and Lawyers' Reasonings* (London, 1964).

No doubt there are many factors that have contributed to what seems to me to be an elementary and persistent form of narrowness. One obvious reason why it persists is that no one has yet constructed an alternative, broad theory of 'lawyers' reasonings' to set against the traditional narrow one. There have, of course, been some developments in relevant areas: the new rhetoric to some extent transcends the division between questions of fact and questions of law;[40] the debates on probabilities and proof,[41] the currently fashionable concern with storytelling;[42] the application of game theory to negotiation,[43] the suggestion that most or all lawyers' skills can be subsumed under the rubric of 'problem-solving' are just some examples. One striking aspect of these particular developments is that they have resulted in separate bodies of literature that have grown up largely independently of each other.

At first sight, it seems fairly straightforward to sketch an agenda for a general theory of lawyers' reasonings which would subsume all of these various activities and discourses under one head. For example, do not negotiation, appellate advocacy, arguments about questions of fact, law, and disposition, law reform, and constitution-making all involve the application of the same general principles of practical reasoning? Insofar as questions arise about the uses and limits of 'rationality' and competing conceptions of the rational, these would form part of the task of constructing such a theory. An agenda for constructing a normative theory of lawyers' reasonings might include: in respect of what kinds of activities, in what contexts, do lawyers typically purport to use reason? What constitute valid, cogent and appropriate reasonings in each context? What are the similarities and differences between each of these various kinds of reasoning and how are they related to each other? Are they all examples of some generalizable notion of practical reasoning? Can they all be subsumed under some general theory of problem-solving? What conception(s) of rationality are presupposed by such theories? Can such conceptions be defended against sceptical attacks and, if so, how?

A general theory of lawyers' reasonings which provided a coherent set of answers to such questions would indeed be broader than standard theories of legal reasoning such as those of Levi, Llewellyn, MacCormick, Dworkin or Alexy. But maybe this is all too simple. First, many of our stock of theories in this area are more or less explicitly limited to common law reasoning and, as such, are closer to particular than to general jurisprudence. It is clear that what is thought

---

[40] C. Perelman, *The Idea of Justice and the Problem of Argument* (London, 1963); Neil MacCormick deals briefly with questions of fact in *Legal Reasoning and Legal Theory* (Oxford, 1978) and in subsequent writings about coherence. There is an extensive philosophical literature on 'practical reasoning' and 'informal logic', see e.g., C. L. Hamblin, *Fallacies* (London, 1970), Douglas N. Walton, *Informal Logic* (Cambridge, 1989).

[41] This is, of course, one part of 'the new evidence scholarship'. For an excellent survey of recent debates and writings about inference and probabilities in several disciplines, see David Schum, *Evidential Foundations of Probabilistic Reasoning* (New York, 1994).

[42] e.g., Bernard Jackson, *Law, Fact and Narrative Coherence* (Merseyside, 1988); *RE*, Ch. 7.

[43] e.g., H.Raiffa, *The Art and Science of Negotiation* (Cambridge, Ma., 1982).

to constitute a valid, cogent, and appropriate argument on a question of law or fact or sentencing varies from legal system to legal system and within legal systems, depending on context, standpoint, and so on. Yet questions about the validity and cogency of arguments are meant to transcend particular cultures and contexts; they purport to provide general principles of reasoning. How does one reconcile the claims to universality of principles of logic with the apparent cultural relativism implicit in comparing and contrasting forms and styles of legal reasonings?

Secondly, this is a philosophical minefield in which it would be naïve to expect consensus. There are many theories of deduction, induction, probability, and so on and many conceptions of rationality. There is no agreed base from which to start to construct a normative theory of lawyers' reasonings as an application of some more general theory; and there is no escaping the philosophical difficulties.

A third concern is empirical. What is the relationship between normative theories of rational argument and psychological theories of decision-making or other kinds of empirical study, such as discourse analysis or jury studies? If broadening involves going beyond the study of rules and particular systems, being more 'realistic' includes getting closer to the actual behaviour of real participants. This general problem of the puzzling relationship between normative and empirical aspects of decision-making is illustrated by a relatively recent development in respect of fact-finding: psychological studies have convincingly shown that juries and other triers of fact in coming to decisions about particular past events typically either construct stories or choose between competing stories presented to them. Stories typically form coherent wholes, while standard theories of argumentation about both questions of fact and questions of law tend to be based on versions of propositional logic. The contrast is sometimes made between the 'atomism' of standard accounts of reasoning and the 'holism' of the psychological accounts. There is thus a seeming tension between normative theories about how people ought to think and empirical theories about how they in fact think. If psychologists could show, as they may well do in respect of certain kinds of operation (for example facial recognition), that people in fact make better judgements when they think holistically, this may pose important challenges at the normative level to standard prescriptive theories of reasoning and some conventional conceptions of rationality. A great deal of writing about judicial processes hovers uneasily between logic, psychology and heuristics. We are only just beginning to come to grips with such issues in legal theory.

These examples may at least illustrate one point: broadening the study of law involves raising one's intellectual sights. Far from being 'soft' ('cauliflower scholarship' or 'Sunday Supplement law', as some denigrators call it), the movement to broaden the study of law points in the direction of an ambitious intellectual agenda. If that is the case, one mistake of those who denigrate the achievements of legal scholarship, English or otherwise, may be that they have underestimated the magnitude of the task, a repetition of the error made in the 1930s by some 'scientific' American Realists.[44]

The current situation is, of course, open to multiple interpretations. From the standpoint of one who remains committed to the development of broader approaches to the study of law, I would construct a story of modest achievement and unfulfilled potential rather than of failure. Some progress has been made, but there is still an unfinished agenda. Academic law has considerable potential, but it has some way to go before it can hope to be reinstated as one of the great humane studies.

How might one construct this rather more optimistic scenario? In respect of the past, the story of academic law in England can be plausibly told in terms of late development in rather unfavourable circumstances. After a slow start, the pioneering generation of law teachers in the late nineteenth century had to struggle to establish the respectability of the subject in the eyes of two sceptical constituencies: colleagues in other disciplines and the practising profession. The leaders adopted the strategy of arrogating to themselves the role of systematizers of the common law; their first scholarly priority was the preparation of basic undergraduate texts.[45] The jurist as Expositor sidelined the Censor and the Craftsman and, hijacked the title of 'Scientist' (despite the fact that exposition was particular and science is general), so that the roles of the external observer, as exemplified by historical jurisprudence, sociology of law, and comparative law, were largely marginalized.

It took a long time for law in the universities to attract able students in large numbers; it was not seen to be entirely convincing either as a vehicle for general education or as a preparation for practice. The most significant changes took place in the 1960s and 1970s, when high demand, the acceptance of the law degree as the normal route to professional qualification (though by no means always to practice), enabled law to share in the general expansion and belatedly to achieve critical mass. The post-Ormrod settlement assigned university law schools a clear, 'academic' role and facilitated their assimilation into the universities; but it also confined their contribution to the first stage of a four-stage process of professional formation. The result was that they were largely sidelined not only in respect of vocational training but also of more advanced studies, such as the training of researchers, specialists, and the judiciary. Unfortunately,

---

[44] Karl Llewellyn, 'The Theory of Legal "Science"', 20 *N Carolina L Rev.* 1 (1941); W. Twining, *Karl Llewellyn and the Realist Movement* (1973, 1985) at 188–96.

[45] David Sugarman, 'Legal Theory, the Common Law Mind and the Making of the Textbook Tradition', in William Twining (ed.), *Legal Theory and Common Law* (1986) Ch. 3. It is too simple to say that a new pluralism in legal scholarship replaced a monolithic orthodoxy which conceived of exposition of legal doctrine as the beginning and end of 'legal science'. This does not do justice to the individuality, the tradition of dissent, and the cosmopolitanism of many of the very small band of pioneers who helped to establish law in the universities in the late 19th c. and in the interwar period. Nor does it allow for the survival and increased sophistication of expository work.

the period of expansion largely coincided with a period of almost perpetual economic crisis in higher education.

During the 1970s and 1980s university and polytechnic law schools were, with few exceptions, essentially undergraduate teaching institutions and much of the early efforts of innovative academic lawyers were invested in designing new courses and preparing new kinds of educational materials. This produced some excellent scholarship,[46] but development was constrained by the limited role of law schools and the economics of publishing: despite the recent increased involvement of university presses in law publishing, most academic law books have still to be addressed to a student market which is based on a restricted curriculum.

For a period university and polytechnic law schools fell between stools in that they were neither treated as genuine professional schools, as in the United States, nor as full-fledged academic departments, providing a general education for undergraduates and specialized advanced studies at postgraduate level, as happened in the better law faculties in Continental Europe. Instead they were viewed and used by their clientele as little more than primary schools for the profession. In the 1980s law schools began to diversify their roles and their clientele. Postgraduate studies expanded; more and more institutions became involved in the second or vocational stage of professional formation; and there was a significant increase in mixed degrees with a European component. The skills movement has so far concentrated on elementary teaching of basic skills—another form of primary education—but it represents a significant step in the direction of becoming more grown-up; it has also stimulated some promising new lines of research.

By the early 1990s there was an increasing feeling among academics that university law schools had by and large outgrown the three-year undergraduate degree at 18 plus. Changes in legal practice and increased competition for entry to the legal profession created a potential crisis in universities: if the undergraduate law degree continued to be regarded as mainly vocational and law schools were essentially undergraduate teaching institutions, it was possible that demand for legal education might fall and that at least some law schools would be in danger of losing their economic base. Faced with this situation, law schools collectively need to consider a number of options: to diversify their clientele, their functions, and their sources of funding; to make the undergraduate degree more credible as a vehicle for general education in order to compete more seriously for students with disciplines such as history and English; or to contract. Whether this is a genuine crisis or an opportunity to develop further in the direction of being multifunctional institutions dealing with all aspects of law in society at a variety of levels was, by 1994, an open question.

In the light of this story, perhaps we should be impressed rather than depressed by what has been achieved in legal scholarship in the past thirty years,

---

[46] Geoffrey Wilson, op. cit., at 821.

not least in respect of diversification. And, more than most academics, lawyers have some grounds for optimism: the subject-matter of our discipline is ubiquitous, important, intellectually challenging, and accessible; it has a rich mass of constantly renewed primary sources that have to date been generally underexploited by scholars, including legal scholars.[47] It is constantly fed by problems and materials from outside the discipline—what some people call 'the real world'. Its economic base is reasonably secure because of high demand, alternative markets for legal education, association with a generally profitable and powerful occupational group, and because it has relatively low overheads, even if it is not quite as cheap as its traditional image. The community of legal scholars is strengthened by the contributions of practising lawyers and judges, at least some of whom can genuinely be said to be learned. There are signs that law is becoming more part of the intellectual mainstream. Above all, the modern English law school is a very recent creation, which has only recently been assimilated into the university and is only just in process of coming of age. Whether or not there should be a Nobel Prize for law is unimportant, not least because the advancement of learning is a collective enterprise, often involving teamwork, multidisciplinary perspectives, and the gradual accretion of contributions by many participants, most of whom remain anonymous. But there is no reason why law as an institutionalized discipline cannot make significant contributions to human welfare and human understanding.

[47] *BT*, Ch. 5.

Index

Abel, R. 8, 23
Abu Rannat, Mohamed Chief Justice 29
academic law, *see* discipline of law
academic lawyers 32–3, 70–1, 309, 310, 344–6
access 21, 237–79, 287
  access courses 264, 278
  barriers to 239, 242–3, 253–65, 269
  courts, role of 272
  conversion courses 244, 257
  criteria of selection 242–3
  financial aid 278
  gatekeepers 240, 245, 305
  to justice 247–8
  to legal services 76, 333
  linear model of professional formation 245
  lotteries 238, 270 n.
  multiple routes of entry 243, 258, 267, 278
  problems of analysis 239–46
  quotas 249, 264
  remedies 245, 277–8
  second chances 245–6, 278
  social desirability 248
  statistics 252–3, 278
  versus excellence 258, 271, 274–7, 279
  see also admissions criteria, discrimination, positive action
Ackerman, Bruce 178
ACLEC, *see* Lord Chancellor's Advisory Committee on Legal Education and Conduct
adjudication, theory of 120–1, 123–4, 176
Adler, Mortimore 92, 94
admissions criteria 237–8, 242–3, 287
  academic record 269
  aptitude tests 268–9, 278–9
  Law School Admissions Test (LSAT) 268 n., 269 n., 308
  merit 266 n., 276
  rationales of 248
adversary system 322
advocacy 3, 289 n.
  ethics of 312, 322–3
  see also skills
affirmative action, *see* positive action
African Constitutions 47–8
Allen, C. K. 166
aggrandisement effect 77, 324
American Bar Association (ABA) 180, 266, *see also* MacCrate Report

American law, as fiction 183
Ames, J. B. 70
Amos, Sheldon 159
analytical jurisprudence, *see* jurisprudence
Anderson, Terence 97 n., 99, 195
animals, liability for, *see* torts
Annan, Noel (Lord) 3
anthropology 174
anti-discrimination measures 258–62, *see also* discrimination, positive action
appellate courts 49, 66, 112, 220–1
apprenticeship 12, 184, 196, 270, 275, 326–7
aptitude tests, *see* admissions criteria
Aristotle 105, 318, 323
Arnold, G. F. 94
Arthurs, Harry, *see* Law and Learning
Armitage, Sir Arthur 13
Ashby, Sir Eric 64, 67, 84 n.
Asheville Conference 78–80, 85, 192
Atiyah, P. S. 9, 29, 36–8, 173–7
  Accidents, Compensation, and the Law 37, 54–62, 341
Austen, Jane 204
Austin, J. L. 3
Austin, John 1, 133, 155–65, 172, 178
autopoiesis 282, *see also* system
ayatollah 212–13

Baconian, *see* probability
Bad Man, *see* Holmes, O. W.
Bar finals, *see* professional examinations
Bar Vocational Course (BVC) 184, 289 n., 332
Barotse 174
Barnes, David W. 91
Bayes Theorem, *see* probability
Becher, Tony 341
Behrens v. *Bertram Mills Circus* 27
Bentham, Jeremy 1, 77, 109, 112, 135, 151–65, 216
  'citizen of the world' 151, 177–8
  evidence 48, 93, 95, 102, 114–22, 124–5, 127
  fictions 122
  Fragment on Government 151–3
  jurisprudence, types of 151–5, 178
  lawyers 246–7, 316
  morals and legislation 260
  pannomion 124, 153–4
  paraphrasis 167
  see also utilitarianism

Printed in the United Kingdom
by Lightning Source UK Ltd.
108849UKS00001B/65